ROGRADSKAYA

Bol Nevka Бол Невка

Neva Нева

ENT

GOSTI

Petrogradskaya
See pp66–75

Palace Embankment
See pp76–97

Gostinyy Dvor
See pp98–115

0 metres	600
0 yards	600

ST PETERSBURG

EYEWITNESS TRAVEL

ST PETERSBURG

Main Contributors **Catherine Phillips**
Christopher and Melanie Rice

LONDON, NEW YORK,
MELBOURNE, MUNICH AND DELHI
www.dk.com

Project Editor Anna Streiffert

Art Editor Marisa Renzullo

Editor Ella Milroy

Designers Gillian Andrews, Carolyn Hewitson,
Paul Jackson, Elly King, Nicola Rodway

Visualizer Joy Fitzsimmons

Map Coordinators Emily Green, David Pugh

Picture Research Brigitte Arora

DTP Designers Samantha Borland, Sarah Martin, Pamela Shiels

Main Contributors

Catherine Phillips, Christopher and Melanie Rice

Photographers

Demetrio Carrasco, John Heseltine

Illustrators

Stephen Conlin, Maltings Partnership, Chris Orr & Associates,
Paul Weston

Printed and bound in China

First published in the UK in 1998
by Dorling Kindersley Limited,
80 Strand, London WC2R 0RL, UK

15 16 17 18 10 9 8 7 6 5 4 3 2 1

Reprinted with revisions 2000, 2001, 2004, 2007, 2010, 2013, 2015

Copyright 1998, 2015 © Dorling Kindersley Limited, London

A Penguin Random House Company

A CIP catalogue record is available from the British Library.

ISBN 978 1 4093 7191 5

Floors are referred to throughout in accordance with European
usage, i.e. the "first floor" is the floor above ground level.

MIX
Paper from
responsible sources
FSC™ C018179

**The information in this
DK Eyewitness Travel Guide is checked regularly.**

Every effort has been made to ensure that this book is as up-to-date as possible
at the time of going to press. Some details, however, such as telephone numbers,
opening hours, prices, gallery hanging arrangements and travel information, are
liable to change. The publishers cannot accept responsibility for any consequences
arising from the use of this book, nor for any material on third party websites, and
cannot guarantee that any website address in this book will be a suitable source of
travel information. We value the views and suggestions of our readers very highly.
Please write to: Publisher, DK Eyewitness Travel Guides, Dorling Kindersley,
80 Strand, London, WC2R 0RL, UK, or email: travelguides@dk.com.

Front cover main image: Church on Spilled Blood

◄ Detail of the mosaics on the ornate vaulted ceiling of the Church on Spilled Blood

Contents

Griffons on Bank Bridge, made by
local sculptor Pavel Sokolov

Introducing
St Petersburg

St Petersburg
Area by Area

Mosaic Tympanum on the exterior of
the Church on Spilled Blood

The distinctive façade of the Smolnyy Cathedral and the adjacent convent buildings

Travellers' Needs

The exquisite Lantern Study in the Pavlovsk Palace, designed by Voronikhin

Survival Guide

Traditional Russian wooden
matryoshka dolls

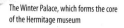

The Winter Palace, which forms the core of the Hermitage museum

HOW TO USE THIS GUIDE

This guide will help you to get the most from your visit to St Petersburg, providing expert recommendations as well as detailed practical information. *Introducing St Petersburg* maps the city and sets it in its geographical, historical and cultural context, with a quick-reference timeline on the history pages giving the dates of Russia's rulers and significant events. *St Petersburg at a Glance* is an overview of the city's main attractions. *St Petersburg Area by Area* starts on page 56 and describes all the important sights, using

maps, photographs and illustrations. The sights are arranged in two groups: those in the central districts and those a little further afield. The guided walks reveal three characteristics of the city – the canals, the Neva and the islands. *Beyond St Petersburg* describes sights requiring one- or two-day excursions. Hotel, restaurant, shopping and entertainment recommendations can be found in *Travellers' Needs*, while the *Survival Guide* includes tips on everything from transport and telephones to personal safety.

Finding Your Way Around the Sightseeing Section

Each of the seven sightseeing areas is colour-coded for easy reference. Every chapter opens with an introduction to the area it covers, describing its history and character. For central districts, this is followed by a

Street-by-Street map illustrating a particularly interesting part of the area; for sights beyond the city limits, by a regional map. A simple numbering system relates sights to the maps. Important sights are covered by several pages.

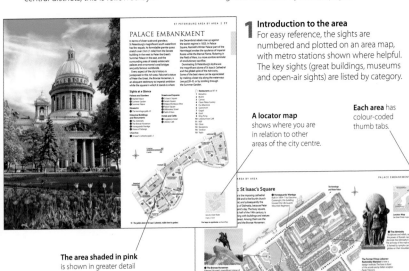

1 **Introduction to the area**
For easy reference, the sights are numbered and plotted on an area map, with metro stations shown where helpful. The key sights (great buildings, museums and open-air sights) are listed by category.

A locator map
shows where you are in relation to other areas of the city centre.

Each area has colour-coded thumb tabs.

The area shaded in pink
is shown in greater detail on the Street-by-Street map.

2 **Street-by-Street map**
This gives a bird's-eye view of interesting and important parts of each sightseeing area, with accurate drawings of all the buildings within them. The numbering of the sights ties in with the preceding area map and with the fuller descriptions on the pages that follow.

A suggested route for a walk is shown in red.

St Petersburg Area Map

The coloured areas shown on this map *(see pp16–17)* are the five main sightseeing areas into which central St Petersburg has been divided for this guide. Each is covered in a full chapter in the St Petersburg Area by Area section *(pp56–133)*. They are also shown on other maps throughout the book. In *St Petersburg at a Glance (pp34–51)*, for example, they help you locate the most interesting museums and palaces or where to see the city's many delightfully designed bridges. The maps' coloured borders match the coloured thumb tabs on each page of the section.

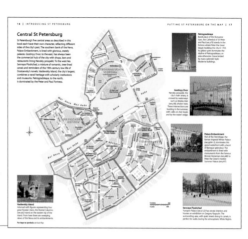

Numbers refer to each sight's position on the area map and its place in the chapter.

Practical information lists all the information you need to visit every sight, including a map reference to the Street Finder maps *(pp240–7)*.

3 Detailed information on each sight
All the important sights are described individually. They are listed to follow the numbering on the area map at the start of the section. The key to the symbols summarizing practical information is on the back flap.

Visitors' Checklist provides the practical information you will need to plan your visit.

Story boxes highlight unique aspects or historical connections of a particular sight.

4 St Petersburg's major sights
These are given two or more full pages in the sightseeing area in which they are found. Buildings of interesting architecture are dissected to reveal their interiors; museums and galleries have colour-coded floor plans to help you find important exhibits.

Stars indicate the best features or works of art.

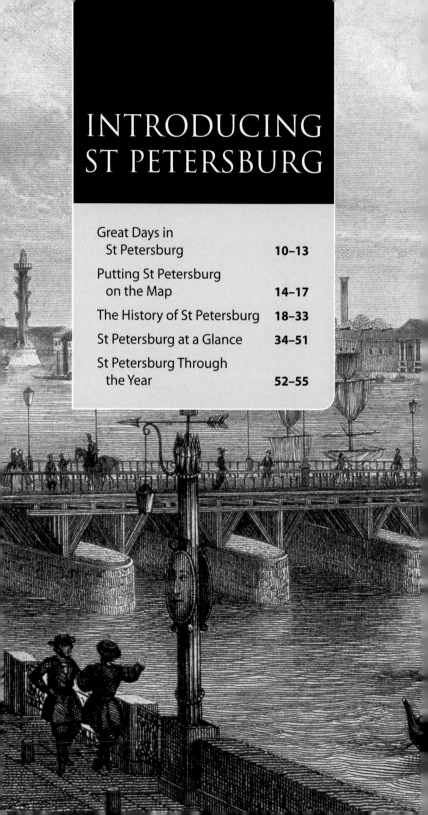

INTRODUCING ST PETERSBURG

GREAT DAYS IN ST PETERSBURG

In just over 300 years St Petersburg has had many faces. Peter the Great's folly, built on a swamp and intended to turn Russia's face towards the West, soon became a magnificent city reflecting the majesty of the Russian Empire. Then it was the "Cradle of the Revolution", where Lenin came to power. During World War II it was a symbol of national pride. Today it is Russia's cultural capital, with a wonderfully preserved heritage and an international arts programme. Taken together, the first three itineraries detailed below show the influences that shaped the city: imperial, Russian and Soviet. The others walk you through the city with a much more mixed offering. There is a day tour, a two-day tour, a three-day tour and a five-day tour. Follow the one that appeals to you, or simply dip in and out and be inspired.

Rastrelli's masterly main staircase at the Winter Palace

Imperial City

Two adults allow at least 6,000 roubles

- Art and opulence
- Grand squares and views
- Remembering Rasputin

Morning

The day starts at the centre of the city with the Baroque **Winter Palace** (see pp94–5), once the official residence of the imperial family and now the heart of the **Hermitage** museum (see pp86–93). Concentrate on the magnificent state rooms, where the Tsars received important guests. Do not miss the view over vast **Palace Square** (see p85), which incorporates the glorious sweep of the General Staff Building, formerly home to the state ministries and now part of the museum. Walk along the embankment to **Krokodil** (see p190) for lunch.

Afternoon

Head back along Galernaya ulitsa to **Senate Square** (see p80) – the **Bronze Horseman**, a statue of Peter the Great, rears up at its centre. There are fine views across the river to Vasilevskiy Island, lined with rich mansions and handsome institutions.

Turn round, and take in **St Isaac's Cathedral** (see pp82–3), topped by a gilded dome. It took from 1818 to 1858 to construct this colossal structure, which, since the Soviet era, has been designated a museum.

Under 1 km (half a mile) west, the **Yusupov Palace** (see p122) has an exhibition on Grigoriy Rasputin, the "holy man" murdered here by Prince Felix Yusupov. Dine at nearby **Romeo's Bar & Kitchen** (see p191), one of the city's best Italian restaurants, or for a more modest outlay, at **1913** (see p191) – the year the Romanovs celebrated 300 years on the throne.

Russian City

Two adults allow at least 4,800 roubles

- Icons and incense
- A traditional lunch
- Shopping for souvenirs

Morning

This itinerary takes in the best traditional Russian sights of a city where European influences can be more evident than Russian. Start at the **Russian Museum** (see pp106–9), the world's finest collection of Russian art. Marvel at the **Church on Spilled Blood's** (see p102) interior, then enjoy a traditional Russian lunch at **Brasserie de Metropol** (see p189).

The Russian Revival-style Church on Spilled Blood

◀ St Petersburg – View of the Troitskiy Bridge, by 19th-century artist J Schroeder

Afternoon

Inspired by the morning's sights, nip across to the **Souvenir Market** *(see p201)*, which sells everything from icons to fur hats.

Then take the green metro line from Gostinyy Dvor to Ploshchad Aleksandra Nevskovo to **Alexander Nevsky Monastery** *(see pp132–3)*. Many notable Russians, including Tchaikovsky and Dostoevsky, are buried here. As the afternoon fades, you may like to attend a magical candlelit choral service at the Church of the Annunciation.

Round off the day with a visit to nearby **Russky Len** *(see p201)*, a shop selling wonderful Russian linen.

In the evening, visit the ballet *(see p204)* or dine at **Bellevue Brasserie** *(see p189)*, which overlooks the Hermitage and Palace Square. For both, book ahead.

The still-operational mint at Peter and Paul Fortress

Soviet City

Two adults allow at least 2,700 roubles

- **Revolutionary heritage sites**
- **Monuments to the People**
- **Soviet-themed dining**

Morning

To indulge a fascination for Leningrad, "Cradle of the Revolution", start at the city centre's edge at the **Smolnyy Institute** *(see pp130–31)*, home of the Revolution and later of the Communist Party. Opposite, catch bus No. 46 and ride past the monument to Dzerzhinsky, father of the Soviet secret police, past the **Field of Mars** *(see p96)* where the dead of the Revolution are buried, and across the river to the **Museum of Russian Political History** *(see p74)*. The **Cruiser Aurora** *(see p75)*, whose guns sounded the 1917 Revolution, is moored a short distance away. For lunch, try Georgian **Salkhino** *(see p187)*.

Afternoon

A little further north, the small **Kirov Museum** *(see p74)* is devoted to the head of the city's Communist Party, Sergey Kirov, whose assassination in 1934 prompted a wave of executions.

To appreciate the Soviet glorification of the People's achievements, take the metro to Moskovskaya and the **Victory Monument** *(see p133)*, whose awesome underground Memorial Hall shows life during the Siege of Leningrad. Then take the metro back to Tekhnologicheskiy Institute and ride the red line between Avtovo and Ploshchad Vosstaniya, where each station tells a part of the history of the city *(see p226)*. Finally, dine at **Kvartirka** *(see p188)* or **Russian Kitsch** *(see p186)*.

A Family Day Out

Family of 4 allow at least 4,500 roubles

- **Awesome views**
- **Gruesome specimens**
- **Food in a forest**
- **Skating or the circus**

Morning

The day starts with a stiff climb up to the colonnade of **St Isaac's Cathedral** *(see pp82–3)* for panoramic city views. Then cross the Neva to the **Strelka** *(see pp60–61)* of Vasilevskiy Island to take in one of the museums there *(see pp62–3)*: the **Zoological**, the **Institute of Russian Literature** or the **Kunstkammer**.

A pleasant walk across the river takes you to **Petrogradskaya** *(see pp66–75)*. Head to the inexpensive **Pelmeni Bar**

for a filling lunch or, for something lighter, try vegetarian **Fruktovaya Lavka** *(see p186)*.

Afternoon

The focus of Petrogradskaya is the **Peter and Paul Fortress** *(see pp68–9)*, with its opulent cathedral and grim history. Attractions include the tombs of the Romanovs, prison cells, displays on the history of the city, Peter the Great's rowing boat, and a rampart climb. In summer, the park surrounding the fortress has all kinds of family attractions.

Also in the park is **Gornyy Oryol** *(see p186)*, a restaurant designed as a fairy-tale castle, located near the entrance to the zoo.

After supper, take the metro to Krestovskiy Ostrov, then a short walk to the western spit of **Yelagin Island** *(see pp138–9)*, where there are fine sunsets and an ice rink in winter. Or, if it is too cold, make a visit to the **circus** *(see p203)*.

The Avtovo metro station celebrates post-war car production

Two Days in St Petersburg

- Enjoy sweeping city views from Trinity Bridge
- Explore the unique art collections at the Hermitage
- Marvel at the sight of the Grand Cascade in Peterhof

Day 1

Morning Stroll through the historic city of St Petersburg, from **Anichkov Bridge** (p39) to **Nevskiy prospekt** (pp48–51). From here, visit the grand shopping arcade at **Gostinyy Dvor** (pp110–11), and catch a glimpse of the Style-Moderne architecture of **Yeliseev's** (p111) on your way. Once you reach the **Admiralty Garden** (p48), turn left towards the colossal **St Isaac's Cathedral** (pp82–3) to admire its lavish interiors and remarkable ceiling paintings.

Afternoon After lunch, head through **Palace Square** (p85) to the renowned **Hermitage** (pp86–95), one of the largest museums in the world. Here you can explore the **Winter Palace State Rooms** (p87) and the **Pavilion Hall** (p87).

Day 2

Morning Start by visiting **Trinity Bridge** (p37), from where you can enjoy glorious views of the city. Next, head to the nearby **Peter and Paul Fortress** (pp68–9).

Façade of the mosque at the Peter and Paul Fortress, St Petersburg

Enter the fortress through **Ivan Gate** (p69), and spend the morning lost in this intriguing complex. Don't forget to visit the beautiful **Cathedral of SS Peter and Paul** (pp70–71), where the Romanovs are entombed.

Afternoon Board a hydrofoil at the Hermitage Embankment for a scenic, 30-minute journey to **Peterhof** (pp150–53). On arrival at Peterhof's Lower Gardens, take a walk along the delightful **Marine Canal** (p150). Beyond the immaculate flower beds, view the **Grand Cascade** (p153), a dazzling water structure that fronts the resplendent **Great Palace** (p151). Afterwards, visit the **Upper Gardens** (p150), which feature many magnificent fountains and ornamental ponds.

Three Days in St Petersburg

- Visit one of the world's largest art collections at the Hermitage
- Admire the stunning Catherine Palace
- Enjoy a scenic boat trip from St Petersburg to Peterhof

Day 1

Morning Begin your day at **Palace Square** (p85), where you can admire the wonderful buildings and architecture. Then, devote the rest of your morning to the opulent **Hermitage** (pp86–95). This former residence of the tsars now houses one of the world's largest art collections, and offers visitors a rich cultural experience. Stop by the splendid **Winter Palace State Rooms** (p87) and the **Pavilion Hall** (p87).

Afternoon Take a walk along **Nevskiy prospekt** (pp48–51), which runs through the heart of St Petersburg. Make a detour along the way, to visit the **Church on Spilled Blood** (p102). The church was built as a memorial to Alexander II on the spot where he was assassinated.

Mosaic floor in the Pavilion Hall at the Hermitage, St Petersburg

Day 2

Morning Take a minibus (*marshrutka*) from Moskovskaya Metro Station to **Pavlovsk** (pp160–63), an expansive park dotted with ornamental pavilions and statues. Look out for the **Apollo Colonnade** (p160) and the **Étoile** (p161). Don't forget to visit the **Pavlovsk Palace** (pp162–3), built in the 18th century.

Afternoon Take a taxi from Pavlovsk to nearby **Tsarskoe Selo** (pp154–7) to visit the magnificent **Catherine Palace** (pp154–5), built for Tsarina Elizabeth. Of the many regal rooms within, the most striking are the **Great Hall** (p154), the **Amber Room** (p155) and the **Green Dining Room** (p155).

Day 3

Morning From the Hermitage Embankment, board a hydrofoil to **Peterhof** (pp150–53), the magnificent palace of Peter the Great. The **Marine Canal** (p150) draws visitors towards Peterhof's centrepiece – the **Grand Cascade** (p153), beyond which stands the spectacular **Great Palace** (p151).

Afternoon Head across **Trinity Bridge** (p37), towards the **Peter and Paul Fortress** (pp68–9). Enjoy wonderful views of the city on your way. At the fortress, visit the Baroque **Cathedral of SS Peter and Paul** (pp70–71). If the weather permits, join sunbathing locals on the beach.

Five Days in St Petersburg

- Look out from the bell tower at Smolnyy Convent
- Admire the bizarre displays at the Kunstkammer
- Wander through the imperial estate of Pavlosvsk

Exterior of the Cathedral of Our Lady of Kazan at Nevskiy prospekt, St Petersburg

Day 1

Morning Cross the **River Neva** *(p86)* using the **Trinity Bridge** *(p37)*, and head to the imposing **Peter and Paul Fortress** *(pp68–9)*. Step into the elegant magnificence of the bright **Cathedral of SS Peter and Paul** *(pp70–71)*, which houses the tombs of the Romanov family. Then, explore the grim history of this fortress, which was once a prison for political dissidents.

Afternoon Get a feel of historic and contemporary St Petersburg, with a stroll along the bustling **Nevskiy prospekt** *(pp48–51)*. The city's most renowned street since the 18th century, it features an array of historic monuments, churches and fine buildings. Look out for the **Cathedral of Our Lady of Kazan** *(p113)*, the statue of **Catherine the Great** *(p112)*, and the **Gostinyy Dvor** *(pp110–11)*. Stop for a meal at the shopping arcade.

Day 2

Morning The famous **Palace Square** *(p85)* provides an easy starting point, from which you can visit the grand buildings of the **Hermitage** *(pp86–95)*. Spend the morning discovering the city's rich cultural heritage at this opulent museum.

Afternoon Take a hydrofoil from Heritage Embankment to **Peterhof** *(pp150–53)*. Wander through the beautiful landscaped gardens, and catch a glimpse of the **Grand Cascade** *(p153)* and the stunning **Great Palace** *(p151)*.

Day 3

Morning Start the day with a tour of the **Church on Spilled Blood** *(p102)*, and admire its marvellous onion-shaped domes. Afterwards, walk to the nearby **Russian Museum** *(pp106–9)*, housed in Mikhaylovskiy Palace. This splendid 19th-century complex has one of the greatest collections of Russian art on display.

Afternoon Catch the metro to Chernyshevskaya, from where you can walk to the **Smolnyy Convent** *(p130)*. Explore the charming cathedral, and climb the bell tower for a panoramic view of St Petersburg. Later, spend time at the adjoining **Smolnyy Institute** *(pp130–31)*, an impressive Neo-Classical building that became Lenin's seat of power from 1917–18.

Day 4

Morning Travel to the vast estate of **Pavlovsk** *(pp160–63)* where you can meander through romantic ruins and pavilions.

Afternoon Hop into a taxi and head to **Tsarskoe Selo** *(pp154–7)*. Tour the estate's fabulous **Catherine Palace** *(pp154–5)*, and explore the **Amber Room** *(p155)*, the **Great Hall** *(p154)*, and the **Green Dining Room** *(p155)*.

Day 5

Morning Begin with a trip to the **Admiralty** *(p80)*, a former fortified shipyard. Then, head across **Palace Bridge** *(p38)* to **Vasilevskiy Island** *(pp58–65)*. Enjoy a walk through the eastern end of this pleasant historic quarter, the **Strelka** *(pp60–61)*. Visit the **Kunstkammer** *(pp62–3)*, built to exhibit Peter the Great's infamous collection of oddities. The **Rostral Columns** *(p62)* are another distinct feature in this area.

Afternoon After lunch, head to the **Stieglitz Museum** *(p129)*, a short walk east of the **Summer Garden** *(p97)*. The museum's collection features art and craft displays from all over Europe. Further east is the 19-century Cathedral of the Transfiguration *(p129)*, worth a visit for its ornate interiors.

The magnificent Grand Cascade, standing before the Grand Palace, in Peterhof

Putting St Petersburg on the Map

The Russian Federation, or Russia as it is usually known, is the world's largest country, covering an area of 17.4 million sq km (6.7 million sq miles). Situated in its northwest corner, St Petersburg is Russia's second city, with a population of just under five million. Once Russia's capital and known as its "Window on the West" *(see pp22–3)*, the city was built on the marshy lands where the Neva joins the Gulf of Finland. Of the 12 countries bordering Russia, Estonia and Finland are St Petersburg's closest neighbours.

White Sea

Arkhangels

NORWAY

FINLAND

Lake Ladoga

See inset map, right

Vologo

Oslo

Kristian-sand

Frederikshavn

SWEDEN

Dalälven

Stockholm

Gothenburg

Oskarshamn

Helsinki

Tallinn

Pärnu

Tartu

ESTONIA

Pskov

Lovat

ST PETERSBURG

Novgorod

M11

M10

Volga

Mosco

M9

DENMARK

Malmö

Copenhagen

Baltic Sea

Liepāja

Riga

LATVIA

M20

M12

M1

Klaipėda

LITHUANIA

Smolensk

T

Hamburg

Szczecin

Koszalin

Kaliningrad

Vilnius

Orsha

Minsk

Orël

BELARUS

M20

Berlin

Odra

POLAND

Olsztyn

Białystok

Gomel

GERMANY

A2

Warsaw

M1

M13

Pripyat

A4

Wrocław

Radom

M17

Kiev

Dnepr

Prague

A3

Danube

CZECH REPUBLIC

Brno

Lviv

UKRAINE

A8

Munich

Vienna

Bratislava

SLOVAKIA

Košice

Dnestr

AUSTRIA

A10

Budapest

HUNGARY

Oradea

Targu Mureş

MOLDOVA

Chisinau

M

Odessa

ITALY

SLOVENIA

Osijek

Timişoara

ROMANIA

Venice

Bologna

CROATIA

BOSNIA-HERZEGOVINA

Belgrade

Piteşti

Bucharest

Black Sea

Florence

Sarajevo

SERBIA

Ruse

Varna

Ancona

Split

Adriatic Sea

MONTENEGRO

KOSOVO

Niš

BULGARIA

Burgas

Rome

A14

Dubrovnik

Skopje

MACEDONIA

Sofia

A1

Naples

Bari

S106

Tirana

ALBANIA

A2

Istanbul

Bursa

Ank

GREECE

TURKEY

St Petersburg and Environs

0 km   50
0 miles   50

Pechora
Pechora
Ukhta
Pechora
Vycheyda
pinega
Syktyvkar
Kotlas
Kirov

Primorsk
M10
A123
Vaskelovo
Lake
Ladoga
Sestroretsk
A129
Novaya
Ladoga
Gulf of Finland
A18
ST PETERSBURG
M18
Sosnovyy
Bor
Kirovsk
A121
Pulkovo
A18
Kolpino
Gatchina
M11
Tosno
M10
Kirishi
Volosovo
M20
Vyritsa
A115

Kazan
slavl
Ufa
Magnitogorsk
Sibay
Ural
Vladimir
Ulyanovsk
Orsk
Ryazan
Samara
Orenburg
M5
RUSSIAN
Aktobe
Yrgyz
FEDERATION
Uralsk
Shubarkudyk
Shalkar
M5
Saratov
Zhem
Balashov
KAZAKHSTAN
Don
Makat
Mikhaylovka
M5
Atyrau
Aral
Sea
Volgograd
Beyneu
Ustyurt plateau
Volga
Donets
Astrakhan
Caspian
Sea
ov
Rostov-na-Don
Elista
Fort-
Shevchenko
pol
Aktau
a of
zov

Key

≡≡≡ Motorway
≡≡≡ Major road
≡≡≡ Minor road
─── Railway
─── International boundary
     Ferry route

0 km   180
0 miles   180

Putting Russia on the Map

Arctic
Ocean
St Petersburg
RUSSIAN FEDERATION
EUROPE
KAZAKHSTAN
CHINA
AFRICA
INDIA
Pacific
Ocean

Central St Petersburg

St Petersburg's five central areas as described in this book each have their own character, reflecting different sides of the city's past. The southern bank of the Neva, Palace Embankment, is lined with glorious, stately palaces. Gostinyy Dvor, to the east, has always been the commercial hub of the city with shops, bars and restaurants lining Nevskiy prospekt. To the west lies Sennaya Ploshchad, a mixture of romantic, tree-lined canals and reminders of the 19th-century low life of Dostoevsky's novels. Vasilevskiy Island, the city's largest, combines a naval heritage with scholarly institutions and museums. Petrogradskaya, to the north, is dominated by the Peter and Paul Fortress.

Vasilevskiy Island
Adorned with figures representing four great Russian rivers, the Rostral Columns *(see p62)* stand on the eastern tip of the island. From here there are sweeping views of the Neva and its embankments.

For keys to symbols *see back flap*

Petrogradskaya
Burial place of the Romanov tsars, the Cathedral of SS Peter and Paul (see p70) stands in the fortress where Peter the Great began building the city in 1703. Its gilded spire dominates the skyline of Petrogradskaya, an area otherwise characterized by many splendid Style-Moderne buildings.

Gostinyy Dvor
Nevskiy prospekt, the city's main artery, is crossed by waterways such as Moyka river (see p38), shown here. These intersections are bustling in the summer, with cafés on river boats and by the water's edge.

Palace Embankment
Part of the Hermitage, the former imperial Winter Palace (see pp94–5), dominates this grand waterfront with a burst of Baroque splendour. The embankment is lined with monuments from the famous Bronze Horseman (see p80) to Peter the Great's modest Summer Palace (see p97).

0 metres   600
0 yards   600

Sennaya Ploshchad
Yusopov Palace (see p122) has ornate interiors and houses an exhibition on Gregory Rasputin. The surrounding area, with quiet streets lining its canals, is perfect for walks during the atmospheric White Nights.

Map labels:
POSADSKAYA ULITSA
PETROGRADSKAYA NAB
SAMPSONIEVSKIY MOST
UL KUYBYSHEVA
УЛ КУЙБЫШЕВА
PENKOVAYA UL
Cruiser Aurora
Ksheshinskaya Mansion
PETROVSKAYA NAB
Trinity Bridge
TROITSKIY MOST
Нева
NAB KUTUZOVA
Summer Palace
SUVOROVSKAYA PL
NAB LEBYAZHEVO KANALA
Fontanka Фонтанка
ULITSA
Field of Mars
НАБЕРЕЖНАЯ РЕКИ МОЙКИ
KONYUS-HENNAYA PL
Church on Spilled Blood
Engineers' Castle
GRIBOEDOVA
Russian Museum
INZHENERNAYA UL
KLENOVAYA ULITSA
TSENTRALNYY RAYON
MAY KONYUSHENNAYA UL
GRIBOEDOVA
ITALYANSKAYA UL
Nevskiy Prospekt
НЕВСКИЙ ПРОСПЕКТ
САДОВАЯ
Fontanka Фонтанка
KANALA
Gostinyy Dvor
Gostinyy Dvor
ULITSA
НАБЕРЕЖНАЯ РЕКИ ФОНТАНКИ
ADOVAYA
LOMONOSOVA
UL ZODCHEVO ROSSI
APRAKSIN PER
TORGOVYY PER
НАБЕРЕЖНАЯ РЕКИ ФОНТАНКИ

THE HISTORY OF ST PETERSBURG

Founded in 1703, within ten years St Petersburg had become capital of the vast Russian Empire and quickly gained a reputation as one of Europe's most beautiful cities. In the 20th century it underwent three name changes, three revolutions and a 900-day siege. For a city less than 300 years old, it has an amazing history.

Some 850 years before St Petersburg became capital of Russia, local Slavic tribes invited the Viking chieftain Rurik to rule them. His successor founded Kiev, which grew into a great princedom. In 988 Grand Prince Vladimir adopted Orthodox Christianity, with profound consequences; Orthodoxy was to become a cornerstone of Russian identity. Paradoxically, Russia only emerged as a united entity during the 250-year domination of the Muslim Mongols. In 1237 these fierce tribes conquered all the principalities except Novgorod. In the 14th century the Mongols chose Moscow's power-hungry grand prince, Ivan I (1325–40), to collect tribute from other subjugated principalities. This sealed the fate of the Mongols for, as Moscow thrived under their benevolence, she also became a real threat.

Mongol warriors in a 14th-century manuscript illustration

Within 50 years, an army led by Moscow's Grand Prince Dmitriy Donskoy won a first victory over the Mongols, and the idea of a Russian nation was born.

During the long reign of Ivan III (1462–1505) the Mongols were finally vanquished and Moscow's prestige increased. Ivan the Terrible (1533–84) was the first to be called "Tsar of All the Russias". Yet his reign, which began in glory, ended in disaster. Ivan killed his only heir, and the so-called Time of Troubles followed as Russia came under a succession of weak rulers and Polish usurpers invaded Moscow.

The First Romanovs

To end this strife, in 1613 the leading citizens chose Mikhail Romanov to be tsar, thus initiating the 300-year Romanov rule. Under Mikhail, Russia recovered from her upheavals, but his greatest legacy was his son Aleksey. Intelligent and pious, Aleksey modernized the state, encouraging an influx of foreign architects, codifying laws and asserting the power of the state over the church.

800	1000	1200	1400	1600

862 Rurik establishes Viking stronghold at Novgorod

863 Cyril and Methodius create early version of Cyrillic

1147 Moscow is founded

1480 Ivan III stops paying tribute to Mongols

1462–1505 Reign of Ivan III

1605–13 Time of Troubles

Boris Godunov

988 Prince Vladimir converts to Orthodox Christianity

1108 Town of Vladimir is founded

1223 First Mongol raid

1240 Mongol rule established in Rus

1242 Alexander Nevsky defeats the Teutonic Knights

1533–84 Reign of Ivan IV the Terrible

1598 Boris Godunov claims title of tsar after 12 years as regent

1613 Mikhail Romanov becomes first tsar of the Romanov dynasty

◀ Peter the Great instructing his workers during the building of St Petersburg (Alexander von Kotzebue, 1862)

Peter the Great

In the transition from a medieval to a more modern state, the future Peter the Great, founder of St Petersburg, was born. After his father Aleksey's death, Peter's childhood was overshadowed by severe rivalry between his mother's family, the Naryshkins, and that of his father's first wife, the Miloslavskiys. At the age of ten Peter ascended the throne, but the Streltsy Guards, influenced by the Miloslavskiys, started a bloody revolt. As a result Peter's sickly half-brother Ivan became his co-tsar, and Ivan's sister Sophia their regent. The memory of seeing his family brutally killed caused his hatred of Moscow and distrust of its conservative, scheming society.

Peter the Great (1682–1725)

When Ivan died in 1696, the 24-year-old Peter had grown into a giant of a man with a tempestuous combination of willpower and energy. Long hours spent drilling toy soldiers as a child developed into a full-scale reform of the Russian army. But Peter's dream was of a Russian navy. In 1697, he went on a European tour to study shipbuilding and other wondrous achievements. To everyone's dismay the young tsar spent more hours working at the docks than socializing at court. On his return to Russia he lost no time in bringing in westernizing reforms.

A New Capital

It was Peter's determination to found a northern port with an unrestricted passage to the Baltic that led to war with Sweden, at the time one of the strongest countries in Europe. By May 1703 Peter had secured the Neva river and began to build the Peter and Paul Fortress and a shipyard opposite *(see pp22–3)*. Only an autocrat with Peter's drive could have succeeded in building a city on this fetid

View of St Petersburg in the early 17th century, with the Admiralty shipyard to the left

Life at Elizabeth's Court

When Elizabeth was not busy looking over architectural plans, she would lie around on her bed, gossiping with a group of ladies whose chief task it was to tickle her feet. Her restless nature meant that her courtiers had to endure endless hunts and skating parties, and were required to keep her company at all hours. Her riotous cross-dressing masquerades were notorious, as was her vast wardrobe, allegedly containing over 15,000 dresses.

Tsarina Elizabeth going for a stroll at Tsarskoe Selo, surrounded by eager courtiers

bogland, where building materials were in short supply and disastrous floodings regular. More than 40,000 Swedish prisoners-of-war and peasants laboured and perished here, their bones contributing to the city's foundations.

Whether or not it was always Peter's intention to make this his new capital, it only became possible after his decisive victory at Poltava in 1709 put an end to the Swedish threat. St Petersburg was named capital of Russia in 1712 and, by Peter's death in 1725, there were 40,000 inhabitants in the city and many more in the surrounding labour encampments.

The Petticoat Period

For most of the rest of the 18th century Russia was ruled by women, whose taste did much to set the celebrated architectural tone of St Petersburg.

During the brief reigns of Peter's wife Catherine I (1725–27) and his grandson Peter II (1727–30), the court abandoned this frontier city for the more comfortable life in Moscow. But when the throne passed to Anna, daughter of Peter's co-tsar Ivan, she decided to create a recognizably European court in St Petersburg. Anna was 37 at the time, and had spent most of her life in Germany. This was obvious in her choice of ministers and favourites, of whom many were German. Fashion and style, however, were imported from France and opera from Italy. Though she herself was serious, plain and somewhat cruel, Anna did much to put the court on a footing with the most frivolous in Europe, as well as encouraging a flowering of culture.

Tsarina Elizabeth, daughter of Peter the Great, was the ideal successor to this twittering court. Elizabeth was attractive, energetic and cheerful, a combination that endeared her to almost everyone, especially the Guards who helped secure her place on the throne. She left the affairs of state to a series of well chosen advisors. The only element of seriousness lay in Elizabeth's perhaps surprising piety, which at times led her to retire temporarily into a convent. Her chief legacy is the splendid Baroque architecture she commissioned, mainly designed by her favourite architect Rastrelli *(see p95)*.

Elizabeth (1741–61)

1721 Peace of Nystad ends war with Sweden

1733 Cathedral of SS Peter and Paul is finished after 12 years' work

1738 Russia's first ballet school is founded in St Petersburg

1745 Tsarevich Peter marries the future Catherine the Great

1757 St Petersburg Academy of Arts is founded

1720 | 1730 | 1740 | 1750

1717 Peter travels to Holland and France

1725 Catherine I is empress after death of Peter the Great

1730–40 Reign of Anna

1727–30 Reign of Peter II

1741 Anna's successor Ivan VI is deposed; Elizabeth takes power, supported by Guards' officers

1754 Rastrelli's Winter Palace is begun

Anna Ivanovna, daughter of Ivan V

A Window on the West

Determined to drag his country out of the medieval period, and inspired by the few Westerners he met in Moscow, Peter the Great was the first tsar to travel to Europe. He returned with many ideas for reforms and architectural novelties which he put into practice in his new city. In 1710, when the Swedish threat was over, the reluctant imperial family and government were moved to this chilly, damp outland. But Peter was adamant and soon a rational street plan, stone buildings and academies made St Petersburg a thriving capital in which fashions and discoveries from Europe were tried out before filtering through to the rest of Russia.

Extent of the City
▨ 1712   ☐ Today

Plan of the New City
This map of 1712 shows Peter's original plan for his capital, with Vasilevskiy Island as centre. This was abandoned due to the hazards of crossing the Neva, and the city spread out around the Admiralty instead.

The Carpenter Tsar
During his 1697–8 tour of Europe, Peter (to the left in this picture) spent months at the Deptford Docks, labouring with his men to learn the basics of shipbuilding.

Based on Amsterdam, the original city grid was meant to follow a strict network of canals but this had to change (*see p59*).

Menshikov Palace

New Fashions
Peter's desire to westernize Russia led to a rule forcing his courtiers to have their bushy beards shaved off.

The Streltsy Rebellion

As a result of a malicious rumour that Peter's relatives planned the murder of his half-brother Ivan, in 1682 the Streltsy Guard regiments invaded the Kremlin. A horrifying massacre took place in front of the 10-year-old Peter who saw his advisor and members of his family murdered. This traumatic event is probably what caused Peter's facial tic and certainly his wish to build another capital city. In 1698 he took a terrible revenge by torturing over a thousand Streltsy Guards to death.

Brutal murders in the Kremlin, 1682

The Battle of Poltava
The struggle with Sweden for control over the Baltic led to the Great Northern War. Nine years after the embarrassing defeat at Narva, Peter the Great's army reforms bore fruit. In 1709 he won a decisive battle over Charles XII at Poltava, and thereby Russia's first victory over a major European power.

Where to see Peter the Great's City

Some of the buildings from the earliest days of St Petersburg still exist in the city centre, including the rustic Peter the Great's Cabin (*p75*), the Summer Palace (*p97*) and the Baroque Menshikov Palace (*p64*). Much of Peter and Paul Fortress (*pp68–9*) also dates from this time. It is also well worth visiting Monplaisir, Peter's first home at Peterhof (*pp150–53*).

Peter the Great's workshop, the Summer Palace

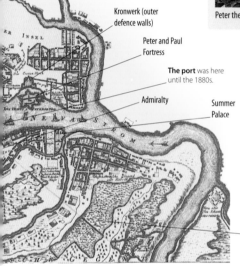

Kronwerk (outer defence walls)

Peter and Paul Fortress

The port was here until the 1880s.

Admiralty

Summer Palace

Marshy soil and a lack of local stone made construction difficult. Thousands of labourers died during the first stages.

Wine Goblet
The tsar, who could hold his drink, enjoyed pressing alcohol on his guests until they passed out. This elegant crystal goblet belonged to his close friend Alexander Menshikov and is engraved with his coat of arms.

Mice Bury the Cat
Coloured woodcuts, *lubki*, served as political cartoons in Peter's day. The tsar was always portrayed as a cat on account of his moustache.

Catherine I
After an unsuccessful first marriage, Peter was drawn to a Lithuanian girl who had followed the army back from the wars in 1704. Her healthy good looks were brought to the tsar's attention by Alexander Menshikov (*see p64*). Although only two daughters survived, their marriage was happy and Catherine succeeded Peter as the first woman on Russia's throne.

Catherine the Great

Catherine, a German princess, was chosen by Elizabeth as wife for her successor, the petty-minded Peter III. When Peter ascended the throne in 1761 Catherine had resided in Russia for 18 years and was fully fluent in Russian. She had made it her duty to steep herself in the Russian culture which she later came to adore. Six months into Peter's reign, Catherine and her allies in the Imperial Guard deposed the tsar. He was assassinated within days and she was crowned Catherine II.

Catherine the Great in 1762

By Catherine's death at the age of 67, her reputation as an enlightened leader (see p26) had been overshadowed by her illiberal reaction to the news of the French Revolution in 1789 and by scandalous rumours concerning her later love affairs. However, she left a country vastly enlarged after successful campaigns against Turkey and Poland.

War and Peace

During the Napoleonic Wars, under Catherine's grandson Alexander I, Russia finally took her place alongside the other great European powers.

Despite his part in the murder of his father Paul, much was expected of the new tsar who was in thrall to the ideals of enlightened government. Russia was by now desperately in need of reform. Of particular concern was the plight of the peasantry, who were tied to the land in serfdom. However, the necessities of war subsumed everything, and no inroads were made against the Russian autocracy during Alexander I's reign.

Determined to harness the wave of Russian patriotism, Alexander joined Britain and marched against Napoleon in Austria in 1805. After the crushing defeat at the battle of Austerlitz, however, the inexperienced tsar retreated, his army having lost 11,000 men.

At the Peace of Tilsit, signed in 1807, Napoleon divided Europe into French and Russian spheres, lulling Alexander into a false sense of security. In 1812 the French emperor invaded Russia, but was defeated by its size and climate. The Russian army followed his forces to Paris, taking part in the allied campaign which led Napoleon to abdicate in 1814. In celebration, Alexander commissioned a series of imposing public edifices in a fitting Empire style.

Murder of Paul I, 1801. Despite all his precautions, Catherine's unstable, paranoid son was murdered in a coup in his own fortified palace (see p103)

1760	1780	1800
1762 Death of Elizabeth. Peter III becomes emperor but is murdered after six months. His wife takes the throne as Catherine II	**1783** Annexation of the Crimea	**1787–92** 2nd Russo-Turkish War	**1801** Paul I murdered. Alexander I becomes tsar	**1805–7** War with France ends with Treaty of Tilsit
1767 Catherine II publishes her *Bolshoy Nakaz*	**1773–5** Pugachev Rebellion	**1782** Falconet's statue, the Bronze Horseman, is completed	**1796** Death of Catherine II; Paul I accedes	**1812** Napoleon invades Russia
	1768–74 1st Russo-Turkish War		*Alexander I (1801–25)*	**1816** Alexander clamps down on reform

Decembrist rebels defeated by tsarist troops, 1825

The Decembrist Rebellion

Officers of the Russian army who had witnessed the freedoms of democratic Europe were frustrated by Alexander's failure to consider constitutional reform. When his stern brother Nicholas was declared tsar in 1825, these liberals rallied their soldiers to support the older brother Constantine, who had given up his rights to the throne, in the hope that he would be more open-minded. They made a stand on 14 December on what is now Senate Square *(see p80)*. Troops loyal to the tsar were instructed to fire on the rebels, killing hundreds before the leaders surrendered. The new tsar, Nicholas I, treated them with the severity which was to become the hallmark of his reign. Five leading figures were hanged, and over a hundred exiled to Siberia.

A City of Rich and Poor

For much of the 19th century, a walk along Nevskiy prospekt offered a microcosm of an increasingly divided society. Striding past drunks, beggars and prostitutes, the city's courtiers, cocky young officers and leading citizens headed for shops selling imported fashionable accessories, or to the distinguished delicatessen Yeliseev's to buy caviar and champagne. They often lived beyond their means, mortgaging their serfs and lands to keep up with the astronomical costs of their luxurious lives. This was also a city in which the salary of a low-ranking government clerk was never sufficient to feed a family. In the countryside, tension was growing among the serfs tied to the large estates of the aristocracy. With such blatant inequality, pressure for political reform was inevitable.

After the unrelenting autocracy of Nicholas I, the "Iron Tsar", liberals welcomed the reign of his fair-minded son Alexander II. In 1861, the tsar passed the Edict of Emancipation, abolishing serfdom, but requiring peasants to buy their land at far from advantageous terms. Thus industrialization finally took off as peasants flocked to the big cities to work in factories, only to be met by even worse living conditions.

The Napoleonic Invasion

Napoleon's Grand Army of 600,000 men reached Moscow in September 1812, after the victory at Borodino, but was defeated by the tactics of non-engagement devised by the great Russian hero General Kutuzov. Finding himself in a city abandoned by its rulers and set on fire by its people, and with the Russian winter ahead, Napoleon was forced into a retreat over the frozen countryside. He eventually reached the border, with only 30,000 men left alive.

French army retreating from Moscow 1812

1822 Abolition of Masonic and secret societies

1833 Pushkin publishes *The Bronze Horseman*

1855 Death of Nicholas I; Alexander II succeeds him

1853–6 Crimean War

Leo Tolstoy

1865–9 Tolstoy writes *War and Peace*

1820

1840

1860

1825 The Decembrist Rebellion. Nicholas I becomes tsar

1851 The "Nicholas Railway" opens between Moscow and St Petersburg

1861 Emancipation of serfs

1864 Reforms in local government, law and education

818 Construction of t Isaac's Cathedral starts

The Enlightened Empress

Born a minor German princess, Catherine II was a learned and energetic woman. She recognized the importance of the great Enlightenment philosophers Voltaire and Diderot, with whom she corresponded. She bought impressive collections of European art for the Hermitage (see pp86–95), libraries for Russia's scholars and talked much about reducing the burden on Russia's serfs. However, a peasant uprising in the 1770s and news of the French Revolution in 1789 put paid to her liberal notions and, when she died, the majority of Russians were just as badly off as before.

Extent of the City
🁢 1790   ☐ Today

The Temple alludes to Catherine's passion for Neo-Classical architecture.

A medal is presented to Count Orlov for his victory over the Turks at Chesma in 1770.

Royal Guards Swear Allegiance
On 28 June 1762, Catherine usurped the throne of her unpopular husband Peter III in a palace coup. The guards regiments flocked to support her and the tsar was assassinated on 6 July.

Catherine the Great
Catherine II "the Great" (1762–96) pursued an expansionist foreign policy. Russia's first naval victory, leading to the annexation of the Crimea, is commemorated allegorically on this fabric.

Count Alexey Orlov, brother of Catherine's one-time lover Grigoriy, played an important role in her takeover of the throne.

Catherine's Instructions
In 1767 the 36-year-old Catherine published her 22-chapter *Great Instruction (Bolshoy Nakaz)*. The book is a collection of ideas on which a reform of Russia's legal system was to be based.

Pretender Pugachev
The greatest threat to Catherine's reign was caused by the Cossack Pugachev who claimed to be Peter III. He was arrested, but escaped to lead a widespread peasant uprising which broke out in 1773 and only ended with his execution in 1775.

The New Academy of Sciences
Catherine, who founded over 25 major academic institutions in Russia, also commissioned new buildings for those already existing. Quarenghi built the Neo-Classical Academy of Sciences in 1783–5.

Where to see the Neo-Classical City

Catherine had the Marble Palace (see p96) and the Tauride Palace (see p130) erected for two of her lovers, and added the Small and Large Hermitage and the theatre (see p86) to the Winter Palace. Her architect Cameron designed the Cameron Gallery and the Agate Rooms at Tsarskoe Selo (see p154–7) and Pavlovsk Palace (see pp160–63).

Grecian Hall at Pavlovsk, created by Charles Cameron in 1782–6

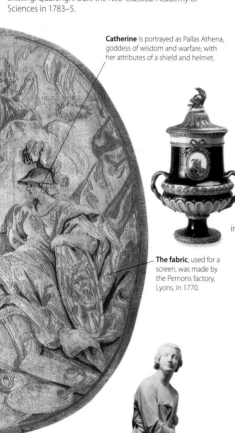

Catherine is portrayed as Pallas Athena, goddess of wisdom and warfare, with her attributes of a shield and helmet.

Empire-Style Vase (1790)
Porcelain was much prized at court. In 1744 the first Russian producer, the Imperial Porcelain Factory, opened in St Petersburg.

The fabric, used for a screen, was made by the Pernons factory, Lyons, in 1770.

Mikhail Lomonosov
A philosopher, historian, linguist and scientist, Lomonosov (1711–65) personified the intellectual enlightenment of 18th-century Russia (see p63). This sculpture of him as a boy by the seashore refers to his fisherman origins.

Grigoriy Potemkin (1739–91)
Of all her lovers, Catherine respected and admired Prince Potemkin the most. He was a successful general and an influential counsellor. They remained friends until his death.

Alexander II was murdered by a revolutionary group in 1881. Tragically, he is said to have had the plans for a Russian parliament in his pocket

The Death of Tsarist Russia

Pressure for reform had built up such a head of steam that in 1881, when still no radical changes had taken place, a revolutionary group murdered Alexander II. The reign of Alexander III was one of rabid reaction. The press was under strict censorship and the secret police more active than ever. But workers began to get organized and opposition was growing. Nicholas II took over a country on the verge of breakdown, in spite of the rapid industrialization of the 1890s. The unsuccessful war with Japan (1904–5) was followed by "Bloody Sunday". On 9 January 1905 a peaceful demonstration carried a petition to the tsar only to be met by bullets. News of the massacre spread like wildfire and the 1905 Revolution broke out with strikes all over Russia. To avert further disaster, Nicholas II promised basic civil rights and an elected Duma (parliament) with the right to veto legislation. However, the tsar simply dissolved the parliament whenever it displeased him. This high-handed behaviour, along with the royal family's unpopular intimate friendship with Rasputin (see p123), further damaged the Romanovs' reputation.

The outbreak of World War I brought a surge of patriotism which the tsar sought to ride. But, by late 1916, Russia had lost three and a half million men, morale at the front was low and food supplies at home scarce.

Red Army badge

World of Art Movement

Costume design by Leon Bakst, 1911

The oppressive political climate at the turn of the century did not prevent art from flourishing. A small group of St Petersburg artists, including Bakst and Benois, grew into an influential creative movement under the inspired leadership of Sergey Diaghilev. Western art was introduced in their stylish *World of Art* magazine, while their stage designs and costumes for the Ballets Russes (see p120) brought Russian culture to the West.

Revolution and Civil War

In February 1917 strikes broke out in the capital, now renamed Petrograd. The tsar was forced to abdicate, his family put under arrest and a Provisional Government set up. But revolutionaries returning from exile organized themselves and, in October, an armed revolution overthrew the government (see pp30–31).

1902 Lenin publishes *What is to be Done?*

1881 Alexander II is assassinated by the "People's Will" group. Alexander III becomes tsar.

1898 Social-Democratic Workers' party is founded. Russian museum opens

The Romanov family in 1913

1913 300 anniversa Romanov

1880

1900

1881–2 Anti-semitic pogroms

1894 Alexander III dies, Nicholas II accedes

1903 Pro-violence Bolsheviks (under Lenin) secede from Social-Democratic Workers' party

1905 The 1905 Revolution is followed by the inauguration of the first Duma in 1906

1887 Lenin's brother is hanged for attempt on the tsar's life

1904–5 Russo-Japanese War

1914 Outbreak of WWI; St Petersburg changes name to Petrograd

The leading Bolshevik party proved to be as careless of democracy as the tsar but, in March 1918, they kept their promise to take Russia out of the war. The army was desperately needed at home to fight the developing civil war. The Bolsheviks (Reds) found themselves threatened by a diverse coalition of anti-revolutionary groups which came to be known as the "Whites", initially supported by foreign intervention. It was the threat of the Whites rallying opposition around the royal family that led to their execution in July 1918. But the Whites were a disparate force and, by November 1920, the last troops had abandoned the struggle, leaving a devastated Soviet Russia to face two years of appalling famine. To manage, Lenin had to revise his aggressive "War Communism" nationalization project. His slightly milder New Economic Policy allowed for private enterprise.

The imperial palaces around St Petersburg were totally destroyed by the Germans in World War II. This photo shows Pavlovsk *(see pp160–63)* in 1944

The Stalin Years

In the five years after Lenin's death in 1924, Joseph Stalin used his position as General Secretary of the Communist Party to eliminate all rivals. He then established his long dictatorship.

Joseph Stalin on a propaganda poster from 1933

The terror began in earnest with the collectivization of agriculture which forced the peasants to give up all livestock, machinery and land to collective farms. During this time, and in the ensuing famine of 1931–2, up to 10 million people are thought to have died.

A first major purge of intellectuals took place in urban areas in 1928–9. Then, in December 1934, Sergey Kirov, the party leader in Leningrad, was assassinated on the secret orders of Stalin *(see p74)*. Blamed on an anti-Stalinist cell, the assassination was used as the rationale for five years of purges throughout the country. By the time they were over, some 15 million people had been arrested, many sent to the Gulag (labour camps) and over a million executed.

Stalin's purge of the Red Army boded ill for World War II, for he had got rid of three-quarters of his officers. When the Germans invaded Russia in 1941 they cut off Leningrad in less than three months, subjecting the city to a 900-day siege *(see p133)* which left more than two million people dead, half of them civilians. Leningrad came to be known as a "Hero City".

The Germans were eventually defeated, but the Russian people, who lost 20 million souls to the war, were subjected to a renewed terror by Stalin, which lasted until his death in March 1953.

| **7** The Russian Revolution *(see pp30–31)* | **1929** Collectivization of private land | **1934** Leningrad Party Secretary Kirov is killed; Stalin's purges intensify | **1939** Nazi-Soviet pact |
| **1918** Civil War starts. Capital moves to Moscow | **1924** Lenin dies; Petrograd is named Leningrad | | **1941** Nazis attack Russia; Siege of Leningrad starts | **1947** The term "Cold War" is coined |

1920   **1940**

| Lenin bans opposition after the tadt mutiny | **1925** Trotsky is expelled from the Politburo | **1932** Socialist Realism is the only officially approved style in art | **1944** The Siege ends |
| **1922** Stalin becomes General Secretary of the Party | | | **1942** First performance of Shostakovich's *Seventh Symphony* in besieged Leningrad |

Sergey Kirov

The Russian Revolution

St Petersburg is known as the cradle of the Russian Revolution, a central event in the history of the 20th century. After the 1917 February Revolution which led to the abdication of Tsar Nicholas II, the Provisional Government declared a political amnesty. Exiled revolutionaries such as Lenin and Trotsky flooded into the city. By setting up a network of Workers' and Soldiers' Soviets, representative councils elected by the people, they established an alternative government. In October, when soldiers had deserted from the front in droves, the revolutionary leaders decided on an armed uprising which brought the Communists to power.

Extent of the City
 ▨ 1917   ☐ Today

The Ex-Tsar
Nicholas II, seen here clearing snow at Tsarskoe Selo during his house arrest in March 1917, was later taken with his family to Yekaterinburg where they were murdered.

Soldier of the Red Guard

Looting was tempting for the mob of sailors and soldiers, especially in the palace's well-stocked wine cellars.

Storming the Winter Palace

Late on the evening of 25 October 1917 the battleship Aurora *(see p75) fired some blank shots at the Winter Palace. The Red Guard, trained by Trotsky at the Smolnyy Institute, stormed the palace. Their aim was the arrest of the Provisional Government, unsuccessfully defended by 300 Cossacks.*

The Cossacks, who defended the palace with some cadets and members of the Women's Battalion, were too few to offer any serious resistance.

Lenin, Leader of the People
A charismatic speaker, as shown in this painting by Victor Ivanov, Lenin returned from exile in April to lead the Revolution. By 1918, his Bolshevik faction had shown their determination to rule.

Revolutionary Plate
Various ceramics with revolutionary themes, mixed with touches of Russian folklore, were produced to celebrate every occasion, in this case the Third International.

Propaganda

One hallmark of the Soviet regime was its propaganda. Artists were employed to design posters spreading its message through striking graphics. War Communism during the Civil War (1918–20) was encouraged by posters such as this one, extolling the "Workers' and Peasants' Defence".

Leon Trotsky

The intellectual Trotsky played a leading military role in the Revolution. In 1927, during the power struggle after Lenin's death, he was exiled by Stalin. In 1940 he was murdered in Mexico by a Stalinist agent.

Avant-Garde Art

Even before 1917, Russia's artists had been in a state of revolution, producing the world's first truly abstract paintings. A great example of this new movement is *Supremus No. 56*, painted in 1916 by Kazimir Malevich.

Ministers of the Provisional Government tried to keep order but were arrested.

New Values

Traditions were radically altered by the Revolution; instead of church weddings, couples exchanged vows under the red flag. Loudly trumpeted sexual equality meant that women had to work twice as hard – at home and in the factories.

1917 The February Revolution	**March** The tsar is persuaded to abdicate. Provisional Government is led by Prince Lvov	**October** Bolsheviks storm Winter Palace after signal from *Aurora* and expel Provisional Government	**March** Bolsheviks sign Brest-Litovsk peace treaty with Germany. Capital is moved to Moscow
1917		**1918**	
July Kerensky becomes Prime Minister of Provisional Government	*Cruiser* Aurora	**1918 January** Trotsky becomes Commissar of War — **December** Lenin forms the CHEKA (secret police)	**July** Start of Civil War. Tsar and family are murdered in prison at Yekaterinburg

Cruiser Aurora

The Washington Dove of Peace, a Russian caricature (1953) from the days of the Cold War

Thaw and Stagnation

Three years after Stalin's death his successor Nikita Khrushchev denounced Stalin's crimes at the Twentieth Party Congress and the period known as "The Thaw" began. Political prisoners were released, and Solzhenitsyn's *One Day In the Life of Ivan Denisovich*, about life in the Gulag, was published.

In foreign affairs, things were not so liberal. Soviet tanks invaded Hungary in 1956 to prevent the country seceding from the

First in Space

It was under Krushchev that the Soviet Union achieved her greatest coup against the West, launching the first Sputnik into space in 1957. That same year the dog Laika was the first living creature in space, aboard Sputnik II. She never came down again, but four years later Yuriy Gagarin made spectacular history as the first man in space, returning to a hero's welcome. The Soviets lost the race to put a man on the moon, but their space programme worked as powerful propaganda, backing up the claims of politicians that Russia would soon catch up with and overtake the prosperity of the West.

Sputnik II and the space dog Laika, 1957

Warsaw Pact and, in 1962, Khrushchev's decision to put nuclear missiles on Cuba brought the world to the brink of nuclear war.

When Leonid Brezhnev took over in 1964, the intellectual climate froze once more and the persecution of political dissidents was stepped up. The first ten years of his regime were a time of relative plenty. But beneath the surface a vast black market and network of corruption was growing. The party apparatchiks, who benefited most from the corruption, had no interest in rocking the boat. When Brezhnev died in 1982, the politburo was determined to prevent the accession of a younger generation. Brezhnev was followed by 68-year-old Yuriy Andropov and, when he died, 72-year-old Chernenko.

Glasnost and Perestroika

When 53-year-old Mikhail Gorbachev announced his policies of *glasnost* (openness) and *perestroika* (restructuring), when he took over in 1985, he had no idea what would follow and that the end of the Soviet Union was in sight.

For the first time since 1917 the elections to the Congress of People's Deputies in 1989 contained an element of genuine choice, with rebels such as Boris Yeltsin and human rights campaigner Andrey Sakharov winning seats. In 1991, local elections brought nationalist candidates to power in

Mikhail Gorbachev and George Bush

1950–1954 Korean War	**1961** Stalin's body removed from its place alongside Lenin in Red Square. Yuriy Gagarin is first man in space	**1962** Cuban missile crisis	**1970** Solzhenitsyn wins Nobel Prize for Literature
		1964 Brezhnev becomes General Secretary	**1982** Death of Brezhnev; replaced by Andropov
			1979 USSR invades Afghanistan

1950   **1960**   **1970**   **1980**

1953 Stalin dies	**1957** Sputnik I is launched	**1968** Soviet troops enter Czechoslovakia to suppress "Prague Spring"	**1969** Strategic Arms Limitation Talks (SALT) with USA
1955 Krushchev comes to power. Warsaw Pact is established	**1956** Stalin denounced by Krushchev at 20th Party Congress. Hungarian uprising is crushed		**1984** Andropov is replaced by Chernenko

Leonid Brezhnev (1906–82)

Demonstrations on Palace Square during the 1991 coup

the republics, and democrats in the major Russian local councils. Russia and the Baltic Republics seceded from the Soviet Union, while the people of Leningrad, always in the vanguard of progressive movements and led by the reformist lecturer in law, Anatoly Sobchak, voted to restore the city's original name, St Petersburg.

With his momentous victory in the election for President of the Russian Republic, Yeltsin was able to deal the death blow to the Soviet Union. It came after the military coup against Gorbachev in August 1991, when Yeltsin's stand against tanks in Moscow made him a hero. In St Petersburg no tanks were on the street, but none-theless Sobchak rallied supporters of democracy. By the end of the year, the Soviet Union no longer existed.

The new Russian State Emblem

St Petersburg Today

The economic reforms which Russia has undergone since 1991 have widened the gap between rich and poor and, while some revel in the new opportunities for work and travel, others cry out for a return to Communism and the albeit limited social protection it offered. The social problems are still being resolved. Major international companies flooded in, and by early 1999 relative stability had been achieved. The elec-tions of December 1999 dramatically reduced the power of the Communists, bringing in young liberal reformers and confirming optimism about Russia's future. The religious revival continues, and churches of all denominations have been restored to their original purpose.

In March 2000, Vladimir Putin was elected President of the Russian Federation, and re-elected in 2004. Dmitry Medvedev became President in 2008, with Putin as Prime Minister. In 2012, Putin and Medvedev switched roles, much to the dismay of many Russians who took to the streets in protest. The next elections are scheduled to be held in 2018.

A church wedding, popular again since religion has gained new importance among the young

	1991 Yeltsin becomes President of Russia. Dissolution of the USSR on 25 December	1998 Nicholas II is reburied with his family in SS Peter and Paul Cathedral on 17 July	2004 Putin is re-elected as President for a second term	2008 Georgian–South Ossetian Conflict; Russia recognizes the independence of Abkhazia and South Ossetia	
					2012 Putin becomes President again and Medvedev, Prime Minister
1990		**2000**		**2010**	**2020**
	1990 Gorbachev is elected President of the USSR and awarded the Nobel Peace Prize	2000 Putin becomes President of Russia		2008 Medvedev becomes President of Russia; Putin becomes Prime Minister	
1989 USSR leaves Afghanistan			2004 Beslan Siege; 300 people killed in a Beslan school by Chechen rebels		

ST PETERSBURG AT A GLANCE

A city built on water, St Petersburg offers beautiful scenery and a wide range of sights. The Peter and Paul Fortress *(see pp68–9)*, the city's first building, contrasts with Baroque monasteries and Neo-Classical palaces. The city's short but stormy history is reflected in many of its museums, which display everything from Catherine the Great's fine art collection in the Hermitage to memorabilia of the Revolution in the Kshesinskaya Mansion *(see p74)*.

To help you make the most of your stay, the following 12 pages are a time-saving guide to the best museums and palaces and the most interesting of the many bridges and waterways. The cultural figures that made St Petersburg a city of importance are also featured. Below is a selection of sights that should not be missed by any visitor.

St Petersburg's Top Ten Attractions

Russian Museum
See pp106–9

Mariinskiy Theatre
See p121

Nevskiy Prospekt
See pp48–51

Stieglitz Museum
See p129

Church on Spilled Blood
See p102

The Hermitage
See pp86–95

Cathedral of Our Lady of Kazan
See p113

St Isaac's Cathedral
See pp82–3

Cathedral of SS Peter and Paul
See p70

Alexander Nevsky Monastery
See pp132–3

◄ Statue of Mikhail Barclay de Tolly in front of the Kazan Cathedral

St Petersburg's Best: Bridges and Waterways

Like its waterbound sisters, Amsterdam and Venice, St Petersburg is built around a network of canals and rivers which are still the lifeblood of the city. They contribute to its unique atmosphere by creating eerie mists which rise from the ice-laden waters in winter and, in summer, form a glittering mirror of façades during the glowing sunsets and bright White Nights.

Bridges, necessary for communication between the islands, were also an excellent means to adorn the city with decorative sculptures, elaborate lampposts and wrought-iron work.

A walk or a boat trip *(see pp134–41, pp228–9)* is the best way to enjoy them.

Winter Canal
Laid out in 1718–20, this narrow canal is crossed by three bridges and Yuriy Velten's Hermitage Theatre foyer (1783–7).

PETROGRADSKA
(see pp66–75)

Malaya Neva

NABEREZHNAYA MAKAROVA

KAMENNOOSTRO

BOL PUSHKARSKAYA UL

SREDNIY PR

VASILEVSKIY ISLAND
(see pp58–65)

BOLSHOY PR

UNIVERSITETSKAYA NAB

Bol Neva

DVORTSOVAYA M

PALACE EMBANKMEN
(see pp76–97)

ANGLIYSKAYA NAB

(SAAKIYEVSKAYA PLOSHCHAD

Moyka

SENNAYA PLOSHCHAD
(see pp116–125)

VOZNESENSKIY PROSPEKT

SEN
PLOS

Fontanka

Blagoveshchenskiy Bridge
Rebuilt in 1936–8, this bridge still retains its original cast-iron seahorse railings, designed by Bryullov.

Lion Bridge
One of the earliest of its kind, this pedestrian suspension bridge dates from 1825–6. Its cables are anchored inside four cast-iron lions, by sculptor Pavel Sokolov.

Egyptian Bridge
This bridge spanning the Fontanka was decorated in the Egyptian style fashionable at the time of its construction, in 1826.

| 0 metres | 500 |
| 0 yards | 500 |

Trinity Bridge
The ten-arched Trinity Bridge (1897–1903) is famous for its Style-Moderne lampposts and railing decorations, the work of the skilful French engineers Vincent Chabrol and René Patouillard.

Swan Canal
This tree-lined canal (1711–19) leading out to the Neva is named after the swans which were once drawn to its peaceful waters.

Bridge Passage
Cleverly designed to span the confluence of the Moyka and the Griboedov, the Theatre and Small Stable bridges were constructed by Traitteur and Adam in 1829–31.

Anichkov Bridge
This three-span bridge, carrying Nevskiy prospekt across the Fontanka, was built in 1839–41. At each corner are Pyotr Klodt's impressive sculptures of men taming wild horses.

Lomonosov Bridge
The distinctive domed granite towers, built in 1785–7, originally contained the bridge's opening mechanism. The bridge was rebuilt in 1912, but the towers were kept.

Bank Bridge
Dating from the same time as the Lion Bridge, and designed by the same team, this bridge is adorned by four magnificent cast-iron griffons. Its name derives from the nearby former Assignment Bank.

UL KUYBYSHEVA

ITSKAYA
SHCHAD

Neva

SUVOROVSKAYA
PLOSHCHAD

Mokya

GOSTINYY
DVOR
(see pp98–115)

NEVSKIY PROSPEKT

OVAYA UL

AB REKI FONTANKI

Exploring St Petersburg's Bridges and Waterways

A boat trip on St Petersburg's canals and waterways is one of the highlights of any visit to the city. From the Anichkov Bridge the river boats *(see p228)* loop along the Neva, Fontanka and Moyka rivers, taking in many impressive bridges and landmarks. Alternatively, you can choose your route to explore the city's rich architectural heritage by taking a water bus or taxi *(see p229)*. A pleasant wander along the embankments of the Griboedov Canal leads past imposing 19th-century apartment houses and fancifully decorated bridges. In winter it is sometimes possible (but not advisable) to walk on the frozen Neva.

The ice-laden Neva river in front of the Peter and Paul Fortress

The Neva and its Branches

Greatest of St Petersburg's numerous waterways, the Neva flows from Lake Ladoga in the east through the city to the Gulf of Finland, a distance of only 74 km (46 miles) in total. Vasilevskiy Island, one of more than 100 islands in the Neva Delta, divides the river into two separate branches, Bolshaya (Great) Neva and Malaya (Small) Neva.

Icebound for at least four months of the year, the Neva usually shows the first signs of cracking in March. The official opening of navigation is announced by the port authority in early spring. Before the Revolution the event was marked with great ceremony. The Commander of the Peter and Paul Fortress *(see pp68–9)*, at the head of a naval flotilla, would scoop some icy water into a silver goblet which he presented to the tsar in the Winter Palace *(see pp94–5)*.

Rivers and Canals

Inspired by Amsterdam, Peter the Great kept the many streams of the delta as canals, which also helped to drain the swampy ground. As the city grew, new ones were dug to improve the canal network.

The **Moyka** originally flowed from a swamp near the Field of Mars *(see p96)*. In the 19th century the aristocracy lined its quays with impressive Neo-Classical mansions which are still their main attraction. Canal boats and barges ply the 7-km (4-mile) long **Fontanka**, widest and busiest of the waterways, which was once the border of the city. These two rivers are linked by the **Kryukov Canal**, dug in the 18th century.

The **Griboedov Canal**, first known as the Catherine Canal in honour of Catherine the Great, was designed to move cargo from Sennaya Ploshchad. Today the atmosphere here is more tranquil. The stretch of water running south from the

Finding the Bridges

Map references refer to the Street Finder on pp232–9.

Alexander Nevsky Bridge **8 F3**
Anichkov Bridge **7 A2**
Bank Bridge **6 E2**
Blagoveshchenskiy Bridge **5 B1**
Egyptian Bridge **5 B5**
Lantern Bridge **5 C2**
Lion Bridge **5 C3**
Liteynyy Bridge **3 A3**
Lomonosov Bridge **6 F3**
Palace Bridge **1 C5**
Peter the Great Bridge **4 F5**
Red Bridge **6 D2**
St Panteleymon's Bridge **2 F5**
Singer's Bridge **2 E5**
Small Stable Bridge **2 F5**
Theatre Bridge **2 F5**
Trinity Bridge **2 E4**

Lion Bridge is particularly picturesque. The narrowest waterway is the **Winter Canal**, just to the east of the Winter Palace. Nearby is the delightful **Swan Canal** which runs along the Summer Garden *(p97)*.

Steady industrial growth in the 19th century prompted the construction of a new canal, the **Obvodnyy**, in 1834, to take the increasing number of heavy cargo barges and supply water to the city outskirts.

Neva Bridges

The most central of the Neva bridges is the **Palace Bridge** (Dvortsovyy most). The present structure, built early in the 20th century, replaced a seasonal pontoon bridge which linked the mainland to Vasilevskiy Island. The other bridge to this island, **Blagoveshchenskiy Bridge** (Blagoveshchenskiy

View of the Moyka and its south bank with a water taxi in foreground

Peter the Great Bridge, crossing the Neva near Smolnyy Institute

most, *see p65*) was the first permanent bridge over the Neva. Once known as Lieutenant Schmidt Bridge, it returned to its original name in 2007. The **Trinity Bridge** (Troitskiy most, *see p75*) was built in 1897–1903 by the French Batignolles company. At 582 m (1,910 ft), the Trinity Bridge was the Neva's longest, until the construction of the **Alexander Nevsky Bridge** (Most Aleksandra Nevskovo) in the 1960s, which is some 900 m (2,950 ft). Between these two is the **Liteynyy Bridge** (Liteynyy most) built in 1874–9. In 1917, the city authorities tried to prevent rebel workers crossing the Neva from the Vyborg Side by raising the central bridge span. The tactic failed since the revolutionaries decided to cross on foot over the frozen ice.

Near the Smolnyy Institute is the **Peter the Great Bridge** (Most PetraVelikovo), also known by its Soviet name Bolsheokhtinskiy most. It has a central drawbridge and distinctive steel twin arches, erected in 1909–11.

From April to November almost all Neva bridges are raised at night to give ships access to the Volga (*see pp228–9*).

Decorative Bridges

In the beginning, wooden bridges spanned the canals and rivers of St Petersburg. They were usually known by their colour – red, blue, green, and so on. The **Red Bridge** (Krasnyy most) which carries Gorokhovaya ulitsa over the Moyka, has preserved its original name. Built in 1808–14, this iron bridge is decorated with picturesque lamps on four granite obelisks. Lamps are also a feature of the **Lantern Bridge** (Fonarnyy most) which crosses the Moyka river near to the Yusupov Palace (*see p122*). Here the gilded lampposts are shaped to look like treble clefs. **Singer's Bridge** (Pevcheskiy most) at the other end of the Moyka takes its name from the choir of the nearby Academic Capella (*see p114*). Its engineer, Yegor Adam, also designed the lace-like patterning of the railings.

At the junction where the Griboedov meets the Moyka is an interesting ensemble, formed by the wide **Theatre Bridge** (Teatralnyy most) and **Small Stable Bridge** (Malo-

Konyushennyy most). The latter is cunningly designed to look like two bridges.

Among the more attractive bridges is Georg von Traitteur's pedestrian **Bank Bridge** (Bankovskiy most), crossing the Griboedov. Its cables are held up by two pairs of gold-winged griffons. The **Lion Bridge** (Lvinyy most), also by Traitteur, uses a similar device; in this case the suspension cables emerge from the open jaws of four proud lions.

St Panteleymon's Bridge (Panteleymonovskiy most, *see p101*) spans the Fontanka near the Summer Gardens. It was Russia's first chain bridge (1823–4). The Empire-style decoration has survived and includes gilded fasces and double-headed eagles perched on laurel wreaths. Next to the Nevskiy prospekt, the **Anichkov Bridge** (Anichkov most) is famous for its four vibrant bronze sculptures of wild horses and their powerful tamers, all of them in different poses. Further down the Fontanka, framed by a handsome Neo-Classical square by Carlo Rossi, is the **Lomonosov Bridge** (Most Lomonosova) with its unusual stone turrets.

The **Egyptian Bridge** (Egipetskiy most) spans the Fontanka close to the Kryukov Canal. It is ornamented with bronze sphinxes and bridge-heads resembling the entrance to an Egyptian temple. Originally constructed in 1826, the bridge collapsed under the weight of a passing cavalry squadron in 1905 but was rebuilt in 1955.

Lamppost, St Panteleymon's Bridge

A City Under Water

A 19th-century illustration of one of the many floods in St Petersburg

Peter the Great should have known it was a bad idea to found a city here. The first flood, just three months after he started the fortress in 1703, swept away his building materials. The water rises dangerously high on average once a year, but four floods, in 1777, 1824, 1924 and 1955, wrought massive damage. In 1824 the whole city went under water and 462 buildings were totally destroyed. This inspired Pushkin's poem *The Bronze Horseman* (see p78). Markers showing record water heights can be found by the Winter Canal and the Peter and Paul Fortress. In 1989 construction of a dam was begun to prevent future destruction.

St Petersburg's Best: Palaces and Museums

St Petersburg boasts more than 90 museums, many of them housed in palaces or other buildings of historical importance. Some are well known throughout the world, such as the Hermitage which began as Catherine the Great's private collection of European art. Others, including the Russian Museum and the Summer Palace, highlight local art, history and culture. Some of the most evocative museums are those commemorating the lives and work of famous artists, writers and musicians. This selection represents the most interesting in each category.

PETROGRADSK.
(see pp66–75)

The Hermitage
Incorporating the breathtaking state rooms of the Winter Palace, the world-famous Hermitage holds nearly three million exhibits which range from Fine Arts to archaeological finds.

Malaya Neva

NAB MAKAROVA

SREDNIY PR

VASILEVSKIY ISLAND
(see pp58–65)

BOLSHOY PR

UNIVERSITETSKAYA NAB

Bol Neva

PALACE EMBANKM
(see pp76–9)

ANGLIYSKAYA NAB

ISAAKIYEV-SKAYA PLOSHCHAD

Menshikov Palace
This grandiose Baroque palace on Vasilevskiy Island is testimony to the power of Peter the Great's friend and advisor, Prince Menshikov.

SENNAY PLOSHCH
(see pp116–)

Imperial Country Palaces

To escape the pressures of the capital, successive Russian rulers built sumptuous retreats in the rural hinterland of St Petersburg. These offer a fascinating insight into the lifestyle of the Romanov dynasty.

Tsarskoe Selo's Catherine Palace was built by Rastrelli in a flamboyant Baroque style.

Peterhof's palace and pavilions are enhanced by the splendid cascades and fountains adorning the attractive grounds.

0 km   15
0 miles   15

Pavlovsk's Great Palace is set in an extensive naturalistic landscaped park, embellished with ponds, pavilions and monuments.

Kshesinskaya Mansion
Built for a prima ballerina of the Mariinskiy Theatre, this attractive Style-Moderne mansion now houses the Museum of Russian Political History containing souvenirs from the Revolution.

Summer Palace
Interiors and furniture, such as Peter the Great's original four-poster bed, give an idea of the tsar's relatively modest lifestyle.

Stieglitz Museum
A rich collection of applied art is displayed in Messmacher's magnificent building, which was inspired by palaces of the Italian Renaissance.

Russian Museum
Carlo Rossi's Mikhaylovskiy Palace is the splendid setting for an outstanding collection of Russian art, ranging from medieval icons to contemporary paintings and sculptures. This semi-abstract work, *Blue Crest* by Vasily Kandinsky, dates from 1917.

Pushkin House-Museum
Period furnishings and personal belongings such as this inkstand recreate the atmosphere of Alexander Pushkin's last home.

0 metres   500
0 yards   500

Exploring St Petersburg's Palaces and Museums

The city's palaces range from imperial excess to the tasteful homes of the nobility, while art museums cover the fine and applied arts and folk crafts. The history of St Petersburg, from its foundation as Peter the Great's "window on the West" to its role as the "Cradle of the Revolution", is covered by a variety of museums while its culture is documented in the apartments of writers, composers and artists. More specialist interests, from railway engines and military paraphernalia to insects and whales, also find reflection in the wealth of museums.

Bedroom in the Chinese Palace (1760s), Oranienbaum

Peter the Great's Summer Palace overlooking the Fontanka

Palaces

The fabulous wealth of imperial St Petersburg is reflected in the magnificence of its palaces. No trip to the city is complete without a visit to at least one of the spectacular out-of-town imperial summer residences, **Peterhof** (see pp150–53), **Pavlovsk** (see pp160–63) or the Catherine Palace (see pp154–5) at **Tsarskoe Selo**. These palaces, built and added to in the last 200 years of Romanov rule, illustrate the extravagance of the imperial court and the wealth of the Empire's natural resources. An abundance of gold, lapis lazuli, malachite, marble and other precious minerals decorates many of the rich palace interiors. The palace parks and grounds are landscaped and filled with follies and monuments.

At the centre of the city, the **Winter Palace** (see pp94–5) is home to the Hermitage art museum and epitomizes the opulence of the court. Peter the Great's more intimate **Summer Palace** is nearby (see p97) and

makes a pleasing contrast. Peter's friend and counsellor, Prince Alexander Menshikov, also built two sumptuous residences, the **Menshikov Palace** (see p64) on Vasilevskiy Island, and his summer palace at **Oranienbaum** (see pp148–9), Lomonosov.

Overlooking the Moyka river is the **Yusupov Palace** (see p122) which is famed as the murder scene of Rasputin, the extraordinary peasant who exerted his malign influence over the Russian court.

For those in search of a tranquil setting, a pleasant day can be spent exploring the **Yelagin Palace** (see p128) and the island of the same name.

Art Museums

One of the world's greatest collections of Western art is housed in the **Hermitage** (see pp86–95) which is home to some 3 million pieces of art.

With its collections ranging from Egyptian mummies to Scythian gold, Greek vases, Colombian emeralds and a vast and dazzling array of Old Master, Impressionist and Post-Impressionist paintings, it is essential to be selective.

The **Russian Museum** (see pp106–9) is a showcase for Russian art, including the 20th-century avant-garde and the folk crafts which influenced it. Exhibitions from its holdings are also in the **Mikhaylovskiy Castle** (see p103), **Marble Palace** (see p96) and **Stroganov Palace** (see p114).

The **Academy of Arts** (see p65) exhibits work by past students as well as models of the city's notable buildings.

There are fascinating displays of applied arts from around the world in the **Stieglitz Museum** (see p129) which includes ceramics, woodcarving, ironwork and embroidery. Its interiors and the glass-roofed exhibition hall are equally impressive.

The Cyclist (1913) by Natalya Goncharova, Russian Museum

History Museums

St Petersburg's dramatic 300-year history is proudly recorded in a number of the city's museums. The **Cabin of Peter the Great** (see p75) was the earliest building to be constructed in the city and it offers an intriguing insight into the surprisingly humble lifestyle of this tsar.

A group of historic sights lies within the Peter and Paul Fortress. The **Cathedral of SS Peter and Paul** (see p70) houses the tombs of all but two of Russia's tsars since Peter the Great. The preserved cells of the grim **Trubetskoy Bastion** (see p71) act as a reminder of the hundreds of political prisoners to be confined within the fortress walls. In the **Commandant's House** (see p71), the courthouse where prisoners were once in-terrogated, an exhibition looks at medieval settlements in the area, while the **Engineer's House** (see p70) focuses on daily life in St Petersburg before the Revolution.

A wealth of revolutionary memorabilia, including Stalin-era posters and a huge propa-ganda stained-glass panel, can be found in the **Museum of Russian Political History**. The museum is located within the Kshesinskaya Mansion (see p74) which, in 1917, housed the Bolshevik headquarters. The **Cruiser Aurora** (see p75) also played a part in the Revolution, having fired a warning shot before the storming of the Winter Palace in October 1917.

For an impression of the prestigious pre-revolutionary school where poet Alexander Pushkin was a student, some of the classrooms of the **Lycée** at Tsarskoe Selo (see p157) have been restored to their 19th-century appearance.

On the southern outskirts of the city, in Victory Square (see p133), the **Monument to the Heroic Defenders of Leningrad** poignantly evokes the Siege of Leningrad (1941–4) and acts as an important reminder of the great hardships endured by St Petersburgers during World War II.

Office of Leningrad party secretary Sergey Kirov, Kirov Museum

Special Interest Museums

Remnants of Peter the Great's legendary "cabinet of curiosities" can be found in Russia's oldest museum, the **Kunstkammer** (see p62). Housed under the same roof is a **Museum of Anthropology and Ethnography**, displaying a large collection of artifacts from all over the world. For natural history, the **Zoological Museum** (see p62) encompasses most known life forms, including a unique collection of molluscs and blue corals.

The **Institute of Russian Literature** (see p62) houses manuscripts from Pushkin to Mayakovskiy. The **Artillery Museum** (see p72) covers military hardware, from pikes to ballistic missiles. Train enthusiasts will find plenty to enjoy in the **Railway Museum** (see p125), including an 1835 engine built for the Tsarskoe Selo railway.

The **Museum of Musical Life** in the Sheremetev Palace (see p131) displays period instru-ments and explains the role of the Sheremetev family as leading music patrons in 19th-century St Petersburg. A stunning array of beautiful stage costumes are on display alongside photos, set designs and other theatrical ephemera in the **Theatre Museum** which is situated on Ostrovskiy Square (see p112).

House-Museums

A handful of evocative museums commemorates some of the city's most famous residents. The **Pushkin House-Museum** (see p115), the **Nabokov Museum** (see p124) and the **Dostoevsky House-Museum** (see p132) recapture something of the life and char-acter of their former residents.

The **Anna Akhmatova Museum** in the former service quarters of the Sheremetev Palace (see p131) traces the dramatic life of the poet, who lived here for many years.

For an insight into the life of a powerful Communist official of the 1930s, visit the **Kirov Museum** (see p74). The museum is devoted to the popular leader whose assassination on Stalin's orders initiated the Great Terror (see p29).

Outside the city in **Repino** (see p148), the house of the painter Ilya Repin is set in beautiful woodland on the Gulf of Finland.

18th-century violin and score in Museum of Musical Life, Sheremetev Palace

Celebrated St Petersburgers

As the residence of the Russian imperial family and court from the early 18th century, St Petersburg was the focus of patronage and an almost boundless source of wealth. It was the perfect seedbed for creativity and the flowering of ideas. Institutions such as the Academy of Arts, the University, the Kunstkammer and the Imperial School of Ballet trained generations of cultural figures and scientists to the highest standards. So successful were they that, by the dawn of the 20th century, St Petersburg had become one of the most important cultural centres in Europe.

Grigoriy Kozintsev
Director Kozintsev confirmed his reputation in the West with his interpretation of Shakespeare's *Hamlet* (1964), made at Lenfilm *(see p72)*.

Nikolai Gogol
A merciless satirist of St Petersburg society, Gogol lived on Malaya Morskaya ulitsa *(see p84)* for three years.

Ilya Repin
This outstanding realist painter is seen here teaching life drawing at the Academy of Arts *(see p65)* where he was a professor.

PETROGRADSKA
(see pp66–75)

Malaya Neva

NAB MAKAROVA

SREDNIY PR

VASILEVSKIY ISLAND
(see pp58–65)

BOLSHOY PR

UNIVERSITETSKAYA NAB

Bol Neva

PALAC
EMBANKM
(see pp76–

ANGLIYSKAYA NAB

ISAAKIYEV-SKAYA PLOSHCHAD

Mokya

SENNAYA PLOSHCHAD
(see pp116–125)

VOZNESENSKIY PROSPEKT

Fontan

Pyotr Tchaikovsky
Tchaikovsky graduated from the Conservatory *(see p122)* in 1865 and went on to compose his world-famous operas and ballets.

Anna Pavlova
A prima ballerina at the Mariinskiy Theatre *(see p121)*, Pavlova took Paris by storm in 1909 when she toured in *Les Sylphides* with the Ballets Russes.

Alexander Pushkin
The great poet, who sketched this self-portrait on a manuscript, died in the flat which is now a house-museum *(see p115)*.

Sergey Diaghilev
Driving force behind the Ballets Russes, Diaghilev also produced the influential *World of Art* magazine in his flat on 45 Liteynyy prospekt. He is shown here with Jean Cocteau *(left)*.

Anna Akhmatova
The poet's most famous poem, *Requiem*, is a powerful and moving indictment of the Stalinist regime. Akhmatova, seen here in a portrait by Nathan Altman, lived in the service quarters of the Sheremetev Palace *(see p131)*.

Dmitriy Shostakovich
Shostakovich's *Seventh Symphony* was broadcast live on the radio from the Great Hall of the Philharmonia *(see p100)* in August 1942, while the city was under siege. Many testified to its role in boosting the morale of the besieged citizens.

Fyodor Dostoevsky
The novelist Dostoevsky lived for many years among the slums of Sennaya Ploshchad *(see p124)* which provided the setting for his greatest work, *Crime and Punishment*.

TROITSKAYA PLOSHCHAD

TROUSKIY PR.

Neva

SUVOROVSKAYA PLOSHCHAD

Mokya

Fontanka

NEVSKIY PROSPEKT

GOSTINYY DVOR
(see pp98–115)

SADOVAYA UL.

NAB REKI FONTANKI

0 metres 500
0 yards 500

Remarkable St Petersburgers

The streets of St Petersburg are redolent with literary and artistic associations. Fascinating art collections, house-museums, theatres and concert halls evoke the memory of famous St Petersburgers. The world of the 18th-century genius Lomonosov and 19th-century writers Pushkin and Dostoevsky can be imagined. So too, can the spirit of Russian ballet when dancers such as Anna Pavlova and Vaslaw Nijinsky thrilled the Mariinskiy audiences. During these early years of the 20th century, writers, musicians, dancers and painters flocked to St Petersburg, bringing with them a wealth of creativity.

Symbolist "Silver Age" poet,
Andrei Bely (1880–1934)

Writers

Considered the father of modern Russian literature, **Alexander Pushkin** (1799–1837) was simultaneously intoxicated by St Petersburg's beauty and sensitive to the underlying climate of political suspicion and intolerance which constrained writers in the wake of the Decembrist rebellion of 1825 *(see p25)*. **Nikolai Gogol** (1809–52) responded to these constraints by satirizing the status quo. In *The Nose*, he targeted the city's bureaucrats with their inflated sense of self worth and mind-numbing conformity.

Another aspect of the city altogether is revealed by **Fyodor Dostoevsky** (1821–81). His novel *Crime and Punishment*, one of more than 30 works set in the city, takes place against a back-drop of squalor in the notorious slums of Sennaya Ploshchad *(see p124)*. The story of the murder of an old moneylender was based on a real crime and the novel's publication in 1866 was blamed for a series of subsequent copy-cat killings.

Poetry, which flourished in the "Golden Age" of Pushkin, only regained its ascendancy over the novel in the "Silver Age" during the first decade of the 20th century. Some of the most exciting poets of the period, including **Aleksandr Blok** (1880–1921), **Andrei Bely** (1880–1934) and **Anna Akhmatova** (1889–1966), gathered at The Tower, a flat overlooking the Tauride Gardens *(see p130)*. Bely later wrote *Petersburg*, one of the earliest stream-of-consciousness novels. Akhmatova is honoured by a museum in the Sheremetev Palace *(see p131)* while one of her protégés, **Joseph Brodsky** (1940–96), went on to receive the Nobel Prize in literature in 1987. Brodsky became the bête-noire of the Leningrad literary establishment in the 1960s. The refusal of the authorities to publish his poetry, which they condemned as decadent, finally forced him to emigrate in 1972.

Musicians

The first important composer to emerge from the nationalist movement was **Mikhail Glinka** (1804–57), the earliest composer of Russian opera. In 1862, the Conservatory *(see p122)* was founded by **Anton Rubinstein** (1829–94) and this became the focus of musical life in St Petersburg. **Nikolai Rimsky-Korsakov** (1844–1908) taught here for 37 years and together with composers such as **Modest Mussorgsky** (1839–81), and **Aleksandr Borodin** (1834–87), he was part of "the mighty handful". They were a largely self-taught group aiming to develop a musical language based on Russian folk music and Slav traditions. Many of the operas premiered at the Mariinskiy *(see p121)*.

One of the musical geniuses of the 20th century was **Igor Stravinsky** (1882–1971). He spent much time abroad but, as works like *The Rite of Spring* testify, his cultural roots were firmly in his homeland.

The city's most important concert venue is the Great Hall of the Philharmonia *(see p204)* where **Pyotr Tchaikovsky**'s (1840–93) *Sixth Symphony* was premiered in 1893 and **Dmitriy Shostakovich**'s (1906–75) *Seventh Symphony*, his most famous work, was performed in 1942.

Portrait of composer Mikhail Glinka painted by Ilya Repin in 1887

The Circus (1919) by avant-garde artist Marc Chagall

Artists

From the 18th century, the Academy of Arts *(see p65)* was the centre of artistic life in St Petersburg. **Dmitriy Levitskiy** (1735–1822), **Orest Kiprenskiy** (1782–1836), **Silvestr Shchedrin** (1791–1830), and Russia's first internationally recognized artist, **Karl Bryullov** (1799–1852), were all trained here.

In 1863, a group of students rebelled against the Academy and went on to establish the Wanderers movement *(see p108)*. To some extent the Academy and the Wanderers became reconciled when the most versatile of these artists, **Ilya Repin** (1844–1930), was appointed professor of painting at the Academy in 1893.

Five years later **Sergey Diaghilev** (1872–1929) and painter **Alexandre Benois** (1870–1960) launched the *World of Art* magazine *(see p109)*, proclaiming "Art for art's sake". Another collaborator, **Leon Bakst** (1866–1924), designed the most famous of the Ballets Russes costumes. Bakst also taught **Marc Chagall** (1889–1985) who later settled in France and had a profound impact on art in the West as well as in Russia. Other members of the Russian avant-garde include **Kazimir Malevich** (1878–1935) and **Pavel Filonov** (1883–1941).

Works by all of these artists can be seen at the Russian Museum *(see pp106–9)*.

Dancers and Choreographers

The skills of Russian dancers are legendary and the performances of the Mariinskiy (Kirov) Ballet Company continue to enthral audiences all over the world. Since 1836 the dancers have been trained at the former Imperial School of Ballet *(see p112)*. In 1869–1903 the outstanding choreographer at the Mariinskiy was **Marius Petipa**. He inspired a generation of dancers including **Matilda Kshesinskaya** *(see p74)*, **Vaslaw Nijinsky** (1890–1950) and the legendary **Anna Pavlova** (1885–1931).

Petipa's successor, **Mikhail Fokin** (1880–1942), is famous as the principal choreographer of the Ballets Russes *(see p121)*. The Mariinskiy tradition was revived after the Revolution by another graduate of the School of Ballet, **Agrippina Vaganova** (1879–1951). Her groundwork paved the way for a new generation of dancers including **Rudolf Nureyev** (1938–93) and modern dancers **Galina Mezentseva** and **Emil Faskhoutdinov**.

Film Directors

The Lenfilm Studios *(see p72)* were founded in 1918 on the site where the first Russian cine film had been shown in 1896. In its heyday Lenfilm produced 15 movies a year. Its two most remarkable directors, **Grigoriy**

Poster for The Youth of Maxim (1935) directed by Kozintsev

Kozintsev (1905–73) and **Leonid Trauberg** (1902–90), first joined forces in 1922 and began making short experimental films. The pair then went on to direct *The New Babylon* (1929), remarkable for its montage and lighting effects, and *The Maxim Trilogy* (1935–39). Kozintsev's versions of *Hamlet* (1964) and *King Lear* (1970), with music composed by Shostakovich for both films, mark the height of his success in the West.

The great polymath Mikhail Lomonosov

Scientists

The foundations of modern Russian science were laid in the 18th century by **Mikhail Lomonosov** (1711–65) *(see p63)* who worked for over 20 years in the Kunstkammer *(see p62)*. His treatise, *Elementa Chymiae Mathematica*, published in 1741, anticipates Dalton's theory of the atomic structure of matter.

In 1869, **Dmitriy Mendeleev** (1834–1907), a professor of chemistry, compiled the Periodic Table of Elements.

Many people believe that the world's first radio signal was sent by **Aleksandr Popov** (1859–1906) from the laboratories of St Petersburg University on 24 March 1896.

In 1904, the world-famous physiologist **Ivan Pavlov** (1849–1936) won the Nobel Prize in medicine for his theory of conditioned reflexes, which he demonstrated by experimenting on dogs and their hearing responses.

Nevskiy Prospekt
From the Admiralty to the Griboedov Canal

A pleasant stroll along this first stretch of St Petersburg's main artery reveals a wealth of attractive buildings. A profusion of architectural styles ranges from the Baroque Stroganov Palace to the magnificent Neo-Classical Cathedral of Our Lady of Kazan and the striking Style-Moderne Singer House. The stately avenue was once known as the "Street of Tolerance", referring to the clutch of churches of different denominations that were established here in the late 18th and early 19th centuries. *(See also p110)*

Literary Café Once called the Wolf and Beranger, this café was known for its fashionable clientele. Pushkin left from here for his fatal duel in 1837 *(see p85)*.

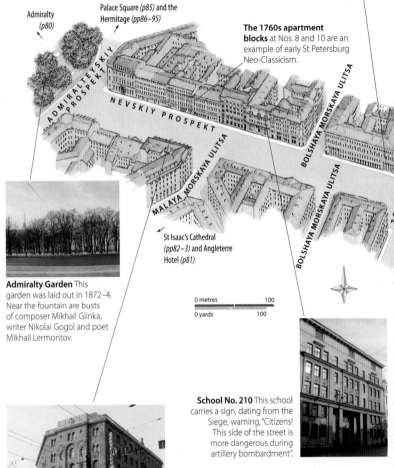

Admiralty *(p80)*

Palace Square *(p85)* and the Hermitage *(pp86–95)*

The 1760s apartment blocks at Nos. 8 and 10 are an example of early St Petersburg Neo-Classicism.

ADMIRALTEYSKIY PROSPEKT

NEVSKIY PROSPEKT

MALAYA MORSKAYA ULITSA

BOLSHAYA MORSKAYA ULITSA

BOLSHAYA MORSKAYA ULITSA

St Isaac's Cathedral *(pp82–3)* and Angleterre Hotel *(p81)*

Admiralty Garden This garden was laid out in 1872–4. Near the fountain are busts of composer Mikhail Glinka, writer Nikolai Gogol and poet Mikhail Lermontov.

0 metres   100
0 yards   100

School No. 210 This school carries a sign, dating from the Siege, warning, "Citizens! This side of the street is more dangerous during artillery bombardment".

Vavelberg House Marian Peretyatkovich's severe granite building (1912) is uncharacteristic of the city's architecture. The upper storeys were inspired by the Palazzo Medici in Florence, the arcades by the Doge's Palace, Venice.

Dutch Church Building The Dutch church was housed behind the central Neo-Classical portico of Paul Jacot's seemingly secular building (1831–7). The elongated wings are still occupied by offices, flats and shops.

Locator Map

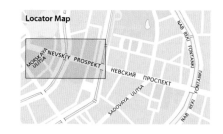

Stroganov Palace The façade of this splendid Baroque palace, one of the oldest buildings on the street (1753), is embellished with sculptural ornaments and the Stroganov coat of arms *(see p114)*.

The Fashion House Marian Lyalevich designed this building for Mertens Furriers in 1911–12. The impact of the Neo-Classical arches is heightened by the beautiful plate glass.

Singer House was built for the Singer Sewing Machine Company in 1902–4 by Pavel Syuzor. The building is distinguished by a glass globe on a conical tower.

➤ Continued *(pp50–51)*

The Lutheran Church (1833) was an important centre for the evangelical community. Converted into a swimming pool during the Soviet era, it is once again open as a church *(see p114)*.

The Griboedov Canal, originally known as the Catherine Canal, was renamed in 1923 after the 19th-century Russian playwright Aleksandr Griboedov.

★ Cathedral of Our Lady of Kazan Ninety-six Corinthian columns, arranged in four rows, form an arc facing Nevskiy prospekt. Andrey Voronikhin's design was inspired by Bernini's colonnade for St Peter's in Rome *(see p113)*.

Nevskiy Prospekt
From the Griboedov Canal to the Fontanka

Nevskiy prospekt has been the main focus for St Petersburg's shopping and entertainment since the mid-18th century. As the prospekt continues towards the handsome Anichkov Bridge on the Fontanka river, cafés, bars, restaurants and cinemas sit alongside three historic shopping arcades, the Silver Rows, Gostinyy Dvor and Passazh. Bustling with life, this stretch of the avenue also has many sights of historic and architectural interest, including the Anichkov Palace.

Passazh Arcade This popular shopping mall is covered by a glass canopy stretching 180 m (590 ft). The arcade opened in 1848 and was reconstructed in 1900.

Church on Spilled Blood (p102)

The Small Hall of the Philharmonia was the city's main concert hall in the early 19th century.

The Church of Saint Catherine (1762–82), by Vallin de la Mothe, is a mixture of Baroque and Neo-Classical styles. It is the oldest Roman Catholic church in Russia.

Belmond Grand Hotel Europe (p103)

Russian Museum (pp106–9)

The Armenian Church (1771–80) is a fine example of Yuriy Velten's decorative Neo-Classical style (see p110).

KANAL GRIBOEDOVA

Nevskiy Prospekt 2 (Griboedova Canal)

MIKHAYLOVSKAYA ULITSA

NEVSKIY PROSPEKT

DUMSKAYA ULITSA

Nevskiy Prospekt 1

Gostinyy Dvor

SADOVAYA ULITSA

Silver Rows Arcade (1784–7)

The Duma Tower was built in 1804 as a watchtower for fires. The Duma building was the centre of local government from 1786–1918.

| 0 metres | 100 |
| 0 yards | 100 |

The Russian National Library houses over 33 million items, including the earliest surviving handwritten Russian book (1057).

Portik Rusca Perinnyie Ryadi Now standing alone, the six-columned portico by Luigi Rusca was originally the entrance to a long arcade of shops. The portico was dismantled during the construction of the metro and rebuilt in 1972.

★ **Gostinyy Dvor** This striking arcade has been St Petersburg's main bazaar since the mid-18th century (see p110). It houses more than 300 outlets which sell everything from clothes and cosmetics to souvenirs and chocolates.

For key to symbols see back flap

Locator Map

★ **Yeliseev's** Famous for its beautiful Style-Moderne decor, this building is home to Yeliseev's delicatessen, and also houses the Akimov Comedy Theatre *(see p111)*.

Beloselskiy-Belozerskiy Palace Now a cultural centre and offices, this sumptuous palace was designed in Neo-Baroque style by Andrey Stakenschneider in 1847–8. The red façade is decorated with Corinthian pilasters and atlantes upholding balconies.

Quarenghi's Stalls were built in 1803–6 as trading rows. They were then handed over to the imperial chancellor and became known as the Cabinet.

Number 66 was occupied by the music publishers Bessel and Co in the 19th century. Tchaikovsky was one of many composers who frequented their offices.

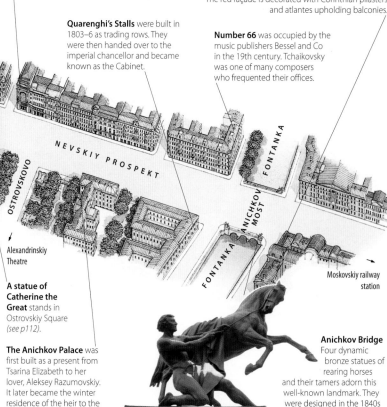

Alexandrinskiy Theatre

A statue of Catherine the Great stands in Ostrovskiy Square *(see p112)*.

The Anichkov Palace was first built as a present from Tsarina Elizabeth to her lover, Aleksey Razumovskiy. It later became the winter residence of the heir to the throne *(see p111)*.

Moskovskiy railway station

Anichkov Bridge Four dynamic bronze statues of rearing horses and their tamers adorn this well-known landmark. They were designed in the 1840s by Pyotr Klodt *(see p37)*.

ST PETERSBURG THROUGH THE YEAR

Whatever the weather, Russians are always ready to celebrate and consequently take their public holidays very seriously. Flowers have great symbolic significance, from mimosa for International Women's Day, to lilac to mark the beginning of summer. Every official holiday, as well as some local festivals such as City Day, are celebrated both in the centre of town and in the many different districts, with regattas, parades and fireworks at night, when the torches on the Rostral Columns (see p62) are lit. Classical music is the central theme of a large number of festivals each year, attracting talented performers from all over the world. But even without an official holiday, Russian people love to get out and about, whether to ski or ice-skate in the winter months or gather mushrooms in late summer and autumn.

Spring

Spring has set in for good when the first sunbathers gather on the beaches outside the Peter and Paul Fortress (see pp68–9) and when, in early April after the waterways have thawed, the city's bridges open to allow ships through.

To warm themselves up after the months of cold, locals celebrate "maslennitsa", the making of pancakes (blini) prior to Lent. They then gather bunches of willow as a symbol of the approaching Palm Sunday. On the eve of Lent, "Forgiveness Sunday", it is common practice to ask forgiveness of those you might have offended during the year. Once the snows have gone, the first trips to the dacha, or country house, are made to put the gardens in order.

Early sunbathers on the banks of the Peter and Paul Fortress

March

International Women's Day (Mezhdunarodnyy zhenskiy den), 8 Mar. Men rush around the city buying flowers for their womenfolk. It is a tradition to

Candles lighting up Russian Orthodox church during Easter service

say s prazdnikom (congratulations on the holiday) to everyone. There are even special performances and concerts and, however sexist it may seem to non-Russians, it is a very popular day.

From the Avant-Garde to the Present (Ot avangarda do nashih dney), mid-Mar. A celebration of 20th-century art and music in a city-wide festival.

Easter Sunday (Paskha). The dates on which Lent and Easter fall change every year. On Easter Sunday, St Petersburg churches are filled with worshippers, the evocative sound of ethereal music and chanting and the smell of incense. Russians traditionally greet each other with Khristos voskres (Christ is risen), to which the reply is Voistine voskres (He is truly risen).

April

Musical Spring in St Petersburg (Muzikalnaya Vesna v Sankt-Peterburge),

mid-Apr. As warm clothing and heavy boots are laid aside after the cold winter months, the public flock to concert halls throughout the city.
Cosmonauts' Day (Den Kosmonavtiki), 12 Apr. Space exploration was one of the glories of the Soviet Union and this occasion is celebrated with fireworks at 10pm.

May

Labour Day (International Workers' Solidarity Day (Den Truda), 1 May. Public holiday.
Peterhof Fountains (Fontany v Petergofe), first weekend in May. Bands and orchestras accompany the switching on of the famous fountains at Peterhof (see p150–53).
Victory Day (Den Pobedy), 9 May. After a sombre ceremony at Piskarevskoe Cemetery (see p128), smartly dressed veterans fill Nevskiy prospekt (see pp48–51) and Palace Square (see p85) in commemoration of the Nazi surrender in 1945.
City Day (Den goroda), last week of May. A great variety of events, mainly taking place around the Peter and Paul Fortress (see pp68–9), mark the founding of the city on 27 May 1703.
Musical Olympus International Festival, late May/early Jun. Young musicians from all over the world are accompanied by St Petersburg's most famous orchestras.

Proud war veteran on Victory Day

Average Daily Hours of Sunshine

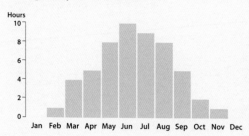

Hours

| Jan | Feb | Mar | Apr | May | Jun | Jul | Aug | Sep | Oct | Nov | Dec |

Sunshine Hours
St Petersburg's climate can vary dramatically from hot, sunny days and occasional heavy downpours during the summer months, to winters with sub-zero temperatures and snow. From mid-June to mid-July, it never gets dark. During the winter months the days are extremely short, but there can be days of bright sunshine.

Summer

A lilac in flower is the real symbol that warm weather has set in and there is an air of excitement once the Field of Mars *(see p96)* comes into bloom. Throughout the warm months, the city is deserted at weekends when people go off to their *dacha*, which is usually a summer house outside the city.

St Petersburg's main festive season is during the acclaimed White Nights in June, when the sun hardly sets and it never quite gets dark. Concerts, ballets and other performances take place all over the city, which fills with thousands of visitors *(see p203)*. The most favoured place to be at night-time is on the embankments of the Neva, which are crowded with revellers watching the bridges being raised around 2am.

June

International Protection of Children Day *(Den Zatschity detey)*, 1 Jun. Performances and events for children are held throughout the city.

Russia Day *(Den Rossii)*, 12 Jun. The day Russia became "independent" of the Soviet Union is marked with fireworks at 10pm.

Trinity Sunday *(Troytsa)*, 50 days after Easter. Believers and atheists alike go to tidy the graves of their loved ones and raise a glass of vodka for their souls.

The White Nights Swing, Jazz Festival, mid-June. A large jam session supported by local and visiting musicians for anyone with an interest in jazz.

Stars of the White Nights, Classical Music Festival *(Zvezdy Belykh nochey)*, Jun. This is the original White Nights festival, with first-class opera, classical music and ballet concerts performed at all major venues.

White Nights, Rock Music Festival *(Belye nochi)*, late Jun. Numerous outdoor rock concerts are held at the Peter and Paul Fortress *(see pp68–9)*.

Festival of Festivals *(Festival-festivaley)*, last week in Jun. This is an international non-

Russian battleships moored on the Neva, Navy Day

competitive film festival showing the best international films released over the past year. The festival attracts film stars from all over the world.

Tsarskoe Selo Carnival *(Tsarskoselskiy karnaval)*, last weekend in June. Funny costumes, music and mayhem fill the centre of Tsarskoe Selo *(see pp154–7)*.

July

Sporting Competitions. St Petersburg is a popular sporting venue for numerous international events, offering everything from tennis to figure skating and yachting.

Navy Day *(Den Voenno-morskovo Flota)*, first Sun after 22 July. The Neva resembles a shipyard, with submarines and torpedo boats adorned with flags and bunting.

August

With schools on holiday and temperatures at their highest, this is a quiet time, with most families escaping to their *dacha* outside the city.

Bridge opening in front of the Peter and Paul Fortress on a White Night

Average Monthly Rain and Snowfall

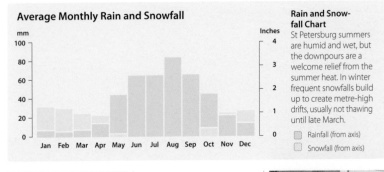

Rain and Snowfall Chart

St Petersburg summers are humid and wet, but the downpours are a welcome relief from the summer heat. In winter frequent snowfalls build up to create metre-high drifts, usually not thawing until late March.

☐ Rainfall (from axis)
☐ Snowfall (from axis)

Autumn

City life begins to gain pace as people return from their *dacha* and families begin to prepare for the start of school.

In September, when theatres reopen after the summer break, the city's cultural life resumes. The Mariinskiy (Kirov) returns from touring, and new plays and operas are premiered. October marks the start of the festival season, with guest musicians and theatre groups from all over the world taking part.

The crisp autumn weather is ideal for gathering mushrooms.

Chanterelle mushrooms

Popular hunting spots can be found to the northwest of the city around Zelenogorsk and Repino (see p148). Enthusiastic mushroom-gatherers rise early to hunt for chanterelles, oyster mushrooms, *podberyozoviki* (brown mushrooms) and *podosinoviki* (orange-cap bolens). The locals are skilled in identifying edible mushrooms while amateur pickers should be aware of the dangers of poisonous ones. An activity with fewer potential side effects might be a trip on the hydrofoil to Peterhof (see pp150–53) to see the magnificent fountains before they are switched off for the winter.

Children dressed up for the first day of school

September
Knowledge Day (*Den znaniy*), 1 Sep. The city is full of children heading for their first day back at school, laden with flowers.

October
International Theatre Festival Baltic House (*Baltiyskiy dom*), Oct. Actors, clowns and pantomime artists gather from the Baltic countries to perform in theatres and on the streets with two weeks of mayhem.

November
Day of National Unity, 4 Nov. A reminder that the Russian Federation is a multinational country with various religions and political parties.
Sound Ways, Modern Music Festival (*Zvukovyye puti*), mid-Nov. A chance to catch up with some of the most avant-garde trends in jazz and contemporary classical music from Russia and the rest of Europe. Musicians invited from abroad abound, and many of Russia's most renowned performers refuse international engagements in order to take part in this home-grown festival.
Christmas Fast, 28 Nov. During this time, vegetarians enjoy countless choices at many restaurants in the city.

Autumn colours in the park at Tsarskoe Selo

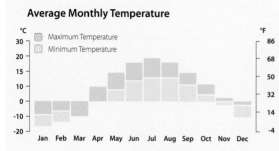

Average Monthly Temperature

- Maximum Temperature
- Minimum Temperature

Temperature Chart

St Petersburg's climate is maritime and milder than might be expected. Summers are warm and often punctuated with hot days as early as May, though during the winter months temperatures often fall well below freezing. St Petersburg's average minimum and maximum temperatures throughout the year are shown in this chart.

Winter

As the ice thickens on the waters and the snow deepens, people head for the outdoors once more. Children's sledges are not expensive to buy, and all other equipment can be hired. Cross-country skiing needs no lessons to make it fun. Tsarskoe Selo *(see pp154–7)* and Pavlovsk *(see pp160–63)* parks provide ski and sledge hire at the ski bases *(lyzhnaya baza)*. Skates can be hired for use in the rink at Moskovskiy Park Pobedy, by Park Pobedy metro station in the south of the city, and also at the Central Park of Culture and Rest (Krestovskiy Ostrov metro station).

The truly hardened members of the local "walruses" swimming club break the ice by the Peter and Paul Fortress *(see pp68–9)* every day to take an early morning dip.

In the midst of winter activities come New Year and Christmas. New Year is the big holiday, while Christmas itself is celebrated according to the Orthodox calendar, on 7 January. Many people also still

Sledging on the frozen Neva outside the Hermitage *(see pp86–95)*

celebrate Old New Year, which falls on 14 January. A seasonal delight is the Christmas ballet, *The Nutcracker*, at the Mariinskiy Theatre *(see p121)*.

December

Constitution Day *(Den konstitutsii)*, 12 Dec. When Yeltsin's new constitution replaced the Brezhnev version, a new constitution day replaced the old one. Fireworks are set off all over town at 10pm.
Musical Encounters in the Northern Palmyra *(Muzykalnyye vstrechi v Severnoy Palmire)*, Dec–Jan. This classical music festival is the last one of the year and is made even more magical by the backdrop of snowy streets and frozen waterways outside.
New Year's Eve *(Novyy god)*, 31 Dec. Still the biggest holiday of the year, New Year's Eve is best celebrated with the local "champagne", Shampanskoe *(see p185)*. This is considered to be a family celebration, with people dressed as Grandfather Frost (the Russian equivalent of Santa Claus) and the Snow Maiden, the traditional bearers of gifts.

January

Russian Orthodox Christmas *(Rozhdestvo)*, 7 Jan. Christmas is celebrated in a quieter fashion than Easter, with a traditional visit to an evening service on Christmas Eve (6th), when the church bells ring out all over the city.

February

Defenders of the Motherland Day *(Den zashchitnikov rodiny)*, 23 Feb. The male equivalent of Women's Day. Men are congratulated and given flowers and presents.

Public Holidays

New Year's Day (1 Jan)

Russian Orthodox Christmas (7 Jan)

International Women's Day (8 Mar)

Easter Sunday (Mar/Apr)

Labour Day (1 May)

Victory Day (9 May)

Independence Day (12 Jun)

Day of National Unity (4 Nov)

Constitution Day (12 Dec)

Drilling a hole through the ice for winter-time fishing

Aerial view of the Church on Spilled Blood in the morning light ▶

ST PETERSBURG AREA BY AREA

VASILEVSKIY ISLAND

It was Peter the Great's intention that Vasilevskiy Island (*Vasilevskiy ostrov*), the largest island in the Neva delta, was to be the administrative heart of his new capital. However, lack of access (the first permanent bridge was not built until 1842) and the hazards of floods and stormy crossings led to the abandonment of Peter's project, and the centre grew up across the river around the Admiralty (*see p80*) instead. The island's original street plan, based on canals that were never dug (*see p22*), survives in the numbered streets known as lines (*linii*), which run from north to south. The focal point of the island is at the east end with the fine ensemble of public buildings around the Strelka, or "spit". The rest of the island developed with the spread of industrialization in the 19th century and it became a middle-class haven. There was also a thriving German community here which is reflected in the Lutheran churches. Today much of the island has a sedate air, with tree-lined avenues, museums and some attractive 19th-century architecture. The northwest part of the island is covered with high-rise buildings.

Sights at a Glance

Museums
- ❷ The Institute of Russian Literature
- ❸ Zoological Museum
- ❹ Kunstkammer
- ❻ Menshikov Palace

Streets and Bridges
- ❼ Bolshoy Prospekt
- ❿ Blagoveshchenskiy Bridge

Historic Buildings and Monuments
- ❶ Rostral Columns
- ❺ Twelve Colleges
- ❾ Academy of Arts

Churches
- ❽ St Andrew's Cathedral

🔲 **Restaurants** *p186*
1. Casa del Myaso
2. Dans le Noir?
3. Fruktovaya Lavka
4. Grad Petrov
5. Ketino
6. Kneipe Jager Haus
7. Maria Karlotta
8. Punkt Pitaniya
9. Restoran
10. Russian Kitsch
11. Staraya Tamozhnya

See also Street Finder map 1

Street-by-Street: the Strelka

The eastern end of Vasilevskiy Island is known as the Strelka, or "spit". Once St Petersburg's main centre of commerce, it has become an area of learning. The Academy of Sciences and St Petersburg University are both situated here, as are various museums, institutes and libraries, housed in the former warehouses and customs buildings. The nautical theme is preserved in the two Rostral Columns. In front of these lighthouses is a lawn, a popular spot for newly-married couples to have their picture taken. From here there are views across the Neva towards the Peter and Paul Fortress (see pp68–9) and the Hermitage (see pp86–95).

The old Stock Exchange and Rostral Columns from across the Neva

The Lomonosov Monument honours Mikhail Lomonosov (1711–65), who taught at the Academy of Sciences.

❺ Twelve Colleges
Originally erected to house the 12 ministries of Peter the Great's government, they now form the main building of St Petersburg University.

The Academy of Sciences was founded in 1724. The present building was constructed by Giacomo Quarenghi in 1783–5.

❹ ★ Kunstkammer
The Kunstkammer houses Peter the Great's collection of biological curiosities. Its tower, crowned by a sundial, is a St Petersburg landmark.

Palace Embankment

❸ Zoological Museum
With over 1.5 million specimens the museum is one of the finest of its kind in the world. The exhibits include a set of stuffed animals that belonged to Peter the Great and a world-famous collection of mammoths.

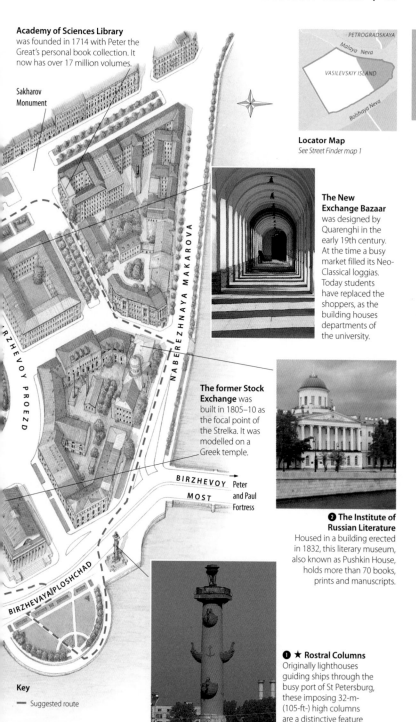

Academy of Sciences Library
was founded in 1714 with Peter the Great's personal book collection. It now has over 17 million volumes.

Sakharov Monument

Locator Map
See Street Finder map 1

The New Exchange Bazaar
was designed by Quarenghi in the early 19th century. At the time a busy market filled its Neo-Classical loggias. Today students have replaced the shoppers, as the building houses departments of the university.

NABEREZHNAYA MAKAROVA

BIRZHEVOY PROEZD

The former Stock Exchange was built in 1805–10 as the focal point of the Strelka. It was modelled on a Greek temple.

BIRZHEVOY → Peter
MOST   and Paul
       Fortress

BIRZHEVAYA PLOSHCHAD

❷ The Institute of Russian Literature
Housed in a building erected in 1832, this literary museum, also known as Pushkin House, holds more than 70 books, prints and manuscripts.

❶ ★ Rostral Columns
Originally lighthouses guiding ships through the busy port of St Petersburg, these imposing 32-m- (105-ft-) high columns are a distinctive feature of St Petersburg's skyline. They are still lit for Navy Day *(see p53)* and other festivals.

Key

— Suggested route

| 0 metres | 100 |
| 0 yards | 100 |

❶ Rostral Columns

Ростральные колонны

Rostralnye kolonny

Birzhevaya ploshchad.
Map 1 C5. 🚌 7, 10, 24, 47, 191, K-209, K-252. 🚊 1, 7, 10, 11.

Situated on the Strelka before the former Stock Exchange, the impressive twin russet-coloured Rostral Columns were designed as lighthouses by Thomas de Thomon in 1810. During the 19th century the oil lamps were replaced by gas torches which are still lit on ceremonial occasions. The columns are decorated with protruding ships' prows in celebration of naval victories. The monumental figures around the base represent four of Russia's rivers: the Neva, Volga, Dnieper and Volkhov.

Rostral Column on the Strelka

❷ The Institute of Russian Literature (Pushkin House)

Институтрусскойлитературы
(Пушкинский Дом)

*Institut Russkoy Literatury
(Pushkinskiy Dom)*

Naberezhnaya Makarova 4. **Map** 1 C5. **Tel** 328 0502. 🚌 7, 10, 47, 187, K-209, K-252. 🚊 1, 7, 10, 11. **Open** 11am–4pm Mon–Fri. 🎫 🌐 English.
Ⓦ pushkinskijdom.ru

Founded at the beginning of the 20th century, this museum houses numerous manuscripts and exhibits connected to Russia's greatest poet, Alexander Pushkin. Known as Pushkin House, the museum focuses on preserving the legacy of Russian literary culture from the distant past to the present. The museum has grown into an unrivalled repository of rare and unusual artifacts connected with some of Russia's greatest writers, including Turgenev, Gogol, Dostoevsky, Tolstoy and Blok. A room is dedicated to the Silver Age poets, displaying work by Anna Akhmatova and Mikhail Bulgakov.

Today Pushkin House contains more than 3 million autographed manuscripts, including 12,000 pages from Pushkin alone. In addition to more than 700,000 books and print editions reflecting the history of Russian literature, the museum also preserves thousands of images, paintings, drawings and objects. Many of these are on view in the galleries, which are decorated with period furniture. In addition to the archives, the institute also publishes new scholarly editions, which are on sale at the museum.

Visitors who wish to take an English-language tour of the museum should be sure to phone ahead.

Manuscripts on display at the Institute of Russian Literature

❸ Zoological Museum

Зоологический музей

Zoologicheskiy muzey

Universitetskaya naberezhnaya 1/3.
Map 1 C5. **Tel** 328 0112. 🚌 7, 10, 24, 47, 191, K-209, K-252. 🚊 1, 7, 10, 11.
Open 11am–6pm Wed–Mon.
🎫 (free Thu). 🚻 📷 🌐 English.
Ⓦ zin.ru

Housed in a former customs warehouse designed by Giovanni Lucchini in 1826, this museum has one of the world's largest natural history collections containing more than 1.5 million specimens. Some of the stuffed animals belonged to Peter the Great's Kunstkammer collection, including the horse he rode at the Battle of Poltava (*see p20*).

Dioramas recreate natural habitats for giant crabs, weasels, polar bears and blue whales. The museum is renowned for its collection of mammoths. One prized carcass was exhumed from the frozen wastes of Siberia in 1902 and is almost 44,000 years old.

Weasel in the Zoological Museum

❹ Kunstkammer

Кунсткамера

Kunstkamera

Universitetskaya naberezhnaya 3.
Map 1 C5. **Tel** 328 0812. 🚌 7, 10, 24, 47, 191, K-209, K-252. 🚊 1, 7, 10, 11.
Open 11am–6pm Tue–Sun. 🎫
🌐 English. Ⓦ kunstkamera.ru

The delicate, sea-green lantern tower of the Baroque Kunstkammer ("art chamber") is visible across this part of Vasilevskiy Island. The building, by Georg Mattarnoviy, was constructed in 1718–34 to exhibit Peter the Great's infamous Kunstkammer collection. While touring Holland in 1697 Peter attended

The restrained Baroque façade of the Kunstkammer (1718–34), Russia's first museum

the lectures of Frederik Ruysch (1638–1731), the most celebrated anatomist of his day. He was so impressed with Ruysch's collection of rarities that on a return visit in 1717, he purchased the entire collection of over 2,000 anatomical preparations. He transported it to St Petersburg and exhibited it to a wide-eyed public, who were enticed by free glasses of vodka. At the time, Peter's collection also included bizarre, live exhibits of deformed or unusual people, including a hermaphrodite. This, Russia's first museum, also included a library, an anatomical theatre and an observatory.

Today the Kunstkammer houses the Museum of Anthropology and Ethnography, with the remnants of Peter's bizarre collection on display in the central rotunda. Included are the heart and skeleton of Peter's personal servant, "Bourgeois", a giant at 2.27 m (7.5 ft), and a cabinet of teeth extracted by the tsar who was an enthusiastic amateur dentist. Most gruesome of all is the collection of pickled oddities which include Siamese twins and a two-headed sheep.

The halls surrounding the Kunstkammer collection contain exhibitions on the peoples of the world. Often neglected by visitors, these marvellously old-fashioned displays present an informative range of artifacts, from an Inuit kayak to Javanese shadow puppets.

⑤ Twelve Colleges
Двенадцать коллегий
Dvenadtsat kollegiy

Universitetskaya naberezhnaya 7.
Map 1 C5. 🚌 7, 24, 47, 129, K-209.
🚋 1, 10, 11. **Closed** to public.

This distinguished Baroque building of red-and-white stuccoed brick is almost 400 m (1,300 ft) in length. It was intended for Peter the Great's newly streamlined administration of 12 colleges or ministries. The single, uninterrupted façade was designed to symbolize the government's unity of purpose, while the curious alignment, at right angles to the embankment, is explained by Peter's unrealized plan for a large square with an unbroken view across the Strelka. Another popular theory is that Prince Menshikov changed the plan in Peter's absence so that the building would not encroach on his grounds. Domenico Trezzini won the competition for the design in 1723, but subsequent bureaucratic wrangling delayed its completion for 20 years. The building's function gradually changed and in 1819 part of it was acquired by St Petersburg University. A string of revolutionaries, including Lenin in 1891, were educated here. Among the famous Russian lecturers to teach here were the chemist Dmitriy Mendeleev (1834–1907) *(see p47)* and the physiologist Ivan Pavlov (1849–1936) *(see p47)*.

Mikhail Lomonosov (1711–65)

Overlooking the Neva, outside the Twelve Colleges, is an engaging bronze statue of the great 18th-century polymath Mikhail Lomonosov (unveiled in 1986). The son of a fisherman, Lomonosov was the first Russian-born member of the nearby Academy of Sciences. A "universal genius", he wrote poetry, systematized Russian grammar and was a pioneer in mathematics and the physical sciences. Thanks to his scientific discoveries, the art of porcelain, glass and mosaic production began in Russia.

A section of the west façade of Trezzini's Twelve Colleges

The southern façade of Prince Menshikov's 18th-century palace

❻ Menshikov Palace
Меншиковский дворец
Menshikovskiy dvorets

Universitetskaya naberezhnaya 15.
Map 5 B1. **Tel** 323 1112. 🚌 7, 24, 47, 191, K-209. 🚊 1, 10, 11. 🚋 1, 10, 11.
Open 10:30am–6pm Tue, Wed, Fri & Sat; noon–9pm Thu; 10:30am–5pm Sun. 🚫 🅿 compulsory (English, French, German available).

The ochre-painted Baroque Menshikov Palace, with its beautifully carved pilasters, was one of the earliest stone buildings in St Petersburg. Designed by Giovanni Fontana and Gottfried Schädel for the infamous Prince Menshikov, the palace was completed in 1720. The palace estate originally extended as far as the Malaya Neva river to the north.

Prince Menshikov entertained here on a lavish scale, often on behalf of Peter the Great, who adopted the palace as a pied-

Prince Menshikov

A leading advisor, comrade-in-arms and friend of Peter the Great, Aleksandr Menshikov (1673–1729) rose from humble origins to his position as the first governor of St Petersburg. After Peter's death in 1725, Menshikov engineered the ascension of Catherine I (Peter's wife, and Menshikov's former mistress) to the throne, thus maintaining his power until her demise. His notorious extravagance and venality eventually caught up with him. Accused of treason, he died in exile in 1729.

à-terre. Guests would cross the Neva by boat and arrive to the grand welcome of a liveried orchestra.

The palace is now a branch of the Hermitage *(see pp86–95)* with exhibitions on early 18th-century Russian culture, revealing the extent to which Peter the Great's court was influenced by Western tastes.

The compulsory tour begins on the ground floor; besides the kitchen there are displays of Peter's cabinet-making tools, period costumes, sturdy oak chests and ships' compasses. Adorning the beautiful vaulted hallway are marble statues imported from Italy which include a Roman Apollo dating to the 2nd century AD.

Upstairs, the secretary's rooms are decorated with 17th-century Dutch engravings of Leyden, Utrecht and Kraków. A series of breathtaking rooms are lined with hand-painted blue and white 18th-century Dutch tiles. Tiles were not only fashionable, but also easy to keep clean. In the tiled bedroom of Varvara (Menshikov's sister-in-law and confidante) is a German-made four-poster bed, with a Turkish coverlet woven from cotton, silk and silver thread. Hanging behind it is an exquisite 17th-century Flemish tapestry.

Menshikov and Peter often received guests in the aptly named Walnut Study which has Persian walnut panelling and commanding views of the Neva. Paintings hang from coloured ribbons, as was the fashion, including a late

17th-century portrait of Peter the Great by the Dutch painter Jan Weenix. The mirrors were a novelty at that time and such displays of vanity were anathema to the Orthodox Church.

The Great Hall, decorated in gold and stucco, is where balls and banquets were held. On one famous occasion, it was the setting for a "dwarfs' wedding" which Menshikov arranged for the amusement of his royal master.

The fine, Style-Moderne *apteka*, just off Bolshoy prospekt

❼ Bolshoy Prospekt
Большой проспект
Bolshoy prospekt

Map 1 A5. Ⓜ Vasileostrovskaya. 🚌 1, 6, 7, 10, 41, 42, 128, 151, 152, K-124, K183, K-346, K-350, K-690. 🚋 10, 11.

This imposing avenue was opened early in the 18th century to connect Menshikov's estate to the Gulf of Finland.

The mix of architectural styles ranges from the elegant Neo-Classicism of St Catherine's Lutheran Church (1768–71) at No. 1 to the simple Troyekurov House (No. 13, 6-ya liniya) in 17th-century Petrine Baroque.

Other buildings of note include St Andrew's food market (1789–90) and two Style-Moderne edifices. One is the former pharmacy, or *apteka* (1907–10) around the corner on 7-ya liniya, and the other is Adolph Gaveman's Lutheran orphanage at No. 55 (1908).

The Academy of Arts (1764–88) on the Neva embankment, an example of early Russian Neo-Classicism

❽ St Andrew's Cathedral

Андреевский собор

Andreevskiy sobor

6-ya liniya 11. **Map** 1 A5. **Tel** 323 3418. 🚌 7, 24, 42, 100, 128, 151, K-62, K-154, K-183, K-200, K-349, K-690. 🚎 10, 11. ♿

First built on the initiative of Peter the Great's second wife, Catherine I *(see p23)*, who donated 3,000 roubles towards its construction, the original church was destroyed by fire.

The present Baroque church with its distinctive bell tower was constructed by Aleksandr Vist in 1764–80. The most stunning feature of the interior is the carved 18th-century iconostasis which incorporates icons from the original church. Next door is

Giuseppe Trezzini's small Church of the Three Saints (1740–60) which is dedicated to SS Basil the Great, John Chrysostom and Gregory of Nazianzus.

❾ Academy of Arts

Академия Художеств

Akademiya Khudozhestv

Universitetskaya naberezhnaya 17. **Map** 5 B1. **Tel** 323 3578. 🚌 7, 47, K-62, K-124, K-154, K-350. 🚎 10, 11. **Open** 11am–7pm Wed–Sun. 📷 📁 🅦 nimrah.ru

Founded in 1757 to train home-grown artists in the preferred Western styles and techniques of art, the Academy spawned a galaxy of talent, including the great painter Ilya Repin *(see p44)* and architects Andrey Zakharov (1761–1811) and Andrey Voronikhin (1759–1814).

The innate conservatism of the Academy tended to discourage innovation and experiment and in 1863 a band of 14 students walked out of their graduation exams in protest. They went on to found a realist art movement and became known as the Wanderers or *Peredvizhniki (see pp108–9)*.

The imposing Academy, built between 1764–1880 by Aleksandr Kokorinov and Vallin de la Mothe, is an example of the transition from

Baroque to Neo-Classicism. Still an art school, it exhibits the work of students past and present, including canvases, architectural drawings and models of many of the city's notable buildings, such as the Smolnyy Convent *(see p130)*.

The splendid Neo-Classical halls and galleries, though faded, retain something of their original grandeur. Of note are the Conference Hall on the first floor, with its ceiling painting by Vasiliy Shebuev, and the adjoining Raphael and Titian galleries, adorned with copies of Vatican frescoes.

Flanking the river stairs outside the Academy are two sphinxes from the 14th century BC. Discovered among the ruins of Thebes in ancient Egypt, they were installed here in 1832. The faces are thought to bear a likeness of the pharaoh Amenhotep III.

❿ Blagovesh-chenskiy Bridge

Благовещенский Мост

Blagoveshchenskiy most

Map 5 B1. 🚌 6, K-154, K-350.

Opened in 1842 with this name, this was the first permanent crossing of the Neva. In 1855 it was renamed Nicholas Bridge but in 1918, after the Revolution, it was called Lieutenant Shmidt Bridge to commemorate a sailor who led an uprising of the Black Sea fleet in 1905. Reconstruction carried out in 1936–8 incorporated Aleksandr Bryullov's original railings, adorned with seahorses and tridents. In 2007 the bridge reverted to its original name.

The treasure of St Andrew's Cathedral, its beautiful Baroque iconostasis

PETROGRADSKAYA

The city was founded on the northern banks of the Neva river in 1703, at the height of the Great Northern War *(see p20)*. Building began with the construction of a wooden fortress and Petrogradskaya, or the Petrograd Side, soon became a marshy suburb of wooden cabins occupied by craftsmen working on Peter the Great's new city.

Nearby, the area around Trinity Square was originally a small merchants' quarter centred around a now demolished church and St Petersburg's first stock exchange.

Petrogradskaya was sparsely populated until the late 1890s when the construction of the Trinity Bridge (Troitskiy most) made the area accessible from the city centre. The bridge caused a housing boom at the height of a fashion for Style-Moderne architecture which is still in evidence today. The population quadrupled and the area became very popular with artists and professionals.

The highlight of Petrogradskaya, which is still largely residential, is the Peter and Paul Fortress.

Sights at a Glance

Museums
- ❷ Engineer's House
- ❹ Commandant's House
- ❻ Trubetskoy Bastion
- ❼ Artillery Museum
- ❿ Kirov Museum
- ⓫ Kshesinskaya Mansion
- ⓬ Cruiser *Aurora*
- ⓭ Cabin of Peter the Great

Gates
- ❶ St Peter's Gate
- ❺ Neva Gate

Cathedrals
- ❸ Cathedral of SS Peter and Paul

Streets, Squares and Parks
- ❽ Aleksandrovskiy Park
- ❾ Kamennoostrovskiy Prospekt
- ⓮ Trinity Square

Restaurants *pp186–7*
1. ChiliPizza
2. Chin Chin Cafe
3. Demyanova Ukha
4. Dozari Bar
5. Flying Dutchman
6. Gornyy Oryol
7. Kommunalka Art-Cafe
8. Korushka
9. Mozzarella Bar
10. Na Zdorovie!
11. Pryanosti & Radosti
12. Salkhino
13. Tbiliso
14. Volna
15. Wishes
16. Yakitoriya

0 metres   400
0 yards   400

See also Street Finder map 2

◀ Interior of the Baroque Cathedral of SS Peter and Paul in the Peter and Paul Fortress

For keys to symbols *see back flap*

Street-by-Street: Peter and Paul Fortress

The founding of the Peter and Paul Fortress on 27 May 1703, on the orders of Peter the Great, is considered to mark the founding of the city. It was first built in wood and was later replaced, section by section, in stone by Domenico Trezzini. Its history is a gruesome one, since hundreds of forced labourers died while building the fortress and its bastions were later used to guard and torture many political prisoners, including Peter's own son Aleksey.

The cells where prisoners were once kept are open to the public, alongside a couple of museums and the magnificent cathedral which houses the tombs of the Romanovs.

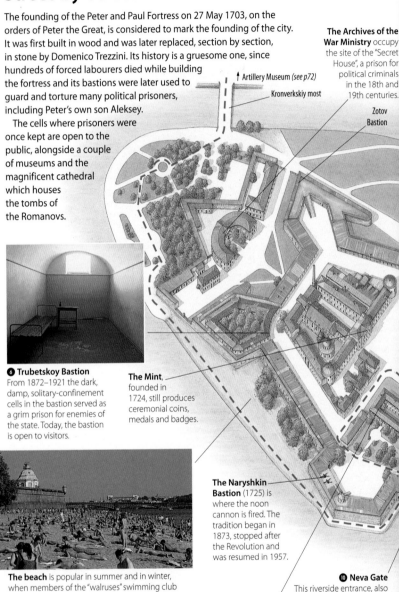

↑ Artillery Museum (see p72)

Kronverkskiy most

The Archives of the War Ministry occupy the site of the "Secret House", a prison for political criminals in the 18th and 19th centuries.

Zotov Bastion

❻ Trubetskoy Bastion
From 1872–1921 the dark, damp, solitary-confinement cells in the bastion served as a grim prison for enemies of the state. Today, the bastion is open to visitors.

The Mint, founded in 1724, still produces ceremonial coins, medals and badges.

The beach is popular in summer and in winter, when members of the "walruses" swimming club break the ice for an invigorating dip.

The Naryshkin Bastion (1725) is where the noon cannon is fired. The tradition began in 1873, stopped after the Revolution and was resumed in 1957.

❿ Neva Gate
This riverside entrance, also known as "Death Gateway", leads to the Commandant's pier from which prisoners embarked on their journey to execution or exile. The Neva river's flood levels (see p39) are recorded under the arch.

❹ Commandant's House
For 150 years this attractive Baroque house was the scene of interrogations and trials of political prisoners. It now houses a museum of local history.

❸ ★ Cathedral of SS Peter and Paul
Marbled columns, glittering chandeliers and painted decor combine with Ivan Zarudnyy's carved and gilded iconostasis to create a magnificent setting for the tombs of the Romanov monarchs.

Locator Map
See Street Finder map 2

The Boat House is now a ticket office and souvenir shop.

Golovkin Bastion

The Grand Ducal burial vault is the last resting place of several Grand Dukes shot by the Bolsheviks in 1919 and of Grand Duke Vladimir who died in exile in 1992.

❶ St Peter's Gate
The entrance to the fortress, by Domenico Trezzini, completed in 1718, features the Romanov double eagle with an emblem of St George and the dragon.

0 metres	100
0 yards	100

Ioannovskiy Ravelin contains a ticket office.

Ivan Gate, in the outer wall, was constructed from 1731–40.

Ioannovskiy most

Kamennoostrovskiy prospekt, Gorkovskaya Metro and Trinity Bridge

Statue of Peter the Great by Mikhail Chemiakin (1991).

Peter I Bastion

❷ Engineer's House
This building, dating from 1748–9, houses temporary exhibitions of artifacts used in everyday life in St Petersburg before the Revolution.

Key

— Suggested route

❶ St Peter's Gate
Петровские ворота
Petrovskie vorota

Petropavlovskaya krepost.
Map 2 E3. Ⓜ Gorkovskaya.
🚌 46, 49, K-46, K-76, K-223.

The main entrance to the Peter
and Paul Fortress is through
two contrasting arches. The
plain Neo-Renaissance Ivan
Gate (1730s) leads to the
more imposing St Peter's Gate
(1708–18), an ornate Baroque
structure with scrolled wings
and a rounded-gable pediment.
Domenico Trezzini redesigned
the Peter Gate, retaining Karl
Osner's expressively carved bas-
relief which allegorizes Peter the
Great's victory over Charles XII
of Sweden (*see p20*). It depicts
St Peter casting down the
winged sorcerer Simon Magus.

St Peter's Gate, entrance to fortress

❷ Engineer's House
Инженерный дом
Inzhenernyy dom

Petropavlovskaya krepost.
Map 2 D3. **Tel** 232 9454, 230 0329.
Ⓜ Gorkovskaya. **Open** 11am–5pm
Thu–Mon, 11am–4pm Tue. ♿
☕ English. 🌐 **spbmuseum.ru**

The Engineer's House, built
in 1748–9, has a changing
exhibition which gives a
fascinating glimpse of daily
life in St Petersburg before
the Revolution. Architectural
backdrops and historical paintings give way to an engaging
miscellany of artifacts, ranging
from model boats to duelling
pistols and court costumes.
   In 1915 there were more
than 100 outlets selling musical
instruments in the city and

An accordion and organ surrounded by Style-Moderne
furniture, Engineer's House

the museum displays an
excellent collection which
includes phonographs, gramo-
phones, symphoniums and
piano accordions of the period.
   A section on vintage tech-
nology features Singer sewing
machines, typewriters, Bakelite
telephones and box cameras.

❸ Cathedral of SS Peter and Paul
Петропавловский собор
Petropavlovskiy sobor

Petropavlovskaya krepost. **Map** 2 D4.
Tel 230 6431. Ⓜ Gorkovskaya.
Open 11am–4pm Mon–Tue,
10am–5pm Thu–Sat, 11am–5pm Sun.
♿ ☕ English. 🌐 **spbmuseum.ru**

Domenico Trezzini designed
this magnificent church within
the fortress in 1712. Employed
by Peter the Great, who wished
to turn his back on traditional
Russian church architecture,

Trezzini produced a
Baroque masterpiece
of singular elegance.
The bell tower was
completed first in
order to test the
foundations and
this served as an
excellent viewpoint
from which Peter
could oversee the
construction work
of his new city.
The cathedral
was completed in
1733, but was badly
damaged by fire in 1756 when
the soaring 122-m (400-ft) spire
was struck by lightning. The
gilded needle spire, crowned
by a weather-vane angel,
remained the tallest structure in
St Petersburg until the building
of a TV transmitter in the 1960s.
   The interior, with its glittering
chandeliers, pink and green
Corinthian columns and
overarching vaults, is a far cry
from the traditional Russian
Orthodox church. Even the
iconostasis is a Baroque flight
of fancy. This masterpiece
of gilded woodcarving was
designed by Ivan Zarudnyy
and executed in the 1720s
by craftsmen from Moscow.
   After Peter's death in 1725,
the cathedral became the last
resting place of the tsars. The
sarcophagi are all of a uniform
white Carrara marble, except
the tombs of Alexander II and
his wife Maria Alexandrovna,

Cathedral of SS Peter and Paul, with Dvortsovyy most in the foreground

which are carved from Altai jasper and Ural rhodonite. Peter the Great's tomb lies to the right of the iconostasis.

The only tsars who are not buried here are Peter II, Ivan VI and Nicholas II. In 1998 a controversial decision was taken to rebury the remains of the last Romanov tsar, his wife and children, and the servants that died together with them, in a chapel by the entrance to the cathedral.

The Grand Ducal Mausoleum, where relatives of the tsars are buried, was added to the northeast of the cathedral at the end of the 19th century.

❹ Commandant's House

Комендантский дом
Komendantskiy dom

Petropavlovskaya krepost. **Map** 2 D4. **Tel** 230 6431. Ⓜ Gorkovskaya. **Open** 11am–5pm Thu–Mon, 11am–4pm Tue. 🅰 🅲 English.

Dating from the 1740s, the plain brick, two-storey Commandant's House served both as the residence of the fortress commander and as a courthouse. Over the years, political prisoners, including the Decembrist rebels *(see p25)*, were brought here for interrogation and sentencing.

The house is now a museum, with a ground-floor exhibition on medieval settlements in the St Petersburg region, and temporary exhibitions upstairs.

❺ Neva Gate

Невскине ворота
Nevskie vorota

Petropavlovskaya krepost. **Map** 2 E4. Ⓜ Gorkovskaya.

This austere river entrance to the fortress was once known as the "Death Gate". Prisoners to be transported to the even more notorious Schlüsselburg Fortress (to the east of St Petersburg) for capital punishment, or to a "living death" in penal servitude, were led down the granite steps and taken away by boat. The appropriately dour, grey gateway dates from 1730–40

Neva Gate leading from the river into the Peter and Paul Fortress

(reconstructed in 1784–7) and is unornamented apart from an anchor in the pediment. In the archway, brass plaques mark record flood levels. The catastrophic inundation of November 1824 is the one commemorated in Pushkin's poem, *The Bronze Horseman (see p80)*.

❻ Trubetskoy Bastion

трубецкой бастион
Trubetskoy bastion

Petropavlovskaya krepost. **Map** 2 D4. **Tel** 230 6431. Ⓜ Gorkovskaya. **Open** 10am–5pm Thu–Tue. 🅰 🅲 English.

Peter the Great's son, the Tsarevich Aleksey, was the first political prisoner to be detained in the grim fortress prison. Unjustly accused of treason in 1718 by his over-bearing father, Aleksey escaped abroad only to be lured back to Russia with the promise

of a pardon. Instead, he was tortured and beaten to death, almost certainly with Peter's consent and participation.

For the next 100 years prisoners were incarcerated in the much feared Secret House, since demolished. In 1872 a new prison block opened in the Trubetskoy Bastion which has existed as a museum since 1924. On the ground floor there is a small exhibition of period photographs, prison uniforms and a model of the guardroom. Upstairs are 69 isolation cells, restored to their original appearance, while downstairs there are two unheated, unlit punishment cells where the recalcitrant were locked up for 48 hours at a time. Once every two weeks, all detainees were taken to the Bath House in the exercise yard for de-lousing. Here prisoners were also put in irons before being carted off to penal servitude in Siberia.

Political Prisoners

The fortress' sinister role as a prison for political activists continued until after the Revolution. Generations of rebels and anarchists were

Leon Trotsky (1879–1940) in the Trubetskoy Bastion

interrogated and imprisoned here, including Leon Trotsky in the wake of the 1905 Revolution. Other prominent detainees were the leading Decembrists in 1825 *(see p25)*, Dostoevsky in 1849 *(see p125)* and, in 1874–6, the anarchist Prince Pyotr Kropotkin. In 1917 it was the turn first of the tsar's ministers, then of members of the Provisional Government. Then, in the Civil War *(see p29)*, the Bolsheviks held hostage four Romanov Grand Dukes who were subsequently executed in 1919.

Rocket launcher in the courtyard of the Artillery Museum

❼ Artillery Museum

Музей Артиллерии

Muzey Artillerii

Aleksandrovskiy Park 7, Kronverkskaya Embankment. **Map** 2 D3. **Tel** 232 0296. Ⓜ Gorkovskaya. **Open** 11am–5pm Wed–Sun. **Closed** last Thu each month. 🎫

This vast, horseshoe-shaped building in red brick stands on the site of the Kronverk, the outer fortifications of the Peter and Paul Fortress (*see pp68–9*). Designed by Pyotr Tamanskiy and constructed in 1849–60, the building was originally used as the arsenal.

More than 600 pieces of artillery and military vehicles include tanks and the armoured car in which Lenin rode in triumph from Finland Station (*see p128*) to Kshesinskaya Mansion (*see p74*) on 3 April 1917. There are uniforms, regimental flags, muskets and small arms dating to medieval times, as well as several rooms devoted to World War II.

❽ Aleksandrovskiy Park

Александровский парк

Aleksandrovskiy park

Kronverkskiy prospekt. **Map** 2 D3. Ⓜ Gorkovskaya. ♿

The park's unique character as a centre of popular culture and entertainment was established in the year 1900 with the inauguration of the Nicholas II People's House. This was where pantomime artists, wild animal trainers, magicians and circus acts entertained the crowds,

while the more serious-minded were drawn to the lecture halls, reading galleries and tea rooms. The *pièce de résistance* was the magnificent domed Opera House (1911), where the legendary bass singer, Fyodor Chalyapin, sometimes gave performances.

Today the Opera House offers less highbrow entertainment, as its change of name to Music Hall suggests. The adjoining 1930s buildings include the innovative Baltic House Theatre, the Planetarium and a waxworks museum.

The park still draws crowds on summer weekends and public holidays, although some of the attractions, especially the zoo, are rather tawdry.

❾ Kamennoostrovskiy Prospekt

Каменноостровский проспект

Kamennoostrovskiy prospekt

Map 2 D1. Ⓜ Gorkovskaya or Petrogradskaya. 🚌 46, K-30, K-76, K-223.

Developed during the construction boom of the late 1890s, this eye-catching avenue is noted for its Style-Moderne architecture. The first house, at No. 1–3 (1899–1904) was designed by Fyodor Lidval. The multi-textured façade, windows of contrasting shapes and sizes, ornate iron balconies and fanciful carvings are the most typical features of this Russian version of Art Nouveau. The

neighbouring house (No. 5) was once occupied by Count Sergey Witte, a leading industrialist who negotiated the peace treaty with Japan in 1905 (*see p28*).

Situated just off the start of the avenue is the city's only mosque (1910–14). Designed by Russian architects, its minarets, majolica tiling and the rough granite surfaces of the walls are fully in keeping with the surrounding architecture. The mosque was, in fact, modelled on the Mausoleum of Tamerlane in Samarkand and involved Central Asian craftsmen.

At No. 10 is the tall portico of the Leningrad Film Studios (Lenfilm). It was on this site, in May 1896, that the Lumière brothers showed the first moving picture in Russia. Since its founding in 1918, some of the most innovative Soviet film

Griffon, No. 1–3 Kamennoostrovskiy

directors, such as Leonid Trauberg and Grigoriy Kozintsev (*see p47*), have worked there. At the intersection with ulitsa Mira, each house has individually designed turrets, spires, reliefs and iron balconies, forming a handsome Style-Moderne ensemble. Other buildings of interest include No. 24 (1896–1912), with its red-brick majolica and terracotta façade; No. 26–28, where Sergey Kirov lived (*see p74*); and on the corner of Bolshoy prospekt, the "Turreted House" with its Neo-Gothic portal.

Turreted House (1913–15), Kamennoostrovskiy prospekt

Style-Moderne in St Petersburg

In vogue throughout Europe from the 1890s to the 1900s, Art Nouveau marked a break with imitation of the past. The movement, known as Style-Moderne in Russia, began in the decorative arts and was then reflected in architecture, where it led to an abundance of ornamental details. Inspired by new industrial techniques, artists and architects made lavish use of natural stone and brick, wrought iron, stucco, coloured glass and ceramic tiles. Dominated by sinuous and undulating lines, with a predominance of floral- and vegetal-inspired elements, even traditional forms such as doors and windows are distorted or given unexpected curves.

In *fin-de-siècle* St Petersburg, the Style-Moderne flourished as the city underwent a building boom, particularly on Petrogradskaya. The city became a showcase for the talents of leading architects such as Fyodor Lidval and Aleksandr von Gogen.

Kshesinskaya Mansion reveals von Gogen's relatively severe version of Style-Moderne. Asymmetrical in composition, it is enlivened with wrought iron and glazed tiles *(see p74)*.

Yeliseev's is evidence of the skill of Gavriil Baranovskiy, who made excellent use of industrial techniques in the creation of large window spaces. The rich exterior detailing is matched by elegant shop-fittings and chandeliers inside *(see p111)*.

28 Bolshaya Zelenina ulitsa is one of the most outstanding examples of the use of stylized animal and fish motifs and a variety of surface decoration techniques. Fyodor von Postel's 1904–5 apartment block is reminiscent of the work of his contemporary, the Catalan architect Gaudí.

1–3 Kamennoostrovskiy pr is the work of St Petersburg's master of Style-Moderne, Fyodor Lidval. Delicate details such as floral and animal reliefs stand out against a background of discreetly elongated proportions and unusual window shapes.

Singer House (1910–14) reveals Pavel Syuzor's use of an unusually eclectic mix of architectural styles. Ornate Style-Moderne wrought-iron balconies and decorative wooden window frames combine with elements of Renaissance and Baroque revivals.

Portrait of Sergey Kirov (1930s), in the Kirov Museum

❿ Kirov Museum
Музей С. М. Кирова

Muzey S M Kirova

Kamennoostrovskiy prospekt 26–28, 4th floor. **Map** 2 D1. **Tel** 346 0217, 346 0289. Ⓜ Petrogradskaya. **Open** 11am–6pm Thu–Mon (5pm Tue). 🖼 🎫 English. 🅦 **spbmuseum.ru**

From 1926–36 this flat was home to one of Stalin's closest political associates, Sergey Kirov. As the charismatic first Secretary of the Leningrad Communist Party, Kirov soon gained national importance. His increasing popularity led Stalin to see in him a potential rival. On 1 December 1934, Kirov was gunned down at his office at the Smolnyy Institute *(see p130)* by Leonid Nikolaev, a party malcontent. Stalin used the assassination as an excuse to launch the Great Purges *(see p29)*, although most historians believe Stalin himself was behind Kirov's murder.

Kirov acquired the status of a martyr after his death, with countless buildings named in his honour. His apartment, preserved as it was in his lifetime, is an example of the near cult status awarded Party leaders, with documents and photographs chronicling his political career, and a touching array of memorabilia including his clothing and favourite books.

⓫ Kshesinskaya Mansion
Особняк М. Кшесинской

Osobnyak M Kshesinskoy

Ulitsa Kuybysheva 4. **Map** 2 E3. **Tel** 233 7052. Ⓜ Gorkovskaya. **Open** 10am–6pm Thu–Tue (8pm Wed). **Closed** last Mon of month. 🖼 🎫 English. 🅦 **polithistory.ru**

This remarkable example of Style-Moderne architecture was commissioned for prima ballerina Matilda Kshesinskaya. Designed in 1904 by the court architect, Aleksandr von Gogen, the building is almost playfully asymmetric, with a single, octagonal tower. Most eye-catching of all are the many contrasting building materials with bands of pink and grey granite, cream-coloured bricks, delicately ornamented iron railings and majolica tiles.

The most impressive interior is the splendid recital hall with its pillared archway and palms. Nearby, the Kshesinskaya memorial room has some of the dancer's possessions, including sketches of Nicholas II.

In March 1917 the mansion was commandeered by the Bolsheviks and became their headquarters and, on Lenin's return to Russia *(see p128)*, he addressed the crowds from the balcony facing the square. The mansion, previously home to a museum glorifying the October Revolution, now houses the Museum of Russian Political History. On the first floor the Bolshevik Party secretariat and Lenin's office have been faithfully restored. Upstairs is a fascinating collection of memorabilia from the revolutionary era, including Communist posters, Nicholas II coronation mugs and even a police file on Rasputin's murder *(see p123)*.

The museum holds an exhibition highlighting crucial events in Russian history. This permanent feature, with audio guides, is extremely popular among visitors.

Matilda Kshesinskaya

One of the finest prima ballerinas ever to grace the stage of the Mariinskiy Theatre *(see p121)*, Matilda Kshesinskaya (1872–1971) graduated from the Imperial School of Ballet *(see p120)* in 1890. She was equally famous for her celebrated affair with the tsarevich, later Tsar Nicholas II, which began soon after she graduated. Kshesinskaya emigrated to Paris in 1920 where she married the Grand Duke Andrey Vladimirovich, another member of the imperial family and the father of her 11-year-old son. It was in Paris that she wrote her controversial memoirs, *Dancing in St Petersburg*, which tells the tale of her affair with the last Russian tsar.

Aleksandr von Gogen's elegant recital hall in the Kshesinskaya Mansion

The historic cruiser *Aurora* (1900), moored in front of the Neo-Baroque Nakhimov Naval Academy (1912)

⑫ Cruiser Aurora

Крейсер Аврора

Kreyser Avrora

Petrogradskaya naberezhnaya 3.
Map 2 F3. **Tel** 230 8440. 🚌 49, K-30, K-183. 🚃 6, 40. **Open** Check for timings

According to the annals of the Revolution, at 9:40pm on 25 October 1917, the cruiser *Aurora* signalled the storming of the Winter Palace *(see p30)*, by firing a single blank round from its bow gun.

The ship entered active service in 1903. It was later converted into a training ship and at the start of the Siege of Leningrad *(see p29)* it was sunk to protect it from German forces. The ship was raised in 1944 and has been a museum since 1956. When open, the famous gun, bell and the crew's quarters can be viewed, along with an exhibition on the ship's history.

⑬ Cabin of Peter the Great

Музей-домик Петра I

Muzey-domik Petra I

Petrovskaya naberezhnaya 6.
Map 2 F3. **Tel** 2304576, 314 0374. Ⓜ Gorkovskaya. **Open** 10am–6pm Wed & Fri–Sun, 1–9pm Thu. **Closed** last Mon of month. ♿ ♿

This pine-log cabin was built for Peter the Great by his soldier-carpenters in just three days in 1703. Peter lived here for six years while overseeing the construction of his new city *(see pp22–3)*. Catherine the Great, ever keen to glorify Peter, had a protective brick shell erected around the cabin.

There are only two rooms, both with period furnishings, and a hallway which doubled as a bedroom. Among Peter's personal possessions are a compass, a frock coat and his rowing boat.

Adorning the steps outside are two statues of the Shih Tze frog-lions, brought from Manchuria during the Russo-Japanese War (1904–5).

⑭ Trinity Square

Троицкая площадь

Troitskaya ploshchad

Map 2 E3. Ⓜ Gorkovskaya. 🚌 46. 🚃 6, 40.

Throughout the early 18th century, the whole of Petro-gradskaya was known as Trinity Island. The name was derived from the Church of the Trinity (built in 1710; demolished 1930s) in Trinity Square, which formed the nucleus of the city's merchant quarter. In 2002–3 the Trinity Chapel was built here to honour the 300th anniversary of St Petersburg. Despite having no direct links to the mainland until the early 20th century, the area flourished with shops, a printing house and the city's first stock exchange.

In the 1905 Revolution *(see p28)* the square witnessed the massacre of 48 workers, killed by government troops. During the Communist era, the square became known as ploshchad Revolyutsii.

From the square, across the widest point of the Neva, the Style-Moderne Trinity Bridge *(see p37)* stretches nearly 600 m (1,970 ft). Its construction led to a building boom on Petrogradskaya *(see p67)* and its completion in 1903 coincided with the city's bicentenary.

The ornate Trinity Bridge, crossing the Neva from Trinity Square

PALACE EMBANKMENT

In terms of sheer scale and grandeur, St Petersburg's magnificent south waterfront has few equals. Its formidable granite quays stretch over 2 km (1 mile) from the Senate building in the west to Peter the Great's Summer Palace in the east, and the surrounding area of stately aristocratic palaces and ornamental canal bridges are justly famous worldwide.

Every aspect of the city's history is juxtaposed in this rich area. Falconet's statue of Peter the Great, the Bronze Horseman, is an eloquent testimony to imperial ambition while the square in which it stands is where

the Decembrist rebels rose up against the tsarist regime in 1825. In Palace Square, Rastrelli's Winter Palace (part of the Hermitage) evokes the opulence of Imperial Russia while the Eternal Flame, flickering in the Field of Mars, is a more sombre reminder of revolutionary sacrifice.

Dominating St Petersburg's skyline are the magnificent dome of St Isaac's Cathedral and the gilded spire of the Admiralty. Some of the best views can be appreciated by making a boat trip along the waterways (see pp228–9), or by strolling through the Summer Garden.

Sights at a Glance

Palaces and Gardens
⑭ Marble Palace
⑯ Summer Garden
⑰ Summer Palace

Museums
⑫ The Hermitage pp86–95

Historical Buildings and Monuments
① The Admiralty
③ The Bronze Horseman
④ Horseguards' Manège
⑨ House of Fabergé

Churches
⑤ St Isaac's Cathedral pp82–3

Streets and Squares
⑥ St Isaac's Square
② Senate Square
⑧ Malaya Morskaya Ulitsa
⑪ Palace Square
⑬ Millionaires' Street
⑮ Field of Mars

Hotels and Cafés
⑦ Angleterre Hotel
⑩ Literary Café

▢ Restaurants pp187–8
1 Borsalino
2 Bushe
3 Canvas
4 Clean Plates Society
5 Da Albertone
6 Gastronom
7 Gogol
8 Gosti
9 King Pong
10 Literaturnoye Café
11 NEP
12 Olivie
13 Receptoria
14 Tandoor
15 Teplo

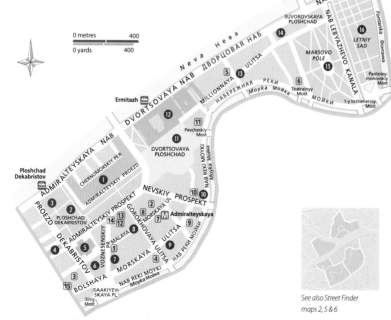

See also Street Finder maps 2, 5 & 6

◄ The golden dome of St Isaac's Cathedral, visible from its gardens

For keys to symbols see back flap

Street-by-Street: St Isaac's Square

The highlight of St Isaac's Square is the imposing cathedral at its centre, which opened in 1858 and is the fourth church to stand on this site. The cathedral, and subsequently the square, were named after St Isaac of Dalmatia, because Peter the Great's birthday fell on this saint's day. The busy square, used as a market place in the first half of the 19th century, is now at the heart of an area teeming with buildings and statues of historical and architectural interest. Among them are the Admiralty, the Mariinskiy Palace and the Bronze Horseman.

❹ Horseguards' Manège
Built in 1804–7 by Giacomo Quarenghi, this building housed the Life Guards' Mounted Regiment.

❸ The Bronze Horseman
Etienne Falconet's magnificent statue of Peter the Great, his horse trampling the serpent of treason, captures the spirit of the city's uncompromising and wilful founder.

❷ Senate Square
Dominating the western side of the square are Carlo Rossi's monumental Senate and Synod buildings, linked by a triumphal arch.

The Glory Columns, topped by bronze angels, were erected in 1845–6.

Myatlev House

The Former German Embassy was designed by Peter Behrens in 1911–12.

❺ ★ St Isaac's Cathedral
The magnificent golden dome of the cathedral is visible all across the city. 100kg (220lb) of gold leaf was needed to cover the dome's surface.

ADMIRALTEYSKAYA NABEREZHNAYA

PROEZD DEKABRISTOV

UL YAKUBOVICHA

ISAAKIEVSKAYA PLOSC

BOLSHAYA

| 0 metres | 100 |
| 0 yards | 100 |

The Hermitage
and Winter Palace

Locator Map
See Street Finder maps 2, 5 & 6

❶ The Admiralty
Sculptures and reliefs, celebrating
the power of Russia's navy,
decorate the Admiralty's façade.
The archway of the main entrance
is framed by nymphs carrying
globes on their shoulders.

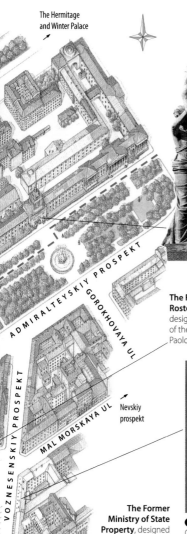

ADMIRALTEYSKIY PROSPEKT

GOROKHOVAYA UL

VOZNESENSKIY PROSPEKT

MAL MORSKAYA UL

Nevskiy
prospekt

**The Former Prince Lobanov-
Rostovskiy Mansion** is now a
design institute. The lions in front
of the arcade are by Italian sculptor
Paolo Triscorni.

**The Former
Ministry of State
Property**, designed
by Nikolay Yefimov
in 1844, is a fine
example of Neo-
Renaissance
architecture.

❼ Angleterre Hotel
Originally built in the 1850s, the Angleterre Hotel *(see
p178)* was the site of the first major public protest in
the history of the Soviet Union. The hotel has been
restored to its 19th-century splendour.

MORSKAYA UL

REKI MOYKI

Siniy most *(see p81)*

**The Mariinskiy
Palace,** named in
honour of Maria,
daughter of Nicholas I,
now houses the
St Petersburg city hall.

❻ St Isaac's Square
Overlooking the
square is Pyotr
Klodt's statue of
Tsar Nicholas I. The
reliefs on the pedestal
depict episodes from
his reign. Tellingly,
two of them show
the suppression
of rebellions.

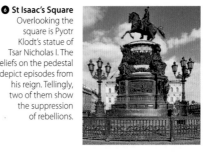

Key

— Suggested route

❶ The Admiralty
Адмиралтейство
Admiralteystvo

Admiralteyskaya naberezhnaya 2.
Map 5 C1. 🚌 7, 10, 24, 100, 191,
K-169, K-187, K-209, K-252. 🚎 1, 5,
7, 10, 11, 17, 22.

Having founded a city and built
a fortress, Peter the Great's next
priority was to create a Russian
navy to guarantee access to the
sea and dominance over Sweden.

The Admiralty began life as
a fortified shipyard built on this
site between 1704–11. Two
years later, some 10,000 men
were employed in building the
first battleships.

One of Russia's most inspired
architects, Andrey Zakharov,
began to rebuild the Admiralty
in 1806. The remarkable façade
is 407 m (1,335 ft) in length and
is adorned with an abundance
of sculptures and reliefs which
document the glory of the
Russian fleet. Zakharov retained
some of the original features,
including the central gate
tower and spire which he
recast in Neo-Classical style
with columned porticos and
pavilions. The heightened spire
was gilded and topped with a
model frigate. This has become
a symbol of the city, just like the
trumpet-blowing pair of angels
on the portals of the façade
overlooking the Neva.

In the 1840s, shipbuilding
was moved downstream and
the Admiralty was handed
over to the Russian navy. It has
been occupied by the Naval
Engineering School since 1925.

Tower and spire of the Admiralty (1806–23)

❷ Senate Square
Сенатская Площадь
Senatskaya ploshchad

Map 5 C1. 🚌 3, 10, 22, 27, 71, 100,
K-169, K-187, K-306. 🚎 5, 22.

The momentous Decembrist
uprising took place here on
14 December 1825 *(see p25)*.
During the inauguration of
Nicholas I, Guards officers intent
on imposing a constitutional
monarchy attempted to stage a
coup d'état in the square. After a
confused stand-off which lasted
several hours, the rebel forces
were routed with grapeshot by
the new tsar and loyalist troops.
Five of the ringleaders were
later executed and 121 others
exiled to Siberia, thus effectively
ending Russia's first revolution.

The imposing Neo-
Classical buildings that
command the western
side of Senate Square
were intended to
harmonize with the
Admiralty. Designed
by Carlo Rossi between
1829–34, they were the
headquarters of two
important institutions
which were originally
created by Peter the
Great: the Supreme
Court, or Senate, and
the Holy Synod which
was responsible for
the administration
of the Orthodox Church.
The two buildings,
which now house
historical archives,
are linked to each
other by a triumphal
arch supported by Corinthian
columns and decorated with
a Neo-Classical frieze and
a plethora of statuary.

The Bronze Horseman (1766–78)

❸ The Bronze Horseman
Медный Всадник
Mednyy Vsadnik

Senatskaya ploshchad. **Map** 5 C1.
🚌 3, 10, 22, 27, 71, 100, K-169, K-187,
K-306. 🚎 5, 22.

The magnificent equestrian
statue of Peter the Great was
unveiled in Senate Square
in 1782, as a tribute from
Catherine the Great. The statue
is known as the Bronze Horseman after Pushkin's famous
poem. A French sculptor,
Etienne Falconet, spent more
than 12 years overseeing this
ambitious project. The pedestal
alone weighs 1,625 tonnes and

The Bronze Horseman by Pushkin

The famous statue of Peter the Great is brought to life in Alexander
Pushkin's epic poem *The Bronze Horseman* (1833). In this haunting
vision of the Great Flood of
1824 *(see p39)*, the hero is
pursued through the mist-
shrouded streets by the
terrifying bronze statue.
Pushkin's words evoke the
domineering and implacable
will for which the tsar was
renowned: *"How terrible he
was in the surrounding gloom!
… what strength was in him!
And in that steed, what fire!"*

1956 stamp of Pushkin and the statue that
inspired his poem

was hewn from a single block of granite, which was hauled from the Gulf of Finland. It bears the simple inscription "To Peter I from Catherine II" in Latin and Russian. A serpent, symbolizing treason, is crushed beneath the horse's hooves.

❹ Horseguards' Manège

Конногвардейский манеж

Konnogvardeyskiy manezh

Isaakievskaya ploshchad 1. **Map** 5 C2. **Tel** 312 2243, 571 4157 (ticket office). **Open** variable. 🚌 3, 22, 27, 71, 100, K-169, K-187, K-306. 🚎 5, 22. 🖼 🖥

The enormous indoor riding school of the Life Guards' Mounted Regiment was built by Giacomo Quarenghi in 1804–7 to resemble a Roman basilica. Two clues to the building's original function are the dynamic frieze of a horse race beneath the pediment and the statues on either side of the portico. The statues of the unclad twin sons of Zeus reining in wild horses are copies from the Quirinale Palace in Rome. The Holy Synod, scandalized by this display of nakedness so near to St Isaac's Cathedral, ordered their removal. The statues were re-erected in 1954.

Next to the manège, which is now used as an exhibition hall, are two marble pillars surmounted by bronze angels cast in Berlin, which were sent over from Germany as a gift in 1840.

❺ St Isaac's Cathedral

See pp82–3.

❻ St Isaac's Square

Исаакиевская площадь

Issakievskaya ploshchad

Map 5 C2. 🚌 3, 10, 22, 27, 71, 100, K-169, K-187, K-306. 🚎 5, 22.

Dominated by Auguste de Montferrand's majestic St Isaac's Cathedral, this impressive square was created during the reign of Nicholas I, although a few of its earlier buildings date from the 18th century. The monument to Nicholas I at its centre was

St Isaac's Cathedral, statue of St Nicholas I and the Angleterre, St Isaac's Square

also designed by Montferrand. Erected in 1859 and sculpted by Pyotr Klodt, it depicts the tsar in the uniform of one of Russia's most prestigious regiments, the Kavalergardskiy guards. The pedestal is embellished with allegorical sculptures of his daughters and his wife, who represent Faith, Wisdom, Justice and Might.

On the western side of the square, at No. 9, is the Myatlev House, a Neo-Classical mansion dating from the 1760s, which belonged to one of Russia's most illustrious families. The French encyclopedist Denis Diderot stayed here in 1773–4 following an invitation from Catherine the Great. In the 1920s it became the premises of the State Institute of Artistic Culture where some of Russia's most influential avant-garde artists, including Kazimir Malevich and Vladimir Tatlin *(see p109)*, worked.

The impressive granite-faced building alongside is the former German embassy, designed in 1911–12 by the German architect Peter Behrens.

Across the 100-m- (330-ft-) wide Blue Bridge (Siniy most), which was the site of a serf market until 1861, the Mariinskiy Palace *(see p79)* dominates the southern end of the square.

❼ Angleterre Hotel

Гостиница Астория

Gostinitsa Astoriya

Malaya Morskaya ulitsa 24. **Map** 6 D2. **Tel** 494 5666. 🚌 3, 10, 22, 27, K-169, K-306. 🚎 5, 22. See Where to Stay, p178.

Now one of St Petersburg's leading hotels, the seven-storey Angleterre was designed by Fyodor Lidval in the Style-Moderne *(see p73)* in 1910–12.

American writer John Reed, author of the famous eyewitness account of the Revolution *Ten Days that Shook the World*, was staying here when the Bolsheviks seized power.

In 1925, the poet Sergey Yesenin, husband of Isadora Duncan, hanged himself in the annexe, after daubing the walls of his room with a farewell verse in his blood "To die is not new – but neither is it new to be alive".

The hotel's banqueting hall was to be the venue for Hitler's prematurely planned victory celebration, so sure was he that he would conquer the city.

Restored Style-Moderne foyer in the Angleterre Hotel, on the eastern edge of St Isaac's Square

❺ St Isaac's Cathedral

Исаакиевский собор

Isaakievskiy sobor

St Isaac's, one of the world's largest cathedrals, was designed in 1818 by the then unknown architect Auguste de Montferrand. The construction of the colossal building was a major engineering feat. Thousands of wooden piles were sunk into the marshy ground to support its weight of 300,000 tonnes and 48 huge columns were hauled into place. The cathedral opened in 1858 but was deconsecrated and became a museum of atheism during the Soviet era. Officially still a museum today, the church is filled with hundreds of 19th-century works of art.

Angels with Torch
Ivan Vitali created many of the cathedral's sculptures, including the pairs of angels supporting gas torches which crown the four attic corners.

KEY

① **St Catherine's Chapel** has an exquisite white marble iconostasis, crowned by a sculpted Resurrection (1850–4) by Nikolay Pimenov.

② **Malachite** and lapis lazuli columns frame the iconostasis. About 16,000 kg (35,280 lbs) of malachite decorate the cathedral.

③ **The north pediment** is ornamented with a bronze relief (1842–4) of the Resurrection designed by François Lemaire.

④ **This chapel** honours Alexander Nevsky, who defeated the Swedes in 1240 *(see p19)*.

⑤ **The mosaic icons** on the iconostasis are by Bryullov, Neff and Zhivago.

⑥ **The silver dove** (1850) hanging in the cupola is a symbol of the Holy Spirit.

⑦ **Portraits of apostles and evangelists**

⑧ **Statue of St Matthew**

⑨ **The relief** of St Isaac blessing the Emperor Theodosius and his wife Flaccilla is by Ivan Vitali. On the extreme left, Montferrand is depicted clutching a model of his cathedral.

⑩ **Red granite columns**, each weighing 114 tonnes, were transported from Finland by specially constructed ships.

⑪ **The vast interior** covers 4,000 sq m (43,000 sq ft).

⑫ **The walls** are adorned with 14 coloured marbles and 43 other types of semi-precious stones and minerals.

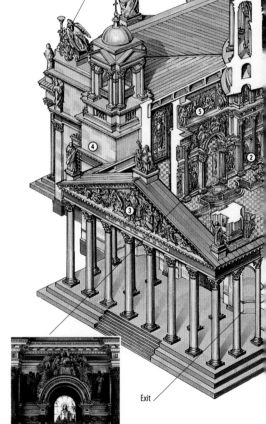

Exit

★ **Iconostasis**
Three rows of icons surround the royal doors through which a stained-glass window (1843) is visible. Above the doors is Pyotr Klodt's gilded sculpture, *Christ in Majesty* (1859).

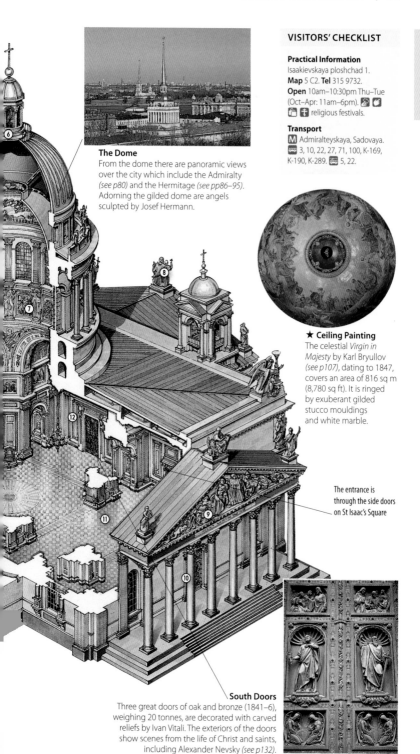

The Dome
From the dome there are panoramic views over the city which include the Admiralty *(see p80)* and the Hermitage *(see pp86–95)*. Adorning the gilded dome are angels sculpted by Josef Hermann.

★ Ceiling Painting
The celestial *Virgin in Majesty* by Karl Bryullov *(see p107)*, dating to 1847, covers an area of 816 sq m (8,780 sq ft). It is ringed by exuberant gilded stucco mouldings and white marble.

The entrance is through the side doors on St Isaac's Square

South Doors
Three great doors of oak and bronze (1841–6), weighing 20 tonnes, are decorated with carved reliefs by Ivan Vitali. The exteriors of the doors show scenes from the life of Christ and saints, including Alexander Nevsky *(see p132)*.

Malaya Morskaya ulitsa with No. 13 in the middle

❽ Malaya Morskaya Ulitsa

Малая Морская у лица

Malaya Morskaya ulitsa

Map 6 D1. 🚌 3, 10, 22, 27, K-306. 🚎 5, 22.

Malaya Morskaya Ulitsa used to be referred to as ulitsa Gogolya after the great prose-writer, Nikolai Gogol (1809–52) who lived at No. 17 from 1833–6. It was here that Gogol wrote *The Diary of a Madman* and *The Nose*, two biting satires on the archetypal Petersburg bureaucrat "drowned by the trivial, meaningless labours at which he spends his useless life". Gogol's bitingly humorous, fantastical and grotesque tales reveal a nightmarish and deeply pessimistic view of modern urban life.

The composer Pyotr Tchaikovsky *(see p44)* died in the top-floor apartment of No. 13 shortly after the completion of his *Pathétique* symphony in November 1893. Officially he was supposed to have died of cholera, but it is commonly believed that he committed suicide, due to pressure from Conservatory colleagues wishing to avoid a scandal after Tchaikovsky's alleged homosexual affair.

The house at No. 23 was occupied by the novelist Fyodor Dostoevsky *(see p125)* from 1848–9. It was here that he was arrested and charged with political conspiracy for his participation in the socialist Petrashevsky Circle *(see p125)*. Today, the street manages to exude a 19th-century feel despite the many busy shops and businesses.

❾ House of Fabergé

Дом Фаберже

Dom Faberzhe

Bolshaya Morskaya ulitsa 24. **Map** 6 D1. **Closed** to public. 🚌 3, 22, 27. 🚎 5, 22.

The world-famous Fabergé jeweller's was established in Bolshaya Morskaya ulitsa in 1842 by Gustav Fabergé, of French Huguenot origin. It was not until the 1880s that his sons Carl and Agathon abandoned conventional jewellery-making for intricate and exquisitely crafted *objets d'art* of a highly innovative design. Most famous of all their works are the imaginatively designed Easter eggs made for the tsars.

In 1900 Carl moved the business from No. 16–18 into purpose-built premises at No. 24, where it remained until the Revolution. The exterior, designed by his relative, Karl Schmidt, has striking triangular roof gables and multi-textured stonework. The original showroom, with its squat red granite pillars, was on the ground floor. It is still a jeweller's, but with no connection to Fabergé. In the workshops above, young apprentices were trained by master craftsmen in the arts of enamelling, engraving, stone cutting and jewelling.

In 1996, the 150th anniversary of Carl Fabergé's birth was marked by the unveiling of a memorial plaque at No. 24 and of a monument, designed by the sculptor Leonid Aristov and others, on the corner of Zanevskiy prospekt and prospekt Energetikov.

Fabergé Eggs

In 1885 Alexander III commissioned the Fabergé brothers to create an Easter egg for Tsarina Maria Fyodorovna. Inside the shell of gold and white enamel was a beautifully sculpted golden hen. A tradition was established and, by the Revolution, there were 54 Fabergé Easter eggs, no two of which were alike. The *pièce de résistance* is the Siberian Railway Egg, commissioned by Nicholas II in 1900. The Bonbonnière Egg was commissioned by Kelch, a wealthy industrialist, for his wife Varvara in 1903. Regrettably, the only eggs on public display in Russia today are in the State Armoury of the Kremlin in Moscow.

The Kelch Bonbonnière Egg

Death of a Poet

In November 1836 Pushkin received an anonymous letter which awarded him the title of "Grand Master of the Most Serene Order of Cuckolds". It had been sent by Georges d'Anthès, a ne'er-do-well cavalry officer who for some time had been

Aleksey Naumov's painting of Pushkin, fatally wounded after his duel

making overtures towards Pushkin's wife, the beauty and socialite Natalya Goncharova. Pushkin challenged d'Anthès to a duel and, on the afternoon of 27 January 1837, he met his opponent in snow-bound woodland to the north of the city. D'Anthès fired first and Pushkin was mortally wounded. He died two days later, aged 38. D'Anthès was later reduced to the ranks and banished from Russia.

Sign outside the Literary Café

⑩ Literary Café
Литературное кафе
Literaturnoe kafe

Nevskiy prospekt 18. **Map** 6 E1.
Tel 312 6057. **Open** 11am–11pm Sun–Thu, 11–1am Fri & Sat.
Ⓜ Nevskiy Prospekt. ♿

Also known as the Café Wulf et Beranger after its original owners, this café is famous for its association with Alexander Pushkin, Russia's greatest poet *(see p45)*. It was here that Pushkin met his second, Konstantin Danzas, before setting out for his ill-fated duel with Baron d'Anthès. The café was a popular haunt for St Petersburg writers from its beginning, frequented by Fyodor Dostoevsky and the poet Mikhail Lermontov (1814–41), among others.

Despite its hallowed literary importance and elegant setting, in Vasiliy Stasov's handsome building of 1815, the café itself does not merit the high prices.

⑪ Palace Square
Дворцовая площадь
Dvortsovaya ploshchad

Map 6 D1 🚌 7, 10, 24, 191, K-209. 🚎 1, 7, 10, 11.

Palace Square has played a unique role in Russian history. Before the Revolution the square was the setting for colourful military parades, often led by the tsar on horseback. In January 1905, it was the scene of the massacre on "Bloody Sunday" *(see p28)* when gathered troops fired on thousands of unarmed demon-strators. Then, on 7 November 1917, Lenin's Bolshevik sup-porters secured the Revolution by attacking the Winter Palace *(see pp30–31)* from the square, as well as its west side. It is still a favourite venue for political meetings and cultural events such as rock concerts *(see p53)*.

The resplendant square is the work of the inspired architect Carlo Rossi *(see p112)*. Facing the Winter Palace on its southern side is Rossi's magnificent General Staff Building (1819–29), the headquarters for the Russian army. Rossi demolished an entire row of houses to make room for it. The two graceful, curving wings (the eastern one now a branch of the Hermitage) are connected by a double arch leading to Bolshaya Morskaya ulitsa. The arch is crowned by a sculpture of Victory in her chariot (1829), by Stepan Pimenov and Vasiliy Demut-Malinovskiy. Forming the eastern side of this striking architectural ensemble is the Guards Headquarters, designed by Aleksandr Bryullov in 1837–43. To the west lies the Admiralty *(see p80)*.

The Alexander Column in the centre of the square is dedicated to Tsar Alexander I for his role in the triumph over Napoleon *(see pp24–5)*. On the pedestal are inscribed the words "To Alexander I, from a grateful Russia". The red granite pillar is balanced by its 600-tonne weight, making it the largest free-standing monument in the world. The column was designed by Auguste de Montferrand in 1829 and it took 2,400 soldiers and workmen two years to hew and transport the granite. It was erected in 1830–34. The column is topped by a bronze angel, and together they stand 47 m (154 ft) high.

The Alexander Column and General Staff Building in Palace Square

⓬ The Hermitage

Эрмитаж

Ermitazh

One of the largest museums in the world, the Hermitage occupies a grand ensemble of buildings. The most impressive is the Winter Palace *(see pp94–5)*, to which Catherine the Great added the more intimate Small Hermitage. In 1771–87, she built the Large Hermitage to house her growing collection of art. The Theatre was built in 1785–7, the New Hermitage in 1839–51. The New and Large Hermitages were opened by Nicholas I in 1852 as a public museum. From 1918 to 1939 the Winter Palace was slowly incorporated into the museum ensemble. In the late 1990s the majestic, Neo-Classical General Staff Building was added. It houses the collections of 19th- and 20th-century art.

★ Raphael Loggias
Catherine was so impressed by engravings of Raphael's frescoes in the Vatican that in 1787 she commissioned copies to be made on canvas. Small alterations were made, such as replacing the Pope's coat of arms with the Romanov two-headed eagle.

Atlantes
Ten 5-m- (16-ft-) tall granite Atlantes hold up what was the public entrance to the Hermitage museum from 1852 until after the Revolution.

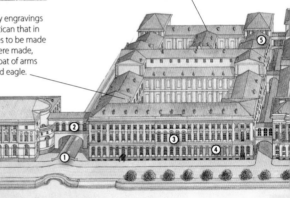

Theatre
During Catherine's reign, there were regular performances held in Quarenghi's theatre. Today it hosts conferences and concerts *(see p204).*

KEY

① **The Winter Canal** *(see p38)*

② **A gallery** spanning the canal connects the theatre to the Large Hermitage and forms the theatre foyer.

③ **The Large Hermitage** was designed by Yuriy Velten to house Catherine's paintings.

④ **Court ministries** were located here until the 1880s.

⑤ **The New Hermitage** (1839–51) was designed by Leo von Klenze to form a coherent part of the Large

Hermitage. It is the only purpose-built museum within the whole complex.

⑥ **The Small Hermitage** (1764–75), by Vallin de la Mothe and Yuriy Velten, served as Catherine's retreat from the bustle of the court.

⑦ **Palace Square**

⑧ **River Neva**

⑨ **The Winter Palace** (1754–62) was the official residence of the imperial family until the Revolution.

Hanging Gardens

This unusual raised garden is decorated with statues and fountains. During the Siege of Leningrad *(see p29)* Hermitage curators grew vegetables here.

VISITORS' CHECKLIST

Practical Information
Dvortsovaya ploshchad 2.
Map 2 D5. **Tel** 710 9079.
Open 10:30am–6pm Tue–Sun;
10:30am–9pm Wed. (last adm:
1 hr before closing). 🎧 🎫 English
(571 8446 to book). ♿ 📷 🖥
🌐 hermitagemuseum.org

Transport
🚌 7, 10, 24, 191, K-209. 🚊 1, 7, 10, 11.

Winter Palace Façade

Rastrelli embellished the palace façades with 400 columns and 16 different window designs.

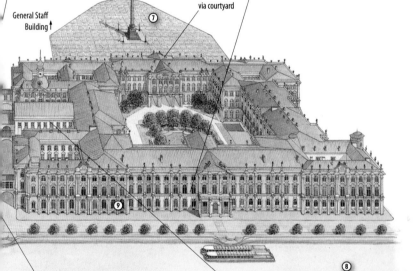

General Staff Building ↑

Main entrance via courtyard

⑦

⑨

⑧

★ Pavilion Hall

(1850–58) Andrey Stakenschneider's striking white marble and gold hall replaced Catherine's original interior. It houses Englishman James Cox's famous Peacock Clock (1772), which was once owned by Catherine's secret husband, Prince Grigory Potemkin.

★ Winter Palace State Rooms

The tsars spared no expense in decorating rooms such as the Hall of St George. These rooms were not intended for private life, but were used instead for state ceremonies.

The Hermitage Collections

Catherine the Great purchased some of Western Europe's best collections between 1764 and 1774, acquiring over 2,500 paintings, 10,000 carved gems, 10,000 drawings and a vast amount of silver and porcelain with which to adorn her palaces. None of her successors matched the quantity of her remarkable purchases. After the Revolution, the nationalization of both royal and private property brought more paintings and works of applied art, making the Hermitage one of the world's leading museums.

The Knights' Hall (1842–51) is used for displays of armour and weapons from the former imperial arsenal.

Entrance for tours and guided groups

First Floor

Stairs to ground floor

Raphael Loggias *(see p86)*

The Gallery of Ancient Painting (1842–51) is decorated with scenes from ancient literature. It houses a superb display of 19th-century European sculpture.

Skylight Rooms

Ground Floor

European Gold Collection

★ **Litta Madonna** (c.1491)
One of two works by Leonardo da Vinci in the museum, this masterpiece was admired by his contemporaries and was frequently copied.

The Hall of Twenty Columns (1842–51) is painted in Etruscan style.

Gallery Guide

Enter via Palace Square, then cross the main courtyard; group tours use other entrances. Start with the interiors of the Winter Palace state rooms on the first floor to get an overview of the museum. For 19th- and 20th-century European Art use either of the staircases on the Palace Square side of the Winter Palace. Note that collections may move.

Main entrance

★ **Abraham's Sacrifice** (1635)
In the 1630s Rembrandt was painting religious scenes in a High Baroque style, using dramatic and striking gestures rather than detail to convey his message.

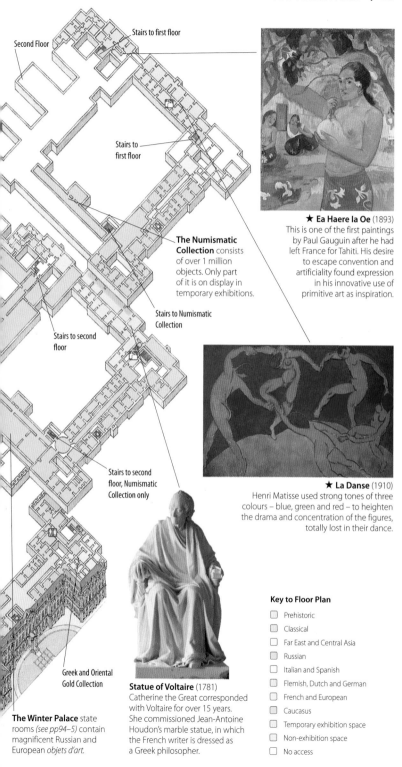

Second Floor

Stairs to first floor

Stairs to first floor

The Numismatic Collection consists of over 1 million objects. Only part of it is on display in temporary exhibitions.

Stairs to Numismatic Collection

Stairs to second floor

Stairs to second floor, Numismatic Collection only

Greek and Oriental Gold Collection

★ **Ea Haere Ia Oe** (1893)
This is one of the first paintings by Paul Gauguin after he had left France for Tahiti. His desire to escape convention and artificiality found expression in his innovative use of primitive art as inspiration.

★ **La Danse** (1910)
Henri Matisse used strong tones of three colours – blue, green and red – to heighten the drama and concentration of the figures, totally lost in their dance.

Statue of Voltaire (1781)
Catherine the Great corresponded with Voltaire for over 15 years. She commissioned Jean-Antoine Houdon's marble statue, in which the French writer is dressed as a Greek philosopher.

The Winter Palace state rooms *(see pp94–5)* contain magnificent Russian and European *objets d'art*.

Key to Floor Plan

- ☐ Prehistoric
- ☐ Classical
- ☐ Far East and Central Asia
- ☐ Russian
- ☐ Italian and Spanish
- ☐ Flemish, Dutch and German
- ☐ French and European
- ☐ Caucasus
- ☐ Temporary exhibition space
- ☐ Non-exhibition space
- ☐ No access

Exploring the Hermitage Collections

It is impossible to absorb the Hermitage's vast, encyclopedic collection in one or even two visits. Whether it be Scythian gold, antique vases and cameos, or Iranian silver, every room has something to capture the eye. The furniture, applied art, portraits and rich clothing of the imperial family went to make up the Russian section, which also includes the superb state rooms. The collection of European paintings was put together largely according to the personal taste of the imperial family, while most of the 19th- and 20th-century European art, notably the Impressionists, Matisse and Picasso, came from private collections after the Revolution.

Scythian gold stag dating from
7th–6th century BC

Prehistoric Art

Prehistoric artifacts found all over the former Russian Empire include pots, arrowheads and sculptures from Palaeolithic sites, which date back nearly 24,000 years, and rich gold items from the time of the Scythian nomads living in the 7th–3rd centuries BC.

Peter the Great's famous Siberian collection of delicate gold work includes Scythian animal-style brooches, sword handles and buckles. Objects continued to be discovered in Siberia and in 1897 a large stylized stag, which once decorated an iron shield, was found at Kostromskaya. This and other gold pieces are held in the European Gold Collection (for which a separate ticket is required). Copies are on display in the Scythian rooms.

Greek masters also worked for the Scythians, and from the Dnepr region came a late 5th-century comb decorated with amazingly naturalistic figures of Scythians fighting, as well as the late 4th-century Chertomlyk Vase with scenes

depicting animal taming. Excavations in the Altai, notably at Pazyryk in 1927–49, uncovered burials nearly 2,500 years old. Many perishable materials were preserved by the frozen land, including textiles, a burial cart and even a man's heavily tattooed skin.

Gonzaga Cameo (285–246 BC),
made in Alexandria

Classical Art

The large number of Graeco-Roman marble sculptures range from the famous Tauride Venus of the 3rd century BC, acquired by Peter the Great in 1720, to Roman portrait busts. The

smaller objects, however, are the real pride and joy of the Classical department.

The collection of red-figured Attic vases of the 6th–4th centuries BC is unequalled anywhere in the world. Exquisitely proportioned and with a lustrous shine, they are decorated with scenes of libation, episodes from the Trojan War, and, in one case, a famous image of the sighting of the first swallow (c.510 BC).

In the 4th and 3rd centuries BC, Tanagra was the centre for the production of small, elegant terracotta figurines. They were discovered in the 19th century and became so popular that fakes were produced on a grand scale. The Russian ambassador in Athens, Pyotr Saburov, put his collection together in the 1880s before the copies appeared, making it unusually valuable.

Catherine the Great's true passion was for carved gems, which she bought en masse. In just ten years, she purchased some 10,000 pieces. The largest and most stunning gem in the Classical collection, however, is the Gonzaga Cameo, which was presented by Napoleon's ex-wife Josephine Beauharnais to Tsar Alexander I in 1814.

The Greek and Oriental Gold Collection contains some items of 5th-century gold jewellery made by Athenian craftsmen. They used a filigree technique for working gold so finely that the detail can only be seen through a magnifying glass.

Far East and Central Asia

This selection of more than 180,000 artifacts covers a wide range of cultures, from ancient Egypt and Assyria, through Byzantium, India, Iran, China, Japan and the marvels of Uzbekistan and Tajikistan. The most complete sections are those where excavations were conducted by the Hermitage, mainly in China and Mongolia before the Revolution, and in Central Asia during the Soviet period.

Dating back to the 19th century BC, at the time of the Middle Kingdom, is a seated

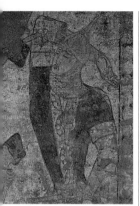

8th-century fresco of a wounded warrior from Tajikistan

of western oil painting, as in the *Portrait of Fatkh-Ali Shah* (1813–14). Uzbekistan and Tajikistan revealed marvellous frescoes in complexes of 8th-century buildings at Varaksha, Adjina-Tepe and Pendzhikent. Rare Mughal jewelled vessels, Iranian weapons and Chinese gold objects are displayed in the Greek and Oriental Gold Collection. These rooms are undergoing a three-year renovation.

Russian Art

Although major Russian works of art were transferred to the Russian Museum (*see pp106–9*) in 1898, everything else that belonged to the imperial family was nationalized after the Revolution. This included anything from official portraits and thrones to looking glasses and petticoats. Over 300 items of apparel belonging to Peter the Great alone survive. Later, the museum also began acquiring medieval Russian art, including icons and church utensils.

The tsars from Peter the Great onwards invited foreign craftsmen and artists to train locals. Peter studied with them

Universal sundial (1714–19) from Peter the Great's collection

porphyry portrait of Pharaoh Amenemhet III. The star of the Egyptian collection is an extremely rare, small, wooden statue of a standing man from the 15th century BC.

From the Far East – Japan, India, Indonesia, China and Mongolia – comes an array of objects ranging from Buddhist sculptures and fabrics to a display of tiny netsukes (ivory toggles). Excavations at the cave temple of the Thousand Buddhas near Dun Huan in western China revealed 6th–10th-century icons, wall paintings and plaster sculptures, including the lions that once guarded the cave. During the 13th-century Mongol invasion, the town of Khara-Khoto was destroyed and taken over by the surrounding desert. The sand preserved many usually perishable objects, from 12th-century silks to woodcuts.

From Byzantium come early secular items, such as icons, religious utensils and a 5th-century ivory diptych with scenes from a Roman circus.

Iran produced a large number of silver and bronze vessels, many of which were taken by medieval traders to Siberia and the Urals where they were rediscovered by specialists in the 19th century. There is also a large collection of traditional Persian miniatures and a rich display of 19th-century Persian court portraits that mix traditional elements with those

Steel dressing table set from Tula dating from 1801

and his fascination for practical things is reflected in his large collection of sundials, instruments and wood-turning lathes which includes the universal sundial by Master John Rowley. A bust by Bartolomeo Carlo Rastrelli (1723–30), however, portrays Peter as the mighty and cruel emperor.

Russian artists were soon combining traditional art forms with European skills to create such intricate marvels as the openwork walrus ivory vase by Nikolay Vereshchagin (1798), and the large silver sarcophagus and memorial to Alexander Nevsky, truly Russian in scale (1747–52).

The gunsmiths of Tula (south of Moscow) perfected their technique to such an extent that they began producing unique furniture in steel inlaid with gilded bronze, such as the decorative, Empire-style dressing table set (1801).

The state interiors (*see pp94–5*) are the pride of the Russian department, revealing the work of Russian and foreign craftsmen from the mid-18th to the early 20th century. The discovery of large deposits of coloured stones in the Urals inspired Russian artists to decorate whole rooms with malachite and to fill every corner of the Winter Palace with marble vases. It was through these rooms that the imperial family paraded on state occasions, greeting courtiers and ambassadors en route in the Field Marshals' Hall.

Italian and Spanish Art

The display of Italian art contains some fine pieces. A few early works reveal the rise of the Renaissance in the 14th and 15th centuries and the styles then in vogue. Simone Martini's stiff *Madonna* (1340–44) contrasts with Fra Angelico's more humane fresco of the Virgin and Child (1424–30).

In the late 15th and early 16th century, artists disputed the merits of line, as practised by the Florentine school, and the merits of colour, virtue of the Venetians. The former can be seen in the *Litta Madonna* (c.1491) and the *Madonna Benois* (1478) by Leonardo da Vinci, a marble *Crouching Boy* by Michelangelo (c.1530) and two early portraits of the Virgin by Raphael (1502 and 1506). Venice is represented by *Judith* by Giorgione (1478–1510) and an array of works by Titian (c.1490–1576). The Skylight Rooms are packed with vast Baroque canvases, including works by Luca Giordano (1634–1704) and Guido Reni (1575–1642), and even larger 18th-century masterpieces by Tiepolo. The works of the Italian sculptor Antonio Canova (1757–1822) (*Cupid and Psyche*, *The Three Graces*) stand in the Gallery of Ancient Painting.

The Spanish collection is more modest, but Spain's greatest painters can all be

seen, from El Greco with *The Apostles Peter and Paul* (1587–92), through to Ribera, Murillo, and Zurbarán with *St Lawrence* (1636). The portrait of a courtier, *Count Olivares*, painted c.1640 by Velázquez, contrasts with a much earlier genre scene of a peasant's breakfast (1617–18).

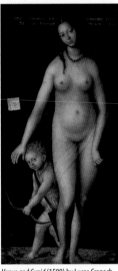

Venus and Cupid (1509) by Lucas Cranach the Elder

Flemish, Dutch and German Art

The small collection of early paintings from the Netherlands includes a marvellous, jewel-like *Madonna and Child* (1430s) by

the Master of Flemalle. He is thought to have been the teacher of Rogier van der Weyden, who is represented by *St Luke Painting the Madonna* (c.1435).

Over 40 works by Rubens include religious subjects (*The Descent from the Cross*, 1617–18) and scenes from Classical mythology (*Perseus and Andromeda*, 1620–21), as well as landscapes and an immensely obese *Bacchus* (1636–40). His portraits, such as the *Infanta's Maid* (1625), reveal the link with his famous pupil Van Dyck, whose paintings include a series of formal, full-length portraits and a dashing and romantic self-portrait from the late 1620s.

The Dutch section is rich in Rembrandts. Within a short period of time he produced the dramatic *Abraham's Sacrifice* (1636), the gentle *Flora* (1634) and the brilliant effects of *The Descent from the Cross* (1634). One of his last works was the *Return of the Prodigal Son* (1668–9), which has an emotional depth unseen before.

Among the many small genre paintings is Gerard Terborch's *Glass of Lemonade* from the mid-17th century. All the usual elements of a genre scene are imbued with psychological tension and heavy symbolism.

In the German collection, it is the works of Lucas Cranach the Elder which captivate the viewer. His *Venus and Cupid* (1509), the stylish *Portrait of a Woman in a Hat* (1526) and the tender *Virgin and Child Beneath an Apple Tree* reveal the varied aspects of his talent.

French and English Art

French art was de rigueur for collectors in the 18th century. Major artists of the 17th century, including Louis Le Nain and the two brilliant and contrasting painters Claude Lorrain and Nicolas Poussin, are well repre-sented. Antoine Watteau's elegant *Embarrassing Proposal* (c.1716), *Stolen Kiss* (1780s), by Jean-Honoré Fragonard and François Boucher's fleshy and certainly far-from-virtuous heroines repre-sent the more wicked side of

A Young Man Playing a Lute, by Michelangelo Caravaggio (1573–1610)

Still Life with the Attributes of the Arts (1766), by Jean-Baptiste Chardin

18th-century taste, but Catherine the Great preferred didactic or instructional works. She bought *Still Life with the Attributes of the Arts* (1766) by Chardin and, on the advice of Denis Diderot, Jean-Baptiste Greuze's moralizing *The Fruits of a Good Education* (1763). She also patronized sculptors, purchasing works by Etienne-Maurice Falconet (*Winter*, carved 1771) and Jean-Antoine Houdon (*Voltaire*, 1781).

Catherine also acquired English works, including a portrait of the philosopher John Locke (1697) by Sir Godfrey Kneller, who was also author of a portrait of Pyotr Potemkin (1682) in Russian 17th-century court dress. From Sir Joshua Reynolds Catherine commissioned *The Infant Hercules Strangling the Serpents* (1788). Her most daring purchase was of works by the still largely unknown Joseph Wright of Derby. *The Iron Forge* (1773) is a masterpiece of artificial lighting, but *Firework Display at the Castel Sant'Angelo* (1774–5) is a truly romantic fiery spectacle. She provided much work for English cabinet-makers and carvers of cameos. She became one of Josiah Wedgwood's most prestigious clients, ordering the famous Green Frog Service for her Chesma Palace *(see p132).*

The Green Frog Service, Wedgwood (1773–4)

19th- & 20th-Century European Art

Although the royal family did not patronize the new movements in art in the 19th century, there were far-sighted private individuals whose collections were nationalized and entered the Hermitage after the 1917 Revolution. Thanks to them, the Barbizon School is represented by works such as Camille Corot's charming silvery *Landscape with a Lake*, French Romanticism by two richly coloured Moroccan scenes of the 1850s by Delacroix. But Nicholas I himself did acquire work by the German Romantic painter Caspar David Friedrich, among them *On the Prow of the Ship* (1818–20).

Two collectors, Ivan Morozov and Sergey Shchukin, brought the Hermitage its superb array of Impressionist and Post-Impressionist paintings. Monet's art can be admired both in his early *Woman in a Garden* (1860s) and in the later, more exploratory, *Waterloo Bridge, Effect of Mist* (1903). Renoir and Degas perpetually returned to women as subjects, as in Renoir's charming *Portrait of the Actress Jeanne Samary* (1878) and Degas' pastels of women washing (1880s–90s). Pissarro's *Boulevard Montmartre in Paris* (1897) is typical of his urban scenes.

A change in colour and technique appeared as artists investigated new possibilities. Van Gogh used deeper tones in his *Women of Arles* (1888) and stronger brushstrokes in *Cottages* (1890). Gauguin turned to a different culture for inspiration, and his Tahitian period is represented by enigmatic works, such as *Ea Haere la Oe* (1893). In *The Smoker* (c.1890–2) and *Mont Ste-Victoire* (1896–8), Cézanne introduced experiments with plane and surface which were to have a strong influence on the next generation.

Matisse played both with colour and surface, in the carpet-like effect of *The Red Room* (1908–9) and the flatness of the panels *La Musique* and *La Danse* (1909–10). His visit to Morocco introduced new light effects, as in *Arab Coffeehouse* (1913), but it was Picasso who took Cézanne's experiments one stage further. In early works such as *Visit* (1902) from his Blue Period, Picasso concentrates on mood, but the surface destruction of the Cubist period of 1907–12, including *L'Homme aux Bras Croisés*, fills a whole room.

L'Homme aux Bras Croisés, painted by Pablo Picasso in 1909

The Winter Palace

Preceded by three earlier versions on this site, the existing Winter Palace (1754–62) is a superb example of Russian Baroque. Built for Tsarina Elizabeth, this opulent winter residence was the finest achievement of Bartolomeo Rastrelli. Though the exterior has changed little, the interiors were altered by a number of architects and then largely restored after a fire gutted the palace in 1837. After the assassination of Alexander II in 1881, the imperial family rarely lived here. During World War I a field hospital was set up in the Nicholas Hall and other state rooms. Then, in July 1917, the Provisional Government took the palace as its headquarters, which led to its storming by the Bolsheviks (see pp30–31).

★ **Small Throne Room**
Dedicated in 1833 to the memory of Peter the Great, this room houses a silver-gilt English throne, made in 1731.

KEY

① **North façade overlooking the Neva**

② **The Nicholas Hall,** the largest room in the palace, was always used for the first ball of the season.

③ **The Field Marshals' Hall** (1833) was the reception room where the devastating fire of 1837 broke out.

④ **The Hall of St George** (1795) has monolithic columns and wall facings of Italian Carrara marble.

⑤ **The 1812 Gallery** (1826) has portraits of Russian military heroes of the Napoleonic War, most by English artist George Dawe.

⑥ **The Armorial Hall** (1839), with its vast gilded columns, covers over 800 sq m (8,600 sq ft). Hospital beds were set up here during World War I.

⑦ **The French Rooms,** designed by Bryullov in 1839, house a collection of 18th-century French art.

⑧ **South façade on Palace Square**

⑨ **The White Hall** was decorated for the wedding of the future Alexander II in 1841.

⑩ **West wing**

⑪ **The Gothic Library** and other rooms in the northwest part of the palace were adapted to suit Nicholas II's bourgeois lifestyle. This wood-panelled library was created by Meltzer in 1894.

⑫ **The Rotunda** (1830) connected the private apartments in the west with the state apartments on the palace's north side.

★ **Main Staircase**
This vast, sweeping staircase (1762) was Rastrelli's masterpiece. It was from here that the imperial family watched the Epiphany ceremony of baptism in the Neva, which celebrated Christ's baptism in the Jordan.

Alexander Hall
Architect Aleksandr Bryullov employed a mixture of Gothic vaulting and Neo-Classical stucco bas-reliefs of military themes in this reception room of 1837.

Bartolomeo Rastrelli

The Italian architect Rastrelli (1700–71) came to Russia with his father in 1716 to work for Peter the Great. His rich Baroque style became highly fashionable and he was appointed Chief Court Architect in 1738. During Elizabeth's reign, Rastrelli designed several buildings, including the Winter Palace, the Palace of Tsarkoe Selo *(see pp154–9)* and Smolnyy Convent *(see p130)*. Unlike Elizabeth, Catherine the Great preferred Classical simplicity and Rastrelli retired in 1763, after she came to power.

Dark Corridor
The French and Flemish tapestries here include *The Marriage of Emperor Constantine*, made in Paris in the 17th century to designs by Rubens.

The Gold Drawing Room
Created in the 1850s, this room was extravagantly decorated in the 1870s with all-over gilding of walls and ceiling. It houses a display of Western European carved gems.

★ Malachite Room
Over two tonnes of ornamental stone were used in this sumptuous room (1839) which is decorated with malachite columns and vases, gilded doors and ceiling, and rich parquet flooring.

⓭ Millionaires' Street
Миллионная у лица
Millionnaya ulitsa

Map 2 E5.

Millionaires' Street takes its name from the aristocrats and members of the imperial family who once inhabited its opulent residences. Since the main façades and entrances overlook the river, some house numbers correspond to the embankment side.

On the eve of the Revolution, No. 26 (on the embankment) was the home of Grand Duke Vladimir Aleksandrovich who was responsible for firing on peaceful demonstrators on Bloody Sunday *(see p28)*. His consort, Maria Pavlovna, was one of Russia's leading society hostesses who gave soirées and balls that eclipsed even those of the imperial court. The building (1867–72), which was designed by Aleksandr Rezanov in the style of the Florentine Renaissance, is now the House of Scholars.

Putyatin's house, at No. 12 Millionaires' Street, witnessed the end of the Romanov dynasty. It was here that Grand Duke Mikhail Aleksandrovich, Nicholas II's brother, signed the decree of abdication in March 1917. Next door, No. 10, was where French novelist Honoré de Balzac stayed in 1843, while courting his future wife, Countess Eveline Hanska. The mid-19th-century house was designed by Andrey Stakenschneider for his own use.

The delicately sculpted façade of No. 10 Millionaires' Street

Gala staircase of the Marble Palace, built of stone quarried in the Urals

⓮ Marble Palace
Мраморный дворец
Mramornyy dvorets

Millionnaya ulitsa 5 (entrance from the Field of Mars). **Map** 2 E4. **Tel** 595 4248. 🚌 46, 49, K-76. **Open** 10am–6pm Mon, Wed & Fri–Sun; 1–9pm Thu. 🎫 English. 🌐 **rusmuseum.ru**

The Marble Palace was built as a present from Catherine the Great to her lover Grigoriy Orlov who had been instrumental in bringing her to power in 1762 *(see p24)*. An early example of Neo-Classical architecture, dating from 1768–85, the building is considered to be Antonio Rinaldi's masterpiece.

The palace takes its name from the marbles used in its construction. Most of the interiors were reconstructed in the 1840s by Aleksandr Bryullov, although the gala staircase and the Marble Hall are Rinaldi's work. The latter has marbled walls of grey, green, white, yellow, pink and lapis lazuli, and a ceiling painting, the *Triumph of Venus* (1780s) by Stefano Torelli.

The palace, which housed a Lenin museum for 55 years, is now a branch of the Russian Museum *(see pp106–9)*. On display are temporary exhibitions of work by foreign artists and modern art bequeathed by

the German collectors Peter and Irene Ludwig. Their collection includes a Picasso, *Large Heads* (1969), and work by post-war artists Jean-Michel Basquiat, Andy Warhol, Ilya Kabakov and Roy Lichtenstein.

In front of the palace stands a curious equestrian statue of Alexander III by Prince Pavel Trubetskoy. Unveiled on Ploshchad Vosstaniya in 1911, the ridiculed statue was removed from its original site in 1937 and its vast pedestal was cut up to create statues of new heroes, such as Lenin.

⓯ Field of Mars
Марсово Поле
Marsovo Pole

Map 2 F5. 🚌 46, 49, K-76.

Once a vast marshland, this area was drained during the 19th century and utilized for military manoeuvres and parades, fairs and other festivities. It was appropriately named after Mars, the Roman god of war. Between 1917 and 1923 the area, by then a sandy expanse, was nicknamed the "Petersburg Sahara". It was landscaped and transformed into a war memorial. The

Eternal Flame, Field of Mars

granite *Monument to Revolutionary Fighters* (1917–19), by Lev Rudnev, and the Eternal Flame (1957) commemorate the victims of the Revolutions of 1917 and the Civil War *(see p29)*. The west of the square is dominated by an imposing Neo-Classical building erected by Vasiliy Stasov in 1817–19. This was formerly the barracks of the Pavlovskiy Guards which were founded by Tsar Paul I in 1796. The military-obsessed tsar is said to have only recruited guardsmen with snub noses like his own. The Pavlovskiy officers were among the first to turn against the tsarist government in the 1917 Revolution *(see pp30–31)*.

Today the huge square is a popular spot for locals in the summer evenings, when the flowers are in bloom.

⓰ Summer Garden

Летний сад

Letniy sad

Letniy Sad. **Map** 2 F4. 🚌 46, 49, K-76, K-212. **Open** May–Sep: 10am–10pm daily; Oct–Mar: 10am–8pm daily. ♿ 🔲

In 1704 Peter the Great commissioned this beautiful formal garden which was among the first in the city. Designed by a Frenchman in the style of Versailles, the *allées* were planted with imported elms and oaks and adorned with fountains, pavilions and some 250 Italian statues dating from the 17th and 18th centuries. A flood in 1777 destroyed most of the Summer Garden and the English-style garden which exists today is largely the result of Catherine the Great's more sober tastes. A splendid feature is the fine filigree iron grille (1771–84) along the Neva embankment, created by Yuriy Velten and Pyotr Yegorov.

For a century the Summer Garden was an exclusive preserve of the nobility. When the garden was opened to "respectably dressed members of the public" by Nicholas I, two Neo-Classical pavilions, the Tea House and the Coffee House, were erected overlooking the Fontanka. These are now used for temporary exhibitions of art.

Nearby, the bronze statue of Ivan Krylov, Russia's most famous writer of fables, is a favourite with Russian children. It was sculpted by Pyotr Klodt in 1854 with charming bas-reliefs on the pedestal depicting animals from his fables.

Ivan Krylov's statue amid autumn foliage in the Summer Garden

⓱ Summer Palace

Летний дворец

Letniy dvorets

Naberezhnaya Kutuzova. **Map** 2 F4. **Tel** 314 0374. **Open** May–Nov: 11am–5:30pm Wed–Mon. **Closed** last Mon of each month. 🚌 46, 49, K-76, K-212. 🖼 🖊

Built for Peter the Great, the modest two-storey Summer Palace is the oldest stone building in the city. It was designed in the Dutch style by Domenico Trezzini and was completed in 1714. The Prussian sculptor Andreas Schlüter created the delightful maritime bas-reliefs (1713) as an allegorical commentary on Russia's naval triumphs under Peter the Great's stewardship.

Grander than his wooden cabin *(see p75)*, Peter's second St Petersburg residence is still by no means comparable to the magnificent palaces built by his successors. On the ground floor, the reception room is hung with portraits of the tsar and his ministers and contains Peter's oak Admiralty Chair. The tsar's bedroom has its original four-poster bed with a coverlet of Chinese silk, and an 18th-century ceiling painting showing the triumph of Morpheus, the god of sleep. Next door is the turnery which contains some original Russian lathes as well as an elaborately carved wooden meteorological instrument, designed in Dresden in 1714.

The palace boasted the city's first plumbing system with water piped directly into the kitchen. The original black marble sink can still be seen, along with the beautifully tiled kitchen stove and an array of early 18th-century cooking utensils. The kitchen opens onto the exquisite dining room, imaginatively refurbished to convey an atmosphere of domesticity. It was used only for small family gatherings since major banquets were held at the Menshikov Palace *(see p64)*.

An original staircase leads up to the first floor and the more lavish suite of Peter's second wife, Catherine. The throne in the aptly named Throne Room is ornamented with Nereides and other sea deities. The glass cupboards in the Green Room once displayed Peter's fascinating collection of curiosa before it was transferred to the Kunstkammer *(see p62)*.

The remarkable stove in the Summer Palace's tiled kitchen

GOSTINYY DVOR

The Great Bazaar, Gostinyy Dvor, was the commercial heart of St Petersburg at the beginning of the 18th century and today it still hums with activity. A profusion of smaller retail outlets soon appeared on and around Nevskiy prospekt. Thriving communities of foreign merchants and businessmen also took up residence in the neighbourhood.

Until the mid-19th century, shops in this area catered almost exclusively for the luxury end of the market, fulfilling the limitless demand, created by the royal and aristocratic households, for gold and silverware, jewellery

and haute couture. Increasing commercial and financial activity created a new middle class of business entrepreneurs. By the Revolution, banks proliferated around Nevskiy prospekt, their imposing new offices introducing diverse architectural styles to a largely Neo-Classical setting. Today the wheels of capitalism are turning again and Nevskiy prospekt still attracts a wealthy clientele. In contrast to the bustling commercial atmosphere of much of the area is the calm oasis of Arts Square, with the Russian Museum and other institutions which act as a reminder of the city's rich cultural life.

Sights at a Glance

Churches
1. Church on Spilled Blood p102
7. Armenian Church
15. Cathedral of Our Lady of Kazan
17. Lutheran Church

Museums
2. Mikhaylovskiy Castle
3. Russian Museum pp106–9
19. Pushkin House-Museum

Streets and Squares
4. Arts Square
6. Nevskiy Prospekt
11. Ostrovskiy Square
12. Ulitsa Zodchego Rossi

Markets and Shops
8. Gostinyy Dvor
9. Yeliseev's
14. Apraksin Market

Palaces
10. Anichkov Palace
13. Vorontsov Palace
16. Stroganov Palace

Hotels
5. Belmond Grand Hotel Europe

Historic Buildings
18. Academic Capella
20. Imperial Stables

Restaurants pp188–90
1. Aragvi
2. Bellevue Brasserie
3. Brasserie de Metropol
4. Caviar Bar and Restaurant
5. Erivan
6. Fartuk
7. Fiolet
8. Iz pechi
9. Jack & Chan
10. Jamie's Italian
11. Kavkaz-Bar
12. Kilikia
13. Kvartirka
14. L'Europe
15. Mama Roma
16. Meat Head
17. Park Giuseppe
18. Pelmeniya
19. Pirogovy Dvorik
20. Rada & K
21. Suliko
22. Tsar
23. Yat

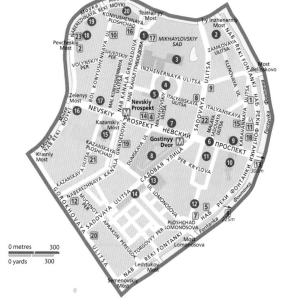

See also Street Finder map 6

◀ Richly decorated façade on the southern portico of the 19th-century Church on Spilled Blood   For keys to symbols see back flap

Street-by-Street: Around Arts Square

The aptly named Arts Square, one of Carlo Rossi's finest creations, is surrounded by buildings revealing the city's impressive cultural heritage. The grand palace housing the Russian Museum is flanked by theatres and the Philharmonia concert hall. Behind it is the leafy Mikhaylovskiy Garden, a haunt of St Petersburg's intellectuals. The gardens stretch down to the beautiful Moyka river which together with two other waterways, the Griboedov and Fontanka, create a shimmering frame for this picturesque area.

❶ ★ **Church on Spilled Blood**
Colourful mosaics and elaborate stone carving are the main features of the church's exterior, which emulates traditional 17th-century Russian style.

Mikhaylovskiy Garden

NABEREZHNAYA REKI MO

MO

❸ ★ **Russian Museum**
Located in Rossi's Mikhaylovskiy Palace, this famous gallery boasts a fabulous collection of Russian painting, sculpture and applied art. The grand staircase and White Hall are original features.

KANAL GRIBOEDOVA

NAB KANALA GRIBOEDOVA

INZHENERNAYA ULI

ITALYANSKAYA ULITSA

Statue of Pushkin (1957)

Nevskiy prospekt

❹ **Arts Square**
The square's present name derives from the number of cultural institutions situated here. On the western side, the Mikhailovsky Theatre opened in 1833 for opera performances.

The Great Hall of the Philharmonia is one of the major concert venues in St Petersburg (see p204).

❺ **Belmond Grand Hotel Europe**
This famous St Petersburg hotel was constructed by Ludwig Fontana in 1873–5. Mighty atlantes adorn its eclectic façade which stretches all the way down to Nevskiy prospekt.

Locator Map
See Street Finder map 6

The Panteleymon Bridge was rebuilt in 1907–8 to support a new tramway but it retains its original Empire-style decor by Lev Ilyin (see p39).

The bird statue, cast in 1995 by Rezo Gabriadze, refers to a popular rhyme about vodka drinking.

Statue of Peter the Great (1747)

❷ Mikhaylovskiy Castle
Originally built for Paul I in 1797–1801, this castle was acquired by the Guards Corps of Engineers in 1823. Today it forms part of the Russian Museum and displays historical portraits.

Key

 Suggested route

| 0 metres | 100 |
| 0 yards | 100 |

Nevskiy prospekt

The Museum of Hygiene, with macabre displays of preserved human organs, was set up in 1919 to teach the public about health and hygiene.

The Circus or *"tsirk"* began performing in the 19th century when it was known as the Ciniselli Circus. It still offers traditional performances (see p203) in its historic venue by the Fontanka. Its original façade was reinstated in 2003.

❶ Church on Spilled Blood

Храм Спаса-на-Крови
Khram Spasa-na-Krovi

The Church on Spilled Blood, also known as the Resurrection Church of Our Saviour, was built on the spot where on 1 March 1881 Tsar Alexander II was assassinated *(see p28)*. In 1883 his successor, Alexander III, launched a competition for a permanent memorial. The winning design, in the Russian Revival style favoured by the tsar himself, was by Alfred Parland and Ignatiy Malyshev. The foundation stone was laid in October 1883.

A riot of colour, the overall effect of the church is created by the imaginative juxtaposition of materials. Inside, more than 20 types of minerals, including jasper, rhodonite , porphyry and Italian marble are lavished on the mosaics of the iconostasis, icon cases, canopy and floor. The interior reopened in 1998 after more than 20 years of restoration.

VISITORS' CHECKLIST

Practical Information
Nab kanala Griboedova 2b. **Map** 2
E5. **Tel** 315 1636. **Open** May–Sep:
10:30am–11:30pm (Oct–Apr:
11:30am–6pm) Thu-Tue. 🚫
📷 📹

Transport
Ⓜ Gostinyy Dvor, Nevskiy Prospekt.

Mosaic Tympanum Mosaic panels showing scenes from the New Testament adorn the exterior. They were based on designs by artists such as Viktor Vasnetsov and Mikhail Nesterov.

The tent-roofed steeple is 81 m (265 ft) high.

Coat of Arms
The 144 mosaic coats of arms on the bell tower represent the regions, towns and provinces of the Russian Empire. They were intended to reflect the grief shared by all Russians in the wake of Alexander's assassination.

Intricate Detailing
The flamboyant Russian Revival style of the exterior provides a dramatic contrast to the Neo-Classical and Baroque architecture which dominates the centre of St Petersburg.

Jewellers' enamel
was used to cover the 1,000 sq m (10,760 sq ft) surface of the five domes.

Glazed ceramic tiles enliven the façade.

Mosaic portraits of the saints are set in tiers of *kokoshniki* gables. Almost 7,000 sq m (75,300 sq ft) of mosaics embellish the church's extravagant exterior.

Twenty dark red plaques of Norwegian granite are engraved in gilt letters with the most outstanding events of Alexander II's reign (1855–81). Among the historic events recorded are the emancipation of the serfs in 1861 and the conquest of Central Asia (1860–81).

Window Frames
The windows are flanked by carved columns of ornate Estonian marble. The casings are in the form of double and triple *kokoshniki* (tiered decorative arches).

South façade of Mikhaylovskiy Castle and statue of Peter the Great

❷ Mikhaylovskiy Castle

Михайловский замок

Mikhaylovskiy zamok

Sadovaya ulitsa 2. **Map** 2 F5. **Tel** 570 5112. 46, K-76, K-212. **Open** 10am–6pm Mon, Wed & Fri–Sun; 1–9pm Thu. book by phone.

The imposing red-brick castle overlooking the Moyka and Fontanka rivers is also known as the Engineers' Castle. It was erected in 1797–1801 by Vasiliy Bazhenov and Vincenzo Brenna for Tsar Paul I. The tsar's obsessive fear of being assassinated led him to surround his new residence with moats and drawbridges, and to build a secret underground passage to the barracks on the Field of Mars *(see p96)*. Unfortunately, all these precautions proved futile and, after living in his fortified castle for just 40 days, Paul fell victim to a military conspiracy which resulted in his murder *(see p24)*.

In 1823 the fortress was acquired by the Guards Corps of Engineers. The school's most famous graduate was the writer Fyodor Dostoevsky *(see p125)*. Today the castle serves as a branch of the nearby Russian Museum. It is used to house temporary exhibitions.

The Church of the Archangel Michael is accessed via the exhibition and is a good example of Brenna's Neo-Classical style.

In front of the castle stands a bronze statue of Peter the Great on horseback, designed by Bartolomeo Carlo Rastrelli and cast in 1747.

❸ Russian Museum

See pp106–9.

❹ Arts Square

Площадь Искусств

Ploshchad Iskusstv

Map 6 F1. Nevskiy Prospekt, Gostinyy Dvor.

Several of the city's leading cultural institutions are located on this leafy Neo-Classical square, hence its name. The attractive square was designed by Carlo Rossi in the early 19th century to harmonize with the magnificent Mikhaylovskiy Palace (now the Russian Museum) which stands on its northern side.

On the opposite side of the square is the Great Hall of the St Petersburg Philharmonia, also known as the Shostakovich Hall *(see p45)*. This is where the Philharmonic Orchestra has been based since the 1920s *(see p204)*. Constructed by Paul Jacot in 1834–9, it started as a Nobles' Club where concerts were held.

Among the works premiered here were Beethoven's *Missa Solemnis* in 1824 and Tchaikovsky's *(see p44) Pathétique* in 1893.

On the square's western side is the Mikhailovsky Theatre *(see p204)*, rebuilt by Albert Kavos in the mid-19th century. In the centre of the square is a sculpture of one of Russia's greatest literary figures, Alexander Pushkin *(see p45)*. The statue was executed by leading post-war sculptor, Mikhail Anikushin.

Belmond Grand Hotel Europe's elegant Style-Moderne restaurant *(see p190)*

❺ Belmond Grand Hotel Europe

Гранд Отель Европа

Grand Otel Evropa

Mikhaylovskaya ulitsa 1/7. **Map** 6 F1. **Tel** 329 6000. Nevskiy Prospekt, Gostinyy Dvor. See Where to Stay, p178.

One of Russia's most famous hotels, the ornate Grand Hotel Europe (1873–5) was designed by Ludwig Fontana. The building owes much of its character to alterations made in the 1910s by Style-Moderne architect Fyodor Lidval.

Before the Revolution, the hotel's magnificent restaurant was a favourite rendezvous for members of the diplomatic corps and secret police. In the 1970s, the hotel café became a popular meeting place for young intellectuals and artists.

Pushkin's statue in front of the Russian Museum, Arts Square

Visitors admiring works of art on display in the Russian Museum ▶

❸ Russian Museum

Русский Музей
Russkiy Muzey

The museum is housed in the Mikhaylovskiy Palace, one of Carlo Rossi's finest Neo-Classical creations, which was built in 1819–25 for Grand Duke Mikhail Pavlovich. Alexander III's plans to create a public museum were realized by his son, Nicholas II, when the Russian Museum opened here in 1898. Today, the museum holds one of the world's greatest collections of Russian art.

The Benois Wing, named after its main architect Leontiy Benois, was added in 1913–19.

Stairs to ground floor

★ Princess Olga Konstantinovna Orlova (1911)
By the turn of the 20th century, Valentin Serov was the most successful portrait painter in Russia.

Entrance

Temporary exhibitions of 20th-century art are often displayed.

Stairs to first floor of Benois Wing

A Meal in the Monastery (1865–76)
Vasiliy Perov's canvas exposes the hypocrisy of the Orthodox clergy, with the juxtaposition of good and evil, rich and poor, false piety and true faith.

Gallery Guide

The main entrance on Arts Square leads to the ticket office on the lower ground floor. The exhibition starts on the first floor. It is arranged chronologically, starting with icons in Room 1. It continues on the ground floor of the main building and Rossi Wing, then the first floor of the Benois Wing. Exhibitions are changed regularly.

Folk Art Toy (1930s)
This clay toy from Dykomovo is part of the colourful selection of folk art which also includes lacquer boxes, painted ceramics and textiles.

★ **The Last Day of Pompeii** (1833)
Karl Bryullov's Classical subject
embodies the aesthetic principles of the
Academy of Arts. This vivid depiction of
the eruption of Vesuvius won him the
Grand Prix at the Paris Salon.

VISITORS' CHECKLIST

Practical Information
Inzhenernaya ulitsa 4.
Map 6 F1. **Tel** 595 4248.
Open 10am–6pm Mon,
Wed & Fri–Sun; 1–9pm Thu. 🦽
📞 phone for details. 🎧 English
(Tel: 314 3448). 📷 📖
🎧 English. 🌐 **rusmuseum.ru**

Transport
Ⓜ Nevskiy Prospekt, Gostinyy
Dvor. 🚎 3, 7, 22, 24, 27, 191,
K-212, K-289. 🚊 1, 5, 7, 10, 11, 22.

Stairs to
ground floor

14
15
12
16
13
17
11
10
9
8
7
1 2 3 6
5
4

The White Hall
contains original
Empire-style
furniture by
Carlo Rossi.

Rossi Wing   Start of exhibition

★ **Barge-Haulers on the Volga** (1870–73)
Ilya Repin was the most famous member
of the Wanderers, a group of artists
dedicated to social realism and
Russian themes. His powerful
indictment of forced labour imbues the
oppressed victims with sullen dignity.

44 43 42 41
40 39
54
34
32
35
31
36
37
30
38
29 28
27
26
25
24
23
22
21
18 19
20

Entrance points from
lower-ground-floor
ticket office

Phryne at the Festival of Poseidon in Eleusin
(1889) Henryk Siemiradzki's paintings are fine
examples of late European Neo-Classicism. He
is renowned for his academic scenes of life
in ancient Greece and Rome.

The portico of eight
Corinthian columns is
the central feature of
Rossi's façade. Behind
is a frieze of Classical
figures, designed by
Rossi and executed
by Demut-Malinovskiy.

Stairs to
first floor

The main entrance
is through a small
door leading to the
lower ground floor,
with a ticket office,
a cloakroom,
toilets and a café.

Key to Floor Plan
☐ Old Russian art
☐ 18th-century art
☐ Early 19th-century art
☐ Late 19th-century art
☐ 20th-century art
☐ 18th–20th-century sculpture
☐ Folk art
☐ Temporary exhibitions
☐ Non-exhibition space

Exploring the Russian Museum

Housing one of the world's greatest collections of Russian art, the museum originally comprised officially approved works from the Academy of Arts *(see p65)*. When the museum was nationalized after the Revolution, art was transferred from palaces, churches and private collections. By the 1930s, Socialist Realism had become state policy and avant-garde works were stored away, to re-emerge with the advent of *perestroika* in the 1980s.

Portrait of E I Nelidova (1773), by Dmitriy Levitskiy

The Angel with the Golden Hair, an icon from the early 12th century

Old Russian Art

The museum's fine collection begins with icons dating from the 12th–17th centuries. Russian icons derive from the Orthodox tradition and thus, just like Byzantine icons, tend to be sombre, marked by an absence of movement and a remote, mystic characterization of the saints. A superb example is one of the earliest icons, *The Angel with the Golden Hair*, in which the large, expressive eyes and delicate modelling of the Archangel Gabriel's face convey a sense of ethereal grace.

The Novgorod School *(see p167)* encouraged a much bolder and brighter style with a greater sense of drama and movement. And yet it is the poetically expressive and technically refined work of Andrey Rublev (c.1340 – c.1430) that is considered by many to mark the pinnacle of Russian icon painting.

18th–19th-Century Art

The first secular portraits (which owed much to the static quality of the icons) appeared in the second half of the 17th century. It was, however, under Peter the Great that Russian painting fully cast off from its Byzantine moorings. Peter the Great himself was the first patron to send young artists, often serfs, to study abroad. Secular art began to gain momentum in 1757 with the establishment of the Academy of Arts *(see p65)* which placed a heavy emphasis on classical and mythological subjects.

European influence permeates the work of Russia's first important portrait painters, Ivan Nikitin (1688–1741) and Andrey Matveev (1701–39). The art of portraiture matured with Dmitriy Levitskiy (1735–1822), among whose best-known works is a series of portraits of noble girls from the Smolnyy Institute.

Russian landscape painting was stimulated by the Romantic movement and in particular artists who sought inspiration abroad, including Silvestr Shchedrin (1791–1830) and Fyodor Matveev (1758–1826).

Ivan Aivazovskiy's (1817–1900) vast marine paintings, however, have something purely Russian in their scale and mood. Romanticism also influenced history painters such as Karl Bryullov (1799–1852), as in his depiction of *The Last Day of Pompeii*.

In 1863 a group of students, led by Ivan Kramskoy (1837–87), rebelled against the conservatism of the Academy of Arts. Seven years later they set up the Association of Travelling Art Exhibitions, and came to be known as the Wanderers *(Peredvizhniki)*, or the Itinerants. They demanded that painting should be more socially relevant, and were fundamentally committed to Russian subject matter.

The most versatile of the Wanderers was Ilya Repin *(see p44)* whose bold canvas *Barge-Haulers on the Volga* combines a visually powerful attack on forced

Knight at the Crossroads (1882), by Viktor Vasnetsov

The Six-Winged Seraph (1904), by Mikhail Vrubel

labour with a romantic view of the Russian people. Meanwhile, *A Meal in the Monastery* by Vasiliy Perov (1833–82) is a satirical and equally effective attack on social injustice.

The nationalist element led history painters such as Nikolay Ge (1831–94) and Vasiliy Surikov (1848–1916) to turn to Russian history for inspiration, treating their subjects with a new psychological understanding, as in Ge's canvas of 1871–2, in which Peter the Great interrogates his sullenly resistant son.

The general Slavic revival also breathed new life into landscape painting, concentrating on the beauties of the Russian countryside. The master of the genre was Isaak Levitan (1860–1900), whose *Golden Autumn Village*, dated 1889, is almost Impressionist in style, a sign perhaps that the ascendancy of the Wanderers was coming to an end.

Viktor Vasnetsov (1848–1926) turned to Russia's heroic, and often legendary, pre-European past, in realistically painted canvases such as *Knight at the Crossroads*. A haunting metaphor for Russia's uncertain future, the painting reveals that Vasnetsov was unable to avoid the *fin-de-siècle* melancholy and mysticism which was so potently expressed in the work of the next up-and-coming generation of artists, notably the Symbolists.

20th-Century Art

The dark, brooding canvases of Symbolist Mikhail Vrubel (1856–1910) combine Russian and religious themes with a more international outlook. Vrubel used colour and form to depict emotion and in *The Six-Winged Seraph* he employs a broken, vibrant, surface to express tension.

Another major contribution to 20th-century art was the "World of Art" movement, founded by Alexandre Benois and Sergey Diaghilev in the 1890s *(see p28)*. It rejected the notion of "socially useful art" in favour of a new tenet, "art pure and unfettered", and also opened up Russian painting to Western influences. Many members of the group, including Benois and Leon Bakst, designed stage sets and

Portrait of the Director Vsevolod Meyerhold (1916), Boris Grigorev

costumes for Diaghilev's Ballets Russes *(see p120)*.

The Russian avant-garde grew out of these local influences, plus the art of Cézanne, Picasso and Matisse. Mikhail Larionov (1881–1964) and Natalya Goncharova (1881–1962) both made brilliant use of Russian folk art as inspiration for primitivist works such as Goncharova's *Bleaching Canvas* (1908). They often altered their style in response to changing stimuli and later turned to Futurism's cult of the machine, as in Goncharova's *Cyclist* (1913) *(see p42)*.

The link between innovation in painting and the arts in general at this time is strikingly depicted in Boris Grigorev's angular portrait of Meyerhold, himself renowned for his radical approach to theatre.

Kazimir Malevich's (1878–1935) fascination with the juxtaposition of simple geometric shapes inspired the Suprematist movement. Vasily Kandinsky (1866–1944), a leading member of Munich's Blaue Reiter group, was also a key figure in the growth of Russian abstract art.

Marc Chagall (1887–1985), El Lissitskiy (1890–1941) and Alexander Rodchenko (1891–1956) are also represented.

Due to the high demand for the loan of avant-garde works abroad, the selection on view changes regularly.

Folk Art

Folk art became a strong influence on the development of modern Russian art in the 1860s when the wealthy industrialist and patron Savva Mamontov established an artists' colony at Abramtsevo, near Moscow. Vasiliy Polenov (1844–1927), Ilya Repin and Viktor Vasnetsov were among the painters encouraged to work alongside, and learn from, the serf craftsmen on the estate. The museum's collection of folk art is wonderfully diverse and includes exquisitely embroidered tapestries, traditional headdresses, painted tiles, porcelain toys, and lacquered spoons and dishes.

❻ Nevskiy Prospekt
Невский проспект
Nevskiy prospekt

Map 6 D1–8 D3. Ⓜ Nevskiy Prospekt, Gostinyy Dvor. See also pp46–9.

Russia's most famous street, Nevskiy prospekt, is also St Petersburg's main thorough-fare and artery. In the 1830s, the novelist Nikolai Gogol *(see p44)* declared with great pride: "There is nothing finer than Nevskiy Avenue…in St Petersburg it is everything…is there anything more gay, more brilliant, more resplendent than this beautiful street of our capital?". In this respect very little has actually changed, for Nevskiy prospekt's intrinsic importance still prevails today.

Laid out in the early days of the city, it was first known as the Great Perspective Road, running 4.5 km (3 miles) from the Admiralty *(see p80)* to the Alexander Nevsky Monastery *(see pp132–3)*. In spite of roaming wolves and uncon-trollable flooding from the Neva *(see p39)* which made the avenue

navigable in 1721, fine mansions, such as the Stroganov Palace *(see p114)* were built. Shops and bazaars, catering for the nobility, and inns for travelling merchants followed. A magnet attracting rich and poor alike, by the mid-18th century the ave-nue had become the place to see and be seen, to meet for gossip, business and pleasure.

Today, the street still teems with people until late into the night throughout the year. Many of the city's sights are close to the stretch between the Admiralty and Anichkov Bridge *(see pp48–9)*. Some of the best shops *(see pp196–7)* can be found along the stretch between the Fontanka and Vosstaniya. Nevskiy prospekt also offers a wealth of cultural interest: the Small Philharmonia concert hall *(see p204)*, the Russian national library, Beloselskiy-Belozerskiy Palace *(see p51)* and a wide variety of museums, theatres, churches, including the Church of St Catherine *(see p50)*, shops, cinemas and eateries.

The portico of the Armenian Church, built between 1771–9

❼ Armenian Church
Армянская церковь
Armyanskaya tserkov

Nevskiy prospekt 40–42. **Map** 6 F1. **Tel** 710 5061. Ⓜ Gostinyy Dvor. **Open** 9am–9pm.

Yuriy Velten designed the lovely blue-and-white Armenian Church of St Catherine, with its Neo-Classical portico and single cupola. The church, which opened in 1780, was financed by a wealthy Armenian businessman called Ioakim Lazarev, who acquired the money from the sale of a Persian diamond which Count Grigoriy Orlov purchased for Catherine the Great *(see p24)*.

Closed in 1930, the building has now been returned to the Armenian community and visitors are welcome to attend a service.

❽ Gostinyy Dvor
Гостиный двор
Gostinyy dvor

Nevskiy pr 35. **Map** 6 F2. **Tel** 710 5408. Ⓜ Gostinyy Dvor. **Open** 10am–10pm daily. Ⓦ **bgd.ru**

The term *gostinyy dvor* originally meant a coaching inn, but as trade developed around the inns, with travelling merchants setting up their stalls, it later came to mean "trading rows". The original wooden structure of this *gostinyy dvor* was destroyed by fire in 1736. Twenty years later, Bartolomeo

The historic Singer House located on the bustling Nevskiy prospekt

Rastrelli designed a new building but the project proved too costly and ambitious. Building recommenced in 1761 and continued until 1785. Vallin de la Mothe created the striking sequence of columned arcades and massive porticos. The prominent yellow building forms an irregular quadrangle which is bounded on one side by Nevskiy prospekt. The combined length of its façades is nearly 1 km (3,300 ft).

In the 19th century the gallery became a fashionable promenade where more than 5,000 people were employed. Serious damage during the Siege of Leningrad *(see p29)* led to major reconstruction, making it more like a modern department store. Even now, it has retained its layout of "stalls" of individual trading units. It offers a wide range of products, making it a central supplier of basic goods and souvenirs *(see p197)*.

Style-Moderne stained-glass windows in Yeliseev's

Moderne building, designed by Gavriil Baranovskiy in 1901–3, it is adorned with bronzes, heroic sculptures and huge windows. A plaque by the main door honours the grandsons.

Today the second floor of the building is home to the Akimov Comedy Theatre, while the ground floor houses a shop that offers a range of expensive food delicacies.

❿ Anichkov Palace

Аничков дворец
Anichkov dvorets

Nevskiy prospekt 39. **Map** 7 A2. Ⓜ Gostinyy Dvor. 🚌 3, 7, 22, 24, 27, 191. 🚎 1, 5, 7, 10, 11, 22. **Closed** to public except for special events.

In the early days, the broad Fontanka river was lined by palaces accessible mainly by boat. One of them was the Anichkov Palace (1741–50), remodelled in Baroque style in 1754. The palace was a gift from Tsarina Elizabeth to her lover Aleksey Razumovskiy. It was named after Lieutenant Colonel Mikhail Anichkov who set up camp on this site at the time of the founding of the city. Over the years the palace was rebuilt and altered many

times, according to the tastes of each successive owner. After Razumovskiy's death, Catherine the Great in turn gave the building to her lover, Prince Potemkin *(see p27)*. In the early 19th century, Neo-Classical details were added by Carlo Rossi.

The palace then became the traditional winter residence of the heir to the throne. When Alexander III became tsar in 1881, he continued to live here, however, rather than move to the Winter Palace as was customary. After his death, his widow Maria Fyodorovna stayed on until the Revolution.

The palace originally had large gardens to the west but these were curtailed in 1816 when Ostrovskiy Square *(see p112)* was created and two Neo-Classical pavilions were added. The elegant colonnaded building overlooking the Fontanka to the east was commissioned by Giacomo Quarenghi in 1803–5. It was initially built as an arcade where goods from the imperial factories were stored before being allocated to the palaces. Later it was converted into government offices and now also houses the Cultural Centre of Children's Creative Work.

Columned arcades in the popular shopping centre, Gostinyy Dvor

❾ Yeliseev's

Елисеевский гастроном
Yeliseevskiy gastronom

Nevskiy prospekt 56. **Map** 6 F1. **Tel** 456 6666. Ⓜ Gostinyy Dvor. **Open** 10am–11pm daily. 🌐 **kupetzeliseevs.ru**

The successful Yeliseev dynasty was founded by Pyotr Yeliseev, an ambitious peasant who, in 1813, opened a wine shop on Nevskiy prospekt. By the turn of the century his grandsons owned a chocolate factory, numerous houses, inns and this famous former food store. The city's most opulent Style-

Quarenghi's addition to the Anichkov Palace from Nevskiy prospekt

Porticoed façade of Alexandrinskiy Theatre (1828–32), Ostrovskiy Square

⓫ Ostrovskiy Square
Площадь Островского
Ploshchad Ostrovskovo

Map 6 F2. Ⓜ Gostinyy Dvor. ▩ 3, 7, 22, 24, 27. ▦ 1, 5, 7, 10, 11, 22.
Russian National Library: **Tel** 310 7137. **Open** 9am–9pm. Theatre Museum: **Tel** 571 2195. **Open** 11am–7pm Thu–Mon, 1–9pm Wed. **Closed** last Fri of each month and public hols. ▦ ▣
W **theatremuseum.ru**

One of Russia's most brilliant architects, Carlo Rossi, created this early 19th-century square, which is now named in honour of the dramatist Aleksandr Ostrovskiy (1823–86).

The focal point of the square is the elegant Alexandrinskiy Theatre *(see p204)*, designed in the Neo-Classical style which Rossi favoured. The portico of six Corinthian columns is crowned by a chariot of Apollo, sculpted by Stepan Pimenov.

The building was the new home to Russia's oldest theatre company, set up in 1756. Plays premiered here, and still performed today, include Nikolai Gogol's *The Inspector General* (1836) and Anton Chekhov's *The Seagull* (1901). In Soviet times the theatre was renamed the Pushkin Theatre.

In the garden is a monument to Catherine the Great, the only one in the city. It was designed principally by Mikhail Mikeshin and unveiled in 1873. The statue depicts Catherine surrounded by statesmen and other worthies, and includes the female president (1783–96) of the Academy of Sciences, Princess Yekaterina Dashkova.

The benches behind the monument are packed during the summer months with chess players and spectators. On the west side of the square, opposite the Anichkov Palace *(see p111)* is an elegant colonnade decorated with Classical sculptures. This is the extension of the Russian Library, made by Rossi in 1828–34. Founded in 1795, the library currently holds more than 28 million items. A prized possession is the personal library of the French philosopher Voltaire, which Catherine the Great purchased to show her appreciation of her sometime mentor and correspondent.

In the southeast corner of the square, at No. 6, is the Theatre Museum which traces the evolution of the Russian stage from its origins in mid-18th-century serf and imperial theatres. Amid the eclectic array of playbills, photographs, costumes, set designs and other artifacts, there are also some set designs by one of the great innovators of modern theatre, the director Vsevolod Meyerhold (1874–1940).

⓬ Ulitsa Zodchego Rossi
У лица Зодчего Росси
Ulitsa Zodchevo Rossi

Map 6 F2. Ⓜ Gostinyy Dvor.

There could be no better memorial to Carlo Rossi than the near perfect architectural ensemble of identical arcades and colonnades forming "Architect Rossi Street". The 22-m- (72-ft-) high buildings stand precisely 22 m (72 ft) apart and stretch for 220 m (720 ft). In 2008 the street had its 180-year anniversary. Seen from ploshchad Lomonosova, the perspective hypnotically coaxes the eye towards the Alexandrinskiy Theatre.

At No. 2 is the home of the former Imperial School of Ballet, now named after the teacher Agrippina Vaganova (1879–1951), one of the few dancers not to emigrate after the Revolution. The school began in 1738 when Jean-Baptiste Landé began training orphans and palace servants' children to take part in court entertainment. It has produced many of Russia's most celebrated dancers *(see p120)*, including Anna Pavlova and Rudolf Nureyev.

19th-century photograph of ulitsa Zodchego Rossi (1828–34)

Architect Carlo Rossi

Carlo Rossi (1775–1849) was one of the last great exponents of Neo-Classicism in St Petersburg. He found an ideal client in Alexander I, who shared his belief in the use of architecture to express the power of the ruling autocracy. By the time of his death, Rossi had created no fewer than 12 of St Petersburg's impressive streets and 13 of its squares, including Palace Square *(see p85)*. Rossi's status as Alexander I's favourite architect encouraged rumours that Rossi was the offspring of an affair between Tsar Paul I and Rossi's Italian ballerina mother.

Central corpus of Vorontsov Palace

⓭ Vorontsov Palace

Воронцовский дворец
Vorontsovskiy dvorets

Sadovaya ulitsa 26. **Map** 6 F2. **Closed** to public. Ⓜ Gostinyy Dvor, Sennaya Ploshchad.

The most exclusive military school in the Russian Empire, the Corps des Pages, occupied the Vorontsov Palace from 1810–1918. Among those privileged enough to study here were a number of the Decembrists *(see pp24–5)* and Prince Felix Yusupov *(see p123)*. Today the palace houses the Suvorov Military Academy.

Designed by Bartolomeo Rastrelli *(see p95)*, the handsome palace, which once stood in its own extensive grounds, was built in 1749–57 for Prince Mikhail Vorontsov, one of Tsarina Elizabeth's leading statesmen. Rastrelli's graceful wrought-iron railings are among the earliest examples of their kind in Russia.

⓮ Apraksin Market

Апраксин двор
Apraksin dvor

Sadovaya ulitsa. **Map** 6 E2. Ⓜ Gostinyy Dvor, Sennaya Ploshchad, Sadovaya, Spasskaya.

Founded in the late 18th century, the market takes its name from the Apraksin family who owned the land it was built on. When fire destroyed the original wooden stalls in 1862, the arcade was erected. By 1900 there were more than 600 outlets selling everything from food, wine and spices to furs, furniture and haberdashery. The large street market has now

moved to Rustavelli Street, far from the city centre. The historic Apraksin Market is being reconstructed; in the meantime arcade shops continue to open.

⓯ Cathedral of Our Lady of Kazan

Собор Казанской Богоматери
Sobor Kazanskoy Bogomateri

Kazanskaya pl 2. **Map** 6 E1. **Tel** 314 4663. Ⓜ Nevskiy Prospekt. ▤ 3, 7, 22, 24, 27, 191. ▤ 1, 5, 7, 10, 11, 22. **Open** 9am–7:30pm daily. 🎫 ♿

One of St Petersburg's most majestic churches, the Cathedral of Our Lady of Kazan was commissioned by Paul I and took over a decade to build (1801–11). The impressive design by serf architect Andrey Voronikhin was inspired by St Peter's in Rome. Its 111-m- (364-ft-) long, curved colonnade disguises the orientation of the building, which runs parallel to Nevskiy prospekt, conforming to a religious stipulation that the main altar face east. In Voronikhin's original design he intended to duplicate the colonnade on the south side.

The cathedral is named after the miracle-working icon of Our Lady of Kazan. The icon is now kept in the cathedral.

The interior decoration is generally subdued. Its most impressive features are the great 80-m- (262-ft-) high dome and the massive pink Finnish granite columns with bronze capitals and bases. Occupied in the Communist era by a Museum of Atheism, the building was returned to exclusive religious use in 1999.

Completed in 1811, the cathedral is intimately linked with the wars against Napoleon *(see p24)* fought during the same period. In 1813 Field Marshal Mikhail Kutuzov (1745–1813), mastermind of a successful retreat from Moscow following the invasion of Napoleon's Grand Army in 1812, was buried here with full military honours. Kutuzov has been immortalized in Tolstoy's great novel *War and Peace* (1865–9). His statue and that of his comrade-in-arms, Mikhail Barclay de Tolly (1761–1818), both by Boris Orlovskiy, have stood outside the cathedral since 1837.

Pink granite columns and mosaic floor in main nave, Kazan Cathedral

⑯ Stroganov Palace
Строгановский дворец
Stroganovskiy dvorets

Nevskiy prospekt 17. **Map** 6 E1.
Tel 571 8238. Ⓜ Nevskiy Prospekt.
🚌 3, 7, 22, 24, 27, 191. 🚎 1, 5, 7, 10,
11, 17. **Open** 10am–6pm Mon, Wed &
Fri–Sun; 1–9pm Thu. ♿

This Baroque masterpiece
was designed in 1752–4 by
Bartolomeo Rastrelli *(see
p95)*. Commissioned by the
enormously wealthy Count
Sergey Stroganov, the palace
was occupied by his descendants until the 1917 Revolution.
The vast Stroganov fortune was
amassed mainly through the
monopoly the family held on
salt, which they mined from
their territories in the north
of the Russian Empire.

The pink and white palace,
which overlooks both Nevskiy
prospekt and the Moyka river,
was one of the city's most
impressive private residences.
The magnificent river façade is
decorated with Doric columns,
cornices, pediments and inven-
tive window surrounds.

The Stroganovs were noted
collectors of everything from
Egyptian antiquities and Roman
coins to icons and Old Masters.
The palace was nationalized
after the Revolution and then
preserved for ten years as
a museum of the life of the

Neo-Romanesque portal of the Lutheran Church (1832–8)

decadent aristocracy. When it
was closed, some of the objects
were auctioned in the West, and
the rest were transferred to
the Hermitage *(see pp86–95)*.
The building now belongs
to the Russian Museum *(see
pp106–9)* and has temporary
exhibitions and a collection
of waxwork figures.

⑰ Lutheran Church
Лютеранская церковь
Lyuteranskaya tserkov

Nevskiy prospekt 22–24. **Map** 6 E1.
Ⓜ Nevskiy Prospekt.

Set back a little from Nevskiy
prospekt, the attractive, twin-
towered Lutheran church is
dedicated to St Peter. Built in its

present form during the 1830s,
the church served St Petersburg's
ever-growing German community
(see p59). The prize-winning design
by Aleksandr Bryullov is in an
unusual, Neo-Romanesque style.

From 1936 the church
was used as a vegetable store
until, in the late 1950s, it was
converted into a swimming
pool. The basin was carved out
of the nave floor, the gallery
lined with spectator benches
and there was a high diving
board under the apse. The
building has now been handed
back to the German-Lutheran
Church of Russia. The church
has been fully restored and
now offers regular services.

The Academic Capella concert hall

⑱ Academic Capella
Академическая капелла
Akademicheskaya kapella

Naberezhnaya reki Moyki 20. **Map** 2
E5. **Tel** 314 1058. Ⓜ Nevskiy Prospekt.
Open for concerts only. ♿ ✉ See
Entertainment, p196.

Enclosed within a courtyard off
the Moyka river is this ochre-
coloured concert hall with a
façade in the French Classical
style of Louis XV. The Academic
Capella was designed by
Leontiy Benois in 1887–9 as the
residence of the Imperial Court
choir. Founded during the reign
of Peter the Great, the choir is as
old as the city itself. Its former
directors have included the
distinguished Russian composers Mikhail Glinka (1804–57)
and Nikolai Rimsky-Korsakov
(1844–1908).

With its excellent acoustics,
the Academic Capella can
claim to be one of the best
concert halls in the world.
Outside is the aptly named
Singers' Bridge (Pevcheskiy
most), which was designed
by Yegor Adam in 1837–40.

Elaborate west façade of the Stroganov Palace overlooking the Moyka river

Personal effects in Pushkin's study, Pushkin House-Museum

⓳ Pushkin House-Museum

Музей-квартира А. С. Пушкина

Muzey-kvartira AS Pushkina

Naberezhnaya reki Moyki 12. **Map** 2 E5. **Tel** 571 3531. **Open** 10:30am–6pm Wed–Mon. **Closed** last Fri of each month and public hols. 🧳 📷

Every year on the anniversary of Alexander Pushkin's death (29 January 1837), loyal devotees of Russia's greatest poet come to lay floral tributes outside his apartment. Pushkin was born in Moscow in 1799, but spent many years of his life in St Petersburg and the museum is one of several places in the city with which the poet is associated.

From the autumn of 1836 until his death, Pushkin lived in this fairly opulent apartment overlooking the Moyka, with his wife Natalya, their four children and Natalya's two sisters. It was here on the couchette in the study that he bled to death after his fateful duel with d'Anthès *(see p85)*.

Some half-dozen rooms on the first floor have been refurbished in the Empire style of the period. By far the most evocative is Pushkin's study, which is arranged exactly as it was when he died. On the writing table is an ivory paper knife given to the poet by his sister, a bronze handbell and a treasured inkstand *(see p41)*. Embellished with the figure of an Ethiopian boy, the inkstand is a reminder of Pushkin's great grandfather, Abram Hannibal. Bought by the Russian ambassador in Constantinople as a slave in 1706, Hannibal served as a general under Peter the Great. He was the inspiration for the unfinished novel *The Negro of Peter the Great* on which Pushkin was working at the time of his death.

On the wall in front of his desk is a Turkish sabre presented to Pushkin in the Caucasus, where he had been exiled in 1820 for his radical views. Ironically it was there that he spent some of his happiest years. It was there too that he began his most famous work, *Eugene Onegin*, a novel in verse written in 1823–30.

The most impressive feature of the apartment is the poet's library which contains more than 4,500 volumes in a staggering 14 European and Oriental languages. Among these are works by the authors whom Pushkin most admired, including Shakespeare, Byron, Heine, Dante and Voltaire.

⓴ Imperial Stables

Конюшенное Ведомство

Konyushennoe Vedomstvo

Konyushennaya ploshchad 1. **Map** 2 E5. Church: **Open** 10am–7pm daily. ✝ 📷

The long, salmon-coloured building running parallel to the Moyka embankment is the former imperial stables. Originally built in the first part of the 18th century, the stables were reconstructed by Vasiliy Stasov in 1817–23.

The only part of the building open to the public lies behind the central section of the long south façade, crowned by a silver dome and cross. This is the church where Alexander Pushkin's funeral took place on 1 February 1837. Its Neo-Classical interior is in the form of a basilica and is decorated with yellow marble pillars. It is now a fully functional Orthodox church.

North façade of Imperial Stables (left) and Little Stable Bridge on the Moyka

SENNAYA PLOSHCHAD

The western part of St Petersburg is an area of contrasts, home to some of the city's wealthiest residences and most poverty-stricken dwellings. The palatial architecture along the English Embankment is a world away from the decrepit living quarters around Sennaya ploshchad, which have changed little since Dostoevsky *(see p125)* described them. In between lies the old maritime quarter, once inhabited by Peter the Great's shipwrights, many of whom were English. This area extended all the way from the New Holland warehouses to St Nicholas'

Cathedral, which stands on the site of the naval parade ground. Theatre Square has been a hub of entertainment since the mid-18th century. It is dominated by the prestigious Mariinskiy Theatre and the Rimsky-Korsakov Conservatory, where many of Russia's greatest artists began their careers. Before 1917, the streets leading off the square were home to theatre directors, actors, ballerinas, artists and musicians. Today, performing artists are once more returning to live here, attracted by the peace of the tree-lined canals.

Sights at a Glance

Cathedrals
2 St Nicholas' Cathedral

Historic Buildings and Areas
1 Mariinskiy Theatre
3 Rimsky-Korsakov Conservatory
5 Choral Synagogue
6 New Holland
8 Main Post Office

Palaces
4 Yusupov Palace

Streets and Squares
7 The English Embankment
9 Bolshaya Morskaya Ulitsa
10 Sennaya Ploshchad

Museums
11 Railway Museum

Restaurants *pp190–91*
1 1913
2 Arcobaleno
3 Conchita Bonita
4 Entree
5 Khochu Kharcho
6 Krokodil
7 Mindal Café
8 Romeo's Bar & Kitchen
9 Russian Vodka Room No. 1
10 Salhino
11 Senoval
12 Zig Zag

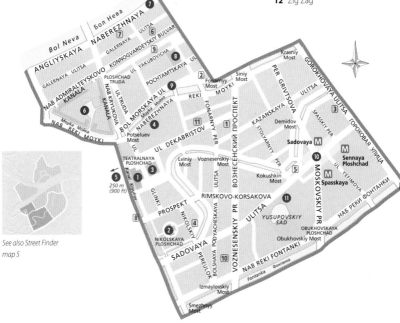

See also Street Finder map 5

| 0 metres | 600 |
| 0 yards | 600 |

◄ The opulent Red Drawing Room in the Yusupov Palace

For keys to symbols *see back flap*

Street-by-Street: Theatre Square

Theatre Square was once known as Carousel Square and was frequently used as the site for fairs and festivals. During the 19th century when St Petersburg became the cultural capital of Russia, the Mariinskiy Theatre and Rimsky-Korsakov Conservatory were established, and the neighbourhood became home to many artists. Today, the tradition of entertainment is still thriving and Theatre Square remains a focal point for theatrical and musical life *(see p204)*. Nearby, the tree-lined canal embankments and the gardens surrounding the beautiful St Nicholas' Cathedral are enchanting places to stroll.

The Monument to Rimsky-Korsakov, who taught at the Conservatory for 37 years, was designed by Veniamin Bogolyubov and Vladimir Ingal and erected in 1952.

❹ Yusupov Palace
Historic site of the gruesome murder of Rasputin *(see p123)*, this grand palace belonged to the wealthy Yusupov family. Its opulent interiors include this Italian marble staircase and a tiny Rococo theatre.

Mariinskiy II
theatre *(see p121)*

❸ Rimsky-Korsakov Conservatory
Tchaikovsky, Prokofiev and Shostakovich *(see p45)* were among the talents nurtured by Russia's first conservatory, founded in 1862 by pianist and composer Anton Rubinstein.

Monument to
Mikhail Glinka
(see p46)

❶ ★ Mariinskiy Theatre
This theatre has been home to the world-famous Mariinskiy (Kirov) Opera and Ballet Company since 1860. Hidden behind its imposing façade is the sumptuous auditorium where many of Russia's greatest dancers *(see p120–21)* have performed.

The Lion Bridge (Lvinyy most) is one of a number of quaint and curious suspension bridges on the narrow, tree-lined Griboedov Canal *(see p38)*. These bridges are well-known meeting places, notably for romantic trysts.

Locator Map
See Street Finder map 5

The House of Mikhail Fokin at No. 109 is where the renowned ballet-master and choreographer lived before the Revolution.

The Benois House belonged to an artistic dynasty which included the co-founder of the World of Art movement, Alexandre Benois *(see p109)*.

The Belfry, an elegant four-tiered structure with a gilded spire, was built to mark the main entrance to St Nicholas' Cathedral.

❷ St Nicholas' Cathedral
A fine example of 18th-century Russian Baroque, the lofty upper church is richly decorated with icons, gilding and this carved iconostasis. The lower church, beautifully lit with candles, is also open for worship.

NAB KANALA GRIBOEDOVA

SKOVO-KORSAKOVA

NIKOLSKIY PEREULOK

KANAL GRIBOEDOVA

Key

— Suggested route

SADOVAYA ULITSA

0 metres 100
0 yards 100

The former Nicholas Market, characterized by its long arcade and steep roof, was constructed in 1788–9. In the 19th century it became an unofficial labour exchange as many unemployed workers gathered here.

Ballet in St Petersburg

Admired throughout the world, Russian ballet traces its origins back to 1738 when a French dancing master, Jean-Baptiste Landé, established a school in St Petersburg to train the children of palace employees. The Imperial School of Ballet, as it soon became known, flourished under a string of distinguished foreign teachers, culminating in Marius Petipa (1818–1910). Petipa first joined the school in 1847 as a principal dancer and later choreographed over 60 ballets, inspiring such famous dancers as Matilda Kshesinskaya (see p74). Following the 1905 Revolution, a reaction against Classicism led to an increasing number of defections from the imperial theatres to the new private companies like Sergey Diaghilev's Ballets Russes. The dispersion of talent increased after the Bolsheviks seized power in 1917 and many artists went into exile abroad. Fortunately for Soviet Russia, the distinguished prima ballerina Agrippina Vaganova remained to train the next generation of dancers. St Petersburg's Russian Ballet Academy now bears her name (see p112).

Anna Pavlova's (1885–1931) most famous role, The Dying Swan, was created especially for her by Mikhail Fokin. In 1912 Pavlova left Russia to form her own touring company, spreading her enthusiasm for ballet across Europe and beyond.

Vaslaw Nijinsky (1890–1950) had one of his greatest roles as the golden slave in Schéhérazade which took Paris by storm in 1910. A principal of the Ballets Russes before World War I, he revolutionized male roles. His incomparable technical skills and expressive qualities influenced future generations of dancers.

Rudolf Nureyev (1938–93), seen here in Sleeping Beauty at the Mariinskiy, defected to the West in 1961. As both choreographer and dancer, Nureyev continued to enthral audiences for over 30 years until his death in 1993.

The Mariinskiy Ballet, usually known abroad as the Kirov, is now reviving some of the original productions of the Ballets Russes, including their version of *Giselle*, previously not shown in Russia.

One of Russia's most important cultural institutions, the Mariinskiy Theatre

The Ballets Russes

The legendary touring company which revolutionized ballet between 1909 and 1929 was the brainchild of the impresario and art critic Sergey Diaghilev *(see p45).* Diaghilev found a kindred spirit in the choreographer Mikhail Fokin, who shared his vision of a spectacle that would fuse music, ballet and decor in a seamless artistic whole.

Diaghilev had the pick of dancers from the Mariinskiy and, in 1909, he brought his Ballets Russes to Paris. The company went from strength to strength with successful tours worldwide.

Diaghilev's new company had a remarkable impact on the contemporary art world. The ballets of Fokin, in particular, prepared audiences for greater innovation and experiment. Exciting contributions from costume and set designers Léon Bakst and Alexandre Benois, the composer Igor Stravinsky and the dancers Vaslav Nijinsky, Anna Pavlova and Tamara Karsavina all played a part in expanding the artistic horizons. After Diaghilev's death in 1929, the Ballets Russes fragmented but its ethos and traditions have been preserved in many of today's leading companies.

Early 20th-century programme for the Ballets Russes

❶ Mariinskiy Theatre

Мариинский театр

Mariinskiy teatr

Teatralnaya ploshchad 1 and Dekabristov ulitsa 34 & 37. **Map** 5 B3. **Tel** 346 4141. 🚌 2, 3, 6, 22, 27, 71, K-1, K-2, K-62, K-124, K-154, K-169, K-186, K-350. 🚊 5, 22. **Open** For information on performances, see p204. 🎭 💻 🏛 ✉ 🖥 **mariinsky.ru**

Named in honour of Tsarina Maria Alexandrovna, wife of Alexander II, the theatre is known abroad by its Soviet title, the Kirov, while at home it has reverted to its original name, the Mariinskiy Theatre. In addition to the original building, there is also a concert hall nearby and a second stage, the Mariinskiy II.

Imperial eagle on the royal box

The building was erected in 1860 by the architect Albert Kavos, who designed the Bolshoy Theatre in Moscow. It stands on the site of an earlier theatre which was destroyed by fire. In 1883–96, the Neo-Renaissance façade was remodelled by Viktor Schröter, who added most of the ornamental detail. The pale blue-and-gold auditorium, where so many illustrious dancers have made their debut, creates a dazzling impression. Its architectural decoration of twisted columns, atlantes, cherubs and cameo medallions has remained unchanged since the theatre's completion, and the imperial eagles have been restored to the royal box. The ceiling painting of dancing girls and cupids by Italian artist Enrico Franchioli dates from c.1856, while the superb stage curtain was added during Russian ballet's golden age in 1914. Equally remarkable is the glittering festive foyer, decorated with fluted pilasters, bas-reliefs of Russian composers and mirrored doors.

Although the Mariinskiy is better known abroad for its ballet company, it is also one of the country's leading opera houses. Most of the great 19th-century Russian operas were premiered here, including Mussorgsky's *Boris Godunov* (1874), Tchaikovsky's *Queen of Spades* (1890), and Shostakovich's controversial opera *Lady Macbeth of Mtsensk* (1934).

The Mariinskiy's luxuriant stage curtain, designed by Aleksandr Golovin in 1914

❷ St Nicholas' Cathedral

Никольский собор

Nikolskiy sobor

Nikolskaya ploshchad 1/3. **Map** 5 C4.
Tel 714 0862. 🚌 2, 3, 22, 27, 49, 71,
181, K-2, K-19, K-154, K-212.
Open 7am–7pm daily.

This stunning Baroque cathedral by Savva Chevakinskiy, one of Russia's great 18th-century architects, was built in 1753–62. Founded for sailors and Admiralty employees housed in the neighbourhood, and named after St Nicholas, the patron saint of sailors, the cathedral became known as the "Sailors' Church".

The striking exterior is decorated with white Corinthian pilasters and surmounted by five gilded cupolas. Nearby, within the cathedral's leafy grounds and overlooking the intersection of the Kryukov and Griboedov canals, is a slender four-tiered bell tower crowned by a spire.

Following the Russian tradition, there are two churches within the cathedral. The lower church, intended for daily use, is lit by icon lamps, candles and chandeliers, creating a magical effect. The icons (1755–7) are the work of the brothers Fedot and Menas Kolokolnikov. The upper church, used on Sundays and for weddings, is brighter and has a Baroque exuberance, with gilt and stucco ornamentation and Italianate paintings. The most impressive feature is the magnificent gilded iconostasis dating from 1755–60.

The pale blue and white Baroque façade of St Nicholas' Cathedral

Islamic arches and coffered ceiling in the Moorish Room, Yusupov Palace

❸ Rimsky-Korsakov Conservatory

Консерватория имени Римского-Корсакова

Konservatoriya imeni Rimskovo-Korsakova

Teatralnaya ploshchad 3. **Map** 5 B3.
Tel 571 8574. 🚌 2, 3, 6, 22, 27, 71,
K-1, K-2, K-62, K-124, K-154, K-169,
K-186, K-350. 🚊 5, 22. **Open** for
performances only. 🎭 📷 by appt
(**Tel** 312 2507).

Russia's oldest music school, the conservatory was founded in 1862 by the piano virtuoso Anton Rubinstein (1829–94). The present building was designed in 1896 by Vladimir Nicolas.

Among those to graduate from the school before the Revolution were Tchaikovsky *(see p44)* and Sergey Prokofiev. In the Soviet years, the school continued to flourish, and the greatest musical figure to emerge from this era was composer Dmitriy Shostakovich (1906–75) *(see p45)*.

In the forecourt outside are two statues. On the left, a 1952 memorial honours the school's influential teacher, Nikolai Rimsky-Korsakov. On the right, the statue of Mikhail Glinka (1906) by Robert Bach is a reminder that the conservatory stands on the original site where Russia's first opera, Glinka's *A Life for the Tsar*, was premiered in 1836 in the old Kamennyy (Stone) Theatre.

❹ Yusupov Palace

ЮсуповскиС дворец

Yusupovskiy dvorets

Naberezhnaya reki Moyki 94.
Map 5 B3. **Tel** 314 9883. 🚌 3, 22, 27.
Open 11am–5pm daily. 🎧 English
(audio tours only).

Overlooking the Moyka, this yellow, colonnaded building (1760s) was designed by Vallin de la Mothe. The palace was acquired in 1830 by the aristocratic Yusupov family to house their superb collection of paintings. Major work was then carried out on the interior by Andrey Mikhaylov and Ippolito Monighetti.

The interiors, notable among them the exotic Moorish Room, with its fountain, mosaics and arches, can be viewed by guided or audio tour only. Separate tickets are needed for the tour of the cellars, which house an exhibition on Grigoriy Rasputin, the infamous "holy man" who was murdered here by Prince Felix Yusupov.

The elegant, Rococo-style family theatre seats just 180, and attending a concert *(see p204)* is an experience in itself.

The Grim Death of Rasputin

The Russian peasant and mystic Grigoriy Rasputin (1869–1916) exercised an extraordinarily powerful influence over the court and government of Russia (*see p28*). The mysterious circumstances of his dramatic death on 17 December 1916 are legendary. Lured to Yusupov's palace on the pretext of a party, Rasputin was poisoned, then shot by Prince Felix Yusupov and left for dead. Returning to the scene the prince found Rasputin still alive and a struggle ensued before Rasputin disappeared into the courtyard. Pursued by the conspirators he was shot another three times and brutally battered before being dumped in the river. When his corpse was found three days later, clinging to the supports of a bridge, water in his lungs indicated death by drowning.

❺ Choral Synagogue
Хоральная Синагога
Khoralnaya Sinagoga

Lermontovskiy prospekt 2.
Map 5 B3. **Tel** 713 8186.
🚌 3, 6, 22, 27, K-1, K-169.

In 1826 Tsar Nicholas I decreed that all Jews, save 29 employed on behalf of the Court, be exiled from the city. Further "purifications" took place in the 1830s. However, after Nicholas' death in 1855 the Jewish population grew rapidly and in 1879 a site was approved for a permanent house of prayer.

Designed in Moorish style by architects Ivan Shaposhnikov and Viktor Shreter, the Synagogue opened in 1893, by which time the Jewish community had reached 16,500, nearly 2 per cent of the city's population. Accommodating 1,200 or more, the Synagogue was the only Jewish place of prayer to survive the repressions of the 1930s.

Vallin de la Mothe's impressive arch on the Moyka, leading into New Holland

It continued to function during the Siege of 1941, the community remaining largely intact while other Jewish communities in Eastern Europe were decimated. Today, the Synagogue still has an active community.

❻ New Holland
Новая Голландия
Novaya Gollandiya

Naberezhnaya reki Moyki. **Map** 5 B2. 🚌 3, 6, 22, 27, 70, 100, K-169, K-350. **Closed** for restoration until 2017.

Created when the Kryukov canal was constructed between the Moyka and Neva rivers in 1719, this triangular island was originally used for storing ship timber. The name is in honour of the Dutch shipbuilders who inspired Peter the Great's naval ambitions.

In 1765, the original wooden warehouses were rebuilt in red brick by Savva Chevakinskiy. At the same time Vallin de la Mothe designed the austere but romantic arch facing onto the Moyka which creates an

atmospheric entrance to the timber yard. Barges would pass through the arch and into a turning basin beyond, then return loaded with timber along the canals towards the Admiralty shipyards. A cultural complex with theatres, exhibition halls and educational centres, is now being built here.

❼ The English Embankment
Английская набережная
Angliyskaya naberezhnaya

Map 5 A2. 🚋 6, 11, K-124, K-154, K-350.

English merchants settled here in the 1730s, and were soon followed by craftsmen, architects, artists, innkeepers and factory owners. By 1800 the area was one of the city's most fashionable addresses.

It still boasts impressive buildings. The Neo-Classical mansion at No. 10 was the fictional setting for the debutante ball of Natasha Rostova in Tolstoy's novel *War and Peace*. No. 28 was occupied by the lover of ballet dancer Matilda Kshesinskaya (*see p74*), and is the former headquarters of the Socialist-Revolutionary Party. On ploshchad Truda, the former palace of Grand Duke Nikolai Nikolaevich (son of Nicholas I) was given in 1917 to the trades unions.

Quarenghi's grand porticoed façade, at No. 32 on the English Embankment

❽ Main Post Office
Главпочтамт
Glavpochtamt

Pochtamtskaya ulitsa 9. **Map** 5 C2.
Tel 315 8022. 🚌 3, 22, 27, 70, 100,
K-169, K-187, K-306. 🚎 5, 22.
Open 24 hours daily.

The building's main exterior
feature is the arched gallery
spanning Pochtamtskaya ulitsa.
Built as an extension to Nikolay
Lvov's main building, the gallery
was added by Albert Kavos
in 1859. Under the Pochtamt
(Post Office) sign on the arch
is a clock showing the time in
major cities around the world.

Inside the post office, behind
Lvov's porticoed Neo-Classical
façade of 1782–9, is a splendid
Style-Moderne hall characterized by decorative ironwork
and a glass ceiling. The hall was
created in the early 20th century
when a roof was constructed
over what had originally been
the courtyard stables.

Porticoed façade, Main Post Office

❾ Bolshaya Morskaya Ulitsa
Большая Морская улица
Bolshaya Morskaya ulitsa

Map 5 C2. 🚌 3, 22, 27, K-187, K-209.
🚎 5, 22.

Always one of St Petersburg's
most fashionable streets, shady
Bolshaya Morskaya ulitsa is the
choice of the artistic elite to this
day. It has some exceedingly
handsome 19th-century
mansions hidden away
between St Isaac's Square
(see p81) and Post Office
Bridge (Pochtamtskiy most).

Stone atlas at No. 43 Bolshaya Morskaya
ulitsa (1840)

The mansion at No. 61 was built
by Albert Kavos in the 1840s for
the St Petersburg Stage Coach
Company. No. 52, nearby, was
acquired by the Russian Union
of Architects in 1932. Built by
Aleksandr Pel in 1835–6, it was
formerly the residence of the
celebrated patron of the arts
Aleksandr Polovtsov, who built
up the impressive collection of
the Stieglitz Museum *(see p129)*.
The striking late 19th-century
interiors with mahogany panelling, tapestries and carved
ceilings were designed by
Maximilian Messmacher and
Nikolay Brullov and can be
admired from the Osobnyak
Polovtseva restaurant within.

Just across the street, No. 47
is a particularly fine example of
Style-Moderne architecture with
sculpted stone rosettes and

delicate iron tracery. This is the
work of Mikhail Geisler and Boris
Guslistiy, dating from 1901–2.
It was in this mansion that
the celebrated émigré novelist
Vladimir Nabokov (1899–1977)
grew up, and there is a small
museum to him on the first
floor. Admired for his linguistic
ingenuity in both English
and Russian, Nabokov hit the
headlines across the world with
the publication of *Lolita*, his
succès de scandale of 1959.

Next door at No. 45 is the
Union of Composers, the former
home of socialite Princess
Gagarina who lived here in
the 1870s. The mansion was
reconstructed in the 1840s by
Auguste-Ricard de Montferrand,
and it retains elements of the
original 18th-century building.

Montferrand also built the
former residence of millionaire
industrialist Pyotr Demidov at
No. 43. A mass of Renaissance
and Baroque elements,
the façade also bears the
Demidov's coat of arms.

❿ Sennaya Ploshchad
Сенная площадь
Sennaya ploshchad

Map 6 D3. Ⓜ Sennaya Ploshchad,
Sadovaya, Spasskaya.

This is one of the oldest
squares in St Petersburg.
The square's name, meaning
Haymarket, derives from the
original market where livestock,
fodder and firewood were
sold and which opened in the
1730s. A 10-minute stroll
from Nevskiy, the area around
the square was inhabited by
the poor, and the market was
the cheapest and liveliest in
the city (the so-called "belly
of St Petersburg"). The oldest
building, at the centre of the

Style-Moderne mosaic frieze at No. 47 Bolshaya Morskaya ulitsa (1901–2)

Fyodor Dostoevsky

One of Russia's greatest writers, Fyodor Dostoevsky *(see pp45–6)* was born in 1821 in Moscow but spent most of his adult life in St Petersburg, where many of his novels and short stories are set. A defining moment in his life occurred in 1849 when he was arrested and charged with revolutionary conspiracy. After eight months of solitary confinement in the Peter and Paul Fortress *(see pp68–9)*, Dostoevsky and 21 other "conspirators" from the socialist Petrashevsky Circle were subjected to a macabre mock execution before being exiled to hard labour in Siberia until 1859. The sinister experience is recalled in his novel *The Idiot* (1868). He died in 1881.

The guardhouse on bustling Sennaya ploshchad

square, is the former guard-house, a single-storey Neo-Classical building with a columned portico, which dates to 1818–20. The guardsmen's duties ranged from supervising the traders to flogging serfs, mostly for minor misdemeanours. By that time the neighbourhood had become synonymous with dirt, squalor, crime and vice. At No. 3 is the site of "Vyazemskiy's Monastery", the nickname for a notorious tenement overrun with pubs, gambling dens and brothels in the 1850s and 1860s.

This was the squalid world so vividly evoked in Fyodor Dostoevsky's masterpiece *Crime and Punishment*. As the contemptuous hero of the novel, Raskolnikov, wanders around the market, he absorbs the "heat in the street… the

airlessness, the bustle and the plaster, scaffolding, bricks and dust… that special St Petersburg stench… and the numerous drunken men" which "completed the revolting misery of the picture". The novel was finished in 1866 while Dostoevsky was living at Alonkin's House (No. 7 Przhevalskovo ulitsa), to the west of the square.

During the Soviet era the square was given a new image, stallholders were banished, trees were planted and it was optimistically renamed Peace Square (ploshchad Mira). The five-storey, yellow and white apartment blocks that surround the square today were also built then, in Stalin's version of Neo-Classicism. Sadly, in 1961, the square's most attractive monument, the Baroque Church of the Assumption, built in 1765, was pulled down to make way for one of the city's earliest metro stations.

⑪ Railway Museum
Музей железнодорожного транспорта *Muzey zheleznodorozhnovo transporta*

Sadovaya ulitsa 50. **Map** 6 D3. **Tel** 315 1476. Ⓜ Sennaya ploshchad, Sadovaya, Spasskaya. **Open** 11am–5pm Sun–Thu. **Closed** last Thu of month. 🔲 English.

More than 6,000 fascinating exhibits illustrate the history of the Russian railway system since 1813. The most interesting sections of the museum deal with the earliest railways, including Russia's first from Tsarskoe Selo to St Petersburg which began running in 1837, and the 650-km (404-mile) line from Moscow to St Petersburg (1851).

Exhibits include models of the first Russian steam engine, built by the Cherepanovs in 1834, and of an armoured train used by Trotsky to defend the city during the Civil War *(see p29)*. An insight into luxury travel in the late tsarist period can be gained from the walk-through section of a first-class sleeping compartment with Style-Moderne decoration.

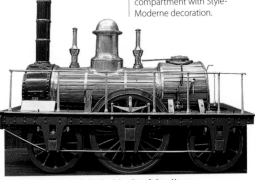

Model of 1830s engine for the Tsarskoe Selo railway, Railway Museum

FURTHER AFIELD

While the majority of St Petersburg's sights are centrally located, the outlying areas of the city have a number of places of architectural, cultural and historical importance.

To the east is the Smolnyy district, taking its name from the tar yard which supplied the city's shipbuilding industry in the 18th century. The highlight of this area is Rastrelli's dazzling Baroque Smolnyy Convent. Nearby, the Smolnyy Institute is famed for its historic role as the Bolshevik headquarters during the October Revolution *(see pp30–31)*. Southeast

of the centre lies the Alexander Nevsky Monastery where many of Russia's celebrated artists, architects and composers are buried.

The southern suburbs offer a strikingly different perspective of the city, with rows of grandiose 1930s–50s houses, a reminder that Stalin sought to destroy the city's historical heart by relocating the centre to the area around Moskovskaya ploshchad. The south also has the Chesma Church and the 1970s Victory Monument, a memorial to the suffering of St Petersburgers during the Siege of Leningrad.

Sights at a Glance

Palaces
1 Yelagin Palace
6 Tauride Palace
9 Sheremetev Palace

Museums
4 Stieglitz Museum
10 Dostoevsky House-Museum

Churches
5 Cathedral of the Transfiguration
7 Smolnyy Convent
11 Alexander Nevsky Monastery
12 Chesma Church

Historic Buildings and Monuments
2 Piskarevskoe Memorial Cemetery
3 Finland Station
8 Smolnyy Institute
13 Victory Monument

0 kilometres 3

0 miles 3

Key

Central St Petersburg

Motorway

Major road

Minor road

Railway

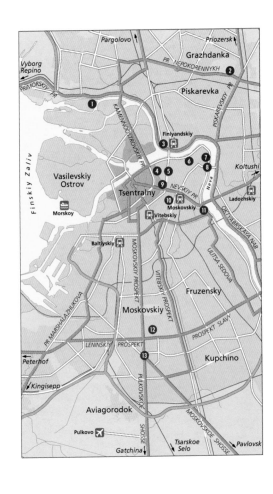

◄ The snow-covered grounds of the Alexander Nevsky Monastery

For keys to symbols *see back flap*

East façade of Yelagin Palace with Srednaya Nevka river in foreground

❶ Yelagin Palace
Елагин дворец
Yelagin dvorets

Yelagin ostrov 1. **Tel** 430 1131.
Ⓜ Krestovskiy Ostrov. **Open** 10am–
6pm Tue–Sun. **Closed** last Tue of
month. 🐾 ♿ to ground floor. 📷

One of the northernmost islands
of St Petersburg, Yelagin Island is
named after a court official who
built a palace here at the end of
the 18th century. Alexander I
then bought the island in
1817 for his mother, Maria
Fyodorovna, and commissioned
Carlo Rossi to rebuild the palace.
The magnificent Neo-Classical
palace (1818–22), enlivened
on the east façade by a half
rotunda flanked by Corinthian
porticoes, is part of an ensemble
which includes an orangery, a
horseshoe-shaped stable block
and porticoed kitchens.

The palace interior was
destroyed by fire during World
War II but is now restored to its
former glory. The Oval Hall is
resplendent with statuary and
trompe l'oeils while the rooms
leading from it are exquisitely
decorated with stucco, *faux
marbre* and painted friezes,
executed by gifted artists
and craftsmen.

Statue of Mother Russia (1956–60),
Piskarevskoe Memorial Cemetery

In the Soviet period, the whole
of the wooded island became
the Central Park of Culture and
Rest (see pp138–9). Festivals and
public entertainments are held
here, and there is an exhibition
of decorative art in the palace's
former stables.

❷ Piskarevskoe Memorial Cemetery
Пискаревское
мемориальное кладбищe
*Piskarevskoe memorialnoe
kladbishche*

Prospekt Nepokorennykh 72–74.
Tel 247 5716. Ⓜ Akademicheskaya.
🚌 80, 123, 138, 178. **Open** 9am–6pm
daily (May–Sep: 9am–9pm daily).
Memorial halls: 9am–6pm daily. 📷

This vast, bleak cemetery is a
memorial to the two million
people who died during the
Siege of Leningrad, 1941–4
(see p29). With little food and no
electricity, water or heating, the
citizens of Leningrad perished
in vast numbers from starvation,
cold and disease. Corpses
were dragged on sledges to
collection points from where
they were taken for burial to
mass cemeteries on the outskirts of town. Piskarevskoe was
the largest, with 490,000 burials.

Today the cemetery is a place
of pilgrimage for those who
lost relatives and friends during
those desperate times. The
memorial complex, designed
by Yevgeniy Levinson and
Aleksandr Vasiliev, opened in
1960, on the 15th anniversary
of the end of the war. Two
memorial halls, one of which
contains an exhibition on the
Siege, flank the stairs down to
a 300-m- (984-ft-) long avenue,
which culminates in a towering,

heroic bronze statue of Mother
Russia by Vera Isayeva and
Robert Taurit. On the wall
behind are verses composed
by Olga Bergholts, herself
a survivor of the Siege. The
funereal music broadcast
over the whole cemetery adds
to the sombre atmosphere.

On either side of the avenue
are 186 grassy mounds, each
with a granite slab marking
the year and indicating, with
a red star or hammer and sickle,
whether those interred were
soldiers or civilians.

Locomotive 293, Finland Station

❸ Finland Station
Финляндский вокзал
Finlyandskiy vokzal

Ploshchad Lenina 6. **Map** 3 B3.
Ⓜ Ploshchad Lenina. See also p223.

On the night of 3 April 1917,
the exiled Vladimir Lenin and his
Bolshevik companions arrived at
Finland Station after travelling
from Switzerland on a sealed
train. A triumphant reception
awaited their return to Russia
and, on leaving the station,
Lenin spoke to cheering crowds
of soldiers, sailors and workers.
A statue erected outside the
station in 1926 depicts Lenin
delivering his speech.

The modern terminal was
opened in the 1960s. On platform 5 there is a huge glass case
containing Locomotive 293
which Lenin rode when fleeing
the capital for a second time in
July 1917. After spending the
summer as a fugitive in Russian
Finland, Lenin returned on the
same train and spurred on the
October Revolution (see pp30–31).

❹ Stieglitz Museum

Музей Штиглица

Muzey Shtiglitsa

Solyanoy pereulok 13–15. **Map** 3 A5.
Tel 273 3258. 46, K-76, K-100,
K-217. **Open** Sep–Jul: 11am–4:30pm
Tue–Sat. **Closed** last Fri of month.

The millionaire industrialist
Baron Aleksandr Stieglitz
founded the Central
School of Industrial
Design in 1876.
His aim was to
provide a top-
quality collection
of original works for
the use of Russian
students of applied
arts and design.

With a large budget
and the good taste of
Stieglitz's son-in-law, Aleksandr
Polovtsov (*see p124*), the collection, unusual in covering
both Western European and
Oriental art, soon outgrew the
school and in 1896 a Museum
of Applied Arts opened next
door. This magnificent building,
designed by Maximilian
Messmacher, was inspired
by Italian Renaissance palaces.
Inside, the halls and galleries
were decorated in an impressive variety of national and
period styles, echoing French
and German Baroque and,

19th-century crystal vase, Stieglitz Museum

above all, Italian Renaissance
monuments, such as St Mark's
Library in Venice, the Raphael
Loggias of the Vatican and the
Villa Madama, also in Rome.

After the Revolution the
school was closed and the
museum became a branch of
the Hermitage (*see pp86–95*).
Serious damage to the building
was inflicted during the Siege
of Leningrad (*see
p29*). At the end
of the war the
school was
revived to train
gilders and carvers
for the huge res-
toration programme
needed to repair
the damaged city.

Situated on the
ground floor, the
exhibition features opulent
displays of glassware, ceramics
and majolica, as well as
porcelain from all the great
European manufacturers. One
room, decorated in the style of
the medieval Terem Palace in
the Kremlin, provides a superb
backdrop for a collection of
embroidered dresses and
headgear made by Russian
peasant women.

Some pieces of decorative
metalwork including locks, keys
and craft tools date back to the
Middle Ages. The workmanship

seen on the wooden furniture
is breathtaking. The Neo-Gothic
cabinet is a beautiful example.
Its finely inlaid doors, depicting
church naves in perspective, open
to reveal sculpted biblical scenes.

One way to end your visit
is with a look at the stunning
Grand Exhibition Hall with its
curving staircase of Italian marble and magnificent glass roof.

❺ Cathedral of the Transfiguration

Спасо-Преображенский собор

Spaso-Preobrazhenskiy sobor

Preobrazhenskaya ploshchad 1. **Map** 3
B5. **Tel** 579 6010. Chernyshevskaya.
46, K-76, K-90, K-177, K-258. 3,
8, 15. **Open** 8am–8pm daily.

Despite its monumental Neo-
Classicism, and the surrounding
fence made of guns captured
during the Russo-Turkish wars
(*see p24*), Vasiliy Stasov's church
has an intimate air as it nestles
in its leafy square. The original
church on this site was built by
Tsarina Elizabeth to honour the
Preobrazhenskiy Life-Guards,
but it was rebuilt after a fire in
1825. Today, the church is
famous for its excellent choir,
which is second only to that
in the Alexander Nevsky
Monastery (*see pp132–3*).

Dolls in 17th–19th-century Russian folk costumes, in front of the Terem Room, Stieglitz Museum

❻ Tauride Palace
Таврический дворец
Tavricheskiy dvorets

Shpalernaya ulitsa 47. **Map** 4 D4.
Ⓜ Chernyshevskaya. 🚌 46, 136.
Closed to public.

This finely proportioned palace by Ivan Starov was built in 1783–9 as a present from Catherine the Great to her influential lover Prince Grigoriy Potemkin *(see p27)*. Potemkin had successfully annexed the Crimea (Tauris) to Russia in 1783 and was given the title of Prince of Tauris, hence the palace's name.

Uncompromising in its lack of external ornamentation, the long, yellow building with its distinctive six-columned portico was one of Russia's first Neo-Classical designs. Sadly, the magnificent interiors have been badly damaged both by Catherine's son, Paul I, who turned the palace into a barracks, and by the many reconstructions undertaken.

The palace played a vital role in 20th-century cultural and political life. In 1905, the impresario Sergey Diaghilev *(see p45)* organized the first ever exhibition of Russian 18th-century portraiture here. The following year the palace hosted Russia's first parliament, the State Duma. After the February Revolution of 1917 it became the seat of the Provisional Government, then the Petrograd Soviet of Workers' and Soldiers' Deputies. Today it is still a government building.

The lovely gardens, with winding streams, bridges and an artificial lake, are among the city's most popular parks.

The blue-and-white façade of the Smolnyy Cathedral and the adjacent convent buildings

❼ Smolnyy Convent
Смольный монастырь
Smolnyy monastyr

Ploshchad Rastrelli 3/1. **Map** 4 F4.
Tel 710 3159. 🚌 46, 136.
Open 10:30am–6pm Thu–Tue.
🖼 ♿ 📷 English.

The crowning glory of this architectural ensemble is the stunning cathedral with its dome and four supporting cupolas topped by golden orbs.

As a symbol of her majesty, Tsarina Elizabeth founded the convent where many young noblewomen were to be educated. It was designed in 1748 by Bartolomeo Rastrelli *(see p95)*, who conceived a brilliant fusion of Russian and Western Baroque styles. Work advanced extremely slowly; 50,000 wooden piles were used to secure the foundations in the marshy soil and the architect's model alone, now in the Academy of Arts *(see p65)*, took seven years to build.

Catherine the Great disliked Rastrelli's work and had little sympathy for the late Elizabeth. When she came to power in 1762, funding for the project

stopped. It was only in 1835 that Nicholas I commissioned the Neo-Classical architect Vasiliy Stasov to complete the cathedral. His austere white interior contrasts dramatically with the luxuriant exterior.

Exhibitions are now held here, as well as regular weekly concerts *(see p204)*. There are spectacular views of the city from the cathedral tower.

❽ Smolnyy Institute
Смольный Институт
Smolnyy Institut

Smolnyy proezd 1. **Map** 4 F4. **Tel** 710 3159, 710 3143. 🚌 46, 54, 74, 136, K-15, K-76, K-136. 🚎 5, 7, 11, 15, 16. Smolnyy Museum: **Open** 11am–6pm Mon–Fri by appt only. 🖼 ♿ 📷 English.

Built in 1806–8 to house a school for young noblewomen, the original having outgrown its premises at the Smolnyy Convent, this Neo-Classical building was considered by Giacomo Quarenghi to be his masterpiece.

It was from here, on 25 October 1917, that Lenin directed the Bolshevik *coup d'état* while the second All-Russian Congress of Soviets was convening in the Assembly Hall. The Congress confirmed Lenin in power and this was his seat of government until March 1918. With the Germans advancing and with the outbreak of civil war *(see p29)*, the government left for Moscow. The Institute was taken over by the Leningrad Communist Party. On 1 December 1934, the First Secretary of the party, Sergey Kirov *(see p74)*, was murdered here, an event that was to

View of Tauride Gardens and the Tauride Palace beyond the lake

Isaak Brodskiy's 1927 painting of Lenin, Smolnyy Institute Assembly Hall

provide cover for the purges of the late 1930s *(see p29)*.

The rooms where Lenin lived and worked can be viewed by appointment. The rest of the institute is now the Mayor's Office. The imperial eagle has replaced the hammer and sickle, but the statue of Lenin has survived.

❾ Sheremetev Palace
Шереметевский дворец
Sheremetevskiy dvorets

Naberezhnaya reki Fontanki 34. **Map** 7 A1. Ⓜ Mayakovskaya, Gostinyy Dvor. 🚌 15, 22, 27, K-15, K-90, K-187, K-258. 🚊 3, 8, 15. Anna Akhmatova Museum: **Tel** 571 7239. **Open** 10:30am–6:30pm Tue–Sun. 🖼 🎧 English. Museum of Musical Life: **Tel** 272 4441. **Open** 11am–7pm Thu– Mon, 1–9pm Wed. **Closed** last Wed of each month. 🖼 🎧

The Sheremetev family lived here from 1712, when the palace was built by Field Marshal Boris Sheremetev, until the Revolution. The palace is also known as the Fountain House, or *Fontannyy dom*, because of the many fountains that once adorned its grounds. The Baroque building dates from the 1750s when it was designed by Savva Chevakinskiy and Fyodor Argunov, although numerous later alterations were made.

Field Marshal Sheremetev's descendants were fabulously wealthy, at one time owning some 200,000 serfs. They were among Russia's leading artistic patrons and the palace is now home to the Museum of Musical Life, which charts the family's contribution to the music of the city. In the 18th and 19th centuries, serf composers, musicians and actors from rural estates owned by the family performed in concerts and plays at the palace. Among those to praise the fine Sheremetev choir was the composer Franz Liszt. The museum's exhibits include a variety of period instruments and a number of scores, some of which are compositions by the Sheremetevs themselves.

One of Russia's greatest 20th-century poets, Anna Akhmatova, lived in one of the service blocks of the palace from 1933 to 1941 and then between 1944 and 1954. Her flat is open to the public as the Anna Akhmatova Museum *(Muzey Anny Akhmatovoy)* and is reached through the courtyard of No. 53 Liteynyy prospekt. By the time she moved into the palace, it had been divided into dingy communal apartments. The rooms where she lived and worked display some of her personal possessions, tracing her intriguing life. Recordings of the poet reading her own work can also be heard.

Anna Akhmatova

By 1914 Anna Akhmatova (1889–1966) was a leading light of Russia's "Silver Age" of poetry *(see p46)*. Tragedy gave her work a new dimension when first her husband was shot by the Bolsheviks, and later, her son and her lover were arrested in Stalin's purges. Anna herself was placed under police surveillance and officially silenced for more than 15 years. Her most famous poem, *Requiem* (1935–61), inspired by her son's arrest, was written in fragments and distributed to friends to memorize. Akhmatova's reputation was partially rehabilitated late in her life and she received honorary awards abroad.

Pilastered façade of Sheremetev Palace on the Fontanka embankment

❿ Dostoevsky House-Museum

Музей Достоевского

Muzey Dostoevskovo

Kuznechnyy pereulok 5/2. **Map** 7 B3.
Tel 571 4031. Ⓜ Vladimirskaya. 🚌 3,
8, 15. 🚎 49. **Open** 11am–6pm Tue–
Sun, 1–8pm Wed. 🎦 📷 English.

This evocative museum was
the final home of the famous
Russian writer, Fyodor
Dostoevsky *(see p46)*, who lived
here from 1878 until his death
in 1881. Dostoevsky was then
at the height of his fame, and
it was here that he completed
his last great novel, *The Brothers
Karamazov*, in 1880. Gambling
and debts, however, confined
him to a fairly modest lifestyle
in this five-roomed apartment.

Although Dostoevsky's public
persona was dour and humour-
less, he was a devoted and
affectionate husband and father.
The delightful nursery contains
a rocking horse, silhouettes of his
children and the book of fairy
tales which he read aloud to
them. In Dostoevsky's study are
his writing desk and a reproduction of his favourite painting,
Raphael's *Sistine Madonna*.

Chesma Church (1777–80), a very early example of
Neo-Gothic in Russia

⓬ Chesma Church

Чесменская церковь

Chesmenskaya tserkov

Ulitsa Lensoveta 12. Ⓜ Moskovskaya.
🚌 16. 🚎 29, 45. **Open** 10am–
7pm daily.

There is little Russian about the
highly unusual Chesma Church,
which was designed by Yuriy
Velten in 1777–80. Its fanciful
terracotta-coloured façade is
decorated with thin vertical stripes

of white moulding which
direct the eye upwards
to its zig-zagged crown
and Neo-Gothic cupolas.
The name commemorates
the great Russian naval
victory over the Turks
at Chesma in the Aegean
in 1770. During the
Communist era the church
became a museum to
the battle, but today
the building is once
again used as a church.
On the opposite side of
ulitsa Lensoveta is the Neo-
Gothic Chesma Palace
(1774–77), formerly
Kekerekeksinen, or
Frog Marsh Palace.
Also designed by Velten,
it served as a staging post
for Catherine the Great en route
to Tsarskoe Selo *(see pp154–7)*.
Wedgwood's famous dinner
service with its frog emblem,
now in the Hermitage *(see p93)*,
was designed specially for the
Chesma Palace.

The palace achieved
notoriety when Rasputin's
body lay in state here after his
murder in 1916 *(see p123)*. Now
substantially altered, it serves
as a home for the elderly.

⓫ Alexander Nevsky Monastery

александро-Невская лавра

Aleksandro-Nevskaya lavra

Ploshchad Aleksandra Nevskovo.
Map 8 E4. **Tel** 274 2635. Ⓜ Ploshchad
Aleksandra Nevskovo. 🚌 8, 24, 27,
46, 55, 58, 191, K-156, K-187, K-209.
🚎 1, 14, 16, 22. 🚎 7, 65. Holy Trinity
Cathedral: **Open** 6am–8pm daily.
Church of the Annunciation: **Tel** 274
2635. **Open** 9:30am– 5pm; closes 6pm
in summer. **Closed** Mon & Thu. 🎦
cemeteries & Church of the
Annunciation. 📷

Founded by Peter the Great
in 1710, this monastery is
named after Alexander Nevsky,
the prince of Novgorod, who
defeated the Swedes in 1240.
Peter defeated them in 1709
(see p20).

From the entrance, a path
runs between two large, walled
cemeteries, then across a
stream and into the main

monastic complex. The oldest
building is the Church of the
Annunciation (1717–22),
designed by Domenico Trezzini.
The church was the burial place
for non-ruling members of the
Russian royal family, politicians
and military leaders. A series
of red and white, mid-18th-
century monastic buildings,
including the Metropolitan's
House (1755–8), surround the
courtyard. Among the trees in
the courtyard lie the graves of
atheist Soviet scholars and
leading Communists.

Dominating the essentially
Baroque complex is the twin-
towered and domed Neo-
Classical Holy Trinity Cathedral,
constructed by architect Ivan
Starov in 1776–90. The wide
nave inside is flanked by
Corinthian columns with
statues by Fedot Shubin.
This leads to the impressive
red agate and white marble

iconostasis, which features
copies of works by Van Dyck,
Rubens and others. To the right
of the iconostasis is a silver
reliquary that contains the
remains of Alexander Nevsky,
transferred to the previous

Reliquary with Alexander Nevsky's remains,
Trinity Cathedral

⓯ Victory Monument

Монумент Защитникам Ленинграда *Monument Zashchitnikam Leningrada*

Ploshchad Pobedy. **Tel** 371 2951, 373 6563. **M** Moskovskaya.
🚌 3, 11, 13, 39, 59, 90, 150, 187, K-13, K-100, K-350. 🚊 27, 29, 45.
Memorial Hall: **Open** 11am–6pm Thu & Sat–Mon, 11am–5pm Tue.
Closed last Tue of each month.
📷 book by phone.

Erected in 1975 to coincide with the 30th anniversary of the end of World War II, this is on the site of a temporary triumphal arch built to greet the returning troops. Named the Monument to the Heroic Defenders of Leningrad, it commemorates the victims of the Siege (*see p29*), and its survivors. It was designed by Sergey Speranskiy and Valentin Kamenskiy and sculpted by Mikhail Anikushin. A 48-m- (157-ft-) high obelisk of red granite is near a vast, circular enclosure which symbolizes the vice-like grip of the siege. Sculptures of soldiers, sailors and grieving mothers surround the monument.

An underpass on Moskovskiy prospekt leads to the Memorial Hall. Here solemn music gives way to the persistent beat of a metronome, the wartime radio signal, intended to represent the city's defiant heartbeat. The subdued lighting comprises 900 dim, orange lamps, one for each day of the Siege. Tablets are inscribed with the names of the 650 Heroes of the Soviet Union awarded the title after the war; and a mosaic depicts the women of the city greeting their menfolk at the end of the conflict.

Around the hall a small display of artifacts, including Shostakovich's violin (*see p45*), records the contribution of different sections of the community to the war effort, while an illuminated relief map illustrates the battle lines. Most disturbing is the tiny piece of bread, which was many people's daily ration.

Heroic partisans facing south towards the enemy during the Siege of Leningrad, detail of Victory Monument

church on this site in 1724. Behind the reliquary hangs a painting of Nevsky, who has been venerated as a saint in Russia since the mid-16th century.

Many of the nation's leading cultural figures are buried in the two monastic cemeteries near the main entrance. The city's oldest graveyard, the Lazarus Cemetery, to the east, contains the graves of the polymath Mikhail Lomonosov (*see p47*) and a number of prominent architects, including Andrey Zakharov, Thomas de Thomon, Giacomo Quarenghi, Carlo Rossi (*see p112*) and Andrey Voronikhin. Clustered together along the northern wall of the Tikhvin Cemetery (to the west) are the tombs of some of Russia's most famous composers. Fyodor Dostoevsky (*see p46*) is also buried here, to the right of the entrance.

Tombs of Interest at Tikhvin Cemetery

① Mikhail Glinka (Composer, 1804–57)
② Ivan Krylov (Poet, 1769–1844)
③ Marius Petipa (Choreographer, 1818–1910)
④ Pyotr Klodt (Sculptor, 1805–67)
⑤ Ivan Kramskoy (Painter, 1837–87)
⑥ Pyotr Tchaikovsky (Composer, 1840–93)
⑦ Modest Mussorgsky (Composer, 1839–81)
⑧ Nikolai Rimsky-Korsakov (Composer, 1844–1908)
⑨ Fyodor Dostoevsky (Writer, 1821–81)

0 metres 50
0 yards 50

Main entrance

For keys to symbols *see back flap*

THREE GUIDED WALKS

Many of St Petersburg's sights are best appreciated on foot. The three walks chosen present different aspects of the city's character, though water plays a central part in each.

The first walk follows the Moyka river and the Griboedov Canal, which criss-cross the heart of the city, and reveals the magnificent scale of the buildings erected in the 18th and 19th centuries. It highlights the contrasts between rich palaces and overcrowded apartment blocks, gilded bridges and the dilapidation of the area around Sennaya ploshchad. An alternative way to appreciate the glorious old buildings set on the canals is to take a boat trip (see pp228–9).

The second walk explores Yelagin and Kamennyy islands, where Petersburgers traditionally spend much of their free time. The islands to the north of the centre were once the preserve of the rich, who spent the hot summers in the cool of their *dachas*. Now locals come to walk and row boats in summer, to ski and skate in winter, and simply to breathe the fresh spring air.

The third walk follows the river Neva on the Petrograd side, from where there are awe-inspiring views of the city's grand south waterfront and of the river itself. The walk encompasses some significant historic sites including Trinity Square, the Cabin of Peter the Great and the cruiser *Aurora*.

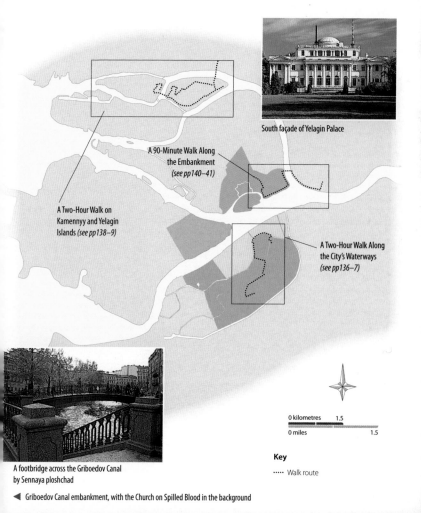

South façade of Yelagin Palace

A 90-Minute Walk Along the Embankment (see pp140–41)

A Two-Hour Walk on Kamennyy and Yelagin Islands (see pp138–9)

A Two-Hour Walk Along the City's Waterways (see pp136–7)

0 kilometres 1.5
0 miles 1.5

Key

..... Walk route

A footbridge across the Griboedov Canal by Sennaya ploshchad

◀ Griboedov Canal embankment, with the Church on Spilled Blood in the background

A Two-Hour Walk Along the City's Waterways

A stroll along the embankments of the Moyka river and the Griboedov Canal is a chance to appreciate the history and splendid architecture of this beautiful city. The two waterways present interesting contrasts. The Moyka winds past the Imperial Summer and Winter Palaces and the lavish mansions of the aristocracy, while the Griboedov is lined with 19th-century apartments, once home to merchants, civil servants and, towards Sennaya Ploshchad (see p124), the working class. The walk also includes a short stretch of the majestic Nevskiy prospekt.

Tips for Walkers

Starting point: Church on Spilled Blood.
Length: 5.8 km (3 miles).
Getting there: Nevskiy Prospekt metro.
Stopping-off points: Bistro Layma, nab kanala Griboedova 16.

View of the Church on Spilled Blood ① and the Griboedov Canal

The Moyka River

Begin the walk at the magnificent Church on Spilled Blood ① (see p102), built over the spot where Alexander II was assassinated in 1881 (see p28). From here, walk around the church beside the park, crossing the canal bridge to Konyushennaya ploshchad. The square is embraced by the elongated façade of the former Imperial Stables ② (see p115). Straddling the junction of the Griboedov Canal and the Moyka river are two ingeniously linked bridges, the Malo-Konyushennyy most (Small Stable Bridge) and Teatralnyy most (Theatre Bridge) (see p39). Cross over these bridges to the north bank of the Moyka and the expansive façade of the Adamini House ③, designed by Domenico Adamini in 1823–7. Between 1916 and 1919 the basement was used by a artists' and writers' club known as "The Bivouac of the Comedians".

Visitors included the avant-garde theatre director Vsevolod Meyerhold and the poets Aleksandr Blok and Anna Akhmatova (see p46).

Turn left onto naberezhnaya reki Moyki and walk past the Round Market ④ built in 1790 by Giacomo Quarenghi, who had shopping arcades as one of his specialities. Continue along the embankment, passing Adam's Bolshoy Konyushennyy most (Great Stables Bridge) to Prince Abamelek-Lazarev's former mansion ⑤ built in 1913–15. The handsome façade, with Corinthian pilasters and graceful reliefs of dancing figures, is by Ivan Fomin. On the opposite bank is the 17th-century apartment block where Pushkin spent the last few months of his life. His flat is now a museum ⑥ (see p115).

At the intersection of Millionnaya ulitsa and the beautiful Winter Canal (Zimnaya Kanavka) are the former barracks of the elite First Regiment of the Preobrazhenskiy Life-Guards. This prestigious corps was formed by Peter the Great in the 1690s.

Across the Winter Canal is the New Hermitage ⑦ (see p86). Ten granite

Quarenghi's arcaded Round Market (1790) ④, overlooking the Moyka river

0 metres 300
0 yards 300

Key

• • • Walk route

View of the tree-lined Griboedov Canal

atlantes bear the weight of the elaborate porch. Returning to the Moyka, the route passes a green, three-storey house ⑧, built by F Demertsov for Alexander I's military advisor and sometime chief minister, Count Aleksey Arakcheev. The Moyka now makes a curve behind the majestic buildings of Palace Square (see p85) which includes the Staff of the Guards Corps ⑨ and the huge crescent of Carlo Rossi's imposing yellow General Staff Building ⑩. Cross the Pevcheskiy most (Singers' Bridge) (see p39) ⑪ and follow the Moyka down to the Zelenyy most (Green Bridge). The yellow building on the other side of the Moyka is the Literary Café ⑫, renowned as a meeting place for writers in Pushkin's day (see p85).

Nevskiy Prospekt

Turn left onto St Petersburg's main street, where a range of architectural styles can be seen. On the left, the elegant façade of Paul Jacot's Dutch Church building ⑬ (see p49) hides a series of shops. Across the road, the superb façade of the

Baroque Stroganov Palace ⑭ (see p114) contrasts starkly with the triple-arched glass frontage of the Style-Moderne Fashion House ⑮ (see p49). The colonnaded forecourt of the Cathedral of Our Lady of Kazan ⑯ (see p113) can be seen further along.

The Griboedov Canal

Cross Nevskiy prospekt by the attractive Singer Sewing Machine Building (see p49) and follow the Griboedov south. When you reach Georg von Traitteur's Bankovskiy most (Bank Bridge) (see p37) ⑰, decorated with golden griffons, cross the canal and continue past the wrought-iron railings to the rear of the former Assignment Bank ⑱ (now occupied by a finance and economics university). Further south the humped Kamennyy most (Stone Bridge) has survived since 1776 despite an attempt to blow it up, by a revolutionary group as Tsar Alexander II passed in his carriage in 1881. Across the Demidov most, on the corner of Kaznacheyskaya ulitsa ⑲ (No.1), is the apartment where Dostoevsky (see p45) wrote *Notes from the House of the Dead* (1861). Also with literary associations, the former Zverkov House ⑳ was where the novelist and dramatist Nikolai Gogol (see p46) lived in the 1830s.

The walk ends in Sennaya ploshchad (see p124), where there are three metro stations.

Apartment block where Dostoevsky lived ⑲, on the Griboedov Canal

Griffons on Bank Bridge (1826), Griboedov Canal

A Two-Hour Walk on Kamennyy and Yelagin Islands

An area of rolling parkland, birch and lime groves and fine river views, the northern islands of the Neva delta offer a retreat from city life. The imperial family built palaces on Kamennyy and Yelagin islands at the end of the 18th century and were soon joined by wealthy aristocratic families. Before the Revolution, many government ministers, industrial magnates and celebrities built themselves a *dacha* here. Today these neglected houses, some intimate, some palatial, in styles ranging from Neo-Gothic to Neo-Classical and Style-Moderne, are being returned to their former glory by the business elite.

③ Wooden façade of Dolgorukov Mansion

rather splendid Style-Moderne mansion in 1913–14. Continue west, and cross the canal bridge to reach the wooden Kamennoostrovskiy Theatre ⑤ which took only 40 days to erect in 1827. Its Neo-Classical portico, rebuilt by Albert Kavos in 1844, is still impressive. The banks of the Krestovka river, with views across to the boatyards of Krestovskiy Island, offer many ideal spots for a picnic (but bear in mind that admission is charged at weekends). To rejoin the walk, return to the path and cross 1-y Yelagin most to Yelagin Island.

Yelagin Island

This island is an oasis of calm, popular with those wishing to escape the city. A tollgate marks the entrance to the grounds of Carlo Rossi's graceful Yelagin Palace ⑥ *(see p128)*. The western

South Kamennyy Island

Begin at Chernaya Rechka metro station and head south to Bolshaya Nevka river, then cross Ushakovskiy most (Ushikov Bridge) to Kamennyy Island, an area of recreation and relaxation. Just across the main road is the small red-brick Church of St John the Baptist ①, designed in Neo-Gothic style by Yuriy Velten in 1776–8. Nearby a yellow gateway leads to the grounds of Kamennoostrovskiy Palace ② (which is now a retirement home) from where Alexander I led the 1812 Russian campaign against Napoleon *(see p28)*.

Follow Kamennoostrovskiy prospekt to the Malaya Nevka river, then turn right on to naberezhnaya Maloy Nevki where there is an imposing wooden mansion ③ at No. 11 with a white-columned portico. The Dolgorukov

Mansion was built in 1831–2 by Smaragd Shustov for the Dolgorukovs, one of Russia's oldest aristocratic families.

From this point you can see across to Aptekarskiy or Apothecary's Island, named after the medicinal herb gardens founded by Peter the Great in 1714. St Petersburg's Botanical Gardens are still located there. Continue along the path, which turns into naberezhnaya reki Krestovki. The house on the left, towards the Malokrestovskiy most (Small Krestovskiy Bridge), is the former home of Sergey Chaev ④, who was the chief engineer of the Trans-Siberian railway. Chaev commissioned the fashionable architect, Vladimir Apyshkov, to build this

① The tower of the Church of St John the Baptist (1776–8)

⑤ Kamennoostrovskiy Theatre's impressive façade (1827)

spit of the island is ideal for viewing the spectacular sunsets over the Gulf of Finland, especially during the White Nights (see p53). If you want to venture further, head south across 2-y Yelagin most to Krestovskiy Island and the Kirov Stadium, Maritime Victory Park and Primorskiy Park Pobedy. Or, to the north, 3-y Yelagin most leads to Primorskiy prospekt and the Tibetan-inspired Buddhist Temple, erected by Gavriil Baranovskiy in 1909–15.

North Kamennyy Island

Return to Kamennyy Island across 1-y Yelagin most, taking the left fork on to Teatralnaya alleya from where you can see the former mansion of Aleksandr Polovtsov ⑦, minister of foreign affairs under Nicholas II. This splendid Neo-Classical mansion with Style-Moderne touches was built by Ivan Fomin in 1911–13. Leave Teatralnaya alleya and cut through the quiet and restful park, passing between the ponds and the canal. Near the junction with Bolshaya alleya are two more early 20th-century mansions. Follenveider's mansion ⑧ on the left, with its

⑦ Early 20th-century Polovtsov Mansion

distinctive tented tower, was designed by Roman Meltzer in 1904 and now belongs to the Danish consulate. Yevgeniya Gausvald's dacha ⑨ dates from 1898 and stands as one of the earliest Style-Moderne buildings in St Petersburg. It was designed by Vasiliy Schöne and Vladimir Chagin. Finally, the last stage of the walk leads along the 2-ya Berezovaya alleya, back to the starting point at Ushakovskiy most and Chernaya Rechka metro.

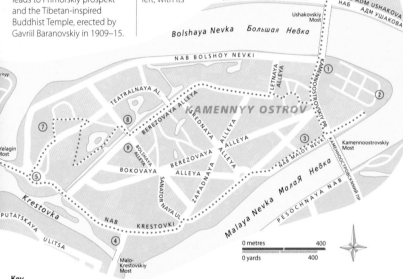

Key

••• Walk route

Tips for Walkers

Starting point: Chernaya Rechka metro station (see p227).
Length: 6 km (3.5 miles).
Stopping-off points: Café in former stables of Yelagin Palace (summer only) and plenty of places to picnic.

The tree-shrouded grassy banks of the Krestovka river

A 90-Minute Walk Along the Embankment

Muscovites envy St Petersburgers their dramatic and open skyline, and this stroll along the northern banks of the Neva offers grand views, not only of the magnificent south waterfront, but also of the Petrogradskaya Side, as seen from Trinity Bridge where it crosses the river at its widest point. In winter the Neva lies frozen, an expanse of whiteness. In warmer months the water pulses hypnotically through the city. The walk encompasses the best of the city's Style-Moderne architecture, the Cabin of Peter the Great, the cruiser *Aurora*, whose guns began the 1917 Revolution, and the train that brought Lenin to Russia.

⑤ View of Peter and Paul Fortress with the Cathedral of SS Peter and Paul

Kamennoostrovskiy Prospekt

From Gorkovskaya metro station, cross the road via the underpass and walk south along Konverskiy prospekt, an avenue noted for its Style-Moderne architecture. Almost immediately, the minarets of the city's only mosque jut up ahead. Sobornaya Mosque ① *(see p72)*, one of Europe's largest, was built in 1913.

Slightly further on, at the junction with ulitsa Kuybysheva, is the Kshesinskaya Mansion ② *(see p74)*, a delicate, asymmetrical Style-Moderne building commissioned in 1906 for the ballerina Matilda Kshesinskaya (Nicholas II's former lover). Once the Bolshevik Party HQ, from whose balcony Lenin addressed the crowds, it now houses the Museum of Russian Political History with exhibits from the revolutionary era.

Take a right down ulitsa Kuybysheva then bear left onto Kamennoostrovskiy prospekt *(see p72)*. To your left is Trinity Square ③ *(see p75)*, the heart of the old city's merchant quarter, and site of the "Bloody Sunday" massacre during the 1905 Revolution, and of the relatively new Trinity Chapel.

Trinity Square

Until the fall of the USSR, the square was known as Revolution Square in memory of the 48 workers who were mown down here by government troops. Walk onto Style-Moderne Trinity Bridge ④ *(see p37)*, which spans the Neva at its widest point and affords fine views of the river and the Peter and Paul Fortress *(see pp68–9)*.

Look out for the needle-sharp steeple of the Baroque Cathedral of SS Peter and Paul ⑤. The bridge was completed in time for the city's bicentenary in 1903 by the French firm Batignol, which also constructed the Eiffel Tower.

Return to the shore, and stroll east along Petrovskaya Embankment, passing the Cabin of Peter the Great ⑥ *(see p75)*. The tiny cabin was built from pine logs in 3 days in May

⑥ Interior of the tiny Cabin of Peter the Great

⑨ The cruiser *Aurora* (1900) moored in front of the Nakhimov Naval Academy

View across the frozen River Neva featuring the golden dome of St Isaac's Cathedral on the south embankment

1703, and Peter lived here for 6 years, supervising the building of his city. The brick shell was added later by Catherine the Great. On the steps outside the cabin are the Manchurian Lions ⑦, two odd statues brought from Manchuria during the disastrous (for Russia) Russo-Japanese War of 1904–5.

Palace. This event brought the Bolsheviks to power in 1917. The battleship also contains a museum.

Further along the embankment, the Neo-Baroque building on the left is the Nakhimov Naval Academy ⑨, built in 1910–11.

Now cross Sampsonievskiy most onto Pirogovskaya naberezhnaya. From here you can catch tram No. 6 to the end of the walk if you wish.

Tips for Walkers

Starting point: Sobornaya Mosque.
Getting there: Gorkovskaya metro station (see p227).
Length: 3.5 km (2 miles).
Stopping-off points: There are places selling snacks along the north embankment, especially around the cruiser *Aurora* and the Cabin of Peter the Great.

Key

••• Walk route

The Cruiser Aurora

Follow the embankment to Petrogradskaya naberezhnaya and the historic old cruiser *Aurora* ⑧ (see p75), famous for firing the shots that signalled the storming of the Winter

Continuing on foot, the embankment leads down to Arsenalnaya naberezhnaya, past the Military Medical Academy ⑩ – built in the time of Tsar Paul I in a High-Classical style. Turn left onto Ploshchad Lenina ⑪. In the square is one of the city's few remaining statues of Lenin.

Statue of Lenin in Ploshchad Lenina ⑪, near Finland Station

Ploshchad Lenina

The majority of statues of Lenin were torn down after the collapse of the USSR. This one was erected in 1926. Note the famous "taxi-hailing" pose that was so popular among architects of monuments to "Grandfather Lenin", as Soviet children were taught to refer to him. Directly opposite the square, on the other side of the river, looms the "Bolshoy Dom", the gloomy former headquarters of the KGB. Here, death sentences were passed on an estimated 47,000 citizens of St Petersburg, who were then executed by firing squad. It is now the FSB's (the KGB's successors) HQ and a prison. Finally, walk across Ploshchad Lenina to Finland Station ⑫ (see p128), home to the train that brought Lenin to Russia to lead the 1917 October Revolution – and to alter the destiny of the largest country on earth. Finland Station also houses the Ploshchad Lenina metro station.

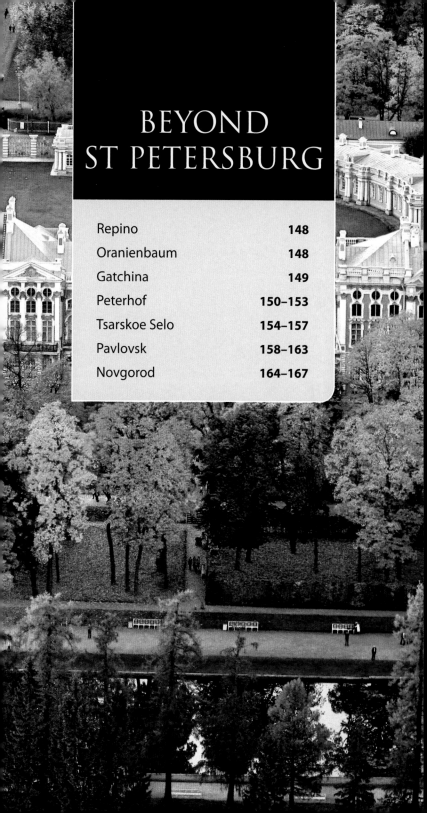

BEYOND ST PETERSBURG

BEYOND ST PETERSBURG

The countryside around St Petersburg is typical of northwest Russia. Among its flat sweeps of land, pine forests and lakes there are sights of cultural interest, including the imperial palaces and the walled medieval city of Novgorod. Venturing away from St Petersburg allows a richer and deeper insight into this splendid land.

Before St Petersburg was founded in 1703, the surrounding landscape was a marshy and inhospitable wilderness, inhabited by wolves. Nevertheless, the area from the Gulf of Finland to Lake Ladoga was of strategic importance for trading and thus one of the reasons for continuous wars between Sweden and Russia. At the time the only city of importance here was Novgorod, an independent and quite wealthy principality *(see p19)*. It has retained its medieval atmosphere, so different from the imperial palaces adorning the countryside south of St Petersburg, each of which reflect the tastes of their owners. Peter the Great's fine residence, Peterhof, is dominated by water; the nearby Gulf and the numerous fountains mirror his maritime interest. Elizabeth wanted vibrant colour and

excess to accommodate her extravagant balls, hence the grand Baroque palace at Tsarskoe Selo. Catherine the Great's love of intimacy led her to add private apartments to Tsarskoe Selo, and the exquisite Chinese Palace at Oranienbaum. Paul I's military mania had him turn Gatchina into a castle, while his wife Maria Fyodorovna created a feminine, elegant residence at Pavlovsk. All the palaces except Oranienbaum suffered devastating damage during World War II *(see p29)*. A great deal of effort has been made to restore them over the last 60 years.

While the aristocracy indulged in their extravagances, the middle classes had more modest country houses. The *dacha* of the artist Repin gives a feel of his more bohemian lifestyle.

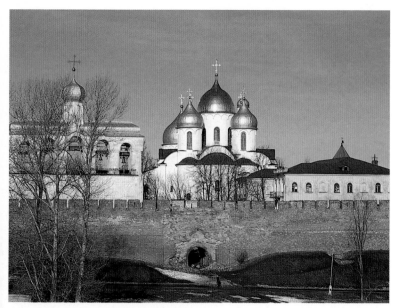

The Novgorod Kremlin with the Cathedral of St Sophia and its belfry

◀ The impressive Grand Cascade in front of the Great Palace, depicting the biblical tale of Samson and the lion

Exploring St Petersburg's Surroundings

Many St Petersburgers leave the city to spend time at their *dacha* or country house for weekends and holidays. But there are several ways of experiencing the countryside around St Petersburg. There are many stunning imperial palaces, spread out like pearls in a necklace south of the city. Each one of them offers splendid interiors as well as beautifully laid out parks and gardens with lakes. Around the artist's studio at Repino is a more typical Baltic landscape, with pine and fir trees stretching down to the pebbly beaches of the Gulf of Finland.

Further away to the south, the medieval town of Novgorod is a great representative of an old Russian city, complete with a walled kremlin and onion-domed churches.

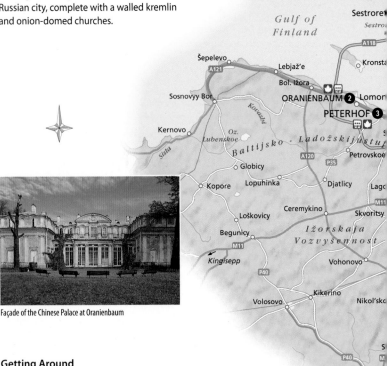

Façade of the Chinese Palace at Oranienbaum

Getting Around

It is relatively easy to get to all of the imperial palaces, and to Repino, by suburban train or by coach *(see p231)*. Driving is less convenient, often taking longer than the train, and driving standards are variable. In summer, a hydrofoil service from the centre offers an alternative way to get to Peterhof *(see pp230–31)*. Each of these sights can easily be visited in a day. Novgorod is situated further away, however, and so it makes sense to spend longer there. Mainline trains depart from Moscow railway station *(see p231)* for Novgorod.

Coastal landscape along the Gulf of Finland

For keys to symbols *see back flap*

Sights at a Glance

1. Repino
2. Oranienbaum
3. Peterhof
4. Gatchina
5. Tsarskoe Selo
6. Pavlovsk
7. Novgorod

Key

Area of main map

St Petersburg

Novgorod

↑ *Priozersk*

P129

V'jun

A120

Vaskelovo

A120

Oz. Lembolovskoe

A121

Arloga

P33

Sertolovo

Oz. Kavgolovskoe

Vartemjagi

Morye

Oz. Hepojarvi

Toksovo

Pargolovo

Kuzmolovskiy

Borisova Griva

Iomyagi

Ozerki

A128

Oja

Vsevolozhsk

A120

Lake Ladoga

A118

Torfjanoj

St Petersburg

Šlisselburg

Novaya Ladoga

Razmetelevo

M18

Kirovsk

M18

Ligovo

Kupchino

Dubrovka

Neva

Pavlovo

Nazija

Vazija

orelovo

Metallostroj

Ust'-Ižora

Otradnoe

Mga

snoe Sel

M10

Kolpino

Gory

TSARSKOE SELO ⑤

Mga

PAVLOVSK ⑥

Sologubovka

Krasnyj Bor

M20

Ulyanovka

P41

Izbora

Šapki

ATCHINA

Fornosovo

Nurma

Tosna

A120

Tosno

Kostuja

Stroenie

inskoe

Vyritsa

P40

Lisino-Korpus

M10

Orvedž

Novgorod 115 km (70 miles) ⑦

Kastenskaja

0 kilometres   20

0 miles   10

Key

═══ Motorway

─── Major road

····· Minor road

━━━ Scenic route

═══ Main railway

─── Minor railway

Gilded cupolas of the chapel of Catherine Palace at Tsarskoe Selo

❶ Repino

Репино
Repino

47 km (29 miles) NW of St Petersburg.
🚆 from Finland Station. 🚌 211 from
Chernaya Rechka metro. Penaty:
Primorskoe shosse 411. **Tel** 432 0834.
Open 10:30am–4pm Wed–Sun. 🅿
📷 English. ♿ ground floor.

Only about an hour's drive from
St Petersburg on Primorskoe
shosse, the northern coastal
road, is a region of lakes, pine-
scented forests and sandy
beaches. Among the green-
painted *dachas* and sanatoria
is Repino, a resort named after
one of Russia's greatest artists,
Ilya Repin (*see p108–9*), who
lived here for over 30 years until
his death in 1930 at the age
of 86. His extraordinary *dacha*,
with its steeply pitched glass
roof and angled windows,
was restored after damage in
World War II and is now open
as a museum.

Named Penaty in honour
of the Roman household
gods, *penates*, the house was
redesigned by Repin himself to
accommodate all that an artist
might need, including a glass-
panelled veranda downstairs,
which was used as a winter
studio. On display in the first-
floor studio are the artist's
brushes and a number of his
works, including an unfinished
portrait of Pushkin (*see p46*) and
Repin's last self-portrait.

Works by the artist adorn the
dining room, including portraits
of the singer Fyodor Chalyapin
and writer Maxim Gorky who
were among Repin's many visitors. A revolving dining table
enabled guests to serve them-

Studio of the eminent artist Ilya Repin at his home in Repino

selves and to store away their
used dishes, since there were no
servants. Anyone failing to obey
this household rule had to give
an impromptu speech from the
lectern in the corner.

In the garden, two small
wooden follies are hidden
among the trees, and Repin's
grave is marked by a simple
cross on the top of a hillock.

❷ Oranienbaum

Ораниенбаум
Oranienbaum

Oranienbaum, 40 km (25 miles)
W of St Petersburg. **Tel** 422 3753,
423 1627 or 422 8016 (excursions).
🚆 from Baltic Station. Grounds:
Open 9am–8pm (free after 5pm).
🅿 Chinese Palace: and Palace of
St Peter III: **Open** Jun–Sep: 10:30am–
6pm Wed–Mon. Sliding Hill Pavilion:
Closed temporarily. 🅿 📷

As the extravagant project of
Peter the Great's closest friend
and main political advisor,
Aleksandr Menshikov (*see p64*),
Oranienbaum was far more
ambitious in conception than
Peter's palace at Peterhof (*see
pp150–53*), which lies just 12 km
(7 miles) to the west. The

grandiose plan bankrupted
Menshikov and, when he fell
from grace in 1727, the estate
entered the state treasury.

The Baroque appearance
of Oranienbaum's Great Palace
has changed little since it was
constructed in 1710–25. Built by
Gottfried Schädel and Giovanni-
Maria Fontana, its sweeping
wings culminate in two
remarkable pavilions. Parts
of the palace and the east
(Japanese) pavilion are open
to the public.

From 1743 to 1761 the estate
became the residence of the
heir to the throne, the future
Peter III, who built himself a
miniature fortress with a small
lake for his "navy" and a parade
ground where he was fond of
playing war games with soldiers.
Peter also commissioned
Antonio Rinaldi to build him
a modest palace.

Peter's wife, Catherine (later
Catherine the Great), abhorred
her isolated existence here, but
after Peter's murder (*see p24*)
she recovered her spirits and
created what she described as
her "personal *dacha*". Built by
Rinaldi in the 1760s and known
as the Chinese Palace, it is
famous for its Rococo interiors
and chinoiserie.

The most unusual building at
Oranienbaum is Rinaldi's Sliding
Hill Pavilion, built in 1762 on
Catherine's initiative. Wooden
sledging hills were a common
source of amusement among
the Russian nobility. Catherine's
visitors would climb the blue
and white pavilion before
descending at top speed by
sledge or toboggan along a
roller-coaster run. The track,

Façade of Menshikov's Great Palace (1710–25), Oranienbaum

500 m (1,640 ft) long, was originally flanked by a colonnade. Sadly, this structure collapsed in 1813 but there is a model in the pavilion.

A pleasant few hours can be spent in the grounds, with their secluded paths, pine woods, ponds and bridges.

Oranienbaum was the only local palace to escape German occupation during World War II (see p29). In 1948, the estate was renamed Lomonosov after the famous 18th-century physicist (see p47) who laid many of the foundations of modern Russian science. The complex has now reverted to its original name, an allusion to the exotic orange trees planted here by Menshikov.

Chinoiserie decorations in Catherine the Great's Chinese Palace, Oranienbaum

❸ Peterhof

See pp150–53.

❹ Gatchina

Гатчина

Gatchina

45 km (28 miles) SW of St Petersburg. from Baltic Station. 431, K-18, K-18a from Moskovskaya metro station. **Tel** +8 813 719 3492. **Open** 10am–6pm Tue–Sun. **Closed** first Tue of month. English (phone to book). gatchinapalace.ru

In 1765, Catherine the Great presented the village of Gatchina to her lover, Prince Grigoriy Orlov. He then

Austere central section of Gatchina Palace

commissioned Antonio Rinaldi to build a Neo-Classical palace which was completed in 1781. When Orlov died, two years later, Catherine transferred the estate to her son and heir Paul (later Paul I). Paul asked his favourite architect Vincenzo Brenna to re-fashion the palace. Brenna's large-scale alterations included the construction of an additional storey and a moat with a drawbridge.

The next Romanov to spend any time here was Alexander III who made it his permanent family residence in the late 19th century. The estate provided a safe and remote haven from the sporadic social unrest which was threatening the capital (see p28). The imperial family led a simple and secluded existence here. In keeping with the increasingly bourgeois tastes of the nobility in the whole of Europe, they scorned the state rooms, confining themselves

instead to the cosy and more intimate servants' quarters. In 1917, immediately after the Bolshevik party had seized power, the proclaimed leader of the Provisional Government, Aleksandr Kerensky, fled to Gatchina where he made a last ditch attempt to rally his supporters. After a week, he deserted his troops and slipped away into exile.

After World War II, in which the palace was badly damaged, Gatchina was used for many years as a military academy. The lengthy and thorough restoration process is ongoing. Of the restored rooms, the three most impressive are the Marble Dining Room, Paul I's gloomy bedroom at the top of one of Brenna's towers and the magnificent White Ballroom. There is also a display of weaponry on the ground floor.

The delightful grounds are the wildest of all the palace parks. Among the attractions are the circular Temple of Venus (1792–3) on the secluded Island of Love and the Birch House (1790s). The latter appears to be a pile of logs, but it actually conceals a suite of exquisite rooms.

The lake has boats for hire and its clean water makes it an ideal spot for swimming.

❺ Tsarskoe Selo

See pp154–7.

Gatchina's sumptuous White Ballroom with its pseudo-Egyptian statues

❸ Peterhof
Петергоф
Petergof

With its commanding views of the Baltic, Peterhof is a perfect expression of triumphalism. Originally designed by Jean-Baptiste Le Blond, the Great Palace (1714–21) was transformed during the reign of Tsarina Elizabeth when Bartolomeo Rastrelli added a third storey and wings with pavilions at either end. He tried to preserve Le Blond's early Baroque exterior, but redesigned the interiors, indulging his love for gilded Baroque decoration. Peterhof stands at the centre of a magnificent landscaped park, with both French and English gardens.

View from palace of Grand Cascade leading down to the Gulf of Finland

The Imperial Suite
The imperial suite lies in the palace's east wing. Peter's Oak Study is one of the few rooms to have survived unaltered from Le Blond's design. Some of the oak panel designs are originals (1718–21) by Nicholas Pineau.

Cottage Palace

Orangery

Roman Fountain

Pyramid Fountain

KEY

① **The Upper Gardens** are framed by borders and hedges and punctuated with ornamental ponds.

② **Mezheumnyy Fountain**

③ **Neptune Fountain**

④ **Oak Fountain**

⑤ **Eve Fountain**

⑥ **Samson Fountain**

⑦ **The Marine Canal** enabled the tsars to sail from the Gulf of Finland up to the Great Palace.

⑧ **Adam Fountain**

★ **The Grand Cascade**
The dazzling cascade (1715–24) is a sequence of 37 gilded bronze sculptures, 64 fountains and 142 water jets *(see p153)*, descending from the terraces of the Great Palace to the Marine Canal and the sea.

Peter the Great's Palace

After his victory over the Swedes at Poltava in 1709, Peter the Great decided to build a palace "befitting to the very highest of monarchs". A visit to Versailles in 1717 furthered Peter's ambitions and he employed more than 5,000 labourers, serfs and soldiers, supported by architects, water-engineers, landscape gardeners and sculptors. Work proceeded at a frenetic pace from 1714 until

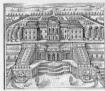

Peterhof was officially opened in 1723. Le Blond's Great Palace was completed in 1721 and has changed considerably over the decades. Catherine the Great commissioned Yuriy Velten to redecorate some of Rastrelli's interiors in the 1770s, including the Throne Room and the Chesma Room.

Jean-Baptiste Le Blond's original two-storey Great Palace

VISITORS' CHECKLIST

Practical Information
Petrodvorets, 30 km (19 miles) W of St Petersburg. **Tel** 420 0073. Great Palace: **Open** 10:30am–6pm Tue–Sun. **Closed** last Tue of each month. Other pavilions: **Open** May–Sep: 11am–5pm Tue–Sun; Oct–Apr: 11am–5pm Sat & Sun. Fountains: **Open** May–early Oct: 10:30am–5pm. 🖾 🗓 🖾 🚻 🖳

Transport
🚇 from Baltic Station *(see p231)* to Novyy Petergof. 🚢 Hermitage (May–Oct) *(see p222)*.

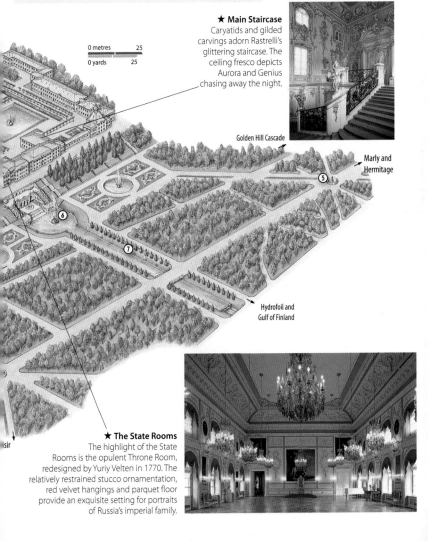

★ **Main Staircase**
Caryatids and gilded carvings adorn Rastrelli's glittering staircase. The ceiling fresco depicts Aurora and Genius chasing away the night.

0 metres 25
0 yards 25

Golden Hill Cascade

Marly and Hermitage

Hydrofoil and Gulf of Finland

★ **The State Rooms**
The highlight of the State Rooms is the opulent Throne Room, redesigned by Yuriy Velten in 1770. The relatively restrained stucco ornamentation, red velvet hangings and parquet floor provide an exquisite setting for portraits of Russia's imperial family.

Exploring Peterhof Park

The grounds at Peterhof include the Upper, Lower and Alexandria parks, covering an area of around 607 hectares (1,500 acres). As well as the numerous palaces and fountains, there are tree-lined avenues, wooded paths and the Baltic shore. Le Blond designed the grounds next to the Great Palace to be laid out in the formal French style with geometrically arranged flower beds, sculptures, summer houses and pergolas. The trees and shrubs, including limes, elms, maples and roses, were imported from all over Russia and abroad.

Cottage Palace in Alexandria Park

own formal garden with sculptures, fountains, a large pond and Niccolò Michetti's Golden Hill Cascade, which was added in 1731–7.

The Hermitage
Standing in splendid isolation on the shores of the gulf, this elegant pavilion (1721–5), by Braunstein, was conceived as a private dining venue for the tsar and his friends. To highlight the need for solitude, the building was raised on a plinth and surrounded by a moat that was crossed by a small drawbridge. The stuccoed façade is decorated with Corinthian pilasters, elaborate wrought-iron balconies and enlarged windows. All the servants were confined to the ground floor and a mechanical device took meals up from the kitchen.

Monplaisir Palace (1714–22), overlooking the Gulf of Finland

Monplaisir
This delightfully unpretentious palace was designed in 1714 by Johann Braunstein. Even after the Great Palace was built, Peter continued to live and entertain at Monplaisir where his guests were usually subjected to a punishing regime of heavy drinking. At breakfast the coffee cups were filled with brandy and by nightfall guests were often discovered wandering drunk in the park.

While not as lavish as those of the Great Palace the interiors are still impressive, in particular the wood-panelled Ceremonial Hall. A painting on its vaulted ceiling depicts Apollo surrounded by characters from a masque. Russian icon painters skilfully carried out the decoration of the exquisite Lacquered Study in the Chinese style, then in vogue. Peter's collection of canvases by Dutch and Flemish artists hang in the rooms and there are wonderful views of the gulf from the tsar's Naval Study.

Adjoining Monplaisir is the Catherine Wing, which was built for Tsarina Elizabeth by Rastrelli in 1747–54. Catherine the Great was staying here in 1762 when her lover, Count Orlov, arrived with news of the coup which was to bring her to the throne (see p26).

Marly Palace
Named after Marly-le-Rois, the king of France's hunting lodge which Peter the Great visited on a tour of Europe in 1717, this beautifully proportioned country residence was built for the tsar's guests. The rooms open to the public include the Oak and Plane Tree studies, Peter's bedroom and the Dining Room. The palace is set in its

Elaborate tiled kitchen in the Marly Palace (1720–3)

Cottage Palace
The romantic landscaped grounds of Alexandria Park, named after Alexandra, wife of Nicholas I, provide a perfect setting for the Cottage Palace. The Neo-Gothic house is more imposing than the term cottage suggests. The Scottish architect, Adam Menelaws, designed it in 1826–9 for Nicholas I and his wife, who wanted a domestic environment in keeping with their bourgeois tastes.

The Gothic theme is pursued throughout, most effectively in the Great Drawing Room with the rose-window motif in the carpet and the lace-like tracery of the stuccoed ceiling. The exquisite 5,200-piece crystal and porcelain dinner service in the Dining Room was made for the royal couple at the Imperial Porcelain factory.

The Fountains at Peterhof

Jean-Baptiste Le Blond submitted his "water plan" to Peter the Great in 1717, by which time the tsar had begun sketching his own ideas. The centrepiece is the Grand Cascade, fed by the underground springs of the Ropsha Hills about 22 km (14 miles) away. The cascade is a celebration of the triumph of Russia over Sweden *(see p21)*, symbolized by Mikhail Kozlovskiy's glorious sculpture of Samson rending the jaws of a lion. An imaginative variety of fountains, mostly concentrated in the Lower Park, includes triton and lion fountains, dragon fountains with chequerboard steps, and smaller fountains with fish-tailed boys blowing sprays of water through conches. Most playful are trick fountains such as the Umbrella which "rains" on those who come too close.

The Adam Fountain, sculpted by Giovanni Bonazza, was commissioned by Peter in 1718, along with a similar statue of Eve. The two fountains suggest the earthly paradise the tsar had recreated at Peterhof.

The Roman Fountains were designed by Ivan Blank and Ivan Davydov in 1738–9. The two-tiered marble fountains were inspired by one in St Peter's Square in Rome.

The Neptune Fountain predates Peterhof by more than 50 years. The Baroque sculpture was erected in 1658 in Nuremberg to mark the end of the Thirty Years War and was sold to Tsar Paul I in 1782 because there was not enough water to make it work.

The Grand Cascade was originally adorned with lead statues which weathered badly and were recast in bronze and gilded after 1799. Shubin, Martos and other noted sculptors worked to create this stunning cascade.

The Pyramid Fountain (1720s) is one of a number of fountains whose jets create a special shape. Over 500 jets of water rise in seven tiers to create an "obelisk" commemorating the Russian victory over Sweden.

❺ Tsarskoe Selo

Царское Село

Tsarskoe Selo

The lavish imperial palace at Tsarskoe Selo was designed by Rastrelli *(see p95)* in 1752 for Tsarina Elizabeth. She named it the Catherine Palace in honour of her mother, Catherine I, who originally owned the estate. The next ruler to leave a mark on the palace was Catherine the Great, and during her reign she commissioned the Scotsman Charles Cameron to redesign the Baroque interiors according to her more Neo-Classical taste. Cameron also built an ensemble of buildings for taking traditional Russian cold and warm baths, containing the Agate Rooms, and the Cameron Gallery. Post-war restoration continues and 35 state rooms are now open, as well as the beautiful park.

★ The Great Hall

Light streams into Rastrelli's glittering hall illuminating the mirrors, gilded carvings and the vast ceiling painting, *The Triumph of Russia* (c.1755), by Giuseppe Valeriani.

Entrance

Atlantes

The stunning 300-m- (980-ft-) long Baroque façade is adorned with a profusion of Atlantes, columns, pilasters and ornamented window framings.

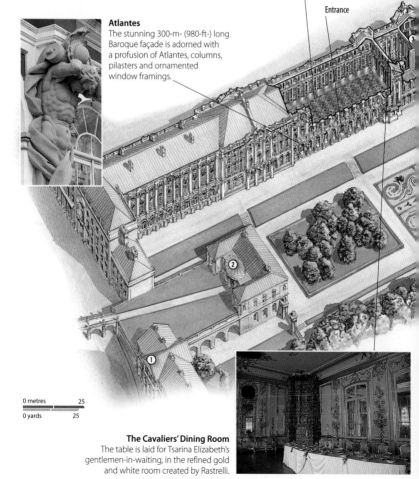

| 0 metres | 25 |
| 0 yards | 25 |

The Cavaliers' Dining Room

The table is laid for Tsarina Elizabeth's gentlemen-in-waiting, in the refined gold and white room created by Rastrelli.

★ **Amber Room**
The original amber panels (1709) by Andreas Schlüter were a gift from Friedrich Wilhelm I of Prussia to Peter the Great. The room has been recreated from photos, complete with carved reliefs and panels in Florentine mosaic.

VISITORS' CHECKLIST

Practical Information
Tsarskoe Selo, 25 km (16 miles) S of St Petersburg. Palace: **Tel** 465 2024. **Open** 10am–5pm Fri–Wed; open noon–2pm & 4–5pm. **Closed** last Mon of month. 🅿 🖼 🖼 🖳 Agate Rooms: **Closed** temporarily. Cameron Gallery: **Open** 10am–5pm Fri–Wed. Park: **Open** daily. 🖼 mid-May–Sep. 🆆 **tzar.ru**

Transport
🚇 from Vitebskiy Station to Detskoe Selo, then 🚌 371 or 382.

To the Lycée and the Church of the Sign *(see p157)*

★ **Green Dining Room**
Cameron's restrained Neo-Classical style contrasts with the Baroque flamboyance of Rastrelli's work. The exquisite stucco bas-reliefs, sculpted by Ivan Martos, were based on motifs from frescoes discovered in Pompeii.

Small Enfilade
A varied selection of furniture and *objets d'art* make up the exhibition in these unrestored rooms. Chinese lacquer furniture and Oriental rugs were among the treasures used to furnish the palace in the 19th century.

KEY

① **The Cameron Gallery** *(see p156)*.

② **The Agate Rooms** *(see p156)* are part of the imperial baths and faced with semi-precious stones from the Urals. (Temporarily closed.)

③ **The Great Staircase (1860)**, by Ippolito Monighetti, ascends to the state rooms on the first floor.

④ **The Royal Chapel** is richly decorated in dark blue and gold. Built by Chevakinskiy in the 1740s, it contains an elaborate six-tiered iconostasis.

⑤ **The Blue Drawing Room** is characterized by blue floral motifs painted on silk. Among the royal portraits hanging here is a painting of Peter the Great by Ivan Nikitin, dating from around 1720.

⑥ **The Picture Gallery** displays canvases by Italian, French, Dutch and Flemish masters of the 17th and 18th centuries.

⑦ **The French-style formal gardens** were laid out in the 1740s. Their formality and symmetry contrasts with the naturalistic English-style landscaping of the park *(see p156)*, created in 1768.

Exploring Tsarskoe Selo

The magnificent parks and gardens of Tsarskoe Selo (the Tsar's Village) were created out of dense forest by thousands of soldiers and labourers. Work began on the formal gardens in 1744 but later, in 1768, Catherine the Great commissioned one of Russia's first landscaped parks. The 567 hectares (1,400 acres) of grounds are dotted with captivating pavilions set around the central lake. The grounds and the town of Tsarskoe Selo, to the northeast of the palace, are also a delight to explore.

Formal gardens in front of Catherine Palace, Catherine Park

Catherine Park

The formal gardens to the southeast of the palace are laid out geometrically with radiating avenues, parterres and terraces, decorative ponds, hedges, elegant pavilions and Classical statuary. Nearest to the palace are Cameron's **Agate Rooms** (1780–87), which are currently closed. Their heavily rusticated lower storey contrasts with the upper tier, modelled on a Renaissance villa. The building takes its name from the agate, jasper and malachite covering the interior.

Girl with a Pitcher by Pavel Sokolov (1816)

The impressive **Cameron Gallery**, built in 1783–7, has a rusticated stone ground floor, surmounted by a Neo-Classical peristyle of 44 Ionic columns. Ranged along the colonnade are bronze busts of ancient philosophers, poets and rulers. In 1792–4 Cameron added a long stone ramp to facilitate access to the gardens for the ageing Catherine the Great. The Neo-Classical **Lower and Upper Baths** were built by Ilya Neyelov in 1777–80. The domed Lower Baths were for the use of courtiers while the exquisite Upper Baths were reserved for members of the imperial family. Construction work on Rastrelli's **Grotto** began in 1749, but the original decoration of the interior with more than 250,000 shells continued well into the 1770s.

The gardens' main avenue leads to the **Hermitage** (1756), a Baroque pavilion built by Rastrelli, where Elizabeth would entertain small groups of guests for dinner.

The romantic landscaped area of the lower park was begun in 1768 by master gardeners such as John Bush, who worked under the overall supervision of the architect, Vasiliy Neyelov. A 16-km (10-mile) waterway was built to feed the numerous canals, cascades and man-made lakes, including the *pièce de résistance*, the **Great Pond**. From Giacomo Quarenghi's pavilion (1786) on the island, musicians would serenade Catherine and her courtiers as they floated by in gilded gondolas.

A naval theme links Vasiliy Neyelov's Dutch, Neo-Gothic **Admiralty** (1773–7) with the 25-m- (82-ft-) high **Chesma Column** which is decorated with ships' prows. The column, designed by Antonio Rinaldi in 1771, commemorates the Russian victory over the Turks in the Aegean.

The reflection of the pink dome and minaret of the **Turkish Bath** shimmers in the placid waters on the far side of the lake. Nearby is Neyelov's colonnaded **Marble Bridge** (1770–76). Perched on a rock overlooking the pond is the **Girl with a Pitcher**, a statue by Pavel Sokolov. The figure inspired Pushkin to write his memorable poem, *Fountain at Tsarskoe Selo,* in which he muses on the girl who has broken her urn and now "sits timelessly sad over the timeless stream".

Evidence of the 18th-century craze for chinoiserie can be found on the border with the wilder Alexander Park where Cameron built his **Chinese Village** in 1782–96. Other examples are Yuriy Velten's **Creaking Pavilion**, designed to creak when visitors entered, and Neyelov's **Great Caprice** (1770s), a hump-backed bridge surmounted by a pagoda-like columned structure.

The Moorish-style Turkish Baths (1852) by Ippolito Monighetti

Creaking Pavilion (1778–86)

The Town of Tsarskoe Selo

This town of 99,000 inhabitants was developed in the 19th century as a summer resort for the aristocracy. In 1937, it was renamed after the poet Alexander Pushkin *(see p45)*, who was educated at the local **Lycée** in 1811–17, and is also referred to as Pushkin town. The school, one of Russia's most prestigious, founded by Alexander I in 1811 to educate members of the nobility.

The attractive **Church of the Sign** (1734) is one of the town's oldest buildings. In a garden next door a statue by Roman Bach depicts Pushkin dressed in the Lycée uniform.

Pushkin and his new bride, Natalya, spent the summer of 1831 in the delightful wooden house, now named **Pushkin's Dacha**. The writer Nikolai Gogol was among the many friends they entertained here.

On the town's western edge is the **Alexander Palace**, commissioned by Catherine for her grandson, the future Alexander I. Designed in 1792 by Giacomo Quarenghi, the austere, Neo-Classical building has a colonnaded façade and protruding wings. It was the residence of Russia's last tsar, Nicholas II and his family from 1904 until their arrest in 1917 *(see p30)*. There is an exhibition inside.

▥ Lycée
Sadovaya 2. **Tel** 476 6411.
Open 10:30am–5pm Wed–Mon.
Closed last Fri of month. ▨

▥ Pushkin's Dacha
Pushkinskaya 2/19. **Tel** 476 6990.
Open 10:30am–5:30pm Wed–Sun.
Closed last Fri of month. ▨

▥ Alexander Palace
Dvortsovaya 2. **Tel** 466 6669. **Open** 10am–6pm Wed–Mon. **Closed** last Wed of month. ▨ ▨ ⓦ tzar.ru

Alexander Pushkin's statue (1900), by Roman Bach

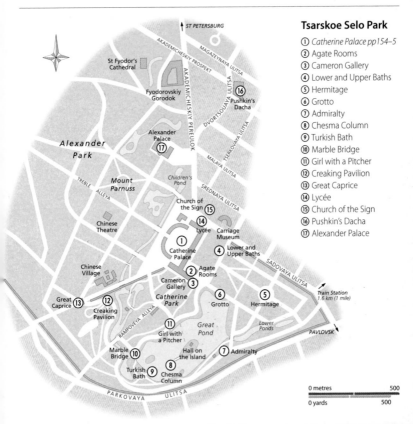

Tsarskoe Selo Park

① *Catherine Palace pp154–5*
② Agate Rooms
③ Cameron Gallery
④ Lower and Upper Baths
⑤ Hermitage
⑥ Grotto
⑦ Admiralty
⑧ Chesma Column
⑨ Turkish Bath
⑩ Marble Bridge
⑪ Girl with a Pitcher
⑫ Creaking Pavilion
⑬ Great Caprice
⑭ Lycée
⑮ Church of the Sign
⑯ Pushkin's Dacha
⑰ Alexander Palace

View of a bridge across a waterway in the beautiful Pavlovsk Park ▶

❻ Pavlovsk

Павловск

Pavlovsk

To celebrate the birth of his heir, Catherine the Great presented her son, the Grand Duke Paul, with these lands in 1777. She also "gave" him her favourite architect, Charles Cameron, to design both palace and park. Work at Pavlovsk (from "Pavel" or Paul) began in 1780 and was continued by Paul's grieving widow, Maria Fyodorovna, long after his death. "English gardens" were at the height of fashion and inspired Cameron's design of a seemingly natural landscape dotted with pavilions (used for informal parties), romantic ruins and attractive vistas around the Slavyanka river.

Cold Baths
This austere pavilion was built by Cameron in 1799 as a summer swimming pool, complete with elegant vestibule, paintings, furniture and rich wall upholstery.

The Apollo Colonnade
Cameron's colonnade (1782–83) encircles a copy of the Apollo Belvedere, above a romantically dilapidated cascade.

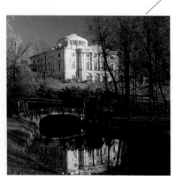

★ Pavlovsk Palace
Cameron's elegant Palladian mansion (1782–6) forms the central block of today's palace *(see pp162–3)*, with wings added in 1789 by Paul's favoured architect, Vincenzo Brenna.

★ Temple of Friendship
This Doric temple (1780) was the first use of Greek forms in Russia.

Pavlovsk Railway Station

Visconti Bridge
One of the most famous bridges which cross the winding Slavyanka, it was designed by Andrey Voronikhin in 1807.

VISITORS' CHECKLIST

Practical Information
Pavlovsk. **Tel** 452 1536. Grounds: **Open** daily. ⚘ May–Nov 10am–5pm. Palace: **Open** 10am–5pm Sat–Thu. **Closed** first Mon of month. ⚘ ⚘ ▢ ⌂ ⚘ English. ⓦ pavlovskmuseum.ru

Transport
▥ from Vitebskiy and Kupchino railway stations, then bus 370, 383, 493, K-286, K-299, K-513 *(see p230)* or from Moskovskaya metro station, then bus K-299, K-505.

The Étoile
The Étoile, the earliest landscaped area in the park, was laid out by Cameron in 1780. The circle of statues represents the nine Muses, protectresses of the arts and sciences.

KEY

① **Cameron's Dairy** (1782) housed both a milking shed and a stylish salon.

② **Aviary**

③ **Three Graces Pavilion**

④ **The Centaur Bridge** by Voronikhin (1805) nestles on a bend of the Slavyanka river.

⑤ **Green Woman Alley**

⑥ **The Beautiful Valley** was the favourite spot of Elizabeth, wife of Alexander I.

⑦ **Paul's Mausoleum** (1808–9) bears the inscription "To my beneficent consort".

⑧ **The Rose Pavilion** was the favourite haunt of Maria Fyodorovna from 1812. She held many concerts and literary evenings in this cottage.

0 metres 200
0 yards 200

Pil Tower and Bridge
Brenna's tower (1795–7) contained a spiral staircase, lounge and library. The bridge was a later addition made in 1808.

Exploring Pavlovsk Palace

Catherine commissioned Charles Cameron to build the Great Palace (1782–6) while Paul and his wife Maria Fyodorovna travelled around Europe incognito as the Comte and Comtesse du Nord. They, meanwhile, bought up everything they saw including French clocks, Sèvres porcelain, tapestries and furniture, to fill their new home. Once back in Russia, they brought in Brenna to add taller, more elaborate wings to Cameron's elegant Palladian mansion, turning it into a true palace.

West façade of the Palladian mansion

Plan of Pavlovsk Palace, First Floor

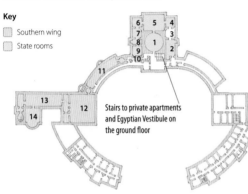

Key

Southern wing

State rooms

Stairs to private apartments and Egyptian Vestibule on the ground floor

1 Italian Hall	**8** Boudoir
2 Paul's Study	**9** State Bedroom
3 Tapestry Room	**10** Dressing Room
4 Hall of War	**11** Picture Gallery
5 Grecian Hall	**12** Throne Room
6 Hall of Peace	**13** Hall of Knights
7 Maria Fyodorovna's Library	**14** Chapel

State Rooms

Nearly all of the palace apartments at Pavlovsk, including the official ones, are relatively modest in scale. They reflect Maria Fyodorovna's intensely

The Italian Hall, originally by Cameron and Brenna, 1789

feminine tastes which have given Pavlovsk a distinct charm rather than grandeur.

A fire in 1803 necessitated some remodelling of the palace interiors by Andrey Voronikhin. The entrance hall, or Egyptian Vestibule, gained its present appearance after he added the painted bronze figures and zodiac medallions. At the top of the stairs is Brenna's State Vestibule, where the bas-reliefs reflected Paul's passion for all things military. It leads onto the Italian Hall, situated beneath the central cupola, with lantern windows and heavy doors of rosewood and mahogany.

The northern row of rooms on this floor were for Paul, the southern ones for Maria. Paul's Study is dominated by Johann Lampi's fine portrait of Maria (1794), who holds a drawing

of six of their children. Beneath it is a model temple of amber, ivory and gilded bronze, made by Maria herself. Next door, the Tapestry Room is named after the Don Quixote tapestries made by Gobelin and presented to Paul by Louis XVI. The mahogany writing table was actually made for Mikhaylovskiy Castle (see p103) but, after Paul's murder there in 1801 (see p24), Maria moved much of the specially designed furniture to Pavlovsk Palace.

The corner rooms are a Hall of War for Paul and Maria's contrasting Hall of Peace, both richly adorned with bas-reliefs and heavy gilding. Between the two lies the magnificent Grecian Hall, Cameron's Neo-Classical masterpiece.

Maria Fyodorovna's rooms commence with a small, comfortable library. The chair at the desk was designed for her by Voronikhin; note the pots built into the spine for flowers. Her Boudoir has pilasters painted with motifs copied from the Raphael Loggias in the Vatican, and a porphyry fireplace.

Maria Fyodorovna's Boudoir, designed by Brenna, 1789

Brenna's Picture Gallery (1789), with chandeliers by Johann Zeck

The State Bedroom was reputedly never slept in, but was part of court ceremony. Opposite the bed is a 64-piece Sèvres toilet set, complete with a coffee cup and an eye bath, which was a gift from Marie Antoinette.

Another present dominates the Dressing Room, a superb set of steel furniture including dressing table, chair, vases and inkstand made by the renowned gun-makers of Tula (1789). This was presented to Maria by Catherine the Great.

Southern Wing

From the elegantly curved picture gallery, built in 1798, there are excellent views. Only a few of the paintings, mostly purchased during the young couple's trip to France, are worthy of special notice, as their taste was for applied art.

The largest room in the palace is the Throne Room, designed by Brenna (1797) after Paul became tsar. Despite its name it was generally used for balls and state dinners. The tables are now laid with part of a 606-piece gilded dinner service. Vast blue Sèvres vases stand on plinths, bought directly from the factory (Paul and Maria spent huge sums on porcelain there alone). The ceiling was painted during restoration after World War II *(see p29)*, and is taken from an original design which was never used.

The Knights of St John chose Paul as Grand Master when they fled Napoleon's occupation of Malta in 1798. This suited Paul's military taste and he commissioned vast lamps, thrones and decorative items (now in the Hermitage), as well as the Hall of Knights, for ceremonies of the Order. The pale-green room is adorned with Classical statues, saved from the Germans in World War II by being buried in the grounds.

The suite of rooms ends with the Imperial Chapel of SS Peter and Paul, a very un-Orthodox church by Brenna (1797–8), decorated with copies of European paintings.

Private Apartments

Located on the ground floor are the private apartments. The Pilaster Room (1800), with its golden pilasters, is furnished with a dark mahogany suite. The Lantern Study, designed a few years later by Voronikhin, is named after its apsed bay window forming the "lantern".

Maria Fyodorovna's Dressing Room leads into the Bedroom (1805) she actually used (as opposed to the State Bedroom upstairs). Pieces of the original silk were saved in the war and used to edge the new curtains.

The small pink and blue Ballroom was for private parties and hung with paintings by the most fashionable artist of the day, Hubert Robert. The General Study, used as a family sitting room, is decorated with portraits of the family. The Raspberry Room, Paul's private study, contains paintings with views of Gatchina Palace, made for Mikhaylovskiy Castle.

The Lantern Study, one of Voronikhin's most successfully designed interiors, 1804

Maria Fyodorovna (1759–1828)

Paul's wife, Maria Fyodorovna, bore 10 children, and Pavlovsk was considered her 11th child. Paul himself preferred Gatchina *(see p149)* and in 1788 Maria was given Pavlovsk entirely. She devoted all her energy to adorning both palace and park, giving precise directions to designers and architects, who bemoaned their lack of independence. Born Sophia of Württemberg-Stuttgart, Maria had a practical German upbringing which she put to good use. Pieces of her own work, from furniture to family portraits, are throughout the palace.

Inkstand (1795) created from an initial design by Maria Fyodorovna

❼ Novgorod

The ancient town of Novgorod (New Town) was founded in 859 by the Varangian (Viking) Prince Rurik *(see p19)*. The city's proud tradition of self-government began in the 11th century and lasted until 1478, when Ivan III subjugated the city. Favourably sited on the River Volkhov with convenient connections from Scandinavia to the Aegean, the city of Novgorod became a powerful trading community during this period. In 1570, Ivan the Terrible put Novgorod to the sword, torturing and massacring thousands of its inhabitants when the city plotted against him. It was, however, the rise of St Petersburg which finally set the seal on Novgorod's decline. Much of the city's splendid cultural heritage, damaged in World War II, has been restored and can be appreciated in the many medieval churches and picturesque streets of the old town.

Bejewelled metal icon cover on display in the Chamber of Facets

The Kremlin

Situated on the left bank, or Sofiskaya Storona (Sophia side), of the River Volkhov, the formidable red-brick walls and cone-topped towers of the oval-shaped Detinets, or Kremlin, date from the 11th to the 17th centuries. According to the prevailing practice at the time, the first stone of the original walls was laid on the body of a living child.

Of the many towers, the 17th-century Kukui is the most remarkable, and also the tallest at 32 m (105 ft). The lower floors once contained a wine cellar and treasury chamber, while the octagonal room beneath the cupola was used, according to chronicles, "for surveying the whole town". At the heart of the fortress is Novgorod's oldest

Kremlin walls, with the silver dome of St Sophia's Belfry (15th century)

and largest church, the strongly Byzantine **Cathedral of St Sophia** (1045–62). It was modelled on the cathedral of the same name in Kiev, but the tendencies of the Novgorod school already appear in the lack of ornament and the scarcity of windows, necessary because of the cold. On the north wall a section of

whitewash has been removed to reveal the original mosaic effect of the grey-yellow stone and brick façade.

The exquisitely sculpted and extremely rare bronze doors adorning the west side were seized as booty in 1187 from the Swedish town of Sigtuna. In the lower left-hand corner there are portraits of the craftsmen, named in the Latin inscription as Riquin and Weissmut. The interior is divided by piers into five aisles, three ending in altar apses. Fragments of early frescoes survive, but the icon-ostasis is one of the oldest in Russia and contains icons from the 11th–17th centuries.

East of the cathedral is **St Sophia's Belfry**, much altered since it was first built in 1439. The bells, now displayed below, were cast in the late 16th and early 17th centuries.

The northwest corner of the Kremlin is occupied by the **Archbishops' Court**, in its heyday a powerful body with its own treasury, police force and military guard. Beneath the 15th-century clock tower an attractive staircase leads to the **Library**, which houses magnificent medieval religious manuscripts. Backing onto the cathedral, the **Chamber of Facets** is the most famous part of this ensemble. A superb reception hall with star-shaped vaulting dates from 1433 and displays treasures from the cathedral, including jewelled mitres and icon covers in precious metals. Within the

The 11th-century Cathedral of St Sophia, the landmark of Novgorod

Kremlin is the **Museum of History, Architecture and Art**, which houses a magnificent collection of 12th–17th-century icons of the Novgorod school. One of the most remarkable is the 12th-century portable icon of the Virgin of the Sign, whose miraculous image is said to have saved Novgorod from the armies of Prince Andrey Bogolyubskiy of Suzdal in 1169. Scenes from the battle are depicted on a vibrant 15th-century icon *(see p167)*. There are also works by leading 18th- and 19th-century artists, including Dmitriy Levitskiy, Karl Bryullov and Vasiliy Serov *(see p108)*. The museum has a number of precious public documents and private letters written on birch bark, some of which date from the 11th century. These give details of ordinary, everyday life and are evidence of the unusually widespread literacy among the city's inhabitants.

In the Kremlin's central square, the huge, bell-shaped **Millennium Monument** was sculpted by Mikhail Mikeshin. The monument was unveiled in 1862, a thousand years after Rurik's arrival in Novgorod. The figure kneeling before the Orthodox cross personifies Mother Russia while, below, the decorative frieze depicts Rurik, Ivan III, Mikhail (the first Romanov tsar), Peter the Great and many others. The frieze around the base shows over 100 figures: heroes, statesmen, artists, composers, princes and chroniclers.

✝ **Cathedral of St Sophia**
Tel (8162) 773556. **Open** 10am–6pm daily.

🏛 **Chamber of Facets:**
Tel (8162) 773608. **Open** 10am–6pm Thu–Tue. 🎫 📷 English by appt.

🏛 **Museum of History, Architecture and Art**
Tel (8162) 773770. **Open** 10am–6pm Wed–Mon. 🎫 📷 English by appt.

The carved Royal Gates of an iconostasis in the Museum of History, Architecture and Art

Yaroslav's Court
Across the River Volkhov was the official seat of the princes, known as Yaroslav's Court. The palace of Yaroslav the Wise (1019–54) has since disappeared but several churches have survived. The area adjacent is Novgorod's commercial centre, once the site of the medieval market, part of whose wall still stands.

The oldest church on this side of the river, **St Nicholas' Cathedral** (1113–36), was built by Prince Mstislav. It dominates the area and once symbolized the prince's power.

Novgorod's merchants were keen to show their recognition of God's hand in their prosperity, and so funded many of the city's churches. **St Paraskeva Pyatnitsa**, erected in 1207 and then rebuilt in 1345, was dedicated to the patron saint of commerce. The more decorative **Church of the Holy Women** and **Church of St Procopius**, both 16th century, were financed by wealthy Moscow merchants. The fanciful tastes of the Muscovite patrons mark a departure from Novgorod's austere style.

Millennium Monument, celebrating Novgorod's 1,000 years of history

Yuriev Monastery walls and bell tower with the silvery domes of the Cathedral of St George in the background

Beyond Yaroslav's Court

In the 12th century, Novgorod boasted over 200 churches, while there are only 30 today. Many of these are hidden away in the quiet hinterland of 19th-century streets to the east of Yaroslav's Court. On Ilyina ulitsa, the arrangement of windows, niches and inset crosses on the **Church of the Saviour of the Transfiguration** façade (1374) is almost whimsical. Inside, there are original frescoes by one of Russia's greatest medieval artists, Theophanes the Greek (1335–c.1410), who came from Constantinople and decorated 40 Russian churches. Andrey Rublev (1360–1430), Russia's most famous icon painter, worked under Theophanes at the beginning of his career.

On the same street, the five-domed **Znamenskiy Cathedral**, or Cathedral of the Sign (1682–8), has an attractive gateway and faded frescoes on the outer walls. The beautiful interior was decorated in 1702 by Ivan Bakhmatov.

The **Church of Theodore Stratilates** on Mstinskaya ulitsa to the north was built in 1360–61 by the widow of a wealthy Novgorod merchant. The delicate purple and pink frescoes contrast with the harsher colours found in most 14th-century Novgorod frescoes. *The Annunciation*, for example, combines sensitivity and charm with religious intensity.

Fresco inside Znamenskiy Cathedral

Further Afield

A pleasant stroll 3 km (2 miles) south along the riverbank leads to the **Yuriev Monastery**. This is the area's largest and most important monastery, founded in 1030 and built on the orders of Prince Vsevolod. Its imposing Cathedral of St George was built in 1119–30 by "Master Peter", the first named architect in Russian chronicles. This beautifully proportioned church, with its three asymmetrical cupolas, was restored in the 19th century, and unfortunately most of the interior murals were lost. There were once 20 monastic buildings in the complex, dating mainly from the 19th century.

In the woods across the road lies the fascinating open-air **Museum of Wooden Architecture**, which displays churches and peasant huts moved from local villages. Of particular interest are the 17th-century two-tiered Kuritsko Church of the Dormition and the tiny wooden church of St Nicholas from Tukhel village.

Yuriev Monastery
Yurevskaya nab. **Tel** (8162) 773020. **Open** 10am–6pm daily.

Museum of Wooden Architecture *(Vitoslavlitsi)*
Yurevo. **Tel** (8162) 773770. **Open** May–Sep: 10am–8pm daily; Oct–Apr: 10am–6pm daily.

A 19th-century peasant hut *(izba)*, Museum of Wooden Architecture

Russian Icon Painting

The Russian Orthodox Church uses icons for both worship and teaching, but never for mere ornament, and there are strict rules for the creation of each image. Icons were believed to be imbued with the force of the saint depicted, and were therefore invoked for protection during wars. Because the content was considered more important than the style, old, revered icons were often repainted again and again. The first icons were brought to Russia from Byzantium. Greek masters came too, to train local painters. The northern schools which developed during the 13th–15th centuries were less restricted by Byzantine canons and have an earthy style linked to Russian peasant life. Novgorod, never under the Mongol yoke and with a thriving economy, was the source of many of the finest icons made for the northern monasteries.

Virgin of Vladimir
The most venerated icon in Russia, this 12th-century work was made in Constantinople. Its huge influence on Russian icon painting cannot be overstated.

Battle of Novgorod and Suzdal
This mid-15th-century work of the Novgorod School is thought to be Russia's earliest historical painting. Icons could have a political purpose – in this case to use Novgorod's great past as a justification for its independence from Moscow. Note the multiple touches of red – a colour central to everyday Russian life and typical for icons of the Novgorod School.

The Iconostasis

The iconostasis screens off the sanctuary from the main part of the church, as if it were a boundary between heaven and earth. In Russian practice it is covered with icons strictly arranged in up to six tiers, each with its own dogmatic purpose.

The Festival Tier shows the 12 major church festivals, such as the Entry into Jerusalem and the Crucifixion. Such pictorial representation aided the faith of the illiterate.

Christ Enthroned

The Deesis Tier, above the Royal Gates, contains Christ Enthroned, flanked by the Virgin and St John interceding on behalf of mortal sinners.

The Royal Gates represent the entrance from the temporal world to the spiritual, between which the priests pass during the service.

The Local Tier is for local saints, those the church is dedicated to and patron saints of major donors.

Old Testament Trinity by Rublev
Andrey Rublev was one of the greatest artists of the Moscow School. He was strongly influenced by recent developments in Byzantine painting, brought to Russia by Greek masters in the late 14th century. His Trinity icon dates from the early 15th century.

TRAVELLERS' NEEDS

WHERE TO STAY

Space in the historic centre of the city may be at a premium, but new hotels continue to open. A number of "mini-hotels" – privately-run establishments with anywhere between 4 to 15 rooms – continue to sprout in or near the centre, and investors have opened large, luxury hotels in outstanding locations. The quality of service in the larger hotels is as good as that on offer in Western Europe. Many tourists visiting in the summer with a package tour, however, are still housed in large, somewhat anonymous hotels outside the centre. These provide reasonable service and full amenities such as restaurants, bars and fitness facilities. Travelling outside the White Nights period cuts costs and opens up the opportunity for booking one of the many excellent deals available at more central hotels. Bookings can be made independently or via an agency. For the summer months, particularly during the White Nights, reservations should be made well in advance for accommodation of all price levels.

Helvetia Hotel, located in a charming early 19th-century building *(see p178)*

Where to Look

There are few large, inexpensive hotels in central St Petersburg. Many of those listed in this section are scattered around the city.

Visitors on a package tour usually find themselves staying in a former Intourist hotel such as the Park Inn by Radisson Pribaltiyskaya or Pulkovskaya, which are situated in modern high-rise areas on the city's outskirts. Mini-hotels and bed-and-breakfast establishments, by contrast, are frequently found in quiet streets near the centre. Independent travellers should consider their priorities from the start, be it location, price or the amenities.

How to Book

Hotel reservations for the White Nights *(see p53)* should be made several months in advance, and as early as possible for the more popular establishments. All the hotels listed here can be booked through online reservation sites such as **Booking.com**. All hotels and agencies recommended can provide visa support *(see p210)*, unless stated otherwise.

Facilities

Rooms in all the hotels listed include at least a shower, television, telephone and Wi-Fi Internet. Most have air conditioning. Large hotels have a luggage room for storing baggage after the midday check-out time. Bars frequently open at night, and extensive fitness and sauna facilities are more or less standard features in bigger establishments.

Price

The most important thing to remember in St Petersburg is that prices in big hotels more than double for the six weeks or so of the White Nights and for the St Petersburg International Economic Forum in early June. These higher prices are quoted throughout the hotel listings *(see pp176–9)*. Normal prices return during the "mid-season", usually April–May and late July–late September. Outside that period, particularly during the "White Days" of winter, there are frequently excellent deals to be had.

Nearly all large central hotels, it should be noted, fall into the luxury category, and offer everything from exclusive single rooms to imperial suites priced at several thousand dollars a night. By opting for a smaller hotel with fewer facilities or a bed and breakfast (usually a small,

Fitness centre at the Belmond Grand Hotel Europe *(see p178)*

basic hotel rather than a family home), you can be just as central for much less money. Many smaller hotels have only shower cabins, not full baths.

Note that prices are not displayed in hotels, and that only some small hotels and hostels take credit cards. It is important to be prepared to pay in cash.

Entrance to the luxurious, modern Corinthia Hotel *(see p178)*

Hidden Extras

Large hotels, which provide visa support and obligatory passport registration *(see p210)* for free, often do not include local taxes or breakfast in the prices they quote. Both of these can be a significant addition to the final bill. (The price categories used in the hotel listings on pages 176–9 include both breakfast and taxes.) Be warned that the cost of making international or even local phone calls from your room in the larger hotels is likely to be prohibitive. On the other hand, phones which use the local network are relatively cheap. Phonecards can be purchased to make international calls from street booths or fixed phones; and Russian pay-as-you-go SIM cards can be bought at most mobile phone shops *(see p218)*.

In smaller hotels, breakfast tends to be included in the price, but you should expect to pay extra for the initial visa support. Calls from phones in small hotels and hostels may be free or very cheap if they use the local tele-phone system. Phonecards can be used to make international calls from such phones.

Security

Some top-range establishments have metal detectors and selective bag searches at entrances. Smaller hotels have a doorman, who may ask to see a visitor's card or identification. Since this is simply a precaution for guests' protection, there is no reason to object.

Most hotels have safes in the rooms and/or security deposit boxes at the front desk. Large sums of money and valuables should always be left in one of these places.

Disabled Travellers

Due to the thick snow in winter, most buildings in St Petersburg have steps leading up to their entrances, making access very difficult for disabled visitors. Most of the elite hotels are fully wheelchair accessible, with staff trained to provide assistance, and other hotels are increasingly adding ramps, widening doors and trying to adapt to meet the needs of disabled travellers.

Room in the Belmond Grand Hotel Europe *(see p178)*

Those with special requirements should contact their preferred hotel before booking.

Children

St Petersburg has never been vaunted as a great children's destination, and few hotels cater specifically for families. However, it is possible to arrange babysitters in all the larger hotels, and, increasingly, in some of the smaller ones. Visitors are advised to check the situation before booking.

The stylish Lounge Bar at the Vedensky Hotel *(see p176)*

Mini-Hotels

Not necessarily budget options because some are very luxurious, St Petersburg's extensive range of mini-hotels, with anything from 4 to 15 or 20 rooms, offer some of the most comfortable and pleasant accommodation. The personalized service is often hard to beat. **Filippov Hotels**, **Hotels on Nevsky** and **Rinaldi Bed & Breakfast** are some of the city's better-known mini-hotels.

The elegant interior of the Petro Palace Hotel *(see p176)*

Budget Accommodation

Truly cheap accommodation is hard to find in St Petersburg. Visitors on a tight budget can choose from the more modest mini-hotels, which usually describe themselves as B&Bs. This usually means they offer a small number of rooms in a converted flat in an ordinary building, with a housekeeper who makes breakfast in the apartment's kitchen. There may be a shared toilet rather than a separate one.

Accommodation agencies such as **Ostwest**, **STN**, **PiterStay** and **City Realty** also offer short-term apartment rental, which can be cheap for a group of friends who are sharing. The apartments are refurbished and centrally located, with anything from one to five rooms, usually with satellite TV.

In many cases, although the apartment has been refurbished, the communal staircase to the building may be a little grubby. This grittiness can be off-putting at first, but it does offer the feel of living in the true St Petersburg.

The best way to cut costs is to travel in the off season instead of during the White Nights. Mini-hotels and short-let apartments

The antique grand piano in the Pavarotti Suite of the Belmond Grand Hotel Europe *(see p178)*

can be extremely cheap at this time of the year, and even the big hotels offer excellent deals. April can be dry and sunny, if still cold, and October can be beautiful, particularly if you catch the brief northern autumn. Travelling in February more or less guarantees the vision of a Russia covered in snow.

Hostels

For the budget traveller seeking comfortable accommodation in a reasonably central location, there are now several hostels to choose from. All offer visa support and registration and are friendly. **Hostel Life** is a popular option for its central location and friendly staff who help organize tours around St Petersburg and beyond. The inexpensive but clean and comfortable **Nord Hostel** is unmatched for location. You could also try **CubaHostel Backpackers**, **Hostel All Seasons**, **Na Muchnom** and **Prima Sport Hotel**.

None of these are "youth" hostels, although young people do tend to dominate in the summer months. In the off season, however, 50 per cent of the guests tend to be over forty.

Staying with Families

For a really good insight into Russian lifestyle, staying with a family can be an interesting and cheap option. The system works very much like any B&B in Europe, with prices including breakfast but no other meals. Extra meals can usually be provided at a small cost.

HOFA (Host Families Association) and **Ostwest** have a wide range of families on their books and a particularly good reputation in this area. Your hosts are likely to be extremely hospitable and will tend to overfeed you rather than otherwise. Many of HOFA's hosts are academics, well educated and speak several languages. Generally, hosts will be keen to talk to you about their life in Russia and Western perceptions of their country.

Many Russian apartments are reached through scruffy entrance halls or decrepit courtyards, but do not let this put you off, as it gives little indication of the quality of the accommodation.

Camping and Outdoor Living

Russians love getting out of town for walks, swimming and mushroom gathering. All are possible on day trips from the city, but staying out of town is more complicated.

St Petersburg's cold winter weather does not make it ideal for camping, though

Park Inn by Radisson Veliky Novgorod *(see p177)*

the forests along the north side of the Gulf of Finland are excellent in milder seasons.

Renting a *dacha* or small house in the country might turn out to be difficult. Most people with modest *dachas* let them to people they know. None of the firms specializing in *dachas* lets them to foreigners, and demand within 100 km (62 miles) of the city far outstrips the properties available. As a result, rental costs can be exorbitant (about US$5,000 per week). In order to find anything at all, book as early as February. The best range of *dachas* (from around US$500 per week) is available through **Alexander**, but you will need to speak Russian, or use a travel company that does, to make a booking. The best option for cheaper living with modern facilities is to rent a chalet attached to a motel. **Retur Camping** offers chalets, camp sites, a swimming pool, sauna, tennis courts and riding.

Extended Stays

Visitors who intend to stay in St Petersburg for a month or more will find the cost of renting apartments much cheaper. While hostels do not offer long-term reductions, companies such as **City Realty** have plenty of flats that are available at more modest rates than those advertised for short lets. Be aware, however, that tourist visas cannot usually be registered *(see p210)* for more than three months, and a longer stay will require a non-tourist visa

Dacha in pine forest near Repino on the Gulf of Finland *(see p148)*

arranged through a company that can legally register you for the period you will be in the country.

Recommended Hotels

The hotels featured in this guide have been selected across a wide price range for their excellent facilities, outstanding location and, often, good value. They are arranged by type of accommodation, and then alphabetically within each price range. Historic hotels are often centuries-old buildings or restored mansions. Luxury options abound, offering the very best in service and amenities. The style-conscious and trendy may prefer hip boutique hotels. Modern lodgings and chain hotels are generally comfortable and have the standard amenities.

DK Choice hotels have been highlighted in recognition of an exceptional feature – a stunning location, notable history, inviting atmosphere or great value.

DIRECTORY

Accommodation Agencies

Alexander
Potemkinskaya ul 13.
Map 3 C4.
Tel 327 1616.
W anspb.ru

City Realty
Muchnoi per 2.
Map 6 E2.
Tel 570 6342.
W cityrealtyrussia.com

Eridan Travel Company
Ul Artilleriyskaya 1,
Business Centre Europa
House, Office 404.
Map 3 B5.
Tel 324 2305.
W prozapad.ru

HOFA Host Families Association
Tavricheskaya ul 5,
Apartment 25.
Map 4 D5.
Tel 7911 7665464.
W hofa.ru

MIR Travel Company
Nevskiy pr 11/2.
Map 6 D1.
Tel 325 2595.
W mir-travel.com

Ostwest
Ligovskiy pr 10.
Map 7 C2.
Tel 327 3416.
W ostwest.com

PiterStay
Naberezhnaya kanala
Griboedova 5.
Map 6 E1.
Tel 913 9099.
W petersburg-apartment.com

STN
Nevisky pr 66/29.
Map 7 A2.
Tel 337 1223.
W 2piter.com

Mini-Hotel Networks

Anabel
Tel 400 2211.
W anabel.ru

Filippov Hotels
Tel 579 7152.
W filippovhotel.ru

Hotels on Nevsky
Tel 703 3860.
W hon.ru

Rinaldi Bed & Breakfast
Tel 325 4188.
W rinaldi.ru

Hostels

CubaHostel Backpackers
Kazanskaya ul 5.
Map 6 E2.
Tel +7 911 921 7115.
W cubahostel.ru

Hostel All Seasons
Yakovlevskiy per 11.
Tel 327 1070.
W hostel.ru

Hostel Life
Nevisky pr 47 (entrance
from Vladimirskiy
prospekt 41).
Map 7 A2.
Tel 318 1808.
W hostel-life.ru

Na Muchnom
Sadovaya ul 25.
Map 6 E2.
Tel 310 0412.
W namuchnom.ru

Nord Hostel
Bolshaya Morskaya ul 10.
Map 6 D1.
Tel 766 1188.
W nordhostel.com

Prima Sport Hotel
Nevskiy prospekt 5.
Map 6 D1.
Tel 345 5070.
W primasport-hotel.com

Useful Website
W russia-hostelling.ru

Camping

Retur Camping
Bolshaya Kupalnaya str.
28, Sestroretsk. 26 km
(16 miles) NW of
St Petersburg.
Tel 434 5022.
W retur-motel.ru

Popular Hotels in St Petersburg

Accommodation in St Petersburg is extremely varied and there are many hotels from which to choose. Unfortunately few of the most affordable are conveniently situated for the city centre and it is important to decide on your priorities, be it location, price, character, service or amenities. This selection represents the city's most popular hotels.

PETROGRADSKA

KAMENNOOSTROVSKIY PROSPEKT

VASILEVSKIY OSTROV

Renaissance St Petersburg Baltic Hotel
Central and prestigious, yet set apart from the hurly-burly of Nevskiy prospekt, the Baltic feels like a small hotel while offering "big" hotel service (see p178).

Domina Prestige Hotel St Petersburg
This hotel (see p176) is tucked away on a small residential street. Stay here and feel like a local, but with all modern comforts.

KIROVSKY

PROSPEKT STACHEK

Azimut Hotel St Petersburg
This 1970s hotel (see p177) offers wonderful views of the city centre from its bar. At sunset or during White Nights the vista is particularly magical.

Rocco Forte Hotel Astoria
One of the city's most luxurious and centrally located hotels, the Astoria (see p177) is perfect for exploring St Petersburg on foot. The attractive building overlooks St Isaac's Square and Cathedral.

Kempinski Hotel Moika 22
Located within the Hermitage museum and a short stroll from most of the city's other attractions, the Kempinski offers its guests an unbeatable combination of historic charm and modern luxury *(see p178)*.

Belmond Grand Hotel Europe
Situated in the heart of the city, this historic hotel *(see p178)* is one of the finest in St Petersburg. Elegant decor and refined service are complemented by many facilities.

Hotel Dostoevsky
Located just a stone's throw from the tourist heart of St Petersburg, the Dostoevsky *(see p177)* combines old and new, historical and modern, in both its design and its service.

0 kilometres   2

0 miles   2

Park Inn by Radisson Pulkovskaya
Comfortable and clean, this vast modern hotel *(see p177)* has many business facilities, including an auditorium. The hotel's main advantage is its proximity to the airport.

TSENTRALNY

Neva

NEVSKIY PR

MOSKOVSKY PROSPEKT

VITEBSKIY PROSPEKT

FRUZENSKY

MOSKOVSKY

PROSPEKT SLAVY

MOSKOVSKOE SHOSSE

Where to Stay

Boutique

Vasilevskiy Island

Trezzini Art Hotel $
Bolshoy prospekt 21, 199004
Tel *332 1035* **Map** 1 A5
W trezzini-hotel.com
Delightful small hotel with classic styling. Rooms are well-furnished and overlook a quiet square.

Petrogradskaya

Sharf Hotel $$
Malyy prospekt 16, 197110
Tel *324 7774* **Map** 1 A4
W sharfhotel.ru
Accommodation in huge, modern apartments with neat rooms and kitchen facilities.

Vedensky Hotel $$
Bolshoy prospekt 37, 197198
Tel *332 4222* **Map** 1 C2
W vedenskyhotel.com
Plush hotel with elegantly furnished rooms. Great location with views of the old town.

Tradition Hotel $$$
Dobrolubova prospekt 2, 197198
Tel *405 8855* **Map** 1 C4
W traditionhotel.ru
Centrally located hotel with large rooms featuring exposed brick walls, underfloor heating and antique-style furniture.

Palace Embankment

Casa Leto Private Hotel $$
Bolshaya Morskaya ulitsa 34, 190000
Tel *600 1096* **Map** 6 D2
W casaleto.com
Tiny establishment that boasts light-filled rooms and many complimentary extras. Superb central location.

The entrance to the magnificent Vedensky Hotel

DK Choice

Petro Palace Hotel $$
Malaya Morskaya ulitsa 14, 190000
Tel *571 2880* **Map** 6 D1
W petropalacehotel.com
Housed in a tastefully renovated and extended 19th-century building, this stylish hotel attracts wealthy Russians as well as tourists. The extensive facilities it offers include a fitness suite, pool and massage services. There are good views of the city from the seventh floor.

Gostinyy Dvor

Mesto Hotel $
Naberezhnaya reki Fontanki 11, 191011
Tel *941 0286* **Map** 7 A1
W mesto-hotel.ru
Outstanding hotel featuring contemporary furnishings and exposed brick walls. Some rooms have kitchenettes.

Sennaya Ploshchad

Hotel 1913 $
Voznesenskiy prospekt 13, 190000
Tel *315 5148* **Map** 5 C2
W restaurant-1913.spb.ru
Atmospheric place with old-fashioned decor, good-sized rooms and a substantial breakfast.

Domina Prestige Hotel St Petersburg $$
Naberezhnaya reki Moyki 99, 190000
Tel *385 9900* **Map** 5 C2
W dominarussia.com
Lavish interior with Classical sculptures in the foyer and bright colour schemes throughout.

Chain

Vasilevskiy Island

Courtyard St Petersburg Vasilevskiy $$
2-ya liniya 61/30, 199178
Tel *380 4011* **Map** 1 A4
W marriott.com
Riverside hotel in an imposing 19th-century building with lovely views and a central location.

Solo Sokos Hotel Palace Bridge $$
Birzhevoy pereulok 2-4, 199044
Tel *335 2200* **Map** 1 B4
W sokoshotels.fi
Smart place offering spacious rooms and great spa facilties. Helpful and attentive staff.

Palace Embankment

Herzen House $$
Bolshaya Morskaya ulitsa 25, 190000
Tel *315 5550* **Map** 6 D2
W herzen-hotel.ru
Modern rooms and free beverages and pastries round the clock. Easy access to the metro and main sights.

Gostinyy Dvor

Atlantic Hotel $$
Kazanskaya ulitsa 14, 191186
Tel *314 4030* **Map** 6 E2
W hotel-atlantic.ru
Unpretentious hotel with modest rooms and a good breakfast.

Sennaya Ploshchad

Arkadia Hotel $$
Naberezhnaya reki Moyki 58a, 190000
Tel *571 6173* **Map** 6 D2
W arkadiahotel.ru
Attractive place in the historic centre with Classical interiors, pretty gardens and a tiny pool.

Gogol Hotel $$
Nab kanala Griboedova 69, 190001
Tel *571 1841* **Map** 6 D3
W gogolhotel.com
Chic, well-run establishment with tasteful decor and parquet floors in a characterful building.

Further Afield

Andersen Hotel $
Chapygina ulitsa 4a, 197022
Tel *740 5140*
W andersenhotel.ru
Located on the Petrogradskaya Side, with good access to the city's sights. Well-furnished rooms.

Bristol Hotel $
Rasstannaya ulitsa 2a, 192007
Tel *242 9900*
W bristol-hotel.spb.ru
Comfortably furnished hotel near transport links. Offers an excellent breakfast.

Stony Island Hotel $
Kamennoostrovskiy prospekt 45, 197022
Tel *337 2434*
W stonyisland.ru
Minimalist-style hotel in a historic building on the elegant main street of the Petrogradskaya Side.

Aparthotel Kronverk $$
Ulitsa Blokhina 9, 197198
Tel *703 3663*
W kronverk.com
Modern hotel in a scenic location on Petrogradskaya, right by the Peter and Paul Fortress.

Azimut Hotel St Petersburg $$
Lermontovskiy prospekt 43/1, 190103
Tel *740 2640*
W azimuthotels.com
Refurbished Soviet-era monolith that towers over the historic quarter. Offers great views of the city.

Holiday Inn St Petersburg Moskovskye Vorota $$
Moskovskiy prospekt 97a, 196084
Tel *448 7171*
W hi-spb.com
Stylish high-rise hotel with good transport links all over the city.

Hotel Dostoevsky $$
Vladimirskiy prospekt 19, 191002
Tel *331 3200*
W dostoevsky-hotel.ru
Elite hotel with most of its rooms overlooking courtyards. Located near Nevskiy prospekt.

Neptun Economy Hotel $$
Naberezhnaya Obvodnovo kanala 93a, 191119
Tel *324 4600*
W neptun.spb.ru
Reliable, no-frills hotel with smart rooms. Excellent fitness complex.

DK Choice

**Novotel
St Petersburg Centre** $$
Ulitsa Mayakovskovo 3a, 191025
Tel *335 1188*
W novotel.com
This ultra-chic block is a stone's throw from Nevskiy prospekt. The ninth-floor executive suites offer superb views. Three rooms have been customized for disabled visitors. The Côte Jardin restaurant offers a Russian take on Mediterranean cooking.

Okhtinskaya Hotel $$
Bolsheokhtinskiy prospekt 4, 195027
Tel *318 0040*
W okhtinskaya.com
Modern building with airy rooms that have great views over the Neva.

Original Sokos Hotel Olympia Garden $$
Batayskiy pereulok 3a, 190013
Tel *335 2270*
W sokoshotels.fi
Run by a reputable Finnish chain, a large characterful place defined by its hardwood floors.

Elegant interior of a room in the Park Inn by Radisson Veliky Novgorod

DK Choice

Park Inn by Radisson Pribaltiyskaya $$
Ulitsa Korablestroiteley 14, 199226
Tel *329 2626*
W parkinn.com
The Park Inn Pribaltiyskaya is a huge, 1980s package-tour hotel, set right on the Gulf of Finland. It boasts splendid views, and a water park with pool and sports facilities. There is also a wellness and spa centre. The hotel provides free shuttle bus service to the city centre.

Park Inn by Radisson Pulkovskaya $$
Pobedy ploshchad 1, 196240
Tel *740 3900*
W parkinn.com
Modern rooms, some of which give views of Victory Monument. Good base for trips to Tsarskoe Selo and Pavlovsk.

Beyond St Petersburg

Hotel Novgorodskaya $
Desyatinnaya ulitsa 6a, Veliky Novgorod, 173007
Tel *(8162) 772260*
W novgorodskaya.nov.ru
Conveniently close to the historic centre. Comfortably furnished rooms. Free Wi-Fi.

Hotel Volkhov $
Predtechenskaya ulitsa 24, Veliky Novgorod, 173007
Tel *(8162) 225500*
W hotel-volkhov.ru
The Volkhov boasts one of the best locations in the historical centre. Buffet breakfast on offer.

Aquamarine Spa Hotel $$
Primorskoye shosse 593-H, Zelenogorsk, 197720
Tel *702 2619*
W hotel-aquamarin.ru
Refurbished Soviet-era hotel with lovely spa facilities.

DK Choice

Park Inn by Radisson Veliky Novgorod $$
Studencheskaya ulitsa 2, Veliky Novgorod, 173020
Tel *(8162) 940910*
W parkinn.com
This well-equipped hotel comprises a large, modern complex with conference halls, tennis courts and a stylish pool. Rooms are pleasantly furnished and many have charming views over the river Volkhov. The spa centre provides sauna and massage treatments. The hotel also offers accommodation in semi-luxurious apartments.

Historic

Vasilevskiy Island

Hotel Shelfort $$
3-ya liniya 26, 199004
Tel *328 0555* **Map** 1 A5
W shelfort.ru
Characterful interiors with beautifully restored traditional tiled stoves. Friendly staff and efficient service.

Palace Embankment

Four Seasons Hotel Lion Palace St Petersburg $$$
Voznesenskiy prospekt 1, 190000
Tel *339 8000* **Map** 5 C1
W fourseasons.com
Opulent hotel housed in a historic building with lavish Russian Empire-style interiors. Spacious and welcoming rooms.

Rocco Forte Hotel Astoria $$$
Bolshaya Morskaya ulitsa 39, 190000
Tel *494 5757* **Map** 6 D2
W roccofortehotels.com
The hotel's graceful interior boasts historic charm. Front-facing rooms offer superb views over St Isaac's Cathedral and the square.

For more information on types of hotels *see page 173*

Taleon Imperial Hotel $$$
Nevskiy prospekt 15, 191186
Tel *324 9911* **Map** 6 D1
W taleonimperialhotel.com
Stunning hotel with rooms
that overlook the river Moyka.

Gostinyy Dvor

Belmond Grand Hotel
Europe $$$
Mikhaylovskaya ulitsa 1/7, 191186
Tel *329 6000* **Map** 6 F1
W grandhoteleurope.com
Luxury hotel with historic interiors,
six restaurants and brilliant service.

Golden Triangle Hotel $$$
*Bolshaya Konyushennaya ulitsa12,
191186*
Tel *490 7710* **Map** 6 E1
W goldtriangle.ru
Elegant hotel with working
fireplaces in some rooms.
Serves hearty breakfast.

Rossi Boutique Hotel $$$
*Naberezhnaya reki Fontanki 55,
191023*
Tel *635 6333* **Map** 6 F2
W rossihotels.com
Charming place with Classical
decor and antique-style furnishing.
River views from most rooms.

Further Afield

Agni Club Hotel $$
Nevskiy prospekt 94/2, 191025
Tel *457 0225*
W agnihotel.ru
In a centrally located 18th-century
building. Comfortable airy rooms.

Helvetia Hotel $$$
Ulitsa Marata 11, 191025
Tel *326 5353*
W helvetiahotel.ru
Superb interior with a blend of
old and new motifs. Pleasant out-
door terrace for summer dining.

Beyond St Petersburg

Hotel Ekaterina $
Sadovaya ulitsa 5a, Pushkin, 196601
Tel *466 8042*
W hotelekaterina.ru
Simple rooms with old-fashioned
furniture in an atmospheric
location within Catherine's Palace.

Luxury
Palace Embankment

Angleterre Hotel $$$
Malaya Morskaya ulitsa 24, 190000
Tel *494 5666* **Map** 6 D2
W hotelangleterre.ru
Stylishly refurbished hotel situated
adjacent to St Isaac's Cathedral.

Key to Price Guide *see page 176*

Renaissance St Petersburg
Baltic Hotel $$$
Pochtamtskaya ulitsa 4, 190000
Tel *380 4000* **Map** 5 C2
W marriott.com
Sumptuous hotel with an intimate
feel, elegantly styled in a subtle
combination of old and new .

Gostinyy Dvor

DK Choice

Kempinski Hotel
Moika 22 $$$
*Naberezhnaya reki Moyki 22,
191186*
Tel *335 9111* **Map** 2 E5
W kempinski.com
Located right opposite the
Palace Square, the Kempinski
offers great views of the
Hermitage from some rooms.
Guests can pamper themselves
with a relaxing Turkish bath or
indulge in international cuisine
at the restaurant that overlooks
St Petersburg.

Sennaya Ploshchad

DK Choice

Alexander House $$$
*Naberezhnaya Kryukova kanala
27, 190068*
Tel *334 3540* **Map** 5 C4
W a-house.ru
Wonderful family guesthouse
run as a boutique hotel, with
each room named after and
decorated in the style of a capital
city. All rooms are comfortably
furnished and most have lovely
views. The common areas have
working fireplaces. Breakfast
can be enjoyed in the rooms.

Opulent interior of the Belmond Grand
Hotel Europe

Ambassador Hotel $$$
*Rimskovo-Korsakova prospekt 5-7,
190068*
Tel *232 8506* **Map** 6 D3
W ambassador-hotel.ru
Splendid hotel with opulent
interiors. The top-floor restaurant
affords fine city views.

Further Afield

Corinthia Hotel $$$
Nevskiy prospekt 57, 191025
Tel *380 2001*
W corinthia.com
Swanky place with three bars.
Popular with visiting celebrities.

Grand Hotel Emerald $$$
Suvorovskiy prospekt 18, 191036
Tel *740 5000*
W grandhotelemerald.com
The Post-Modern exterior of this
hotel hides a Classical interior.
Superb fitness centre with a
sauna, pool and Turkish bath.

Radisson Royal Hotel $$$
Nevskiy prospekt 49/2, 191025
Tel *322 5000*
W radisson.ru
Modern hotel in a historic
building. The rooms as well
as the bar and café overlook
the busy main street.

Beyond St Petersburg

DK Choice

Baltic Star Hotel $$
*Berezovaya alleya 3, Strelna,
198515*
Tel *438 5700*
W balticstar-hotel.ru
Set in the country between
St Petersburg and Peterhof, the
Baltic Star is popular with official
delegations. The interiors of this
modern building are styled histor-
ically. There are 20 cottages for
guests who prefer privacy, as well
as a pool, gym and beauty salon.

Grand Peterhof Spa Hotel $$
*Gofmeysterskaya ulitsa 2, Peterhof,
198510*
Tel *334 8690*
W grandpeterhof.ru
Fantastic spa hotel close to
the historic sights. Rooms are
decorated in Classical style.

President Hotel $$
*Primorskoye shosse 572, Zelenogorsk,
197720*
Tel *433 8682*
W hotel-president.spb.ru
Wonderful place in the woods
with tastefully furnished rooms
and superb spa facilities.

Modern

Vasilevskiy Island

Nashotel $$
11-ya liniya 50, 199178
Tel *323 2231*
🌐 nashotel.ru
Floral themes run through
this brightly decorated hotel.
Exceptionally good service.

Petrogradskaya

Posadskiy Dvor $$
Bolshaya Posadskaya ulitsa 9/5, 197046
Tel *658 0490* **Map** 2 E2
Rooms with basic comforts and
hydro-massage showers. Located
close to top tourist destinations.

Palace Embankment

Admiral Hotel $
Bolshaya Morskaya ulitsa 13, 191186
Tel *315 4502* **Map** 6 D1
🌐 admiralhotels.ru
Pleasant budget hotel in a central
location, offering basic, modern
rooms with en-suite bathrooms.

Amulet Hotel $
Malaya Morskaya ulitsa 7, 191186
Tel *570 1732* **Map** 6 D1
🌐 amulet-hotels.ru
Quiet hotel within walking
distance of the main sights. Simple
rooms with old-style furniture.

Comfort Hotel $$
Bolshaya Morskaya ulitsa 25, 190000
Tel *570 6700* **Map** 6 D2
🌐 comfort-hotel.ru
Wonderfully located at the heart
of the historic centre. Modest
rooms and cheerful service.

Gostinyy Dvor

Korona Guest Centre $$
*Malaya Konyushennaya ulitsa 7,
191186*
Tel *571 0086* **Map** 6 E2
🌐 korona-spb.com
Lovely family-run hotel with
spacious rooms. Offers generous
breakfasts. The staff is helpful.

M-Hotel $$
Sadovaya ulitsa 2, 191023
Tel *448 8383* **Map** 6 F2
🌐 mhotelspb.ru
Nice, large rooms at this simple
hotel. Decent buffet breakfast.

Mini-Hotel Polikoff $$
Nevskiy prospekt 64/11, 191023
Tel *995 3488* **Map** 7 A2
🌐 polikoff.ru
Simple interiors with rooms
overlooking a quiet courtyard.
Situated on the second floor,
but there is no lift.

View of the beautiful Pushka Inn Hotel

Pushka Inn Hotel $$$
Naberezhnaya reki Moyki 14, 191186
Tel *644 7120* **Map** 2 E5
🌐 pushkainn.ru
Housed in a 19th-century
mansion, this delightfully cosy
establishment has immaculate
rooms. Efficient staff.

Sennaya Ploshchad

Hotel Garrah $
Gorokhovaya ulitsa 23, 190000
Tel *571 7845* **Map** 6 D2
🌐 hotel-garrah.ru
Centrally located hotel with big,
cheerfully decorated rooms. It
has good transport links.

> ### DK Choice
>
> **Grand Mark Hotel** $$
> *Galernaya ulitsa 12, 190000*
> **Tel** *570 0536* **Map** 5 C1
> 🌐 grandmarkhotels.com
> Situated in the historic city
> centre within walking distance
> of the main sights, the Grand
> Mark is run by an enthusiastic
> team that ensures their guests
> enjoy a comfortable stay.
> Rooms are small but spotless,
> and include a flat-screen TV.
> Guests are served hearty conti-
> nental breakfasts. Free Wi-Fi.

Happy Pushkin Hotel $$
Galernaya ulitsa 53, 190000
Tel *777 1799* **Map** 5 B2
🌐 happypushkin.com
Compact rooms decorated
in quirky Classical style. Good
breakfast and attentive staff.

Veles Hotel $$
Zastavskaya ulitsa 19, 196084
Tel *334 2525*
Basic mini-hotel offering rooms
with bathtubs as well as family
rooms that include a kitchen.
Friendly and helpful staff. Offers
bike rentals. On-site spa.

Further Afield

Domotelli $
Kolomyazhsky prospekt 15, 197348
Tel *917 5777*
🌐 domotelli.ru
Well-equipped apartments
in various locations, all close
to the Pionerskaya metro.

Hotel Adeliya $
Nevskiy prospekt 82, 191025
Tel *579 9287*
🌐 adeliya.com
Small hotel on a quiet street
with smart rooms. Free Wi-Fi
and private parking.

Cronwell Inn Stremyannaya $$
Stremyannaya ulitsa 18, 191025
Tel *406 0450*
🌐 stremyannaya-hotel.ru
Pristine rooms, fresh bread from
the hotel's bakery and helpful
staff make for a pleasant stay
at this hotel.

Vesta Hotel $$
Nevskiy prospekt 92, 191025
Tel *272 1322*
🌐 vesta-hotel.com
Peaceful central option tucked
away on a quiet street. Great
breakfast and service.

Beyond St Petersburg

Friedental $
*Moskovskoe shosse 10, Pushkin,
196601*
Tel *476 0041*
Small, cosy hotel located in
a residential building close to
the sights. Tempting breakfast.
Parking available.

Home Hostel $
*Zoi Kruglovoy ulitsa 23, Veliky
Novgorod, 173007*
Tel *+7 952 485 6750*
Modest hostel in a local family
home. Characterful dormitory-
styled accommodation with
shared bathrooms.

For more information on types of hotels *see page 173*

WHERE TO EAT AND DRINK

A huge variety of restaurants serving international cuisine line almost every block in the centre of St Petersburg. Most have simple, set menus at lunch and dinner, offering visitors a risk-free opportunity to try out more expensive places. Russian cuisine is still popular, and is available at numerous traditional-style restaurants. Ethnic food from the former Soviet republics and abroad provides an array of vegetarian dishes. Small cafés offer a chance to escape the more garish tourist traps found near some sights. Although getting a plain green salad may still pose a problem, other fresh salads are offered by most restaurants as well as good-quality cafés. For a list of recommended restaurants and cafés, see pp186–93.

The exquisite Art Nouveau interiors of the L'Europe restaurant *(see p190)*

Where to Eat

Restaurants on Nevskiy prospekt tend to be more expensive than those on other streets. A few steps off Nevskiy, however, a variety of eateries line the streets – Bolshaya Konyushennaya, Rubinshteyna, Vladimirskiy prospekt and Ulitsa Vosstaniya – offering something to suit most pockets and tastes. Venture out a little further and the short Ulitsa Belinskogo, for instance, offers at least five highly recommended options.

Types of Restaurant

All large hotels offer good eating opportunities, but hotel restaurants are included in this guide only if they are outstanding or found in places that are short on other options.

Style and fashion can dominate in some restaurants, so the food often suffers and prices can be unreasonably high. Other establishments, however, manage to combine food, decor and service in fine Russian style. Dining trends include "Imperial Russian" amid opulent interiors (Staraya Tamozhnya, see p186), and exotic Caucasian restaurants (Kavkaz-Bar, see p189). Top restaurants serve a mix of European and Russian dishes, with some Asian elements.

The former Soviet republics Georgia and Armenia have left their mark on Russian cuisine. Try Salkhino (see p187) or Lagidze (see p191) for Georgian

Outdoor café in the arcade of Gostinyy Dvor *(see p110)*

food, and Erivan *(see p189)* for Armenian fare. Asian restaurants are numerous, if usually uninspiring; the sushi restaurant Yakitoriya *(see p187)* is a rare exception.

Reading the Menu

Large restaurants and some cafés have menus in English. Any restaurant that accepts credit cards will usually have English-speaking waiters, and, in those places that do not, most waiters try to overcome language difficulties.

Payment and Tipping

All restaurants and cafés show meal prices in roubles. The listings in the guide give an indication of price ranges in roubles as restaurants cannot accept foreign currency by law *(see pp216–17)*. Guests must pay with either cash or a credit card.

Major restaurants accept most credit cards, but it is advisable to check beforehand. Amex and Diners Club cards are almost never accepted. Credit card payment is still limited in Russia, especially in smaller establishments, so it is advisable to carry some cash with you at all times.

Tips are usually 10–15 per cent unless service is already included in the bill. To ensure the waiter receives the tip, it is best to give it in cash, rather than as part of a credit card payment.

Opening Times

Most restaurants in St Petersburg open at noon and stay open until around 11pm or midnight. Increasingly, the more expensive restaurants, and particularly those that are attached to a casino or nightclub *(see pp206–7)*, may stay open well into the early morning hours. Cafés close early, usually around 10pm.

For those who wish to eat after an evening event, many restaurants stay open until the last customer leaves. Many bars, for example Jili-bili *(see p195)*, offer food into the small hours. In addition, if all else fails, the lights of many fast-food outlets, such as Layma *(see p195)*, are often to be found burning after midnight. The city's two 24-hour restaurants are Khochu Kharcho for Georgian cuisine *(see p190)* and Du Nord 1834 for French *(see p191)*.

The beautifully decorated interior of the Russian Room in Demidov *(see p192)*

Street sign for Pirosmani *(see p192)*, located in Petrogradskaya

Making a Reservation

It is always advisable to book ahead, especially during the White Nights *(see p53)* when upmarket restaurants may take bookings weeks in advance. Your hotel concierge can help. Smaller restaurants and cafés do not require reservations, but as they rely on special events such as weddings and birthdays they sometimes close unexpectedly.

Children

Russians are acquiring the habit of taking their children out to dine with them. On the whole, Russians love children, few restaurants will refuse them entry, and staff will often adjust dishes to meet their needs. A number of city eateries, such as Tres Amigos *(see p192)* and Il Patio *(see p195)*, have children's parties and even nannies at weekends.

A cosy room at Botanica is equipped with a play area, books and a TV. Some places advertised to foreigners – but none in this guide – have "entertainment" that is not suitable for children.

Live Music

Most restaurants and cafés have some kind of music on Fridays or Saturdays – DJs or live acts. The listings that follow on pages 186 to 193 note those which have live music on other days as well.

Vegetarians

Traditional Russian food is meat-oriented, but an increasing number of eateries aimed at a more Westernized crowd, such as Krokodil *(see p190)*, include vegetarian options, and Georgian and Armenian cuisines offer a wide range of vegetable and bean dishes. There are several vegetarian dining options in St Petersburg – Rada & K *(see p189)* and Ukrop *(see p191)* are the best.

Smoking

As in the rest of Europe, Russian law forbids smoking in any public space, including bars and restaurants. However, several restaurants allow smoking on terraces or have separate non-smoking areas. In Russia, patrons, as well as business owners, can be fined by the police for breaking the law.

Dress Code

Formal dress is de rigueur only in large and fashionable restaurants, but guests should always be neatly and cleanly dressed. Trainers and tracksuits are acceptable in the less expensive cafés.

Disabled Access

Only a few restaurants have ramps or no stairs at all, but waiters and doormen are used to visitors in wheelchairs and are usually very helpful.

Cafés and bars prove more problematic, with stairs and narrow doors, and certainly no toilets for the disabled. Disabled travellers may find themselves confined to hotel dining or the more expensive eateries and bars.

Recommended Restaurants

The restaurants listed in this guide have been selected for their atmosphere, quality and good value. Establishments range from simple to lavish and cater to different tastes, from traditional, home-cooked recipes to gourmet cuisine. They are listed by area and then by price, with map references and an indication of the main type of cuisine offered.

DK Choice restaurants stand out from the crowd, whether it is for outstanding service, stunning views, intimate atmosphere or renowned chefs. These special places are highly recommended by both local and visiting diners.

WEBSITES

W **tripadvisor.com** is a great source of regularly updated restaurant reviews. Most restaurants have websites, but many are in Russian only, or are poorly maintained. Many places appear on the St Petersburg restaurant site, which has an English-language version at:
W **restoran.ru**

For Russian-speakers, there are now many listings and reviews online. Try: **W** **allcafe.info** and **W** **menu.ru**

The Flavours of St Petersburg

Russia's culinary reputation centres on warming stews, full of wintery vegetables such as cabbage, beetroot and potatoes. Yet St Petersburg was once the capital of a vast empire stretching from Poland to the Pacific and this is reflected in the variety of food on offer there. Aubergine (eggplant) and tomatoes, from the Caucasus in the south, bring in the flavours of the Mediterranean, while spices from Central Asia lend an exotic touch. On the stalls of the city's Kuznechniy Market, caviar and crayfish sit alongside honey from Siberia and melons and peaches from Georgia.

Wild Mushrooms

Caviar, the roe of sturgeon from Russia's warm southern waters

Russian Countryside

Many St Petersburgers have small country houses within easy reach of the city, and spend weekends from spring to early winter tending their immaculate vegetable gardens, or combing the countryside for wild berries and mushrooms. Much of this bountiful harvest is made into preserves and pickles. There is a refreshing soup, *solianka*, in which pickled cucumbers impart an unusual salty taste. Pickled mushrooms in sour cream make a regular appearance on restaurant menus, as do a variety of fresh berry juices.

In a country where food shortages are a fairly recent memory, very little is wasted. *Kvas*, a popular, mildly alcoholic drink is frequently made at home by fermenting stale bread with sugar and a scattering of fruit. Summer visitors should make a point of trying the seasonal cold soup *okroshka*, which is based on *kvas*.

Russia is also a land with hundreds of rivers and lakes, and has a long tradition of fish cookery. Dishes range from simple soups, such as *ukha*, to caviar and sturgeon, and salmon cooked in a bewildering variety of ways.

Pickled mushrooms Spiced cheese Rye bread Gherkins
Blinis
Salted fish Soured cream Pickled herring
A typical spread of *zakuski* (cold appertizers)

Local Dishes and Specialities

Borsch (beetroot soup) and *blinis* (buttery pancakes) with caviar are perhaps two of the most famous Russian dishes – one a peasant dish which varies with the availability of ingredients and the other a staple for the week leading up to Lent, when rich food would be eaten to fatten up before the fast. Much of Russia's cuisine is designed to make use of what is readily to hand or is warming and filling. A popular main course is *kulebiaka*, a hearty fish pie, larded with eggs, rice, dill and onion and encased in a buttery crust. Another is beef stroganoff with its creamy mushroom sauce, created in 18th-century St Petersburg by the chef of the wealthy Stroganoff family.

Beetroot

Borsch Made with meat or vegetable stock, this beetroot soup is usually served with dill and soured cream.

Market vegetable stall in St Petersburg

The Caucasus

The former Soviet states of the Caucasus – Georgia, Azerbaijan and Armenia – are renowned for their legendary banquets, where the tables are laden with an enormous quantity and variety of food and drink. They still supply Russia's cities with a tempting range of fine subtropical produce. Limes, lemons, oranges, walnuts, figs, pomegranates, peaches, beans, salty cheeses and herbs are all shipped in season to St Petersburg's markets and its many Georgian restaurants. The cuisine of Georgia, with its focus on freshly grilled meats, pulses, vegetables, yogurt, herbs and nut sauces – including the hallmark walnut sauce, *satsivi* – is famously healthy and makes a delicious, unusual-tasting treat.

Central Asia

From the Central Asian republics of the old Soviet Union come a range of culinary traditions based on the nomadic lifestyles of Russia's one-time overlords,

Freshly picked lingonberries from Russia's bumper autumn harvest

the Mongol or Tartar Hordes. The meat of fat-tailed sheep, which thrive in the dry desert air, is used to make communal piles of *plov* (pilaf) around which guests sit, eating in the traditional manner with their hands.

Served in St Petersburg's Uzbek restaurants, it shares the menu with warm flat breads, spicy noodle soups, *manti* (tasty dumplings reminiscent of Chinese cuisine) and a variety of melons and grapes, which proliferate in the desert oases, and apricots and nuts, grown in the mountains.

ZAKUSKI

A traditional Russian meal generally begins with *zakuski*, a selection of cold appetizers. These may include pickled mushrooms (*gribi*), gherkins (*ogurtsi*), salted herrings (*seliodka*), an assortment of smoked fish, *blinis* topped with caviar, various vegetable pâtés (sometimes known as vegetable caviars), stuffed eggs (*yaitsa farshirovanniye*), spiced cheese (*brinza*), beetroot salad (*salat iz svyokly*) and small meat pies (*pirozhki*), accompanied by fried rye bread and washed down with shots of vodka. A bowl of steaming soup often follows, before the main course reaches the table.

Kulebiaka Rich, buttery puff pastry is wrapped around a mix of fish, hard-boiled eggs, rice, onion and chopped dill.

Pelmeni These meat-stuffed dumplings may be served in a clear broth, or with tomato sauce or soured cream.

Kissel A mix of red berries is used to make this soft, fruity jelly, which is served topped with a swirl of fresh cream.

What to Drink in St Petersburg

Russian vodka is famous throughout the world and the Russian Standard distillery in St Petersburg is Russia's second largest distillery, the largest being in Moscow. Vodka first appeared in Russia sometime in the 14th or 15th century. Peter the Great *(see p20)* was particularly fond of anise- or pepper-flavoured vodkas and devised modifications to the distillation process which greatly improved the quality of the finished drink.

Tea is Russia's other national drink. Traditionally made using a samovar and served black, tea has been popular in Russia since the end of the 18th century, when it was first imported from China.

A 19th-century Russian peasant family drinking vodka and tea

Clear Vodka

Vodka is produced from grain, usually wheat, although some rye is also used in Russia. Local vodkas dominate in St Petersburg, the best of which are Diplomat, Five Star and Russian Standard. Moscow's Kristall company, which produces Kristall and Gzhelka vodka, is increasingly popular, while Flagman distillery proudly proclaims that it is the official purveyor of vodka to the Kremlin. The range of vodkas available these days is overwhelming. There is one golden rule: if it is under $7 or $8 for half a litre, do not drink it.

Kubanskaya

Vodka is always served with food, often with a range of richly flavoured accompaniments called *zakuski (see p183)*, particularly black bread, pickled cucumbers and herring. Vodka is not always served ice cold, but it should be chilled.

Putinka   Russian Standard   Stolichnaya

Flavoured Vodka

The practice of flavouring vodka has entirely practical origins. When vodka was first produced commercially in the Middle Ages, the techniques and equipment were so primitive that it was impossible to remove all the impurities. This left unpleasant aromas and flavours, which were disguised by adding honey together with aromatic oils and spices. As distillation techniques improved, flavoured vodkas became a speciality in their own right. Limonnaya, its taste deriving from lemon zest, is one of the most traditional, as is Pertsovka, flavoured with red chilli pepper pods. Klukvennaya (cranberry) and Oblepikha (sea buckthorn, an orange Siberian berry) are also favourites. Some of the best flavoured vodkas are made at home by soaking peach stones or whole berries in alcohol for months.

Pepper vodka

Limonnaya

Klukvennaya

Oblepikha

Major Wine Regions

- Wine-growing region
- Moldova
- Ukraine
- Russia
- Georgia
- Armenia
- Azerbaijan
- — International boundaries

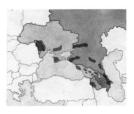

White and red Georgian wine   Shampanskoe

Wine

The Soviet Union was one of the world's largest producers of wine (*vino*), but many of the major wine regions are now republics in their own right. Several indigenous types of grape are cultivated in the different regions, along with many of the more familiar international varieties.

Georgia is considered the best wine-making area. Its wines include those made from the Rkatsiteli grape, characterized by a floral aroma and subtle, fruity flavour, and the Gurdzhaani, which gives a unique, slightly bitter touch. Among its best red wines is the smooth Mukuzani. Moldova produces white, sparkling wines in the south and central regions, while the south is also known for its red wines. Since 1799, Moldova also produces a sweet, champagne-like wine called Shampanskoe.

Other Alcoholic Drinks

Brandy (*konyak*) was originally a by-product of wine-making and commercial production only began in Russia in the 19th century. Armenian brandy is one of the finest, with a distinctive vanilla fragrance resulting from its ageing in 70–100-year-old oak barrels. Georgia and Daghestan also produce good brandies. St Petersburg beer (*pivo*) is among the best in Russia. Baltika, Vena and Stepan Razin make a full range of beers in bottles and on draught. In addition, Tver beers such as Afanasy are well worth trying. Various imported beers are also available.

Baltika Beer   Armenian brandy

Mineral water   Kvas   Cranberry juice

Other Drinks

Kvas is a lightly fermented drink made from rye and barley, consumed by adults and children alike. Russia's vast range of mineral waters (*mineralnaya voda*) includes many with unusually high mineral contents. Mineral waters from the Caucasus are particularly prized. Also widely available are fruit juices (*sok, mors* or *kompot*), including cranberry (*klyukva*). Look out for traditional Russian *sbiten*, made from honey and herbs.

Tea

Russian tea is served black with a slice of lemon and may be drunk from tall glasses or cups. Sweetened with jam or sugar, tea (*chay*) is an ideal accompaniment to rich cakes and pastries. The boiling water for tea traditionally comes from a samovar. The water is used to brew a pot of tea, from which a little is poured into a cup and is then diluted with more hot water.

A glass of tea, with jam (*varenye*) to sweeten it

The Samovar

Made from brass or copper and heated by coals in the central chimney, samovars traditionally provided boiling water for a wide variety of domestic purposes and were an essential wedding gift. Modern electric ones are made of stainless steel and are used mainly for boiling water to make tea. The word samovar comes from *samo* meaning "itself" and *varit* meaning "to boil".

Where to Eat and Drink

Vasilevskiy Island

Fruktovaya Lavka $
Café   **Map** 1 A5
6-ya liniya 23, Vasilevskiy ostrov
Tel 335 4848
Originally a chain of fresh fruit
and vegetables stores, it is now
a string of cafés serving food
made with fresh produce.
Vegetarians have a variety
of soups and salads to choose
from. Plenty of meat dishes too.

Grad Petrov $
German   **Map** 1 C5
*Universitetskaya naberezhnaya 5,
199034*
Tel 326 0137
Cheerful German *kneipe* (pub)
that serves great beer brewed
in the classic style and hearty
German dishes. Try the *Ein Meter
Thüringer* (one-metre sausage
with red cabbage).

Ketino $
Georgian   **Map** 1 A5
8-ya liniya 23, 199004
Tel 326 0196
Excellent restaurant where guests
can sample well-prepared authentic Georgian delicacies. Vegetarian
options are available. Wine can
be expensive. Friendly ambience.

Kneipe Jager Haus $
German
Sredniy pr 64, Vasilevskiy ostrov
Tel 321 3376
Modelled after a traditional
German *kneipe*, this establishment
has the atmosphere of a beer
restaurant in Munich. There
is a great choice of sausages
and international beer on offer.

Punkt Pitaniya $
International   **Map** 1 B5
Bolshoy prospekt 5, 199004
Tel 329 9550
Simple, cheerful place run
by a friendly young team that

guarantees a warm welcome.
Offers generous portions and
excellent desserts.

Casa del Myaso $$
International   **Map** 1 C5
Birzhevoy proezd 6, 199034
Tel 320 9746
Literally translated as the "House
of Meat", this atmospheric basement restaurant, with stylishly
designed vaulted brick ceilings,
has an extensive variety of meat
dishes on offer. There is also
a salad bar with cold snacks.

Maria Karlotta $$
International   **Map** 5 B1
*Universitetskaya naberezhnaya
21, 199034*
Tel 320 2120
Located in a restored palace
that is now a hotel, this elegant
restaurant is named after the
wife of the first architect of
St Petersburg. It boasts an
extensive wine list and excellent
service. The kitchen specializes
in European and Russian cuisine.

Restoran $$
Russian   **Map** 1 C4
Tamozhennyy pereulok 2, 199034
Tel 327 8979
Buff-coloured walls and
wooden tables serve as the
perfect setting for a selection
of flavoured home-made
vodkas and superb game
dishes. The menu features
various Russian classics as well.

Dans le Noir? $$$
International   **Map** 1 B4
Birzhevoy pereulok 4, 199004
Tel 335 2212   **Closed** Mon
Intriguing concept-restaurant
where diners eat in total
darkness. They are guided
and served by blind waiters.
After the meal they can see
pictures of the menu and
find out what they ate.

> **Price Guide**
> The price ranges are for a three-course
> meal for one, including a glass of house
> wine and all unavoidable charges.
>
> | $ | under 1,500R |
> | $$ | 1,500 to 3,000R |
> | $$$ | over 3,000R |

DK Choice

Russian Kitsch $$$
Fusion   **Map** 5 B1
*Universitetskaya naberezhnaya
25, 199034*
Tel 325 1122
A slightly ironic, grand venue
with luxurious trappings from
the period of *perestroika* –
painted ceilings, green marble
and gilt. The food consists of
a mix of caviar and sushi rather
than *pelmeni* and cabbage, but
the popular dance floor is very
Russian. Glass galleries give
views across the Neva.

Staraya Tamozhnya $$$
French   **Map** 1 C5
Tamozhennyy pereulok 1, 199034
Tel 327 8980
Superb place with a general air
of bonhomie. There is a strong
French orientation in its wines
and menu. Serves plenty of meat.

Petrogradskaya

ChiliPizza $
Pizzeria   **Map** 1 C4
Dobrolubova prospekt 8, 197198
Tel 244 5544
Upbeat and reliable restaurant
with a modern interior. Offers
an extensive selection of
appetizing pizza varieties.
Quick and efficient service.

Gornyy Oryol $
International   **Map** 1 C3
Aleksandrovskiy Park 1A
Tel 232 3282
This eatery resembles a fairy-tale
castle with columns, narrow win-
dows, sculptures and fountains.
Specializing in Georgian cuisine,
the menu also boasts Russian and
European dishes. Popular with
wedding parties. Book ahead.

Kommunalka Art-Cafe $
Russian   **Map** 1 C3
Kronverkskiy prospekt 65, 197198
Tel 232 7689
Soviet-themed place decorated
with wacky murals and retro relics.
The menu features hearty portions
of Russian dishes. Local bands
play most weekend evenings.

The interesting decor at the Russian Kitsch, located on Vasilevskiy Island

View of the regal setting at Tandoor

Pryanosti & Radosti $
International   Map 2 E2
Malaya Posadskaya ulitsa 3
Tel *333 4633*
One of the only places in
the city that serves breakfast
24 hours a day, this chic eatery
is appropriate for a romantic
evening or a family meal. Also
popular for its European and
Georgian cuisine.

Yakitoriya $
Japanese   Map 2 F3
Petrovskaya naberezhnaya 4, 197046
Tel *970 4858*
Favourably located near the Peter
and Paul Fortress, Yakitoriya
is part of a vast Russian chain
of Japanese restaurants in the
city. Serves a consistently high
standard of sushi.

Chin Chin Cafe $$
Asian   Map 1 C4
Mytninskaya naberezhnaya 3, 197198
Tel *232 1042*
Offers comfortable armchair
seating in a tastefully styled
interior and imaginative Asian
fusion cuisine. There is a wide
selection of wines and cocktails.

Demyanova Ukha $$
Seafood   Map 1 C3
Kronverkskiy prospekt 53, 197198
Tel *232 8090*
The city's first specialist fish
restaurant retains its premier
position over the competition
by dint of sheer hard work
along with unpretentious,
traditional cooking.

Dozari Bar $$
International   Map 1 C4
Prospekt Dobrolyubova 14a, 197198
Tel *928 6070*
This barge with panoramic
vistas serves classically inspired
Russian and continental cuisine.
It is also a venue for late-night
revelry with live music, karaoke,
an extensive cocktail menu
and bar snacks.

Mozzarella Bar $$
Fusion   Map 1 B3
Bolshoy prospekt 13/4, 196128
Tel *235 3521*
Attracts the hip, young and
casual crowd for its unusual
fusion of Italian and Japanese food
that has something for everyone.
Friendly and efficient staff.

Na Zdorovie! $$
Russian   Map 1 B3
Bolshoy prospekt 13/4, 196128
Tel *232 4039*
Brightly decorated in traditional
Russian style, this is a great
spot to get a taste of the
country's favourite dishes
and drinks. The accompanying
gypsy music makes dining
a pleasant experience.

DK Choice

Salkhino $$
Georgian   Map 2 D2
*Kronverkskiy prospekt 25,
197101*
Tel *232 7891*
This sister restaurant to Ketino
on Vasilevskiy Island offers
generous home cooking by
two Georgian women who
know how to tempt. Their
khachapuri (cheese-filled bread)
is arguably the best in town.
Try the aubergine (eggplant)
stuffed with walnuts. They also
prepare an extensive range
of meat dishes and mouth-
watering home-made desserts.

Tbiliso $$
Georgian   Map 2 D2
Sytninskaya ulitsa 10, 197101
Tel *232 9391*
Highly rated Georgian restaurant
with an authentic menu that
includes such dishes as chicken
seasoned with the delectable
walnut sauce, *satsivi*, and
mamalyga (ground corn
with salted cheese). Waiters
are traditionally dressed.

Volna $$
Fusion   Map 2 F3
Petrovskaya naberezhnaya 4, 197046
Tel *322 5383*
Japanese-style minimalist
eatery serving appealing Asian
fusion cuisine that uses organic
ingredients wherever possible.
Excellent international wines.

Wishes $$
Russian   Map 1 B3
Prospekt Dobrolubova 23, 197198
Tel *232 9883*
Designed to resemble the
interior of a *dacha*, this homely
restaurant prepares lovely
standard Russian dishes such as
sweet and savoury dumplings.

Flying Dutchman $$$
International   Map 1 C4
Mytninskaya naberezhnaya 6, 197198
Tel *336 3737*
The three restaurants on board
this atmospheric replica of the
Flying Dutchman ship have splen-
did views across the Neva to the
Winter Palace. Japanese, Italian
and Russian cuisine.

Korushka $$$
International   Map 2 E3
*Zayachij Ostrov, Petropavlovskaya
Krepost 3, 197046*
Tel *917 9010*
Exquisite dishes served in tranquil
surroundings with great views
across the Neva. Russian and inter-
national fare, along with grilled fish.

Palace Embankment

Bushe $
Café   Map 6 D1
Malaya Morskaya ulitsa 7, 191186
Tel *315 5371*
Tremendously popular café chain
serving delicious freshly baked
breads and pastries as well as light
meals, sandwiches and desserts.

Clean Plates Society $
International   Map 6 D2
Gorokhovaya ulitsa 13, 190000
Tel *934 9764*
Cosy eatery popular for its eclectic
menu. The burgers stand out,
as also the home-made Russian
favourites and Central Asian dishes.
Don't miss the unique hot and
cold non-alcoholic berry drinks.

King Pong $
Asian   Map 5 D1
Bolshaya Morskaya ulitsa 16, 191186
Tel *315 8256*
Spacious laid-back spot with a
broad range of flavourful and
well-prepared dishes from all
across southeast Asia. Has
a separate children's menu.

For more information on types of restaurants *see pages 180–81*

The beautiful dining area in Gosti restaurant, located on the Fontanka River

Tandoor $
Indian **Map** 6 D1
Admiralteyskiy prospekt 10, 190000
Tel *312 3886*
Well-established Indian restaurant with atmospheric interior. Offers generous portions of signature Indian recipes and consistently high standards of service. Vegetarian options available.

Teplo $
Italian **Map** 5 C2
Bolshaya Morskaya ulitsa 45, 190000
Tel *570 1974*
Enormously popular place with a warm homely ambience. Serves faultless Italian dishes as well as some Russian favourites. Advance booking recommended.

Da Albertone $$
Italian **Map** 2 E5
Millionnaya ulitsa 23, 191186
Tel *915 5501*
Conveniently close to the Hermitage, this simple Italian restaurant has some lovely pizzas and consistently good service. Well-equipped children's room.

Gastronom $$
International **Map** 2 F5
Naberezhnaya reki Moyki 1/7, 191186
Tel *314 3849*
Fashionable eatery serving Italian, Russian and Japanese cuisine. It features covered outdoor seating and a stylish interior with vaulted ceilings and comfortable sofas.

Gogol $$
International **Map** 6 D1
Malaya Morskaya ulitsa 8, 191186
Tel *312 6097*
Wonderful 19th century Russian-style decor and welcoming surroundings. Home-made bread and vodka accompany excellent dishes such as rabbit stew and venison with apple sauce.

Gosti $$
Italian/Serbian **Map** 6 D1
Malaya Morskaya ulitsa 13, 191186
Tel *312 5820*
Casual and cosy place offering Italian classics alongside Serbian specialities. Spread over several floors, it has a separate play area for children.

Literaturnoye Café $$
Russian **Map** 6 E1
Nevskiy prospekt 18, 191186
Tel *312 6057*
Historic restaurant from where the idolized Russian poet Alexander Pushkin set off for his fatal duel. Serves traditional, rather heavy recipes.

NEP $$
Russian **Map** 2 E5
Naberezhnaya reki Moyki 37, 191186
Tel *571 7591*
Worth visiting for the nightly cabaret show alone, the NEP is a great place for delicious Russian fare. The decor and the food reflect the classic charm of 1920s Russia.

Olivie $$
Caucasian **Map** 6 D1
Admiralteyskiy prospekt 8, 190000
Tel *925 7714*
Georgian, Armenian and Russian cuisine in a relaxed environment with polite and attentive service. A good venue to try classics such as beef stroganoff.

Borsalino $$$
Italian **Map** 6 D2
Angleterre Hotel, Malaya Morskaya ulitsa 24, 190000
Tel *494 5666*
The restaurant is housed inside the historic Angleterre Hotel that overlooks St Isaac's Cathedral. Authentic and high-quality food.

Canvas $$$
International **Map** 5 C2
Renaissance St Petersburg Baltic Hotel, Pochtamtskaya ulitsa 4, 190000
Tel *380 4000*
Canvas has great city views from its sixth-floor position and focuses on superior-quality food and service. Offers fine, traditional Russian and European cuisine.

Receptoria $$$
French/Italian **Map** 6 D1
Admiralteyskiy prospekt 10, 190000
Tel *312 7967*
Small portions of exquisitely presented French and Italian cuisine in a characterful place with immaculate classic interiors.

Gostinyy Dvor

Iz pechi $
Café **Map** 6 F1
Italyanskaya ulitsa 10/5, 191011
Tel *918 0118*
Popular basement café-bakery serving healthy and delicious traditional Russian pastries and light lunches. Excellent service.

Jack & Chan $
Fusion **Map** 6 F1
Inzhenernaya ulitsa 7, 191011
Tel *982 0535*
This relaxed eatery with mis-matched furniture and a shipping container entrance offers casual dining. Try the prawn and avocado salad with glass noodles.

Kvartirka $
Russian **Map** 7 A2
Nevskiy prospekt 51, 191025
Tel *315 5561*
Fun, Soviet-era themed café with hearty portions of traditional Russian food. Even the service is mock Soviet style, carrying the theme throughout.

Mama Roma $
Italian **Map** 7 A1
Karavannaya ulitsa 3/35, 191011
Tel *314 0347*
Part of a well-run chain of authentic Italian restaurants offering consistently high standards of food. The interior is light and airy. Features a salad bar and business lunch options.

Pelmeniya $
International **Map** 7 A1
Nab reki Fontanki 25, 191011
Tel *415 4185*
Named after Russia's ubiquitous dumpling dish, this fun buffet-style eatery serves dumplings from around the world. Polish, Chinese, Japanese, Georgian and Mongolian versions on the menu.

Pirogovy Dvorik $
Café **Map** 6 E2
Naberezhnaya kanala Griboedova 22/5, 191011
Tel *310 0160*
Bustling café-bakery chain with a wonderful selection of freshly made Russian pastries as well as soups, sandwiches, light meals and desserts.

Rada & K $
Vegetarian **Map** 6 F3
Gorokhovaya ulitsa 36, 191023
Tel *385 1226*
Intimate vegetarian restaurant that attracts a hip young crowd. Serves healthy Indian dishes along with meatless versions of Russian staples such beef stroganoff and *borsch*.

Yat $
International **Map** 2 E5
Naberezhnaya reki Moyki 16, 191186
Tel *+7 921 957 0023*
Homely eatery with friendly staff, kids' play area and a limited menu of wholesome food options to choose from – the artichokes stuffed with almonds are excellent.

Aragvi $$
Georgian **Map** 2 F5
Nab reki Fontanki 9, 191011
Tel *570 5643*
Aragvi features light, elegant interiors and large windows overlooking the Fontanka river. Serves authentic Georgian cuisine, which includes *satsivi* and *khachapuri*.

Brasserie de Metropol $$
International **Map** 6 F2
Sadovaya ulitsa 22/2, 191911
Tel *571 8888*
Elegant place with a spacious classic interior and snug rooms perfect for sampling the home-brewed beer. Broad selection of Russian and international cuisine.

Erivan $$
Armenian **Map** 6 F2
Naberezhnaya reki Fontanki 51, 191011
Tel *703 3820*
Welcoming place, comfortably furnished in Armenian style. Traditional recipes with lots of mutton and veal as well as rarities like brains in olive oil. Vegetarian options available.

Fartuk $$
International **Map** 7 A2
Ulitsa Rubinshteyna 15–17, 191025
Tel *764 5256*
Popular with locals and tourists alike for its relaxed outdoor dining, European-influenced food and home-made lemonade. Book in advance.

Fiolet $$
Fusion **Map** 6 F2
Rossi Boutique Hotel, Naberezhnaya reki Fontanki 55, 191023
Tel *635 6333*
Smart hotel-restaurant that serves an impressive range of remarkably good Asian fusion dishes. The interior blends Classical and contemporary designs. Outdoor terrace for summer dining.

Jamie's Italian $$
Italian **Map** 2 E5
Konyushennaya ploshchad 2, 191186
Tel *600 2570*
Part of Jamie Oliver's empire of Italian eateries around the globe, this restaurant offers the TV chef's no-fuss take on classic Italian food. The service is top-notch.

Kavkaz-Bar $$
Caucasian **Map** 7 A1
Karavannaya ulitsa 18, 191011
Tel *312 1665*
Georgian and Armenian cuisine accompanied by excellent wines and brandies. Some of the best vegetarian kebabs in town can be had here. Superb location and intimate atmosphere.

Kilikia $$
Armenian **Map** 6 E2
Naberezhnaya kanala Griboedova 40, 191023
Tel *327 2208*
Welcoming Armenian restaurant with vaulted brick ceilings and a handy picture menu to guide diners. Pleasing Armenian recipes and attentive service.

Park Giuseppe $$
Italian **Map** 2 F5
Naberezhnaya kanala Griboedova 2b, 191011
Tel *571 7309*
Delightful spot with summer terrace and lovely views across the Moyka. Serves savoury pizzas baked in a wood-burning oven.

Suliko $$
Georgian **Map** 6 E2
Kazanskaya ulitsa 6, 191186
Tel *314 7373*
Central Georgian restaurant tucked away behind the Kazan Cathedral. Frequented by local Georgians, who come to enjoy the hearty traditional fare.

Bellevue Brasserie $$$
International **Map** 2 E5
Kempinski Hotel Moika 22, Naberezhnaya reki Moyki 22, 191186
Tel *335 9111*
On the ninth floor of the hotel, offers fantastic views of Palace Square and the Winter Palace. Excellent modern European menu.

Caviar Bar and Restaurant $$$
Russian **Map** 6 F1
Belmond Grand Hotel Europe, Mikhaylovskaya ulitsa 1/7, 191186
Tel *329 6000*
The city's only caviar restaurant is tiny and showcases the most elegant and varied ways of serving caviar and fish. Try caviar on a delicate *blini* or one of the special Russian regional dishes.

The stylish Caviar Bar, located in the Belmond Grand Hotel Europe

For more information on types of restaurants *see pages 180–81*

DK Choice

L'Europe $$$
International **Map** 6 F1
Belmond Grand Hotel Europe,
Mikhaylovskaya ulitsa 1/7, 191186
Tel *329 6000*
This Art-Nouveau hall with
elegant stained-glass ceiling
is not a re-creation of the city's
glorious past, but the real thing,
beautifully restored. The food
is first-class European. Regular
celebrations of Russian cuisine
and culture include Tchaikovsky
ballet shows on Friday evenings
and vodka tastings.

The impressive hall of L'Europe restaurant

Meat Head $$$
International **Map** 2 E5
Konyushennaya ploshchad 2, 191186
Tel *923 0044*
Plenty of meat on the menu,
including the superb New Zealand
lamb steak. The exposed-brick
ceiling adds character to the place.

DK Choice

Tsar $$$
Russian **Map** 2 F1
Sadovaya ulitsa 12, 191011
Tel *640 1900*
Housed within a former palace,
Tsar occupies a suite of pains-
takingly restored rooms that
offer a sumptuous setting for the
enjoyment of first-rate Russian
classics. Every detail, down to
the cut-crystal glassware and
portraits of Russian nobility,
exudes opulent indulgence.
The service is suitably subdued.

Sennaya Ploshchad

DK Choice

Krokodil $
International **Map** 5 B2
Galernaya ulitsa 18, 190000
Tel *314 9437*
Small and intimate, this
enduringly popular bar and
restaurant has a broad selection
of tempting international dishes
and excellent fish options that
include pike cutlets and salmon
steak. There is a separate no-
smoking dining room.

Senoval $
Café **Map** 5 C3
Ulitsa Dekabristov 13, 190000
Tel *314 6932*
Buzzing underground café-
restaurant frequented by a lively
young crowd attracted to its low

prices and generous servings.
Standard Russian fare on the
platter. Friendly and cheerful staff.

Zig Zag $
American **Map** 6 F3
Gorokhovaya ulitsa 59
Tel *314 3400*
This fun spot resembles a
1950s American diner and
serves food to match, including
a Cobb Salad. The cocktail menu
is full of surprises. Features live
music often.

Arcobaleno $$$
Fusion **Map** 5 C2
Domina Prestige Hotel St Petersburg,
Bolshaya Morskaya ulitsa 54, 190000
Tel *385 1292*
This vibrant, modern hotel-
restaurant offers excellent
Italian fusion cuisine. The bright-
hued interior justifies the name,
which means rainbow in Italian.

Conchita Bonita $$
Mexican **Map** 6 E2
Gorokhovaya ulitsa 39, 190031
Tel *570 6050*
High-energy Mexican bar and
restaurant with phenomenal
cocktails and a reasonable
range of spicy Latin American
specialities such as *taquitos*
and *fajitas*. Decent service.

The elegant Tsar restaurant, located in
a former palace

Entree $$
French **Map** 5 C4
Nikolskaya ploshchad 6, 190068
Tel *572 5201*
This bistro serves beef, duck
and salmon *carpaccio* as well as
a variety of traditional dishes. Visit
the separate café/patisserie to
sample their delicious pastries.

DK Choice

Mindal Café $$
Georgian **Map** 5 B2
Angliyskaya naberezhnaya 26,
190000
Tel *312 3238*
Housed in a stunning historic
mansion with a summer terrace
and glorious views over the
Neva, Mindal Café is the
perfect place to sample
Georgia's exemplary cuisine.
Diners can expect personal
attention and cooking demon-
strations from the well-known
head chef Marina Naumova.

Salhino $$
Georgian **Map** 5 C4
Voznesenskiy prospekt 55, 190068
Tel *314 8682*
Lovely place that is very popular
with locals. It is renowned for
its *chebureks* – deep-fried meat
pastries with a thin, crispy crust.
Children's menu available.

Khochu Kharcho $$
Georgian **Map** 6 D3
Sadovaya ulitsa 39/41, 190031
Tel *310 3236*
One of the city's few 24-hour
restaurants, serves a great range
of delectable Georgian favourites
including *kharcho* – the tradi-
tional Georgian meat soup.

1913 $$$
Caucasian **Map** 5 C2
Voznesenskiy prospekt 13/2, 190000
Tel *315 5148*
The intriguingly named 1913 is
the place for generous portions

of outstanding regional dishes such as *draniki* with bacon and sorrel soup, as well as lobster fricassee.

Romeo's Bar & Kitchen $$$
Italian   **Map** 5 B4
Prospekt Rimskovo-Korsakova 43, 190068
Tel *572 5448*
One of the top Italian restaurants of the city, conveniently close to the Mariinskiy Theatre. The many tempting choices include squid ink ravioli and asparagus with fried eggs.

Russian Vodka Room No. 1 $$$
Russian   **Map** 5 B2
Konnogvardeyskiy bulvar 4, 190000
Tel *570 6420*
Old-world style dining room with modern interpretations of Russian classics. More than 100 different varieties of vodkas feature in the menu. The restaurant also houses a museum of Russian vodka.

Further Afield

Du Nord 1834 $
French
Ligovskiy prospekt 41/83, 191040
Tel *578 1245*
This charming French café is one of the few 24-hour eateries in St Petersburg. It has an appetizing selection of pastries and also serves classic French dishes.

Lagidze $
Georgian
Ulitsa Belinskovo 3, 191014
Tel *579 1104*
Located on one of the city's shortest and best restaurant-lined streets, Lagidze provides Georgian food and wine in a modest but modern interior.

Pelmennaya Dyuzhina $
Russian
Ligovskiy prospekt 30a, 191040
Tel *318 0017*
Part of a successful chain of *pelmini* eateries in town, offering a mind-boggling array of one of Russia's best-known dishes – stuffed dumplings. The wooden furniture adds to the warm ambience.

Schelkunchik $
International
Ligovskiy prospekt 10/118, 191036
Tel *717 6868*
Simple canteen-style eatery with its own micro-brewery. Serves a reliable choice of delectable Russian and international dishes.

Sunduk $
Café
Furshtatskaya ulitsa 42, 191123
Tel *272 3100*
Offbeat art café that boasts an extensive wine list and a filling Russian and European menu. Good live jazz performances keep the atmosphere lively.

Ukrop $
Vegetarian
Ulitsa Marata 23, 191025
Tel *946 3036*
Superb café-restaurant with bright raw-wood interior and an imaginative range of artfully presented vegetarian and vegan fare.

Baklazhan $$
Asian
Ligovskiy prospekt 30a, 191040
Tel *677 7372*
Relaxed, Georgian-inspired restaurant with expertly prepared renditions of Asian classics at reasonable prices. Home-made noodles and baked goods come highly recommended.

Caffe Italia $$
Italian
Prospekt Bakunina 5, 191024
Tel *905 6474*
Expect bona fide Italian cuisine at this popular spot that even has some real Italians on its staff for added authenticity. Spacious interior and cheerful ambience.

Cat Café $$
Caucasian
Stremyannaya ulitsa 22/3, 191025
Tel *571 3377*
Intimate place adorned with cat-related paraphernalia that serves lovely Armenian and Georgian cuisine. Off the beaten track, but well worth a visit.

Claret Café $$
Russian
Helvetia Hotel, Ulitsa Marata 11, 191025
Tel *710 6546*
Delightful small restaurant with chic styling, an open fire and excellent service. Classic Russian fare complemented by a good range of wines.

Karl and Friedrich $$
International
Yuzhnaya doroga 15, Krestovskiy ostrov, 197110
Tel *320 7978*
Fun restaurant-brewery in the woods with outdoor seating. Aimed at families – has a children's entertainer every evening and weekend. Meat-dominated menu and great beer.

Marcelli's $$
Italian
Ulitsa Vosstaniya 15, 191036
Tel *986 9111*
Italian restaurant/café and deli with casual, spacious interior. Founded on a philosophy of serving the best possible food at the most reasonable price.

Geografia $$
Russian
Ulitsa Rubinshteina 5
Tel *340 0074*
This eatery has become popular for its eclectic menu of dishes made using fresh local produce and served in an upscale setting. Extensive wine and cocktail list.

The brightly decorated and popular Baklazhan restaurant

For more information on types of restaurants *see pages 180–81*

Moskva $$
International
Nevskiy prospekt 114, 191025
Tel *937 6497*
Stunning sixth-floor location with panoramic city views from the summer terrace. The vast menu covers recipes from around the world prepared to exacting standards by specialist chefs.

ObedBufet $$
International
Nevskiy prospekt 114, 191025
Tel *961 6311*
Upscale café that boasts salad bars, steam tables, live-cooking stations and a dessert bar. The focus is on freshly prepared, hearty food. Both dine-in and takeaway options available.

Palermo $$
Italian
Naberezhnaya reki Fontanki 50, 191002
Tel *764 3764*
Good Italian family restaurant, offering classic Sicilian recipes with the addition of a few European favourites. Decorated in Italian style with frescoes, it has a great atmosphere, too.

Puri $$
Uzbek/Caucasian
Industrialnyy prospekt 17/1a, 195426
Tel *240 2030*
Serves faultless Uzbek and Caucasian delights, many of which are cooked in a traditional *tandoor* oven. The comfortable Eastern-style interior adds character to the place.

DK Choice

Pirosmani $$
Georgian
Bolshoy prospekt 14 Petrogradskaya, 197110
Tel *235 6456*
This colourful Georgian restaurant is set out like a Georgian hill village, with wattle-and-daub houses, a stained-glass window and ponds. Walls are hung with works by Pirosmani, arguably the best Georgian painter of the 20th century. Try the *lobio* (beans in spicy sauce) washed down with Old Tbilisi wine.

Samsa $$
Uzbek
Leninskiy prospekt 84/1, 198332
Tel *646 7571*
Pleasing Uzbek restaurant with mildly exotic styling where *samsa* (meat pastries) and other savoury Uzbek

staples are on the menu. Diners can watch the cooking process in the open kitchen.

Schengen $$
International
Kirochnaya ulitsa 5
Tel *922 1197*
One of the few restaurants in town that offer traditional Western breakfast every day. The superb chef cooks up delicious, wholesome dishes popular with tourists and locals alike. Great service.

Shinok $$
Ukrainian
Zagorodnyy prospekt 13, 191002
Tel *571 8262*
Decent Ukrainian food served in large portions accompanied by Ukrainian vodka. There is a Ukrainian folk show every evening at 8pm, and lots of jollity. The interior is rustic; the staff, friendly.

Staraya Derevnya $$
Russian
Ulitsa Savushkina 72, 197183
Tel *431 0000*
With an informal interior styled as an old-fashioned apartment, this is one of the friendliest restaurants in town. Enjoy traditional Russian fare with Russian and Gypsy song performances most evenings.

Tony's Kitchen $$
International
Malyy prospekt 88, Vasilevskiy ostrov, 199406
Tel *988 8020*
Spacious, welcoming place spread over two floors with an open summer terrace. Good range of meaty Russian and European dishes, plus hookah options.

Tres Amigos $$
Mexican
Ulitsa Rubinshteyna 25, 191002
Tel *572 2685*
The restaurant has a bizarre mix of decor inspired by Aztecs and beer halls. Good selection of Latin American fare and cocktails. Excellent children's room.

Xren $$
International
Zagorodnyy prospekt 13, 191002
Tel *347 8850*
Four uniquely styled rooms, well prepared and stylishly presented food and a good selection of wines. Marbled beef steaks are a house speciality. DJs every weekend.

DK Choice

Birreria $$$
Italian
Vladimirskiy prospekt 19, 191002
Tel *943 6004*
Magnificent views of Vladimirskiy Cathedral, a superb selection of Italian beers, as well as the chance to watch football matches in style make Birreria a popular place for a meal, drinks or even a sedate lunch. The menu features classic Italian fare, with thin-crust pizzas topping the list, and delectable Neapolitan street food.

Demidov $$$
Russian
Naberezhnaya reki Fontanki 14, 191028
Tel *272 9181*
Touristy, Old Russian-style restaurant. The extensive menu includes everything from quail's eggs to pancakes and caviar. Gypsy music every evening from 8pm.

The charming rustic interior of Shinok

Dickens $$$
English
Naberezhnaya reki Fontanki 108,
2nd floor, 190013
Tel 702 6263
Inviting English pub specializing
in steaks and game dishes. It
offers a small but respectable
wine list, old-world style decor and
lovely views onto the Fontanka.

Ferma $$$
International
Finlyandskiy prospekt 1, 194044
Tel 643 0430
Very upmarket, featuring
concrete walls adorned with
a quirky collection of farming
paraphernalia. Serves a high
standard of Russian and
European cuisine.

Russian Fishing $$$
Russian
Yuzhnaya doroga 11, Krestovskiy
ostrov, 197110
Tel 323 9813
Stylized fisherman's hut with
a pond. Guests can catch their
own fish – trout, sturgeon,
beluga, sterlet – and watch it
being cooked. Attracts families
during the day.

Ryba $$$
International
Ulitsa Akademika Pavlova 5, 197022
Tel 234 5060
Choice of traditional Italian
food including a wide variety
of pastas and pizzas or Asian
wok-based dishes at one of
the highest restaurants in
the city. Breathtaking views
over rooftops.

Troika $$$
Russian
Zagorodnyy prospekt 27, 191180
Tel 407 5343
Lots of glitz and glamour;
good food; but Troika focuses
more on entertainment.
Features elaborate floor
shows with circus acrobatics,
folk songs and Russian dancing.

Beyond
St Petersburg

Dom Berga $
Russian
Bolshaya Moskovskaya ulitsa 24,
Veliky Novgorod, 173000
Tel (8162) 948838
Traditional Russian cuisine in
an atmospheric 19th-century
mansion. A good venue to
sample *Medovukha* – an
old Russian alcoholic drink
made with honey.

The splendid decor at the Dom Berga restaurant

La Chatte Café $
Café
Bolshaya Moskovskaya ulitsa 86,
Veliky Novgorod, 173014
Tel (8162) 998753
Modern café serving cakes and
pastries as well as soups, pizzas,
sandwiches and more substantial
meals. There are cocktails and draft
beer to accompany the food.

Park $
Russian
Zverinskaya ulitsa 23, Pavlovsk, 196621
Tel 452 1073
Pleasant eatery with a good
selection of Russian standards
and upbeat service. Conveniently
located close to the main sights.

Napoli $$
Italian
Ulitsa Studencheskaya 21/43, Veliky
Novgorod, 173014
Tel (8162) 636307
Laid-back Italian restaurant
offering authentic dishes from
various regions of Italy and a
good selection of home-made
pasta. Intimate ambience.

Oldham $$
English
Bolshaya Moskovskaya ulitsa 55,
Veliky Novgorod, 173023
Tel (8162) 900560
Popular English pub and steak
house serving ale on tap and
plenty of delicious pub food.
Convivial atmosphere.

Shalyapin $$
Russian
Ulitsa Nagornaya 1, Repino, 197738
Tel 432 0775
Charming spot with a classic
19th-century interior, serving

irresistible *shashlik* (kebabs).
Vast fireplace in winter and
roof terrace in summer.

Bake'n'Bards $$$
Russian
Litseiskiy pereulok 1/4
Tel 996 0235
In a historical 19th-century house
with preserved interiors that give
the feeling of being in Tsarskoe
Selo during the time of the tsars.
Serves exemplary renditions of
traditional Russian fare.

Daniel $$$
International
Srednyaya ulitsa 2/3, Pushkin, 196601
Tel 466 9116
Wonderful restaurant set in
wooded grounds with covered
outdoor seating amid flower
beds. It provides a fine choice
of Russian and European cuisine.
Excellent service.

Stroganoff Bar & Grill $$$
Russian
Primorskoye shosse 418, Repino,
197738
Tel 432 0575
Designed to resemble a country
mansion, this is a great place
to relax and enjoy some fine
Russian cuisine. It has a children's
playroom and a separate menu
that caters to young taste buds.

XIX Vek $$$
Russian
Srednyaya ulitsa 2a, Pushkin, 196600
Tel 465 2685
Classy restaurant popular with
wedding parties. Just a short
walk from Catherine's Palace,
the place serves superb Russian
food in palatial surroundings.

For more information on types of restaurants *see pages 180–81*

Light Meals and Snacks

Despite their plastic chairs and metal tables, Russian and ethnic cafés often serve very tasty food – from simple sandwiches to hefty meat dishes. Look out for the word кафе (café) and try one. Cautious travellers can experiment in one of the restaurants listed opposite, which frequently offer moderately priced meals between noon and 4pm. A number of bars and "art cafés" with live music *(see p207)* also have excellent kitchens. (In the evening these may be filled with people and noise, but at lunchtime they are calmer.) During the summer many cafés add tables outside – which is great for people-watching. In colder weather, the ground-floor cafés of the Moika or Radisson SAS hotels, Jili-bili or Il Patio are almost as good.

Russian

Traditional Russian dishes such as *borsch* and *draniki* (potato pancakes) are widely offered. *Pelmeni* (dumplings filled with meat) and *vareniki* (dumplings filled with fruit or vegetables) are in a class of their own. Specialist *pelmeni* establishments are truly "local", with no flashy decor or tourists. Try the **Pelmeni Bar** behind the Peter and Paul Fortress. Russian *bliny* and *blinchiki* (flat pancakes) come in both sweet and savoury varieties at the outstandingly cheap **Cherdak**. Some places listed are quite plain, notable mainly for their location: **Priboy** is behind the Hermitage *(see pp86–95)*; **Sadko** is next to the Mariinskiy Theatre; **Café de Clie** is next to the Peter and Paul Fortress. **Gloss Café** serves Asian food and is located in the courtyard of the Stroganov Palace. Near St Isaac's Square *(see p81)* is **Idiot**, a vegetarian café popular with ex-pats. **Dachniki** is cheap, cheerful and busy. **Botanica** is known for its vegetarian dishes and generous portions.

Ethnic Food

Georgian and Armenian foods are popular in St Petersburg. The **Kavkaz-Bar** restaurant *(see p189)* also has an informal café, and other small cafés offer Caucasian dishes. **Mops** is the city's only Thai restaurant. Filling Uzbek food is on offer at **Chaikhana Alo Halol**, a bustling and cheap café located near all the major tourist attractions in the city centre.

Fast Food, Pizza and Pasta

The first Russian fast food was an open sandwich with cheese or salami, or *pirozhki* (small buns) filled with rice, cabbage or something sweet like apple. The best *pirozhki* come from **Stolle**. A slightly cheaper version is available from the **Bulochnaya** on Bolshaya Konyushennaya ulitsa. Always avoid fried *pirozhki* with meat. Never buy them on the street.

In addition to the well-known fast-food chains, local options include the 24-hour **Layma** and **Stolovaya #1 Kopeika**, where customers can choose by pointing. **Teremok** specializes in pancakes. **Troitskiy Most** is a popular and inexpensive vegetarian option. Pizza and pasta houses are popular. (**Il Patio** caters for children.)

Pastries and Sweets

Russians are sweet-toothed, and in private homes tea is never offered without biscuits or cakes. Ice cream – best bought from one of the many street sellers – is enjoyed all year round. **Sladkoezhka** sells a wide range of fresh cream desserts and pastries, and is probably the city's favourite spot for a hit of sugar. Coffee shops, such as **Bushe** and the **Idealnaya Chashka** chain, also offer a variety of cheesecakes and cakes. At **Stirka 40°** customers drink tea while doing their washing (it doubles as the city's only launderette).

Pubs and Bars

Most bars serve a good range of food. In addition to the standard English and Irish pubs, where food is unadventurous, expensive and the clientele is composed mostly of ex-pats, there are now a number of Russian "pubs", such as **Penguin** and **Tolsty Fraer**, that offer a range of excellent local beers. **The Office Pub** offers a rest from the bustle of Nevskiy prospekt, just behind Kazan Cathedral.

One of the joys of summer is to drink beer sitting on one of the pontoons that appear with the warm weather on the canals and rivers, particularly around Nevskiy prospekt. While such places do not usually offer food, they do allow customers to linger and watch the sunset.

Sushi

An enduring craze for sushi bars – which tend to be quite good – means that there are plenty of good alternatives for quick, healthy lunches in St Petersburg. Menus are easy to understand because they include pictures of each dish. Try **Dve Palochki** or **Planet Sushi**.

Eating Out on Day Trips

More effort is required when seeking a place for a modest lunch outside the city. Pavlovsk *(see pp160–63)* and Peterhof *(see pp150–53)* have reasonable cafés in the palaces, although space is limited in summer. Peterhof's tiny **Trapeza** is always a favourite. At Tsarskoe Selo *(see pp154–7)*, there are several cafés along and around Oranzhereynaya ulitsa, leading off the park. Gatchina Palace *(see p149)* has cafés in the grounds and even Oranienbaum *(see p148)* has a tiny café, too. In general, however, the best option is to take a picnic to Gatchina or Oranienbaum. (Delicious takeaway pies can be bought from **Stolle**.) In Novgorod *(see pp164–7)*, the **Golden Ladle** serves many kinds of beer and snacks.

DIRECTORY

Russian

Barberry
Kamennoostrovskiy 10.
Map 2 E2.
Tel 954 0022.

Botanica
Ботаника
Ulitsa Pestelya 7.
Map 3 A5.
Tel 272 7091.

Café de Clie
Kronverkskiy prospekt 27.
Map 2 D2.
Tel 232 3606.

Chaynaya Khizhina
Чайная хижина
Bolshaya Konyushennaya
ulitsa 19 (entrance from
Volynskiy pereulok).
Map 6 E1.
Tel 570 1947.

Cherdak
Чердак
Ligovskiy prospekt 17.
Map 7 C1.
Tel 272 5564.

Dachniki
Дачники
Nevskiy prospekt 20.
Map 6 E1.
Tel 312 9160.

Idiot
Идиот
Naberezhnaya reki
Moyki 82. **Map** 5 C2.
Tel 946 5173.

Jili-bili
Жили-были
Nevskiy prospekt 52.
Map 6 F1.
Tel 314 6230.

Pelmeni Bar
Пельмени-бар
Kronverkskiy prospekt 53a
(entry from ulitsa Markina).
Map 1 C3.
Tel 498 0977.

Priboy
Прибой
Naberezhnaya reki
Moyki 19. **Map** 2 E5.
Tel 571 8285.

Sadko
Садко
Ulitsa Glinki 2.
Map 5 B3. **Tel** 903 2373.

Soiree
Суаре
Ulitsa Zhukovskovo 28.
Map 7 B1. **Tel** 272 3512.

Troitskiy Most
Naberezhnaya reki
Moyki 30.
Map 6 E1.
Tel 921 5978.

Tryn-Trava
Трын-Трава
Nevskiy prospekt 22–24.
Map 6 E1. **Tel** 571 0385.

Ethnic Food

Chaikhana Alo Halol
Чайхана Аъло Халол
Naberezhnaya kanala
Griboedova 52.
Map 6 D2.
Tel +8 952 353 5012.

Gloss Café
Nevskiy prospekt 17.
Map 6 E1. **Tel** 315 2315.

Mops
Мопс
Ulitsa Rubinshteyna 12.
Map 7 A2. **Tel** 572 3834.

Fast Food, Pizza and Pasta

Bulochnaya
Булочная
Bolshaya Konyushennaya
ulitsa 15. **Map** 2 E5.
Nevskiy prospekt 66.
Map 7 A2. **Tel** 314 8559.

Il Patio
Nevskiy prospekt 30.
Map 6 E1. **Tel** 314 3215.
Nevskiy prospekt 182.
Map 8 E3. **Tel** 271 3177.

Layma
Лайма
Naberezhnaya kanala
Griboedova 16. **Map** 6 E1.
Tel 315 5545.

Pelmenia
Пельмения
Tel 415 4185.

Stolle
Штолле
Nevskiy prospekt 11.
Map 6 D1.
Tel 314 7021.

Konyushennyy pereulok
1/6.
Map 2 E5.
Tel 312 1862.

Stolovaya #1 Kopeika
Столовая № 1
Копейка
Nevskiy prospekt 54.
Map 6 F1.
Tel 571 2400.

Teremok (pancakes)
Теремок
Nevskiy prospekt 60.
Map 7 A2.
Tel 363 2332.

Troitskiy Most
Троицкий мост
Kronverkskiy prospekt 35.
Map 2 D2. **Tel** 964 8967.

Coffee, Pastries and Sweets

Bushe
Буше
Ulitsa Vosstaniya 10.
Map 7 B1.
Tel 273 7459.

Café Singer
Кафе Зингер
Nevskiy 28.
Map 6 E1.
Tel 571 8223.

Denisov-Nikolaev Confectionery
Денисов и Николаев
Naberezhnaya kanala
Griboedova 77.
Map 6 D3.
Tel 571 9495.

Idealnaya Chashka
Идеальная чашка
Kamennoostrovskiy
prospekt 2.
Map 2 E2. **Tel** 233 4953.

Sladkoezhka
Сладкоежка
Marata ulitsa 2.
Map 7 B2.
Tel 571 1420.
Sadovaya ulitsa 60.
Map 5 C4.
Tel 310 8144.
Gorokhovaya 44.
Map 6 E3.
Tel 310 8005.

Stirka 40°
Стирка 40°
Kazanskaya ulitsa 26.
Map 6 D2.
Tel 314 5371.

Pubs and Bars

The Office Pub
Офис Паб
Kazanskaya ulitsa 5.
Map 6 E2.
Tel 571 5428.

Penguin
Пингвин
Razezzhaya ulitsa 26.
Map 7 A3.
Tel 926 5527.

Tolsty Fraer
Толстый Фраер
Dumskaya ul 3.
Map 6 E2.
Tel 570 0102.

Sushi

Dve Palochki
Две палочки
Ulitsa Vosstaniya 15.
Map 7 C1.
Tel 335 0222.

Eurasia
Евразия
Nevskiy prospekt 13.
Map 6 D1.
Tel 315 1858.

Planet Sushi
Планета Суши
Nevskiy prospekt 94.
Map 7 B2.
Tel 275 7533.

Day Trips

Golden Ladle
Золотой Ковш
Novo-Luchanskaya ulitsa
14, Novgorod.
Tel (8162) 730599.

Linea
Sankt-Peterburgskiy
prospekt 46,
Petrodvorets
(Peterhof).
Tel 450 7878.

Podvorie
Подворье
Filtrovskoye 16.
Tel 466 8544.

Trapeza
Трапеза
Kalininskaya ulitsa 9,
Petrodvorets (Peterhof).
Tel 450 6393.

SHOPS AND MARKETS

A trip round St Petersburg's shops and markets provides an insight into local life. Even today, shopping in the city requires flexibility and even a sense of adventure: you can never depend on finding what you set out to find, but may confidently expect to end up buying something you never guessed you needed. Imported goods have pushed out many local products. Even so, Russian linen, the city's celebrated Krupsksaya chocolates, vodka, caviar, and Russian crafts and toys all make wonderful gifts. Larger shops are concentrated around main streets such as Nevskiy and Bolshoy prospekts, and metro stations, notably Sennaya Ploshchad and Vasilevskiy Ostrov. However, most buildings are occupied by shops or restaurants at ground level. Do venture in.

Ladies' fashion at one of the numerous upscale boutiques along Nevskiy prospekt

Opening Hours

Hours vary, but shops usually open from 10am until at least 7pm, though "fashionable" outlets may stay open later. A few, mainly cheap food shops, close for lunch. On Sundays department stores remain open, as do other large shops. During the summer, smaller places may reduce their hours and close at weekends. There are 24-hour food shops all over town.

How to Pay

Accepting payment in non-Russian currency is a criminal offence. The only place you might be able to pay in foreign currency is at a tourist market.

There are numerous, reliable exchange offices and ATMs inside metro stations and outside banks (see p216). Moreover, many stores now accept credit cards. However, cash is still the predominant way to pay in Russia, even in large cities. Despite the many signs advertising the option to pay by card, don't be surprised if you are told that the machine is "out of order." In some shops, customers are forced to peer at goods stacked behind the counter. If you would like a closer look, point to what you want and say *"mozhno"* ("may I?"). To purchase something, pay for it at the cash desk and then return to collect the item from the counter with your receipt. Shop assistants will usually realize if you do not speak Russian, and will write down the prices for you to hand to the cashier. Defective goods can generally be returned provided they are accompanied by a receipt.

Bargaining Etiquette

If a set price is displayed at markets, this indicates no bargaining. In all other cases you can usually get some reduction if you haggle, especially since visitors (and prosperous-looking Russians) are likely to be quoted a higher price. Haggling in Russia, however, is a serious matter, so do not bother unless you genuinely intend to buy.

Buying Art and Antiques

Under Russian law, all objects made before 1956, and all objects made from valuable materials such as gold, silver, precious stones and fur, are subject to strict export controls. Works of art, including contemporary watercolours, also fall under this ruling, likewise books published before 1946. Be aware that, although there are green and red channels at the airport customs, and not all suitcases are X-rayed, there are random checks. In practice, customs officials may turn a blind eye to prints and watercolours without frames, and unless a book is extremely rare you are likely to be able to export it without authorization. In all other cases, strict rules are applied. Permission to export both books and art objects can be obtained from a department of the **Ministry of Culture**. This process is relatively speedy. The gallery from which or the artist from whom the item is purchased should always assist with the paperwork.

If you have not obviously tried to cheat customs, any objects not allowed through can simply be handed over to someone who is remaining in St Petersburg. If, however, there is any hint of foul play, the item will be placed in storage at

Second-hand bookshop sign

Russian box-camera (1920s)

Export Permissions

Ministry of Culture
Министерство культуры
Ministerstvo kultury
Malaya Morskaya ulitsa 17.
Map 6 D1. **Tel** 571 0302.
Open 11am–5pm Mon–Fri.

Tertia *(see p201)* has exportable antiques to suit all budgets

the airport, for which, if you wish to reclaim it later, there will be a charge. Any objects that remain unclaimed after a year will be confiscated, as will objects which have obviously been hidden to avoid detection. Valuable pieces may be donated to a museum.

Department Stores

Known as a "univermag" or universal shop, Russian department stores evolved from the old trading rows, which were literally rows of kiosks owned by different traders. Present-day department stores have altered a great deal and now operate as a complex of boutiques and distinct sections. Even though the goods on sale do not differ much from those that are available in European shops, every visitor to St Petersburg should explore **Gostinyy Dvor** *(see p110)*, the oldest shopping centre in the city, and **Passazh** *(see p50)*, a smaller department store. Despite the glitzy goods, however, the narrow passages and layout speak of a different age.

The newer shopping centre such as the **Nevsky Centre** *(see p201)* and **Galeria** are more like Western European and American shopping malls, with upmarket boutiques and food outlets. **DLT** (Dom Leningradskoy Torgovli) *(see p201)* on Bolshaya Konyushennaya is the city's top luxury department store, with a wide selection of designer clothing and fragrance.

Markets and Bazaars

Food can be bought in one of the 11 markets (*rynoks*) dotted around the city. The most centrally located is **Kuznechnyy** *(see p201)*, just off Nevskiy prospekt, which sells flowers, fruit, vegetables, delicious home-made cream cheese and wonderful natural honey which you can sample. Note that prices at markets tend to be higher than at the supermarkets, but buyers do have the option of haggling.

Apraksin Dvor has been the site of a thriving market since the mid-18th century. Today it sells everything from cigars to CDs. While the market is undergoing reconstruction, only the shops that have a roof over them remain open.

Flea markets are perpetually being moved on, though some sellers continue to pop up at the city's main markets. The true seeker of unusual finds amid the trash will set off on a Friday or Saturday morning for Udelnaya metro, where a vast unofficial market sprawls along the railway line.

Souvenir watercolours and prints of varying quality are sold throughout the year at the open-air market, **Vernisazh** *(see p201)*, outside the Church of St Catherine *(see p50)* on Nevskiy prospekt. The official **Souvenir Market** *(see p201)* near the Church on Spilled Blood *(see p102)*, sells a wide selection of *matryoshka* dolls *(see p198)*. You are also likely to find handmade chess sets, watches, fur hats, old cameras and military paraphernalia.

Visitors browse the shelves at the Hermitage museum Shop

Museum Shops

The best museum shop is found inside the **Hermitage** *(see pp86–95)* and sells reproduction prints and objects, books on the city and its art, jewellery and silk scarves, both inside the museum and online: www. hermitagemuseum.org.

The **Russian Museum** *(see pp106–9)* has several outlets, though these are not run by the museum itself. The best is in the Stroganov Palace *(see p114)*.

Of the other shops attached to museums, the best are found in the **Peter and Paul Fortress** *(see pp68–9)* and in the palaces at **Pavlovsk** *(see pp160–63)*, **Peterhof** *(see pp150–53)* and **Tsarskoe Selo** *(see pp154–7)*. These tend to sell souvenirs (rather than reproductions of exhibits and other related objects): amber and semi-precious-stone jewellery, dolls, lacquered boxes and books on the city. The prices are not fixed, so check how much something is worth before starting to haggle.

Souvenirs sold at the tourist market opposite the Church on Spilled Blood

What to Buy in St Petersburg

It is easy to find interesting and beautiful souvenirs in St Petersburg. They range in price from small, enamelled badges, which sell for very little, through to hand-painted Palekh boxes and samovars which can be very expensive. Traditional crafts were encouraged by the state in the old Soviet Union and many items, such as lacquered boxes and bowls, matryoshka dolls, wooden toys and chess sets, are still made by craftsmen and women using age-old methods. Memorabilia from the Soviet era also make good souvenirs and Russia is definitely the best place to buy the national specialities, vodka and caviar.

Samovar
Used to boil water to make tea, samovars come in all shapes and sizes (see p185). A permit is needed to export a pre-1945 samovar.

Vodka and Caviar
An enormous variety of both clear and flavoured vodkas (such as lemon and pepper) is available (see p184). They make excellent accompaniments to black and red caviar (ikra), which are often served with blini (see p182).

Red caviar

Clear vodka

Flavoured vodka

Black caviar

Malachite egg   Amber ring

Semi-Precious Stones
Malachite, amber, jasper and a variety of marbles from the Ural mountains are used to make a wide range of items – everything from jewellery and chess sets to inlaid table tops.

Wooden Toy
These crudely carved wooden toys often have moving parts. They are known as Bogorodskiye toys and make charming gifts.

Matryoshka Dolls
These dolls fit one inside the other and come in a huge variety of styles. The traditional dolls are the prettiest, but those painted as Russian, Soviet and world leaders are also very popular.

Chess Sets
Attractive chess sets made from all kinds of beautiful materials, including malachite, are widely available. This wooden chess set is painted in the same style as the matryoshka dolls.

Lacquered Artifacts

Painted wooden or papier-mâché artifacts make popular souvenirs and are sold all over the city. The exquisite hand-painted, lacquered Palekh boxes can be very costly, but the eggs decorated with icons and the typical red, black and gold bowls are more affordable.

Palekh Box

The art of miniature painting on papier-mâché items originated in the late 18th century. Artists in the four villages of Palekh, Fedoskino, Mstera and Kholui still produce these hand-painted marvels. The images are based on Russian fairy tales and legends.

Painted wooden egg

Bowl with Spoon

The brightly painted bowls and spoons, usually known as "Khokhloma", have a lacquer coating, forming a surface which is durable, but not resistant to boiling liquids.

Russian hand-painted tray

Tuners

Strings

Musical Instruments

Russian folk music uses a wide range of musical instruments. This *gusli* is similar to the Western psaltery and is played by plucking the strings with both hands. Also available are the brightly painted balalaika and the *bayan* (accordion).

Russian Scarf

These brilliantly coloured traditional woollen shawls are good for keeping out the cold of a Russian winter. Mass-produced polyester versions are also available, mostly in big department stores, but these are not as warm.

Gzhel Vase

Ceramics with a distinctive blue-and-white pattern are produced in Gzhel, an area near Moscow. Ranging from figurines to household crockery, they are popular with Russians and visitors alike.

Soviet Memorabilia

An eclectic array of memorabilia from the Soviet era is on sale. Old banknotes, coins, pocket watches and Red Army kits, including belt buckles, badges and other items of uniform, can be found along-side watches with cartoons of KGB agents on their faces.

Pocket watch

Badge with
Soviet symbols

Red Army
leather belt

Where to Shop in St Petersburg

The main department stores in the city centre stock everything from souvenirs to vodka and furs, all of a high quality. For some local products, however, it is best to visit specialist shops, most of which are conveniently located in or near the centre. In a city which prides itself on its intellectuals, books and art are, appropriately, St Petersburg's other main exports. Soviet memorabilia has also become very popular for souvenirs.

Food and Drink

Good vodka is to be had everywhere. Avoid cheaper brands in "amusing" packaging: they are invariably of poor quality. Diplomat and Gzhelka are good, standard brands.

Caviar should be bought only from a food shop or department store. **Gostinyy Dvor** and the **Land** supermarket store on Vladimirskiy prospekt are the most central, reliable places for both vodka and caviar. The many **Gastronom 811** outlets also stock a wide range of alcoholic drinks. All kinds of food shopping can be done at **Kuznechnyy**, which is stacked high with Russian specialities. All kinds of meats and cheeses are on sale at the **Stockmann Delicatessan**.

St Petersburg's **Krupskaya Fabrika** chocolate factory has long been famous in the Soviet Union. The **Chocolate Museum** sells novelties such as famous buildings crafted in chocolate.

Souvenirs and Crafts

In summer, when traders set up stalls by tourist spots, the city is flooded with *matryoshka* dolls, music boxes shaped like a church, painted lacquerware and chess sets. In winter, it can be quiet on the retail front. The **Souvenir Market** and **Vernisazh** market, however, operate all year, and there are good gifts to be found in Gostinyy Dvor and Passazh department stores. Shops in or near museums also stock souvenirs – notably those in the Stroganov Palace (*see p114*) and Tsarskoe Selo (*see pp154–7*). The shop inside the Hermitage (*see pp86–95*) sells higher range goods and excellent art books. Local porcelain from the **Imperial Porcelain Factory** is much prized. The factory makes everything from gaily painted rustic cups to reproduction revolutionary-era porcelain.

Soviet Memorabilia

Artifacts from the Soviet era are now produced specifically for the tourist market. Be careful when buying on the street: many apparently genuine articles are modern reproductions. Original pieces can be picked up at the **Souvenir Market**, though **Nado Zhe** and **Komissionnyy Magazin** antiques shops are more reliable. Or you could try one of the smaller second-hand shops. Soviet badges are easily transportable. A selection of actual Soviet military surplus is available from **Voennyy Kollektsioner**.

Antiques and Art

Although older antiques and many works of art need to be cleared with customs, some pieces, such as small water-colours, may be exempt. Many shops are extortionately expensive, but **Tertia** is an exception, with readily export-able items to suit all pockets, and **Russkie Sezony** is a veritable treasure trove. Only buy an expensive object if you are sure the relevant paperwork and export applications can be obtained (*see p196*). **Antikvariat** should be able to provide the paperwork for purchases made in the centre.

Paintings all require export licences, but as galleries can provide these themselves it is worth dropping in to **Anna Nova**, **S.P.A.S.** or **Borey** to see what they have. The **Union of Artists** has exhibitions by traditional local artists. The **Pushkinskaya 10** art centre stages shows at weekends, some with works for sale.

Books, Film and Music

St Petersburgers perceive their city as an intellectual focal point, with a great literary and artistic past. The centre has been taken over by book chains such as **Bookvoed**, but there are some smaller new and second-hand bookshops. The best are still **Dom Knigi** and the **Writers' Bookshop**. If you need a holiday novel in English, try **Anglia**, Dom Knigi or Bookvoed. More unusual, second-hand English books – usually donated by tourists – can sometimes be found in **Akademkniga** and **Na Liteynom**. **Severnaya Lira** sells sheet music – everything from classical to folk songs – as well as instruments, CDs and books on music. Art books can be bought in Dom Knigi.

DVDs of English-language films and CDs can be purchased in shops such as **Phonoteka**.

Furs and Fashion

Clothes and other accessories are mainly imported. Elegant boutiques occupy part of Gostinyy Dvor and run along streets such as naberezhnaya kanala Griboedova and ulitsa Zhukovskovo. Some local designers have their own boutiques; notably **Tatyana Parfyonova**, whose garments have been purchased by the Russian Museum.

Paloma and the **Marina Sedova Hat Salon** offer hats in everything from straw to fur. Furs are sold in **Lena**, Paloma and on the top floor of Gostinyy Dvor. Russian linen is also a good buy. Elegant shift dresses and the traditional *kosovorotka* (peasant shirt) are found in **Russky Len**. Fashion pieces are sold at **Toto**. Locally made jewellery of semi-precious stones from the Urals and amber from the Baltic is available in jewellers such as Samotsvety.

DIRECTORY

Department Stores

DLT
Bolshaya Konyushennaya ulitsa 21–23.
Map 6 E1.
Tel 648 0848.

Galeria
Галея
Ligovskiy prospekt 30.
Map 7 C3.

Gostinyy Dvor
Гостиный двор
Nevskiy prospekt 35.
Map 6 F2.

Nevsky Centre
Nevskiy prospekt 114–116.
Map 7 B2.
Tel 313 9319.

Passazh
Пассаж
Nevskiy prospekt 48.
Map 6 F1.

Markets

Apraksin Dvor
Sadovaya ulitsa 30.
Map 6 E2.

Kuznechnyy
Кузнечный рынок
Kuznechnyy pereulok 3.
Map 7 A3.

Souvenir Market
Рынок сувениров
Naberezhnaya kanala Griboedova, by Church on Spilled Blood.
Map 2 E5.

Vernisazh
Вернисаж
Nevskiy prospekt 32–4.
Map 6 E1.

Food and Drink

Chocolate Museum
Музей шоколада
Nevskiy prospekt 17.
Map 6 E1. **Tel** 315 1348.

Gastronom 811
Гастроном 811
Nevskiy prospekt 66.
Map 7 A1.
Tel 314 8559.

Krupskaya Fabrika
Кондитерская фабрика им. Н.К. Крупской
Ulitsa Pravdy 6.
Map 7 A3.

Land
Лэнд
Vladimirskiy prospekt 19.
Map 7 A2. **Tel** 324 1324.

Stockmann Delicatessen
Гастроном Стокманн
Nevskiy prospekt 114–116. **Map** 7 B2.
Tel 313 6000.

Souvenirs and Crafts

Imperial Porcelain
Императорский фарфоровый завод
Obukhovskoy oborony prospekt 151.
Map 8 F4. **Tel** 560 8544.
Vladimirskiy prospekt 7.
Map 7 A2. **Tel** 713 1513.
Nevskiy prospekt 160.
Map 8 D3. **Tel** 717 4838.

Soviet Memorabilia

Komissionnyy Magazin
Комиссионный магазин
1-ya Sovetskaya ulitsa 12 (enter through the arch).
Map 7 C2. **Tel** 717 4932.

Nado Zhe
Надо же
Rubinsteina 11.
Map 7 A2. **Tel** 314 3247.

Voennyy Kollektsioner
Военный Коллекционер
Zagorodnyy prospekt 42.
Map 7 A3. **Tel** 315 9351.

Antiques and Art

Anna Nova
Ulitsa Zhukovskovo 28.
Map 7 B1.
Tel 275 9762.

Antikvariat
Антиквариат
Malaya Morskaya ulitsa 21. **Map** 6 D1.
Tel 571 2643.

Borey
Борей
Liteynyy prospekt 58.
Map 7 A1. **Tel** 275 3837.

Marina Gisich Gallery
Fontanka 121.
Map 6 D3.
Tel 314 4380.

Pushkinskaya 10
Пушкинская 10
(The Door Gallery, Naviuila Artis, Art-Liga, New Academy of Fine Arts, Nonconformists' Museum) Ligovskiy prospekt 53.
Map 7 B3.
Tel 764 5371.

Renaissance Antiques
Pestela 8. **Map** 3 A5.
Tel 272 2894.

Russkaya Starina
Русская Старина
Nekrasova 6. **Map** 6 E1.
Tel 273 2603.

Russkie Sezony
Русские сезоны
Liteynyy prospekt 15.
Map 3 A2. **Tel** 275 1749.

S.P.A.S.
С. П.А.С.
Naberezhnaya reki Moyki 93. **Map** 5 C2.
Tel 571 4260.

Tertia
Терция
Italyanskaya ulitsa 5.
Map 6 E1. **Tel** 710 5568.

Union of Artists
Союз художников
Bolshaya Morskaya ulitsa 38. **Map** 6 D2.
Tel 314 7721.

Books, Film and Music

Akademkniga
Академкнига
Liteynyy prospekt 57.
Map 7 A1.
Tel 273 1398.

Anglia
Англия
Naberezhnaya reki Fontanki 38.
Map 7 A2.
Tel 579 8007.

Bookvoed
Буквоед
Ligovskiy prospekt 10.
Map 7 C2.
Tel 346 5327.

Dom Knigi
дом книги
Nevskiy prospekt 28.
Map 6 E1.
Tel 448 2355.

Iskatel
Искатель
Naberezhnaya reki Moyki 51. **Map** 6 E1.
Tel 312 6621.

Na Liteynom
На Литейном
(Books and antiques)
Liteynyy prospekt 61.
Map 7 A2.
Tel 275 3874.

Phonoteka
Фонотека
Ulitsa Marata 28.
Map 7 B3.
Tel 712 3013.

Severnaya Lira
Северная лира
Nevskiy prospekt 26.
Map 6 E1. **Tel** 312 0796.

Writers' Bookshop
Лавка Писателей
Nevskiy prospekt 66.
Map 7 A2. **Tel** 314 4858.

Furs and Fashion

Lena
Лена
Kronverkskaya 7.
Map 6 F1. **Tel** 244 7246.

Marina Sedova Hat Salon
Шляпный салон Марины Седовой
Ligovsky prospekt 27/7.
Map 7 C2. **Tel** 579 3268.

Paloma
Палома
Nevskiy prospekt 19
Map 6 E1. **Tel** 571 6091.

Russkiye Samotsvety
Русские Самоцветы
Bolshoi prospekt 98, Petrogradskaya.
Map 1 D1. **Tel** 291 9011.

Russky Len
Славянский стиль
Pushkinskaya ulitsa 3.
Map 7 B2. **Tel** 325 8599.

Tatyana Parfyonova
Татьяна Парфенова модный дом
Nevskiy prospekt 51.
Map 7 B2. **Tel** 713 3669.

Toto
Nevskiy prospekt 74.
Map 6 E1. **Tel** 579 3590.

ENTERTAINMENT IN ST PETERSBURG

St Petersburg has an impressive and varied choice of entertainment. Its ballet, opera, classical music and theatre are among the best in the world. In addition to the high culture, a thriving and vibrant nightlife is made up of numerous rock and jazz clubs, bars, art cafés, discos, nightclubs and casinos.

Increasingly, international artists are adding St Petersburg to their tours, and mainstream now exists harmoniously alongside underground in music,

theatre and cinema. The St Petersburg Philharmonia and the Mariinskiy (Kirov) ballet and opera (see pp120–21) deserve their impressive international reputations, though this does mean that they are often away on tour.

St Petersburg's entertainment changes with the seasons. In winter there are concerts and other traditional indoor events. Summer starts with the White Nights, followed by a mass of festivals and outdoor events.

The magnificent, gilded interior of the Yusupov Theatre

Entertainment Information

St Petersburg can be quite a difficult city to keep up with, as both official and unofficial events are organized at short notice. For example, theatre programmes are not announced more than a couple of months in advance, so it's important to keep alert in order not to miss the fun.

The best listings in English for local events can be found in *The St Petersburg Times*. This weekly newspaper (see p219) is distributed free of charge on Wednesdays to hotels, foreign bars, most fast-food chains and museums. A much broader range of information is provided in Russian in two biweekly listings magazines: *Afisha* (www.spb.afisha.com) and *Time Out* (www.spb.timeout.ru). Tickets for a wide range of

events can be booked on the Russian-language website www.bileter.ru.

Most traditional theatres and concert halls close down for July, August and part of September because their troupes go on tour. While this may deprive visitors of local performers, some theatres bring in guest troupes from Moscow and abroad. In addition, other venues such as the Hermitage (see p86) and Alexandrinskiy (see p205) theatres launch summer programmes that are aimed at tourists. It is worth noting that, although they are fun, their opera and ballet shows are sometimes not of the highest quality.

Mariinskiy poster pillar

Matinees start at noon and most evening performances at 7pm. To avoid disappointment check tickets carefully so you know when to arrive.

Buying Tickets

Most people buy their tickets with cash and in person. Theatre ticket offices and kiosks can be found all over town, offering tickets up to a month in advance. They display a full programme (in Russian) of all theatre and classical music performances for the next 20 days and are generally open daily from 10am–1pm and 4–7pm. Offices within theatres usually work from 11am–3pm and 4–7pm and sell tickets for all advertised concerts. Non-Russian-speakers should not be nervous: most ticket cashiers will be helpful and patient while you point to the date you want. Tickets can also be booked by your hotel concierge. The Mariinskiy Theatre has an excellent English-language website on which tickets can be bought (www.mariinsky.ru). Similar services for other theatres are offered on www.artis.spb.ru.

A few venues, notably the Mariinskiy (see p121), have price bands, with some tickets set aside at a cheaper rate and available only to Russian citizens. Non-Russians trying to use these may be refused entry or asked to pay the difference in price. Visitors, however, may obtain tickets for sold-out performances at the Mariinskiy Theatre if they go on the day.

As in most cities, touts sell tickets for major events, but beware of possible fakes and inflated prices.

Spectacular performance of the famous *Sleeping Beauty* ballet

Late-Night Transport

The metro closes its doors soon after midnight and buses run until 12:15am (infrequently after 11pm). There is no reliable all-night public transport, so expect to take a taxi late at night. Avoid any taxis which wait outside foreign hotels and bars as they charge extortionate prices (*see pp224–5*).

Children's Entertainment

Many theatres put on plays in Russian especially for children. See the children's section of *Afisha* or *Time Out*. Unfortunately, few give English-language performances except at New Year. No language problems occur at the **Circus**, however, or at the **Dolphinarium** on Krestovskiy Island.

Some of the best shows and concerts for children are held at **Zazerkalye**, while the puppet theatres usually have several productions based on well-known fairy tales.

For the "real" Russian winter experience, try a *troika* (sleigh) ride. These are offered at Pavlovsk (*see pp160–63*) and at **Shuvalovka**, a reproduction Russian village. Located 30 km (19 miles) out of town, Shuvalovka is open throughout the year and includes wooden houses in 17th-century Russian style, a skating rink, ice slides, a working smithy and a museum of peasant life. Take any minibus to Peterhof from Avtovo metro and ask the driver to stop at Shuvalovka.

Festivals

The various White Nights festivals (*see p53*) draw some of the big names of pop and classical music, and ticket prices go up accordingly – as do accommodation rates – during this time. But there are plenty of other worthwhile seasonal festivals. The White Days (taking in Russian Christmas on 7 January, when the city is shrouded in snow) and Shrovetide festivals place the accent on Russian culture.

Numerous jazz festivals (look out for SKIF in April), the long-standing Early Music Festival (Sep and Oct), along with feature and documentary cinema festivals ensure that the city entertainment scene thrives all year round.

Acrobatic performers, St Petersburg's circus

The Russian Circus

Circuses first appeared in Russia in the early 19th century, but it was not until 1876–7 that Russia's first permanent circus building was erected for Gaetano Ciniselli's Italian circus. St Petersburg's circus is still based at this historic site, which was modernized in 1963, and continues to practise the traditional training, skills and animal acts which have made the Russian circus famous throughout the world.

The Arts

For a city renowned worldwide for its rich tradition of ballet and classical music, it is not surprising that St Petersburg has a wide range of cultural events on offer. An evening spent at any of the three Mariinskiy Theatre venues is a highlight of any visit. It is also well worth venturing into the many other theatres, music halls and churches to absorb the city's cultural diversity. Classical music is vastly popular and local orchestras are much in demand the world over. In addition, there are the evocative sounds of church choirs, the lively ambience of folk cabarets, and numerous festivals *(see pp52–5)* held to encourage young musicians, composers, film-makers and dancers.

Mariinskiy Theatre

The **Mariinskiy Theatre** *(see p121)*, the epitome of the best in Russian ballet and opera, is a veritable performing arts complex, encompassing three separate venues. In addition to the historical stage, a nearby concert hall stages both concerts and small-scale operas, while the lavish Mariinskiy II is the city's newest stage and one of Europe's best-equipped. To see the current programme, check the website and keep an eye on the listings.

Ballet

Some of the best dancers in the world come from the **Mariinskiy** *(see p121)*. Tickets for performances by leading ballerinas Ulyana Lopatkina and Diana Vishneva are hard to come by. One of the highlights of the year is the Christmas performance of *The Nutcracker*, danced by children from the Vaganova Ballet School *(see p112)*. Ballet at the **Mussorgsky Opera and Ballet Theatre** and the **Conservatory Opera and Ballet Theatre** *(see p122)* are of more varied quality but still provide good entertainment.

In summer, many troupes perform for tourists in various theatres, but with inconsistent levels of skill. Boris Eifmann's modern ballet company is one of the city's best, often touring abroad and winning critical praise. When at home, they perform at the **Alexandrinskiy Theatre** *(see p112)*.

Opera

Tchaikovsky's opera *Eugene Onegin* and Mussorgsky's *Boris Godunov* remain stalwarts in any repertory. Operas are performed (usually in their original language) at the **Mikhailovsky Theatre** and at the **Mariinskiy**. Look out for local stars Anna Netrebko and Olga Borodina, or the tenor Vladimir Galuzin. Less common works, including 18th-century chamber operas, are performed by **St Petersburg Opera** on their own stage, and at the **Hermitage** and tiny **Yusupov Theatres**. Look out for sparkling productions at the children's theatre **Zazerkalye** *(see p203)*.

Classical Music

The city's classical repertoire is huge. Tchaikovsky, Shostakovich, Mussorgsky and Rimsky-Korsakov lived in St Petersburg and their music is performed here frequently.

The **Great Hall of the Philharmonia** *(see p100)*, the **Small Hall of the Philharmonia** *(see p50)* and the **Academic Capella** *(see p114)* are historic venues for classical concerts. The former is the home of the St Petersburg Philharmonic Orchestra. Other historic locations used for concerts include the Hermitage *(see p86)*, and the palaces of Tsarskoe Selo *(see pp154–7)* and Sheremetev *(see p131)*. By contrast, **Dom Kochnevoy** and **Beloselskiy-Belozerskiy** are intimate spaces for chamber music.

Church Music

The music of an Orthodox choir is one of the most evocative sounds in Russia. The best are heard on Saturday evenings and Sunday mornings at the **Holy Trinity Cathedral** in Alexander Nevsky Monastery *(see pp132–3)* and at the **Cathedral of the Transfiguration** *(see p129)*. Services in the **Cathedral of Our Lady of Kazan** *(see p113)* are also of a high standard. More formal religious music is performed in the **Smolnyy Cathedral** *(see p130)*.

Folk Music

The tourist industry encourages visits to concerts of Russian folk music and dancing, some of which are very good, especially those at the **Nikolaevskiy Palace**. Many restaurants have a folk cabaret, though these can be kitsch and loud. **Podvoryie** restaurant in the grounds of Pavlovsk Palace *(see p160–63)*, however, has an excellent, small ensemble.

Street Music

Democracy has had the unexpected effect of allowing many informal activities such as busking, which has brought some highly talented musicians onto the streets. Today, as skilled players stake their pitches, the sound of music fills the city's streets. The two under-passes beneath Nevskiy prospekt by Gostinyy Dvor are busy busking spots, while other metro stations are popular sites for old ladies singing Russian love ballads.

Theatre

All performances are in Russian. For non-Russian-speakers, productions of classic plays such as *The Cherry Orchard* may be interesting to experience, but more obscure works can be difficult.

Since the days of the Soviet Union, the leading light in the drama world has been the **Bolshoy Drama Theatre** (BDT). The Alexandrinskiy Theatre is the oldest in Russia; one of the newest is the **Molodyozhnyy (Youth) Theatre**. Lev Dodin's direction of the **Malyy Drama Theatre (MDT)** has brought it international fame as the "Theatre of Europe", despite all performances being in Russian (though some are performed in English).

Cinema

Most cinemas now show Hollywood blockbusters, but these are dubbed into Russian rather than subtitled. **The Angleterre Cinema Lounge** often holds showings of undubbed films, as do a few Russian cinemas such as **Dom Kino**, **Avrora** and the

Formula Kino multiplex at Galeria. A large number of film festivals are held in the city every year, and these frequently include films in their original language.

The St Petersburg Times, Afisha and Time Out give full coverage of all festivals, including the main **Festival of Festivals** (see p53).

DIRECTORY

Tickets

Tickets are sold in city kiosks and at individual theatres unless stated otherwise.

Ballet and Opera

Conservatory Opera and Ballet Theatre
Театр оперы и балета Консерватории
Teatr opery i baleta Konservatorii
Teatralnaya pl 3.
Map 5 C3.
Tel 312 2519.

Hermitage Theatre
Эрмитажный театр
Ermitazhnyy teatr
Dvortsovaya nab 34.
Map 2 E5.
Tel 571 5059.
(Tickets from city kiosks and hotels only.)

Mariinskiy Theatre
Мариинский театр
Mariinskiy teatr
Teatralnaya pl 1.
Map 5 B3.
Tel 326 4141.
w mariinsky.ru

Mikhailovsky Theatre
Михайловский Театр
Teatr Mikhailovsky
Pl Iskusstv 1.
Map 6 E1.
Tel 595 4305.
Closed late Jul–Aug.
w mikhailovsky.ru

St Petersburg Opera
Санкт-Петербург опера
Sankt-Peterburg opera
Galernaya ul 33.
Map 5 B2.
Tel 312 3982.

Yusupov Theatre
Юсуповский театр
Yusupovskiy teatr
Yusupov Palace, nab reki Moyki 94. **Map** 5 B3.
Tel 314 9883, 314 1991.

Classical Music

Academic Capella
Академическая Капелла
Akademicheskaya Kapella
Nab reki Moyki 20.
Map 2 E5.
Tel 314 1058.

Beloselskiy-Belozerskiy Palace
Дворец Белосельских-Белозерских
Dvorets Beloselskikh-Belozerskikh
Nevskiy pr 41.
Map 7 A2.
Tel 315 5236.

Dom Kochnevoy
Лом Кочневой
Nab reki Fontanki 41.
Map 6 F2.
Tel 310 2987.

Great Hall of the Philharmonia
Большой зал филармонии
Bolshoy zal Filarmonii
Mikhaylovskaya ul 2.
Map 6 F1.
Tel 710 4257.

Small Hall of the Philharmonia
Малый зал филармонии
Malyy zal Filarmonii
Nevskiy pr 30.
Map 6 F1.
Tel 571 8333.

Church Music

Cathedral of Our Lady of Kazan
Собор Казанской Богоматери
Sobor Kazanskoy Bogomateri
Kazanskaya ploshchad 2.
Map 6 E1.
🕐 9am & 7:30pm daily.

Cathedral of the Transfiguration
Спасо-Преображенский собор
Spaso-Preobrazhenskiy sobor
Preobrazhenskaya pl 1.
Map 3 B5.
🕐 10am & 6pm daily.

Holy Trinity Cathedral
Свято-Троицкий собор
Svyato-Troitskiy sobor
Alexander Nevsky Monastery,
pl Aleksandra Nevskovo.
Map 8 E4.
🕐 10am & 6pm daily.

Smolnyy Cathedral
Смольный собор
Smolnyy sobor
Ploshchad Rastrelli 3.
Map 4 F4.
Tel 577 1421.

Folk Music

Nikolaevskiy Palace
Николаевский дворец
Nikolaevskiy dvorets
Pl Truda 4.
Map 5 B2.
Tel 312 5500.

Theatre

Alexandrinskiy Theatre
Александринский театр
Aleksandrinskiy teatr
Ploshchad Ostrovskovo 6.
Map 6 F2.
Tel 380 8050.
w alexandrinsky.ru

Bolshoy Drama Theatre (BDT)
Большой драматический театр
Bolshoy dramaticheskiy teatr
Nab reki Fontanki 65.
Map 6 F2.
Tel 244 1071.
w bdt.spb.ru

Malyy Drama Theatre (MDT)
МДТ – Театр Евролы
MDT – Teatr Evropy
Ul Rubinshteyna 18.
Map 7 A2.
Tel 713 2078.

Molodyozhnyy Theatre
Молодёжный театр на фонтанке
Molodyozhnyy teatr na Fontanke
Nab reki Fontanki 114.
Map 6 D4.
Tel 316 6564.

Cinema

Angleterre Cinema Lounge
Angleterre Hotel, Malaya Morskaya ulitsa 24.
Map 6 D2.
Tel 494 5990. (Tickets from the hotel concierge.)

Avrora Cinema
Аврора
Nevskiy pr 60.
Map 7 A2.
Tel 315 5254.

Dom Kino
Дом Кино
Karavannaya ulitsa 12.
Map 7 A1.
Tel 314 5614.

Formula Kino
Формула Кино
Galeria, Ligovskiy prospekt 30.
Map 7 C3.
Tel 676 7776.

Mirage
Мираж
Bolshoy pr 35, Petrogradskaya.
Map 1 C2.
Tel 677 6060.

Live Music and Nightlife

St Petersburg was at the heart of the underground Soviet rock scene and many of the best Russian sounds originate here. The nightclub scene offers mostly techno music and mainstream pop, in vast complexes with strobe lights, and attracts the well-paid young and *nouveaux riches*. Some smaller clubs featuring an eclectic mix describe themselves as "art" clubs or cafés, and host live music one night and avant-garde fashion shows or films the next. Some large clubs and casinos accept credit cards. Where hours are not given, check programmes before heading out. Avoid places that admit foreigners or women free.

Art and Café Clubs

Fish Fabrique is probably the oldest art café in town, having survived the ups and downs of recent Russian history. **Brodyachaya Sobaka** has been frequented by poets such as Anna Akhmatova since the Silver Age, and other major poets still come here to perform their works in arts events. **GEZ-21** even manages to fit poetry and philosophy readings in among rock concerts.

Rock Venues

Under the Soviet regime, Leningrad rock was rebellious without being overtly political. Though there is now less emphasis on poetical lyrics that express a spirit of freedom from control and repression, Russian rock still owes much to its rebellious past, while also managing to incorporate the latest in Western music trends.

Kosmonavt hosts international bands, while **A2** is a popular concert venue that hosts local and international acts. Rockabilly gave birth to **Money Honey** and to the **City Club** upstairs (for older rockers), which in turn led to an explosion of rockabilly groups in the city.

Big-name, massed audience rock and pop concerts are usually held in one of the big concert halls such as the **Oktyabrskiy Bolshoy Kontsertnyy Zal**, or the largest of them all, the **Ledovyy Dvorets**. When major international stars come to town, however, they usually perform on a specially erected stage in Palace Square.

Jazz Venues

The father of Petersburg jazz is David Goloshchokin, who set up the **Jazz Philharmonic Hall**. As the name suggests, the jazz played in the hall is mainly very traditional, and, sadly, dancing or talking are prohibited. **JFC** has led the way for improvisation and innovative jazz. Guests here are often musicians with an international reputation. **Jimi Hendrix Blues Club** comes a close second to JFC by virtue of its mixture of blues and rock, and its good food.

Restaurants such as **Sunduk** (*see p191*) often bring in good live performers. **48 Chairs** is a classy, intimate restaurant-club that puts on nightly shows.

Bars with Music

Live music is played in many bars around town, but on the whole a lot of the music in such places is awful. It is best to stick with the established, more reliable clubs.

Liverpool, for example, hosts live bands, not all of whom play Beatles cover versions. In addition, **Manhattan** sometimes has good jazz acts. **Da:da** has two concert halls and its eclectic programming often sees punk music fans in one room, while jazz aficionados sit just next door.

Nightclubs and Discos

Big entertainment complexes such as **Metro** (with three floors) cater mainly to the young and upwardly mobile, playing house, techno and Russian dance music. **Barrel** is an upscale nightclub with guest DJs, karaoke and a restaurant. **MOD** is centrally located and attracts a student crowd at its DJ nights and performances.

Circus Club is situated in the basement of a historical building with old brick arches, and the crowd it attracts is similarly focused on underground music.

Smaller, more diverse clubs, such as the underground **Griboedov**, are still very much of the alternative culture trend, playing a variety of the latest hits from Europe, and hosting fashion shows and other cultural events. **Purga**, literally meaning "snowstorm", celebrates New Year's Eve every night, complete with a midnight countdown. In summer, the club takes the revelry riverside, with nightly cruises. **Zal Ozhidaniya**, which is housed in a former railway station, is one of St Petersburg's few medium-sized venues and attracts international artists.

Gay Clubs

For some reason, few gay clubs in St Petersburg manage to last more than four or five years. **Cabaret** is, however, an exception, remaining popular while other venues come and go; and **Central Station** seems to have made a go of it, too. Gay culture in the city is strongly tied into the art world, and events are advertised at Saturday exhibitions in the New Academy of Fine Arts at Pushkinskaya ulitsa 10.

Billiards and Bowling

Along with bars and night-clubs, a popular night out in St Petersburg is billiards and bowling.

Billiard halls and bowling alleys are casual but upmarket affairs and always serve a full selection of alcohol as well as offering respectable restaurants with extensive menus. Many locals go to these places without ever lifting a pool cue or a bowling ball, instead preferring to enjoy the atmosphere.

DIRECTORY

Art and Café Clubs

Brodyachaya Sobaka
Бродяиая Собака
Italianskaya ulitsa 4.
Map 6 F1.
Tel 312 8047.
w vsobaka.ru

Fish Fabrique
Ligovskiy pr 53.
Map 7 B3.
Tel 764 4857.
Open 3pm–6am daily.
w fishfabrique.ru

GEZ-21
ГЕЗ-21
Ligovskiy pr 53.
Map 7 B3.
Tel 764 5258.
w gez21.ru

Rock Venues

A2
Pr Medikov 3.
Tel 309 9922.
w a2.fm

Backstage Club
Ligovskiy pr 113.
Map 7 B4.
Tel 958 3888.

Kosmonavt
Космонавт
Bronnitskaya ulitsa 24.
Map 6 E5.
Tel 303 3333.
w cosmonavt.su

Ledovyy Dvorets
Ледовый дврец
Pr Pyatiletok 1.
Tel 718 6620.

Money Honey / City Club
Apraksin dvor block 13,
Sadovaya ul 28–30.
Map 6 E2.
Tel 310 0549.

Oktyabrskiy Bolshoy Kontsertnyy Zal
БКЗ Октябрьский
Ligovskiy prospekt 6.
Map 7 C1.
Tel 275 1300.

Yubileynyy Dvorets Sporta
Дворец спорта юбилейный
Pr Dobrolyubova 18.
Map 1 B3.
Tel 602 2005.

Jazz Venues

48 Chairs
Ulitsa Rubinshteyna 5.
Map 7 A2.
Tel 315 7775.
w 48chairs.com

Jazz Philharmonic Hall
Филармония Джазовой музыки
Zagorodnyy prospekt 27.
Tel 764 8565.
Open 7–11pm Tue–Sun.
w jazz-hall.spb.ru

JFC
Shpalernaya ulitsa 33.
Map 3 C4.
Tel 272 9850.
Open 7–10pm daily.
w jfc-club.spb.ru

Jimi Hendrix Blues Club
Джими Хендрикс блюз-клуб
Liteynyy prospekt 33.
Map 3 A5.
Tel 579 8813.
Open noon–midnight daily. Concerts: 8:30pm.

Bars with Music

Da:da
Moskovskiy prospekt 109/3.
Tel +7 921 424 3969.
w clubdada.ru

Datscha
Дача
Dumskaya ul 9.
Map 6 E2.
Open 6pm–6am daily.

Liverpool
Ливерпуль
Ul Mayakovskovo 16.
Map 7 B1.
Tel 579 2054.

Manhattan
Nab reki Fontanki 90.
Map 6 E3.
Tel 713 1945.
Open 1pm–midnight daily.
w manhattanclub.ru

Nightclubs and Discos

Alfa.fm
Ligovskiy pr 50, building 15. **Map** 7 B3.
Tel +7 921 998 9888.

Barrel
Kazanskaya ulitsa 5.
Map 6 E2.
Tel 929 8298
w project-barrel.ru

Circus Club
Konyushennaya Ploshchad 2.
Map 2 E5.
Tel 922 2050.
Open midnight–6am daily. **w** club-circus.ru

Coyote Ugly
Liteynyy prospekt 57.
Map 7 A1.
Tel 272 0790.
w coyoteugly.ru

Estrada
Ul Sadovaya 17.
Map 6 F2.
Tel 931 5101.
Open 6pm–6am daily.

Griboedov
Грибоедов
Voronezhskaya ul 2A.
Map 7 B4.
Tel 764 4355.
Open 2pm–6am.
w griboedovclub.ru

Metro
Метро
Ligovskiy pr 174.
Tel 766 0204.
Open 10pm–6am daily.
w metroclub.ru

MOD
Nab kanala Griboedova 7.
Map 6 E1.
Tel +7 921 881 8371.
w modclub.info

Purga
Пурга
Nab reki Fontanki 11.
Map 7 A1.
Tel 570 5123.
w purga-club.ru

Santa Barbara
Kazanskaya ulitsa 7.
Map 6 E2.
Tel 900 0666.
w santabarbaraclub.ru

Zal Ozhidaniya
Зал Ожидания
Nab Obvodnovo kanala 118.
Tel 333 1068.
w clubzal.com

Gay Clubs

Cabaret (A.K.A. Matrosskaya Tishina)
Кабаре
Razezzhaya ulitsa 43.
Tel 764 0901.
w cabarespb.ru

Central Station
Ulitsa Lomonosova 1.
Map 6 E2.
Tel 312 3600.
w centralstation.ru

Billiards and Bowling

Art Billiard
Арт-Бильярд
Bolshaya Morskaya ulitsa 52.
Map 5 C2.
Tel 312 3077.
w art-billiard.ru.

Bowling City Sennaya
Боулинг Сити Сенная
Ulitsa Yefimova 3.
Map 6 E3.
Tel 380 3005.
w bowlingpark.ru.

The Cellar
Birzhevoi proyezd 2/24.
Map 1 C5.
Tel 335 2207.

Sapsan
Сапсан
Galeria Mall,
Ligovskiy 300.
Map 7 C3.
Tel 600 0331.
w sapsan-bowling.ru

SURVIVAL
GUIDE

PRACTICAL INFORMATION

The street signs and maps of St Petersburg are not as difficult to negotiate as it may first appear when confronted with daunting Cyrillic letters. Not only do hotels, restaurants and all service sectors attempt to compensate by being helpful to foreigners, but the city has English signage pointing out major sights and shops. There are also several tourist information offices located near popular places of interest. On the street, many things will seem unfamiliar, but with patience and determination everything is possible, from making international telephone calls and exchanging money to finding emergency medical treatment. The city has developed at an astonishing pace during the last decade, and as quality improves, prices now often outstrip Western equivalents.

The Grand Cascade of Peterhof Palace during the White Nights

When to Go

The height of the tourist season in St Petersburg is during the famed White Nights (see p53 and p203), from mid-May to mid-July, when the sun barely sets for an hour due to the city's northern location. Prices at this time are at their highest. Fewer tourists visit during the winter.

Visas and Passports

Visas are required for all visitors to Russia. Package tour companies will organize visas for you, but independent travellers need to arrange their own. Document requirements change regularly and it is essential to check these in advance (http://ru.vfsglobal.co. uk). You will need to show proof of an invitation (visa support) from a hotel, tour company or business in Russia. Invitations can be purchased online at **visaable.com** or from **Go Russia**. The easiest option is to pay your travel agency to process the visa for you. Alternatively, fill in the appli-cation yourself and either post it or deliver it in person to the **Russian Visa Centre** in London.

Customs Information

Passports and visas are checked thoroughly at immigration. Visitors must fill out an immigration card, which is available in Russian and English. Part of the completed card is retained by travellers for presentation on departure.

There are no limitations on the amount of money you can bring into Russia; Russian money to the value of 326,000 roubles may be exported. Any items of considerable value, such as diamond jewellery, should be noted on a customs form on entry.

All foreigners must register with **OVIR** (visa registration) within seven working days before travelling and obtain a stamp of registration on their migration card or in their passport. Tourists spending less than seven working days in the country do not need to register.

Tourist Information

Hotels are a good source of tourist information, as are Tourist information offices. **Ostwest** runs a reliable tourist information service, as well as booking accommodation and entertainment. Also try www. saint-petersburg.com, which is a useful English-language website. The bimonthly free guide St Petersburg In Your Pocket and English-language news-papers (see p219) give up-to-the-minute information.

Tourist information kiosks can be found all over the city centre: Palace Square, Ploshchad Vosstaniya, Smolnyy Cathedral, Sadovaya ulitsa and St Isaac's Square. Main offices are at the airport.

Tourists consulting a map to find their way in St Petersburg

Admission Prices

Many museums and theatres, notably the Hermitage (see pp86–95), the Russian Museum (see pp106–9) and the Mariinskiy (see p121) charge foreigners a higher entry fee than Russians. Students and schoolchildren are entitled to discounts.

◀ Aerial view of St Petersburg from St Isaac's Cathedral on the south embankment

The ticket office is often positioned away from the entrance, so look for the "KACCA" sign. Ticket prices vary from about 50 roubles for small state museums to 400 roubles for entrance to the Hermitage. A good-value option is to buy a Tourist Card from tourist information offices. Cards are valid for two days (2,000 roubles) to seven days (4,500 roubles), and offer free entry to many state museums, as well as discounts in some restaurants.

Opening Hours

Most sights are open from 10:30am to 6pm, with no break for lunch, and close one day a week. They also close one day each month for cleaning; see individual museum entries for this information. Last tickets are sold about 1 hour before closing. Parks are usually open from 10am to 10pm, later during White Nights.

ОТКРЫТО

Sign for open (otkryto)

ЗАКРЫТО

Sign for closed (zakryto)

Visiting Churches

Attending an Orthodox service is a fascinating experience. Since services tend to run for several hours, it is generally fine simply to drop in. Certain dress codes must be observed: no shorts; men should remove hats; women should cover their shoulders and chest and preferably wear a hat or headscarf. Women in trousers are accepted in town churches, but small monasteries outside of the city will strictly enforce the no-trousers rule. The most important services are held on Saturday evening, Sunday morning and on major religious holidays.

Most major faiths are represented in the city. Churches tend to be open all day from

St Isaac's Cathedral (see pp80–81), open to visitors

early morning until late. Service times at Catholic and Protestant churches are published in The St Petersburg Times (see p219).

Language

Cyrillic, the alphabet used in the Russian language, is named after the 9th-century monks Cyril and Methodius who invented it. The apparent similarity between Cyrillic and roman letters can be misleading. Some letters are common to both alphabets, others look similar but represent totally different sounds. Various systems of transliteration are in usage, but they do not differ enough to cause serious confusion.

Most people who come into contact with tourists speak some English and passers-by on the street will do their best if asked directions. Knowledge of a few Russian words (see pp260–64) is appreciated.

Etiquette and Smoking

On public transport, it is expected that young men should offer their seats to women with young children or the elderly.

Greetings among friends involve a handshake (between men) or a kiss, or simply saying – "privet" (hi).

Photographic restrictions have more or less disappeared. In museums, expect to buy a ticket for the right to photograph or film inside. Tripods and flashes are not to be used. Photography in the metro is

prohibited as it is seen as a threat to national security. If you do wish to take a photo in the metro, approach a police officer, who may allow you to for a fee, which is unlikely to exceed 100 roubles.

Smoking is prohibited in cinemas, museums, theatres and on public transport, as well as on long-distance trains, railway stations, airports and in restaurants, bars and clubs. Drinking alcohol is prohibited in the street. Russians take great pleasure in smoking and drinking and frequent toasts are required to justify the filling and draining of glasses. At a private home, always toast the hostess (za khozyayku) or the host (za khozyayina).

Public Conveniences

The situation is improving, but most public toilets are quite basic, and most cafés do not have any toilet facilities at all. In such cases, go to the nearest hotel or use the pay toilets located in department stores. The person who takes the money also hands out toilet paper. There are portaloos with attendants situated near several of the major tourist attractions. The fee ranges from 20 to 35 roubles. Baby-changing facilities are an extremely rare amenity in Russia and can be found only in upscale hotels, the biggest shopping malls and Western-owned stores such as IKEA, where they are usually free of charge.

Taxes and Tipping

Roubles are the sole valid currency in Russia (see p217). All cash payments must be made in roubles only and all prices are given in roubles. Credit cards are accepted in most restaurants and hotels, as well as larger shops, though there are some places that will not accept them so it is best to carry cash with you.

Tipping is a matter of choice. Simply pay what you feel is right; 50 or 100 roubles is usually sufficient.

The Hermitage museum offers disabled access to visitors

Travellers with Special Needs

While just a few years ago St Petersburg had almost no facilities for disabled visitors, the situation is gradually improving, though services remain far from ideal and transport in particular is a problem. Of the museums, only the Hermitage and the Russian Museum have disabled access. Many 4- and 5-star hotels are now equipped for disabled guests, with ramps, lifts, wider doorways, handrails and showers with removable sides. **Liberty** specializes in tours around St Petersburg and its suburbs for disabled travellers. The company uses minibuses equipped with a lift or folding ramp to transport wheelchair-users around the city, and can also advise on hotels and restaurants with disabled access and facilities.

Travelling with Children

Russians adore children, and travellers in the company of under-tens are likely to attract a good deal of attention and many compliments. Russian *babushki* (grannies) also think nothing of telling parents of their failings.

The city has many parks and during school holidays temporary playgrounds are sometimes set up around town. There are several playgrounds in the Tauride Gardens *(see p130)*, as well as a playground in the gardens next to the Bronze Horseman *(see pp80–81)*. Museums and public transport are free for under-sevens.

Schoolchildren pay the full fare on transport, but pay a reduced price at museums (proof of being under 18 may be required).

Attractions guaranteed to delight younger travellers are listed in the Children's Entertainment section *(see p203)*.

Young visitors enjoying the view

Senior Travellers

St Petersburg is popular with senior travellers and many hotels offer guided coach trips around the city. Concierges can arrange tickets and transport to ballet and opera performances, as well as to the city's museums and the former imperial estates located outside St Petersburg.

Discounts for pensioners are often available at museums and for other activities such as boat trips, but not for single tickets on transport.

The hotels on St Isaac's Square, such as the Astoria *(see p177)* and Angleterre *(see p178)*, are quiet and in convenient locations, as is the Belmond Grand Hotel Europe *(see p178)*, located close to many sights.

Gay and Lesbian Travellers

Russian society is not in general very tolerant of homosexuality, and men in particular should be aware that public displays of affection may attract unwanted attention. The city does, however, have a thriving gay and lesbian scene, with several gay clubs *(see p206)*.

The **Russian LGBT Network** provides general information on gay and lesbian life in the city. Local organizations **Coming Out** and **Gay.ru** provide information orientated to gay and lesbian visitors. *The St Petersburg Times* includes gay clubs and bars in its club guide, but there are no English-language listings of daily events.

Travelling on a Budget

St Petersburg is no longer a cheap city to visit, and it is increasingly difficult to find things to do on a budget. There are, however, many *stolovayas* (canteens) around the city, where travellers can enjoy traditional Russian food at bargain prices.

There is an increasing number of hostels in the city *(see p172)*, such as Life Hostel on Nevskiy prospekt, from where some of **Peter's Walking Tours** leave. Free English-language walking tours are also available. Several bike-rental offices in the city offer an affordable way to get around, and public transport is inexpensive compared to many Western European cities.

An ISIC (international student card) entitles its holder to discounts in museums and on rail and air travel, although convincing ticket sellers of this may be more trouble than its worth. A visit to the Hermitage is free upon presentation of an ISIC card, and for all visitors on the first Thursday of every month.

Entrance to all parks inside the city is free, as well as to the grounds of the Peter and Paul Fortress *(see pp68–9)*. The Field of Mars *(see p96)* is popular with young people in warmer months.

Time

St Petersburg follows Moscow time, which is 4 hours ahead of Greenwich Mean Time (GMT), and 9 hours ahead of Eastern Standard Time. As of 2014, Russia decided to remain on permanent winter time and abandon the practice of changing the clocks. This decision reverses former plans, which were quite unpopular, to stay on summertime.

Electricity

The electrical current is 220 V. Two-pin plugs are required, but some of the old Soviet two-pin sockets do not take modern European plugs, which have slightly thicker pins. American appliances require a 220:110 current adaptor. Travellers are advised to bring adaptors with them because they can be difficult to find in St Petersburg.

Responsible Travel

While St Petersburg, and Russia as a whole, have a regrettably poor record with regard to the environment, it is easy to travel about the city using green transport, such as trolleybuses and trams. Bikes can be rented from companies such as **Skat Prokat** and Velotour (see p225), although it is best to stick to quieter side roads.

It is possible to visit most of the city's major attractions on foot, either independently or on a walking tour (see p224). At **Sennoi Market**, a small part of the outdoor area is devoted to fruit and vegetables that have been grown locally in the Leningrad Oblast area.

Conversion Table

Imperial to Metric
1 inch = 2.54 centimetres
1 foot = 30 centimetres
1 mile = 1.6 kilometres
1 ounce = 28 grams
1 pound = 454 grams
1 pint = 0.6 litres
1 UK gallon = 4.6 litres

Metric to Imperial
1 centimetre = 0.4 inches
1 metre = 3 feet, 3 inches
1 kilometre = 0.6 miles
1 gram = 0.04 ounces
1 kilogram = 2.2 pounds
1 litre = 1.8 UK pints

DIRECTORY

Embassies and Consulates

Australia
14 Petrovskiy prospekt, office 22–N.
Tel 325 7334.
w dfat.gov.au/ missions/countries/ rupe.html

Canada
Moscow, Starokonju-shenny per 23.
Tel (495) 925 6000.
w canadainternational. gc.ca/russia-russie

Ireland
30 Kuznetsovskaya ulitsa.
Tel (495) 326 9057 or (495) 937 0233.

New Zealand
Moscow, Povorskaya ul 44. **Tel** (495) 956 3579.
w nzembassy.com/ russia

UK
Pl Proletarskoy Diktatury 5.
Map 4 E4.
Tel 320 3200.

US
Furshtatskaya ul 15.
Map 3 B4.
Tel 331 2600.
w stpetersburg. usconsulate.gov

Visas and Passports

Go Russia
Boundary House, Boston Road, London, W7 2QE.
Tel (020) 3355 7717.
w justgorussia.co.uk

Russian Visa Centre
15–27 Gee Street, London EC1V 3RD.
Tel 0905 889 0149.
w ru.vfsglobal.co.uk

Visaable.com
Tel +7 921 369 3412.
w visaable.com

Customs Information

OVIR
Овир
(Tsentralnyy district)
Foreign department,
Pereulok Krylova 5.
Map 6 F2.
Tel 273 2246.
(Central) Ul Kirochnaya 4.
Map 3 B5.
Tel 278 3486.
w visatorussia.com

Tourist Information Offices

Main Office
14 Sadovaya ulitsa.
Tel 310 2822.

Information Pavilions

Ploshchad Rastrelli (in front of Smolnyy Cathedral)
Open 8am–6pm Mon–Fri.
Palace Square
Open 10am–7pm daily.
St Isaac's Square
Open 10am–7pm daily.
Ploshchad Vosstaniya
Open 10am–7pm daily.
Marine Facade passenger terminal
Open 10am–7pm daily (May–Sep).
Kronverkskaya Embankment (opposite Peter and Paul Fortress)
Open 10am–7pm daily.
Pulkovo airport
Open 10am–7pm daily.

Ostwest
Ligovskiy prospekt 10.
Map 7 C2. **Tel** 327 3416.
w ostwest.com

Visit Russia
Tel 309 5760.
w visitrussia.com

Travellers with Special Needs

Liberty
12 Ulitsa Polozova.
Tel 232 8163.
w libertytour.ru

Gay and Lesbian Travellers

Coming Out
Tel (812) 242 5469.
w comingoutspb.ru

Gay.ru
w gay.ru

Russian LGBT Network
191040, St Petersburg, Ligovsky prospekt 87, office 528.
Tel (812) 454 6452.
w lgbtnet.ru

Travelling on a Budget

Peter's Walking Tours
Tel 943 1229.
w peterswalk.com

Responsible Travel

Sennoi Rynok (Sennoi Market)
4a Moskovskiy prospekt.
Tel 310 1209.
Open 8am–7pm daily.

Skat Prokat
7 Goncharnaya ulitsa.
Tel 717 6838.

Personal Security and Health

St Petersburg is a relatively safe city. Petty crime should be the only concern for tourists, and even this can generally be avoided if the usual precautions are taken. Make copies of your passport and visa, note Travellers' cheque and credit card numbers and, for language reasons, keep a card with the address you are staying at in Russia. A multilingual tourist helpline (300 3333) can assist with any issue and is a free number from a mobile phone on the Megafon network by dialling 0333 first. Medical insurance is essential, as local healthcare compares poorly with Western standards, and English-speaking services or medical evacuation via Finland are very expensive. Many medicines are readily available, but it is best to bring specific medication needed.

Police officer *(politsiya)*

Police

Several kinds of police officer operate on St Petersburg's streets. Their uniforms change according to the weather, with the very necessary addition of fur hats and big overcoats in the winter. The street officers *(politsiya)* wear dark-grey uniforms and many carry guns. The riot police or OMON wear blue camouflage fatigues.

Separate from both these are the traffic police, whose uniforms carry the logo ДПС (DPS) on the chest and shoulder. They have the authority to stop any vehicle to check documents.

Both the street police and traffic police supplement their income by fining people for minor infringements of the law, and have been known to stop tourists for document checks and then "forget" to return wallets or mobile phones. This is far more likely to happen to drunk tourists. Avoid the police if possible and stay alert if stopped.

What to be Aware of

To avoid trouble once in St Petersburg, simple rules should be observed, such as not displaying large sums of money; carrying cash in a concealed money belt; and keeping passports, tickets and all valuables in the hotel whenever possible. Security in Western-run hotels is very high, but in all hotels it is advisable to place valuables in the safe. Travellers' cheques *(see p216)* may have an insurance policy but are expensive to use and are easily laundered in Russia.

Avoid the "gypsies" who occasionally group on Nevskiy prospekt, apparently begging. If they do approach, do not stop for them and keep a firm hold of your possessions. Also watch out for pickpockets on the metro and buses. A common tactic is for the culprit to (seemingly accidentally) block your exit from the metro car or bus while another goes through your pockets. Avoid the back doors on buses, which are narrower than those in the centre, and be on guard for people employing these tactics.

Women on their own are unlikely to encounter sexual harassment, though they should ignore kerb-crawlers and avoid taking a cab alone at night. When travelling around, always be alert and safety-conscious, as you would in any city. On the streets be aware of local drivers, who see all pedestrians as a nuisance. Avoid walking on manhole covers, which tend to rock or even collapse under your feet.

In an Emergency

In the event of a fire, call 01. For police, call 02 and for an ambulance, call 03. There is also a combined emergency number, 112.

Lost and Stolen Property

The greatest danger faced by foreigners is that posed by pickpockets and petty thieves. If threatened in the streets it is advisable to hand over belongings on demand.

If you have property stolen, report it to the local police

Police car

Fire engine

Ambulance

station for insurance purposes. They are unlikely to have an interpreter, so ask your hotel for assistance or call the **Tourist Helpline**. The central place to go to for lost property is on Suvorovskiy prospekt. You should take all your documents with you: passport, visa and migration card. You will be required to write a statement, so it is important to call the tourist helpline first for an interpreter to be present. If you lose something on the public transport system, call the main tourist helpline. They will hold items for a limited time, so contact them immediately. If you lose your passport, inform your embassy (see p213). Lost credit or debit cards should be reported to the card issuer (see p216–17).

Hospitals and Pharmacies

There are pharmacies (apteka) located throughout the city, and many are open 24 hours. Some stronger medications can be bought over the counter, so prescriptions are not necessary. Every assistant is a trained pharmacist and can advise alternative drugs. If you have specific requirements, particularly insulin, bring sufficient supplies for your stay.

If you fall ill, seek advice at your hotel, which should have its own doctor. Several companies, notably the **Medem International Clinic** and **Euromed**, specialize in dealing with foreigners. They cover everything from minor emergencies, dental care, X-rays and pre-natal care to medical evacuation. Their charges are high, but they are used to dealing with foreign insurance policies.

If you are in need of immediate attention, head to the casualty department of the **Trauma Clinic of the Central District** just off Nevskiy prospekt. Basic care involving stitches or injections can be given. If you are taken to a local hospital and require further treatment, contact either your consulate or one of the above medical centres. They can either

Sign for pharmacy (apteka)

have you moved or they can oversee your care in the hospital.

Dentists can be expensive. The medical clinics listed opposite are covered by insurance policies. **Dental Palace** will offer dental care, but costs will not be reimbursed.

Health Precautions

Neither visitors nor residents should drink tap water, which contains heavy metals and giardia, a parasite causing stomach problems. To be safe drink bottled water only. If you do pick up giardia, it can be treated with metronidazole.

Russian food is unlikely to do much harm, but avoid the meat pies sold on the streets.

Sexually transmitted diseases are on the rise, so all due caution should be exercised.

Mosquitoes (komari) are rife between June and late September. Burning oils or using plugs that heat chemical tablets are recommended for use at night time.

Travel and Health Insurance

Visitors to St Petersburg are advised to take out travel insurance. Check the conditions of your cover before you travel – if possessions are stolen, you will need a copy of the police report to make an insurance claim. Make a note of the 24-hour emergency medical assistance telephone number that comes with your policy – the company can give advice if you need urgent medical attention. Keep any receipts or prescriptions so that you can claim the expenses on your insurance.

DIRECTORY

In an Emergency

Combined emergency number
Tel 112.

Ambulance (skoraya pomoshch)
Tel 03.

Fire (pozharnaya sluzhba)
Tel 01.

Police (politsiya)
Tel 02.

Lost and Stolen Property

Tourist Helpline
Tel 300 3333. From a mobile, call 0333 (free of charge with the Megafon network).

Hospitals and Pharmacies

24-Hour Pharmacy
Nevskiy pr 98.
Tel 275 8189.
Vladimirskiy pr 16.
Tel 324 4400.
Zagorodnyy pr 21.
Tel 315 2743.

American Medical Clinic
Nab reki Moyki 78. Map 2 E5.
Tel 740 2090.
W amclinic.com

Clinic Complex
Ao Poliklinicheskiy kompleks
Moskovskiy pr 22.
Map 6 D5.
Tel 777 9777.

Dental Palace
Petropavlovskaya ulitsa 4.
Map 2 D1.
Tel 325 7500.
W dentalpalace.ru

Euromed
Suvorovskiy pr 60.
Map 4 E4.
Tel 327 0301.
W euromed.ru

Medem International Clinic & Hospital
Ul Marata 6.
Map 7 2B.
Tel 336 3333.
W medem.ru

Trauma Clinic of the Central District
Travmpunkt pri poliklinike n. 7.
Ulitsa Pravdy 6.
Map 7 A4.
Tel 315 2158.

Banking and Local Currency

Major European debit and credit cards can be used in hotels, as well as in most restaurants and shops in St Petersburg. It is advisable to carry some cash, as there are still places that do not accept credit or debit cards. Roubles are the only legal currency and the city is well equipped with exchange offices and ATMs where visitors can turn their currency into roubles. It is advisable to visit a few exchange points before exchanging money, as commission rates offered do vary.

Banks and Bureau de Change

Roubles can be obtained outside Russia, but rates are better once in the country. There are numerous exchange offices throughout St Petersburg, including at the airport.

Many exchange offices are open for 24 hours a day. A passport has to be shown when changing money. Any visible defect on foreign banknotes, especially vertical tears or ink or water stains, can make them difficult to exchange. Travellers should make sure that all the banknotes they bring into Russia are in good condition, and that any US dollars were issued after 1990.

As bank rates are so good in St Petersburg, visitors should never be tempted to change their money on the streets, however appealing the rates on offer appear to be. The unpleasant truth is that street-changers will try to cheat anyone willing to take the risk.

A few of the foreign banks in St Petersburg offer over-the-counter services. The most reliable Russian bank is **Sberbank**.

Banks are plentiful in St Petersburg. There are often branches offering both cash currency exchange, and cash advances on credit or debit cards. Some of the larger branches also cash travellers' cheques. Sberbank exchange rates are generally among the best available, and there are branches conveniently located all over the city. **Alfa-Bank**, **Citibank** and **Raiffeisen** also offer currency exchange.

A fast and safe, but also rather more expensive, way of transferring cash from abroad to Russia is through wiring via Western Union, which has offices in most major banks located in the city centre.

ATMs

There are ATMs located in major hotels such as the Belmond Grand Hotel Europe and Astoria, as well as in Dom Knigi and Gostinyy Dvor, and at regular intervals along Nevskiy prospekt and other main streets. All VISA/Maestro cards are accepted, though

a fee of about 150 roubles per transaction is levied. As always, it is advisable to be alert to the people around you when withdrawing cash, and to cover the keypad when entering your PIN to avoid becoming the victim of credit-card fraud.

Credit and Debit Cards

It is possible to obtain roubles with a credit card through the larger banks as well as from ATMs located all over the city.

The local commission is between 2 and 5 per cent, plus credit-card charges. (This can work out as cheap or cheaper than bringing cash to change.)

The most accepted cards are VISA, MasterCard and Eurocard. Diners Club and American Express are less widely recognized. Less commission is charged for cash in roubles.

DIRECTORY

Banks

Alfa-Bank
Альфабанк
Nab kanala Griboedova 6/2.
Map 6 E1.
Tel +8 800 200 0000.
W alfabank.ru

Citibank
Nevskiy pr 45/2.
Map 7 B2.
Tel 336 7575.

Raiffeisen Bank
Volynskiy per 3A (entrance from nab kanala Griboedova).
Map 5 A4.
Tel 334 4343.
W raiffeisen.ru
Nevskiy pr 102. **Map** 7 B2.
Tel 334 4343.

Sberbank
Сбербанк
Dumskaya ulitsa 1–3.
Map 6 F2.
Tel 272 9089.
W sberbank.ru

VTB 24
Nevskiy pr 29. **Map** 6 F2.
Tel +8 800 505 2424.
W vtb24.ru

ATMs at a branch of Alfa-Bank

If your credit card is lost or stolen, you should report it immediately to the credit-card company so make sure you keep the relevant telephone number to hand.

It can be difficult to find places to cash travellers' cheques, and banks charge at least 2 per cent to do so. Only the larger banks, such as Alfa-Bank and Sberbank, offer this service. Travellers' cheques can only be used as payment for goods or services in a few of the large hotels, and are acceptable only in US dollars and euros. You will need to present your passport whenever exchanging or paying with travellers' cheques.

Currency

The Russian currency is the rouble (or ruble), written рубль or abbreviated to р or руб. The higher denominations are available in banknotes, which bear images of Russian cities, the lower denominations in coins. The kopek, of which there are 100 in a rouble, is issued in coins.

Banknotes

There are 6 denominations of notes, with values of 10, 50, 100, 500, 1,000 and 5,000 roubles. When changing money check that the notes correspond to those shown here.

10 roubles

50 roubles

100 roubles

500 roubles

1,000 roubles

5,000 roubles

Coins

The revaluation of the Russian rouble in 1998 led to the revival of the long-redundant but much-loved kopek. Traditionally, the rouble had always consisted of 100 kopeks. As well as coins for 1, 2, 5 and 10 roubles, there are now coins for 1, 5, 10 and 50 kopeks.

1 rouble

2 roubles

5 roubles

10 roubles

1 kopek

5 kopeks

10 kopeks

50 kopeks

Communications and Media

St Petersburg is home to many tech-savvy people and most cafés and restaurants have a Wi-Fi connection, which is usually free. There are dozens of mobile phone shops on and around Nevskiy prospekt, where a local SIM card can be purchased cheaply (for about 150 roubles) upon presentation of a passport. Unfortunately, the everyday postal service remains notoriously slow and unreliable, but St Petersburg offers several more efficient alternatives. The abundance of newspapers, magazines and TV channels on offer includes some in English.

Visitors using mobile phones at a park in St Petersburg

International and Local Telephone Calls

The local system, Rostelekom (in Cyrillic "Ростелеком"), is reliable and relatively cheap. Rostelekom phone boxes are green and located on the streets and in some metro stations. Most phone boxes have instructions in Russian only.

Local calls made from private phones are usually free of charge. International calls are much cheaper with a prepaid phonecard such as the Zebra card; these are available to buy from kiosks and post offices and also serve as Internet pay-as-you-go cards. A more efficient alternative is to buy a Russian SIM card for your mobile phone (see opposite).

From a payphone, the Emergency Services can be reached by dialling a two-digit number free of charge: for the fire service dial 01, for the police dial 02 and for the ambulance service dial 03.

Mobile Phones

To find out if a mobile phone will work on Russian networks, check with your local service provider before travelling. If you want to ensure your phone will work while you are away you should have a quad-band phone. Tri-band phones from the EU will usually work in Russia, but US mobile phones may not. Visitors should be aware that "roaming" in Russia is very expensive. It is also more expensive to make and receive calls while abroad.

A cheaper option is to buy a Russian SIM card from any of the mobile phone chains, such as Evroset or Svyaznoi. A SIM card costs about 150 roubles and includes the same sum in credit. A passport must be shown when you buy a SIM card.

The four networks – **MTS**, **Megafon**, Beeline and Tele2 all have sufficient coverage and similar charges. Calls within St Petersburg are much cheaper than rates in Western Europe.

Reaching the Right Number

- To phone **Russia** from abroad, dial 007 followed by the local area code and individual number.
- To phone **St Petersburg**, dial 812 followed by the individual number.
- To phone **Moscow**, dial 495 or 499 followed by the individual number.
- St Petersburg directory enquiries, dial 09.
- There is no international directory enquiries.
- Inter-city call booking, dial 07.
- International call booking, dial 315 0012.
- To phone the **UK**, dial 8 (tone) 1044 followed by the number, omitting first 0 from area code.
- To phone **Canada** or the **US**, dial 8 (tone) 101 followed by the number.
- To phone the **Irish Republic**, dial 8 (tone) 10353 followed by the number.
- To phone **Australia**, dial 8 (tone) 1061 then the number.
- To phone **New Zealand**, dial 8 (tone) 1064 followed by the number.
- To phone **South Africa**, dial 8 (tone) 1027 followed by the number.

Internet

Internet access is available at cafés and clubs throughout St Petersburg such as **Cafe Max** and **5.3 GHz**. Free Wi-Fi access is available both inside the Hermitage museum and within

The interior and grounds of the Hermitage offer free Wi-Fi access

its grounds *(see p86)*. Wi-Fi coverage is widely available in hotels, as well as at the airport. It is generally free, though some hotels may charge where Internet is only available in a specific area.

Postal Services

The state-run, international postal system is generally slow and unreliable. A more efficient, and expensive, service is run by **Westpost**, who also offer door-to-door next-day delivery to Moscow. Anything other than papers must go through customs, which can add an extra day.

DHL and **Fedex** also have offices in the city and take three days to deliver to Europe and four to Australia and the US. The Belmond Grand Hotel Europe *(see p178)* runs a quick postal service, taking three days to the UK via Finland, which costs about 130 roubles per letter.

Ordinary post offices, such as the **Main Post Office** *(see p124)*, which is open daily, and those in hotels, sell normal and commemorative Russian stamps, postcards, envelopes and local phonecards. Russian postboxes are marked **Почта** *(Pochta)* and are plentiful in the city centre. Tourists should use the small, pale-blue postboxes. The yellow postboxes are used for local delivery services only.

Addresses

After 1917, when the city was renamed Leningrad, many streets and sights were renamed to avoid imperial connotations or in order to commemorate new Soviet heroes. Since the city resumed its original name after a referendum in 1991, most streets in the centre have officially reverted to their pre-1917 names. The area surrounding the city, however, is still the Leningrad Region. Many people use both the original and Soviet names; no offence is caused when one is used in preference to another. Some useful words to recognize are **улица** (street) and **проспект** (prospekt).

The St Petersburg Times, a popular local newspaper

Newspapers and Magazines

There are three English-language newspapers and magazines available in the city, which are distributed free to all hotels, major restaurants and most fast-food chains. *The St Petersburg Times* comes out every Wednesday and provides coverage of local events, as well as national Russian news and politics, and detailed culture listings and reviews. Church opening times are listed on its website. A useful source of city information is *St Petersburg In Your Pocket*, a free guidebook aimed at tourists and expats that comes out every two months and can be found in hotels, restaurants and bars.

Foreign papers can be picked up at highly inflated prices from major hotels.

Television and Radio

Russian-language television is dominated by soap operas, detective shows and talkshows. The two St Petersburg-based channels are Channel 5 and 100TV. Russia Today, the state-run English-language channel widely viewed as a mouthpiece for the Kremlin, is available in most hotels. Its hourly weather forecasts are useful. Most hotels in St Petersburg have satellite television and receive many other Western programmes.

The best English-language radio broadcast to the city on shortwave is still the BBC World Service.

TRAVEL INFORMATION

St Petersburg is growing in popularity as a tourist destination, with the local government making concerted efforts to attract foreign tourists. As the number of business travellers increases, the number of flights and alternative means of transport is on the rise. Flying remains the most popular way of travelling to St Petersburg, both for individuals and groups, with the train from Moscow or Helsinki a close second. There is a ferry link with Helsinki and Stockholm, while the Baltic capitals can be reached by coach. Independent travel in Russia is difficult for those who don't speak Russian, and for this reason it is worth considering a package tour. British companies run a variety of tours with specialist guides, which often incorporate St Petersburg and Moscow. Package tours can be expensive, but shopping around can uncover some good deals, particularly on flights with stopovers in Europe or low-season package deals.

Exterior of Pulkovo airport

Arriving by Air

Direct flights from the UK to St Petersburg run seven days a week on **British Airways** and four days on **Rossiya**, the local airline. **Lufthansa**, **SAS** and **Finnair** also serve St Petersburg. There are connecting flights on other airlines departing daily and these can often be a cheaper option. **Scott's Tours** in London are particularly good for budget fares and package deals. The journey from London takes around 3 hours, or about 6 hours with a stopover in a European city.

Direct flights to St Petersburg from Ireland, US, Canada, South Africa and Australia are either very limited or simply do not exist. The usual route from these destinations is to fly via a European city or via Moscow, from where you can transfer to another flight or continue by road or rail.

It is worth noting that travelling from Australia can be fairly complicated. The most usual route is to pick up a European carrier in Singapore, with a stopover in Europe. On landing, passengers are sometimes required to confirm onward flights. You can do this through the airline you are travelling with or through the **Central Air Communication Agency** on Malaya Morskaya ulitsa.

St Petersburg is served by **Pulkovo** airport, which was until recently divided between two buildings set a few kilometres apart along a single runway. In 2013, a new terminal opened that made flying in and out of the city much more convenient. Able to handle up to 7 million arrivals a year, the new Pulkovo airport has done away with the separate terminals in favour of one large central structure.

Despite its modernity and size, there are only 14 jetways, meaning that most arrivals and departures will employ buses to transfer passengers between the plane and the terminal. The greatest improvement for international passengers is that the number of passport desks has increased from 10 to 110, significantly reducing waiting times. A number of business lounges, cafés and duty-free shops offer shopping and refreshment. The Park Inn by Radisson Pulkovo Airport hotel sits just steps away, making it a convenient stop for early departures or overnight stays.

Aeroflot company logo

Transport to and from the Airport

The airport is located 17 km (11 miles) south of the city centre. The major hotels operate cars to pick up individual tourists for a cost of around 1,500 roubles, but this service is no longer as essential as it once was as there is now a regulated taxi system in the arrivals halls of both airports. Look for the stand near the exit door marked *Taxi*, and tell the attendant where you want to go. The dispatcher will state how much the journey will cost (this price will be fixed), provide you with a printed receipt and radio in a driver. You should expect to pay about 1,000 roubles to get to the city centre.

A cheaper option for those who have already changed money at the airport, is to take bus No. 39 from directly outside the arrivals hall to Moskovskaya metro station. Minibuses travel the same route and charge about twice as much (see p223).

Arriving by Rail

Rail is a convenient way to travel from Finland to Moscow and within Russia in general, although European student discount passes provide little or no reduction in fares.

More than ten trains a day run in each direction between Moscow and **Moscow Station** and **Ladozhskiy Station**. Twice daily high-speed trains connect Helsinki and **Finlyandskiy Station**. For those with time and a sense of adventure, it is possible to travel by train between London and St Petersburg via Central Europe (Warsaw, Prague, Berlin). It takes about three days and is almost always more costly than flying. Trains are comfortable and usually run on time, but carriages can be overcrowded and thefts are not uncommon. A costly transit visa is also necessary to travel through Belarus. All visitors to Russia need a visa and obtaining one can be a complicated procedure (see p210).

Trains travelling from Eastern Europe arrive and depart from **Vitebskiy Station**. Tickets for train journeys from St Petersburg should be bought from kiosks at the **Central Train Ticket Office**, **Moscow Station**, or from any other railway station in the city, regardless of destination.

An overnight sleeper compartment

Travelling Between Moscow and St Petersburg

Many visitors fly in to Moscow and out of St Petersburg, or vice versa. The most popular form of transport between the two cities is the train, of which there are ten or more a day. The fastest option is the **Sapsan** train, which takes less than 4 hours to travel between the cities, while night-time trains take from 8 to 12 hours.

Prices vary according to the class of the train – the Sapsan being most expensive – and the type of seat. Most trains have a choice of *coupé* (four-person compartment), *platzkart* (dormitory-style carriages), or *sidyachyy* (open seating). For daytime travel *sidyachyy* is more comfortable and cheaper than *platzkart*. One-way prices for standard trains range from 800 roubles for *sidyachyy* to 2,600 roubles for *coupé*. Sapsan tickets start at 4,200 roubles. Food may be available but it is best to take your own.

Regular commercial flights connecting the two cities take 50–90 minutes. These are run by Aeroflot and independent companies such as Rossiya and Transaero. Prices range from 2,700 roubles for an economy class one-way ticket to 4,200 roubles for business class. Tickets are sold online, at the airport, or at the **Central Air Communication Agency**. In summer, travelling by boat to and from Moscow is possible (see p222).

Rail Tickets and Reservations

Tickets can be bought both at **Moscow Station** and at the ticket office on the Griboedova Canal. Long queues are the norm, unless you are prepared to pay about 300 roubles commission to buy tickets (*coupé* class only) from the Service Centre at Moscow train station. E-tickets can be bought online, at www.eng.rzd.ru and www.russiantrains.com. International rail passes are not usually valid on Russian trains and foreigners are not eligible for discounts.

Arriving by Coach

Comfortable coaches run to and from Helsinki in Finland, offering a cheaper alternative to the train. **Lux-Express** runs two daytime coaches and one overnight in each direction; the journey takes around 8 hours. Coach companies do not always use the city's inconvenient coach station, but will drop off instead at various locations in St Petersburg. Dozens of coaches depart for Finland at 6 or 7am every morning and 10 or 11pm every evening from outside the Bukvoyed bookstore on Ploshchad Vosstaniya. The Baltic states can also all be reached by coach. Journey times vary from 8 to 13 hours.

Coach Tickets and Reservations

Timetables, prices and tickets to the Baltic states can all be found at www.ecolines.net and www.luxexpress.eu/ru. They are also sold at the **Eurolines** and **Ecolines** offices. It is best to book ahead as tickets regularly sell out. Students can claim a 10 per cent discount, with an ISIC card. The **Lux-Express** office also sells tickets.

Sapsan train travelling between Moscow and St Petersburg

Arriving by Sea

Arriving by boat can be one of the most exciting and novel ways to approach St Petersburg. Cruises are an increasingly popular way to visit the city, and there are regular ferry services to Helsinki and Stockholm.

Cruise ships and ferries dock at the **Marine Facade Passenger Terminal** on the north side of Vasilevskiy Island. Trolleybus No. 10 and No. 11 and bus No. 7 run from here to the centre.

In summer, river cruises between St Petersburg and Moscow run along the Volga and across to Lake Ladoga. The trips last about two weeks and make a very pleasurable way to see more of Russia. The cruises are bookable in the UK through **Noble Caledonia** or **Voyages Jules Verne**, and in the US through **Visit Russia**. Ships dock at St Petersburg's **River Terminal**, 10 minutes' walk

St Peter Line cruise ship visiting St Petersburg

from Proletarskaya metro. Cruise companies run buses to and from the city centre.

Ferry Tickets and Reservations

Tickets for the ferry to and from Stockholm and Helsinki can be bought online at www.stpeter line.com. The Princess Maria ferry travels between St Petersburg and Helsinki three to four times a week. The journey takes about

12 hours and costs for a one-way ticket range from 1,200 roubles for a berth in a four-person cabin midweek to 18,000 roubles for a spacious deluxe cabin for two at the weekend. The Princess Anastasia ferry travels once or twice a week to Helsinki, Stockholm and Tallinn before returning to St Petersburg. Ticket prices range from 600 to 20,000 roubles, depending on the timing and type of package booked.

DIRECTORY

Tour Companies

Noble Caledonia
2 Chester Close, London
SW1X 7BE.
Tel (0207) 409 0376.
W noble-caledonia.
co.uk

Scott's Tours
141 Whitfield Street,
London W1T 5EW.
Tel (0207) 383 5353.
W scottstours.co.uk

Visit Russia
Tel 309 5760.
W visitrussia.com

Voyages Jules Verne
21 Dorset Square,
London NW1 6QG.
Tel (0207) 616 1000.
W vjv.com

Arriving by Air

Pulkovo
Пулково
Tel 337 3444.
W pulkovoairport.ru

British Airways
Sotsialisticheskaya
ulitsa 14. **Map** 7 A4.
Tel 313 5044.
Tel 346 8146 (Pulkovo).
W britishairways.com

Central Air Communication Agency

Malaya Morskaya ul 16.
Map 6 D1. **Tel** 571 5669
W cavs.ru.

Finnair
Pulkovo airport.
Tel 303 9898.

KLM
Malaya Morskaya ul 23.
Map 6 D1.
Tel 346 6864.

Lufthansa
Botkinskaya ul 15/1.
Map 3 B2. **Tel** 702 1333.
Tel 325 9140 (Pulkovo).

Rossiya
Nevskiy pr 61.
Map 7 B2.
Tel 733 3800.

SAS
Pulkovo airport.
Tel 324 3244.

Arriving by Rail

All Train Enquiries
Tel 055.

Central Train Ticket Office

Центральные железно-дорожные кассы
Tsentralnye zhelezno-dorozhnye kassy
Nab kanala Griboedova
24. **Map** 6 E2.
Tel 067.

Finlyandskiy Station
финляндский вокзал
Finlyandskiy vokzal
Pl Lenina 6. **Map** 3 B3.

Ladozhskiy Station
Ладожский вокзал
Ladozhskiy vokzal
Zanevskiy pr 73.

Moscow Station
Московский вокзал
Moskovskiy vokzal
Pl Vosstaniya.
Map 7 C2.

Vitebskiy Station
Витебский вокзал
Vitebskiy vokzal
Zagorodnyy prospekt 52.
Map 6 F4.

Travelling Between Moscow and St Petersburg

Sapsan
W eng.rzd.ru
W russiantrains.com

Arriving by Coach

Ecolines
Podezdnoi pereulok 3.
Tel 325 2152.
W ecolines.ru

Eurolines/ Lux-Express
2 Mitrofanyevskoe shosse.
Tel 441 3757.
W luxexpress.eu

Sovavto
Park Inn by Radisson
Pulkovskaya, Ploshchad
Pobedy 1.
Tel 740 3985.

Arriving by Sea

Marine Facade Passenger Terminal
Морской фасад
пассажирский терминал
*Morskoy Fasad
passazhirskiy terminal*
Morskaya Naberezhnaya.
Tel 499 0988.
W portspb.ru

River Terminal
Речной вокзал
Rechnoy vokzal
Prospekt Obukhovskoy
Oborony 195.
Tel 262 0239.

GETTING AROUND ST PETERSBURG

Although public transport in the city is abundant, efficient and very cheap, the most enjoyable way to get around and fully appreciate St Petersburg is on foot. A glance at a map that shows the city has a rational, organized layout, which makes it easier to negotiate. A boat cruise along the waterways can also be a wonderful way to become acquainted with St Petersburg. Nevskiy prospekt is where many of the city's transport routes and main roads meet.

Metro lines, tram, bus and trolleybus routes radiate out from here. It is possible to travel without too much difficulty to almost anywhere in town from this main avenue. Driving is not recommended due to the combination of poor road conditions, aggressive Russian driving and over-enthusiastic traffic police. Cyclists, once virtually unheard of in St Petersburg, are now becoming a common sight, and the city has several bike-rental companies.

Green Travel

The greenest ways to get around St Petersburg are on foot or by bike, both of which are perfectly viable options given the compact size of the historical centre. The public transport system is good enough to make using a car unnecessary and many forms of the transport network are also environmentally friendly, such as the extensive trolleybus and metro routes.

Buses and Minibuses

All services run every 10 minutes, sometimes less often. Bus stops in the city centre are marked either by white-and-yellow signs with a black letter "A" for *avtobus*, or by blue signs depicting a bus. Signs are placed by the side of the road or attached to lampposts. Some routes are duplicated by commercial buses, marked with a "k" before the number, or minibuses (though there are no minibus routes along Nevskiy prospekt).

Fares on these buses are 50 per cent higher than those on non-commercial equivalents, and are paid to the driver when getting on or off – if in doubt just follow what other passengers do. Buses can be hailed or requested to stop anywhere along the route.

Useful routes include the No. 22 bus from the Smolnyy Institute *(see p130)* via St Isaac's Square *(see p81)* to the Mariinskiy Theatre *(see p121)*. Bus numbers 3, 7, 22 and 27 run along most of Nevskiy prospekt between Ploshchad Vosstaniya and the Admiralty.

Open-top **City Tour** red buses offer sightseeing excursions from 9am to 8pm daily. Tickets can be bought on board and are valid for one day, costing 600 roubles for an adult ticket.

Trolleybuses

Trolleybuses offer convenient routes and stops around the city. Stops are marked by small blue-and-white signs suspended from wires or lampposts, indicating the trolleybus numbers. These signs show a Cyrillic "T" for trolleybus, on a white background. Trolleybuses can be boarded at the front, middle or back doors. The front eight seats are reserved for the disabled, the elderly and passengers with children. All fares are collected on board by a conductor.

Trams

Trams are disappearing from many roads in the city centre, but some remain. Stops are marked by red-and-white signs suspended on wires above the rails. Trams can be boarded via any of the doors and tickets bought in cash from the conductor. Trams will automatically stop along the route.

Tickets and Travel Cards

A flat fare is payable on all forms of transport, whatever the length of the journey. Tickets are bought from the conductor or, on commercial transport, from the driver.

The cheapest way to travel, if you are staying a few weeks or more, is to buy a monthly or half-monthly travel card for all forms of transport, including the metro *(see pp226–7)*. Prices range from 1,020 to 2,040 roubles. Separate monthly cards are also sold for each form of transport.

A city trolleybus on Nevskiy prospekt

Walking

In some areas, particularly around Palace Embankment, sights are situated so close together that using public transport from place to place is unnecessary. A few of the more scattered sights are at some distance (20 minutes on foot) from the nearest transport and walking the last stretch is often the most practical option. Apart from the ease, getting around on foot can be a most rewarding way to explore the city, allowing you to soak up the atmosphere and appreciate the fascinating architectural and sculptural detail on many of St Petersburg's buildings.

As soon as the sun appears, in winter as well as in summer, people of all ages emerge onto the streets and into the parks. Locals are very fond of walking, whether it be promenading up and down Nevskiy prospekt, or ambling around the Neva at 2am during the White Nights *(see p53)*. The Summer Gardens *(see p97)* and Mikhaylovskiy Gardens have long been popular with local residents. For longer walks mixed with some architectural interest, two good areas to try are Kamennyy and Yelagin islands *(see pp138–9)*, with their official residences and *dachas*, many of them dating from the early years of the 20th century.

For a romantic stroll around the city away from the traffic, walk along the Moyka or Griboedov canals *(see pp136–7)*. To the south of Nevskiy prospekt, majestic buildings give way to smaller, 19th-century residential blocks,

Visitors on a walking tour of St Petersburg

with trees by the waterside and leafy squares and courtyards.

Drivers have little respect for pedestrians and traffic is the main hindrance to walking. Cars drive on the right-hand side, so look left first when crossing the road. If there is a pedestrian underpass, use it and, if not, look for a light-controlled crossing with red and green figures indicating pedestrian right of way. Crossings without lights are marked by a blue sign showing a pedestrian, but although drivers are obliged by law to stop for pedestrians, this does not mean they will, so the greatest care should be taken when crossing the road.

On the main city streets, dark-blue sponsored name-plates give street names in Russian and English. Elsewhere, black-on-white street names are in Cyrillic only.

Guided Tours

Walking tours in English can be booked through **Peter's Walking Tours**, which offers themed excursions such as

Rasputin, Dostoevsky, World War II and Style-Moderne architecture. They also offer guided cycling tours, popular during the White Nights. Liberty offer tours for disabled travellers *(see p212)*. Many bike-hire companies provide their own tours *(see p225)*. Other English-language excursions are available from **Anglotourismo**, who offer free daily walking tours lasting 3 hours as well as guided boat tours *(see p228)*.

One of the taxi styles

Taxis

St Petersburg does not have a coordinated official taxi system, and private cabs come in a variety of colours. There is no uniform taxi style, but a taxi will have an orange chequered light on the top or an illuminated green light on the windscreen when it is available. The more expensive taxis have a yellow *"taksi"* sign on the roof.

Taxis can be found outside metro stations, major sights and hotels. It is usually cheaper and easier to ask hotel or restaurant staff to order you a private taxi rather than attempting to hail one on the street. Taxis can carry

A pedestrian crossing, one of the safer places to cross Russian roads

four people. There are no official taxi ranks in the city, but plenty on the streets to hail. Private cars and taxis that have not been pre-booked are best avoided if you are travelling alone at night.

Taxis in Russia rarely have meters, so if you book in advance, agree the price with the driver before you get in. It is also best to agree the price with the dispatcher at the time of booking and this will be fixed. Journeys in the city centre should cost no more than 400 roubles. After 1am some taxi companies will offer a 10 per cent discount. A journey from the airport to the city centre will cost 1,000 roubles. There may be an extra charge for passengers with large luggage.

Driving

Driving is not recommended but if you do choose to drive, be aware that local drivers tend to ignore rules of the road and do more or less as they like, so be on your guard. Drive on the right and make no left turns on main roads unless a road sign indicates that it is permitted.

In winter conditions, driving requires studded tyres as chains can be damaged on tram lines and vice versa.

There is no charge for street parking in most parts of the city centre. The Corinthia Hotel *(see p178)* and some hotels have 24-hour secured parking, some with an extra charge for non-guests. There are few public car parks in the city centre, with the exception of two at Ploshchad Vosstaniya and one outside **Moscow Train Station**. Car parks are identified by a white letter "P" on a blue sign. These are short-stay car parks and cost 100 roubles for one hour. Car parks are often open 24 hours.

Be aware that the traffic police can pull over drivers at any time in order to check documents and will more often than not find something wrong with your car and may ask for a bribe. Tourists are required by law to have a notarized translation of their driving licence, as producing just an international driving licence will not suffice.

Cycling

St Petersburg is flat and compact and should be a haven for cyclists. Unfortunately, it is also a city of reckless drivers. If you choose to cycle, wear a helmet and stick to quieter side roads or take part in a led cycle tour. Parts of the Neva embankment with wider pavements, such as the area near Smolnyy Cathedral *(see p130)*, is a popular route with cyclists.

Bikes can be rented from **Skat Prokat** and **Velotour**, who also conduct cycling tours. Bike rental costs 150 roubles per hour or 600–800 roubles per day, plus a refundable deposit. Collect your bike from the office or have it delivered for 500 roubles. This delivery service is offered free of charge when you rent a bike with **Rentbike**.

Cycling, an increasingly popular means of transport

DIRECTORY

Buses

City Tours
Pirogovskaya naberezhnaya 7.
Map 5 C2.
Tel 718 4769.
🌐 citytourspb.ru

Public Transport Agency
Ulitsa Rubinshteyna 32.
Map 7 A3. **Tel** 388 9660.
🌐 orgp.spb.ru

St Petersburg Coach Station
Naberegnaya Obvodnogo kanala 36
Tel 756 5777.

Trams and Trolleybuses

GorElectroTrans
Syzranskaya 15.
Tel 610 2088.
🌐 electrotrans.spb.ru

Guided Tours

Anglotourismo
Tel +7 921 989 4722.
🌐 anglotourismo.com

Peter's Walking Tours
Tel 943 1229.
🌐 peterswalk.com

Taxis

St Petersburg Taxi
Tel 068.

Seven Million
Tel 7 000 000.

Six Million
Tel 6 000 000.

Driving

Moscow Train Station
Московский вокзал
Moskovskiy vokzal
Pl Vosstaniya.
Map 7 C2.

Cycling

Rentbike
Griboedova naberezhnaya kanala 57.
Map 5 A4.
Tel 981 0155.
🌐 rentbike.org

Skat Prokat
Goncharnaya ulitsa 7.
Map 7 C2.
Tel 717 6838.
🌐 skatprokat.ru

Velotour
Tel 981 0155.
🌐 velotour-spb.ru.

Travelling by Metro

Since overland transport is the most efficient means of getting around the city centre, the metro is used mainly to get to and from the outskirts of the city. As a tourist attraction, however, the metro's stunning stations, intended by Stalin to be "palaces for the people", should be high on your itinerary. The metro runs until just after midnight. Travelling in the daytime or late evening will avoid most of the two million people estimated to use the metro each day. With just five lines, negotiating the network is fairly straightforward, especially since there are now basic signs in English. Do watch out for pickpockets on the metro – gangs have been known to target travellers getting off particularly at Nevskiy Prospekt metro station.

Sculpture in Pushkinskaya metro

The Metro as a Tourist Attraction

Thousands of tonnes of marble, granite and limestone were used to face the walls, and sculptures, mosaics and chandeliers were commissioned from leading artists for the St Petersburg metro. The first line – the red line – opened in 1955, and is one of the most fascinating, being the supreme embodiment of Stalinist style and ideals. The line's crowning glory has to be Avtovo, incorporating a wealth of style and detail, even down to the moulded glass columns.

The metro now has 67 stations, ranging in style and ambience from the dim lighting and memorial atmosphere of Ploshchad Muzhestva (Courage Square, 1975) near Piskarevskoe Memorial Cemetery (see p128),

to the 1980s vulgarity of Udelnaya and the cool of Komendantskiy Prospekt (2005).

The Network

The metro is vital for getting to and from hotels outside the city centre and the airport.

The five lines run from the outskirts through the centre, where they intersect at one of six main stations.

Trains run every few minutes during the day and every 5 minutes late at night. The last train leaves the station of origin at midnight. There is no rush hour as such but the metro tends to be full at most times of day, which makes it generally safe as it is always busy. Platforms are not staffed, but there is an attendant in a booth at the bottom of each escalator who can call for assistance.

Because of the many waterways in the city, stations are buried deep underground and long escalators lead down to the platforms.

New stations are still being added to the St Petersburg metro to increase efficiency and link the centre to more areas around the city, reducing travel time.

Finding your Way

Before setting foot in St Petersburg's metro, ensure you have a network map with the Cyrillic and transliterated names to hand. There are English and Russian signs in the metro, but knowledge of the Cyrillic station names will be useful. Turnstiles are located at the top of the escalators on route to the trains, where you can touch in with a magnetic card or pay with a metro token (see Tickets and Travel Cards). Follow the signs in the metro to the platform. Once on the platform, the direction of the trains and a list of all stops along the route are marked on the wall; routes are also displayed inside the carriage.

Busy stations may have safety doors between the platform and the trains. When the train stops, these doors open, and only then do the train doors open.

Before the train doors close, an automatic announcement is made: "Ostorozhno. Dveri zakryvayutsya" (Be careful the doors are closing). As the train approaches a stop, the name of

Signs in both Cyrillic and English in the metro system

the station is announced, this will be in Russian only. Announcements are also made if the station you are approaching is an interconnecting one, allowing you to change lines. Keep count of the stops, in case you do not catch the announcements.

To change to another line, follow the interchange signs for переход (*perekhod* – crossing). The exception is at Tekhnologicheskiy Institut, where the two southbound lines are on parallel platforms, as are the two northbound lines: thus to continue in the same direction on another line you simply cross the central concourse.

Exits are marked выход (*vykhod*). Some stations, such as Moskovskaya (for the airport) and Gostinyy Dvor, have two or more exits.

Magnetic metro card

Tickets and Travel Cards

The most common means of paying for the metro is the token (*zheton*), available to buy from metro stations only. Magnetic cards, which can be topped up with as many trips as needed, are also available. There are no zones in the metro, so as with other forms of transport in the city, there is a flat charge for each journey, regardless of the distance.

Barrier machines are installed at the top of the escalators; most take both cards and tokens. Cards must be touched to the illuminated sensor on top. If you try to go through a machine without paying, an automatic barrier closes in front of you. If you have a large bag or suitcase, you must buy a special luggage token, which allows you to pass through a

St Petersburg's Metro

Комендантский Проспект
Komendantskiy pr

Старая деревня
Staraya derevnya

Крестовский остров
Krestovskiy Ostrov

Чкаловская
Chkalovskaya

Спортивная
Sportivnaya

Приморская
Primorskaya

Василеостровская
Vasileostrovskaya

Парнас
Parnas

Пр Просвещения
Pr Prosveshcheniya

Озерки
Ozerki

Удельная
Udelnaya

Пионерская
Pionerskaya

Черная речка
Chernaya Rechka

Петроградская
Petrogradskaya

Горьковская
Gorkovskaya

Девяткино
Devyatkino

Гражданский пр
Grazhdanskiy Pr

Академическая
Akademicheskaya

Политехническая
Politekhnicheskaya

Пл Мужества
Pl Muzhestva

Песная
Lesnaya

Выборгская
Vyborgskaya

Пл ленина
Pl Lenina

Чернышевская
Chernyshevskaya

Гостиный двор
Gostinyy Dvor

Адмиралтейская
Admiralteyskaya

Невский пр
Nevskiy Pr

Садовая
Sadovaya

Сенная пл
Sennaya

Театральная
Teatralnaya
(under construction)

Спасская
Spasskaya

Владимирская
Vladimirskaya

Звенигородская
Zvenigorodskaya

Пушкинская
Pushkinskaya

Пл Восстания
Pl Vosstaniya

Маяковская
Mayakovskaya

Достоевская
Dostoevskaya

Технологический инст
Tekhnologicheskiy Inst

Лиговский пр
Ligovskiy Pr

Пл Александра Невского
Pl Aleksandra Nevskovo

Воковская
Volkovskaya

Обводный Канал
Obvodnyy Kanal

Букжарестская
Bukharestskaya

Балтийская
Baltiyskaya

Нарвская
Narvskaya

Кировский завод
Kirovskiy Zavod

Автово
Avtovo

Ленинский пр
Leninskiy Pr

Пр Ветеранов
Pr Veteranov

Фрунзенская
Frunzenskaya

Моск ворота
Mosk vorota

Электросила
Elektrosila

Парк Победы
Park Pobedy

Московская
Moskovskaya

Звездная
Zvezdnaya

Купчино
Kupchino

Дунайская
Dunayskaya
(under construction)

Шушары
Shushary
(under construction)

Международная
Mezhdunarodnaya

Проспект Славы
Prospekt Slavy
(under construction)

Елизаровская
Elizarovskaya

Ломоносовская
Lomonosovskaya

Пролеарская
Proletarskaya

Обухово
Obukhovo

Рыбацкое
Rybatskoe

Новочеркасская
Novocherkasskaya

Ладожская
Ladozhskaya

Пр болышевиков
Pr Bolshevikov

Ул дыбенко
Ul Dybenko

wider gate at the metro barrier. At the far right an attendant checks passes and allows you to put your token in a machine which does not have automatic barriers. Those with magnetic cards cannot pass through this machine. Monthly magnetic cards for the metro or for all forms of public transport are valid for 70 metro journeys and an infinite number of journeys on overground transport during a calendar month. Cards, which are valid for 35 metro journeys and unlimited overground transport during a two-week period, can also be bought between the 16th and the 5th of each month. Cards can be bought at any time during the

Metro token

month but are valid only from the 1st to the 15th of each month.

Visitors who plan to stay in the city for a while may find it worthwhile to purchase a personal "smart" card bearing their photograph, to which they can transfer credit to fund future journeys at any metro station. Such cards are not inserted into the barrier machines that check tickets and tokens, but placed briefly onto a sensor marked with a white circle. There are no further ticket checks once you have past through the barriers inside the metro station.

DIRECTORY

St Petersburg Metro
Tel 301 9700.
w metro.spb.ru

Canal and River Cruises

St Petersburg's numerous natural waterways were adapted and extended, to make it resemble Peter the Great's beloved Amsterdam *(see pp22–3)*. Indeed, it would be true to say the city vies with Amsterdam for the title "Venice of the North".

A wide selection of cruises, for small and large groups, in open and closed boats, depart from bridges along Nevskiy prospekt and other parts of the city. They offer marvellous opportunities to see more of the city, especially for those unable to walk long distances. Forming part of any cruise are the broad Fontanka river with its Neo-Classical palaces, the leafy Moyka river with its ironwork bridges, and the Griboedov Canal which twists and turns its way through southwest St Petersburg. Bring a bottle of champagne, a picnic, a warm jumper and just relax.

A river cruise passing the Rostral Columns

General Information

The weather plays a vital role in determining the exact time of year canal cruises start and finish. Most boats operate daily from mid-May to late September. Their routes also vary because regular construction work such as reinforcing the granite embankments, sometimes prevents movement along parts of the canals.

The Gulf of Finland is tidal and this affects the Neva and inland waterways. Strong winds can cause the water level to rise significantly and boat trips may be cancelled under these conditions.

Guided River and Canal Trips

Large, covered cruise boats depart every 30 minutes, between 11:30am and 8pm, from the Anichkov Bridge on Nevskiy prospekt *(see p51)*. Tickets for the next available

boat should be purchased from the kiosk on the embankment, or on board. Trips last 60 minutes and take in the Moyka and Fontanka rivers, and sometimes the Griboedov Canal. Some routes go out onto the Neva, from where there are superb views of the whole city.

Trips usually cost about 600 roubles. Guided tours are available in English from companies such as **Anglo-tourismo**, **Neptun-boat** and **Astra Marine**. Large groups are advised to book in advance, either at a kiosk or by phone, especially during school holidays. Boat trips providing guided tours in English can be booked through any of the major hotels, though this is a more expensive choice.

A popular option are the night-time boat trips along the Neva to watch the bridges opening. No commentary is usually provided on these tours, which depart from the Anichkov

Bridge pier next to the Anichkov Palace at 1:30am and last for about an hour. Blankets are usually provided, but take your own food and drink, as these are rarely available.

Neva Cruises

A variety of boats cruise up and down the Neva. The trips, operating hourly between 10am and 10pm, last an hour. Tickets can be bought on the landing stage or on board for about 500 roubles. The boats leave from in front of the Admiralty *(see p80)* and from near the main entrance of the Hermitage *(see p86–7)*, as well as from the pier of the Peter and Paul Fortress *(see pp68–9)*, from where tickets can be bought for as little as 400 roubles.

Luxury catered cruises can be booked in advance. **MIR** and **Russkiye Kruizy** offer a variety of routes along the Neva and the city's other rivers and canals. Trips along the Neva are a good way to see all the majestic façades that line the river's embankment. Most trips start by going to the Blagoveshchensky Bridge before turning around. Heading back towards Palace Bridge, sights on the left-hand side include the Academy of Arts *(see p65)*, which is easily identifed by the two Egyptian sphinxes in front of it.

The next building to come into view is the yellow Menshikov Palace *(see p64)*, built by Peter the Great's friend Alexander Menshikov. Peter lived in the relatively humble Summer Palace, which can be seen later on the right-hand side in the Summer Gardens.

Shortly after the Menshikov Palace, the side façade of St Petersburg State University comes into view *(see p63)*. The striking turqoise-and-white building soon after is the Kunstkammer *(see p62)*.

On the other side of the river, the Bronze Horseman monument to Peter the Great *(see pp80–81)*, St Isaac's Cathedral *(see pp82–3)* and the Admiralty *(see p80)* can be seen

A cruise along the Neva river

in all their glory. Back on the left, the spit of Vasilevskiy Island is crowned by the stately Stock Exchange building, and completed by the two large red Rostral Columns. Across the Neva is the spectacular Winter Palace (see pp94–5). The next sight on the left is the Peter and Paul Fortress, while shortly afterwards, the enormous blue dome of the city's first mosque can be seen.

On the right is the stunning façade of the Marble Palace (see p96), with the onion domes of the Church on Spilled Blood (see p102) peeping out above it. After the palace, the iconic intricate railings of the Summer Gardens can be admired.

Most sightseeing boats cruise up to Liteiny Bridge or beyond before doubling back to their original starting point.

Departure Points Along Rivers and Canals

Boats depart at regular intervals from the Moyka river, Griboedov Canal and Fontanka river at their intersections with Nevskiy prospekt (see pp48–51), on both sides of the street. Boats departing from the northern side may be about 50 roubles more expensive as they attract more passers-by. Boats also leave from the eastern side of St Isaac's Square, heading in the direction of Nevskiy prospekt. Other boats leave from across from the Field of Mars on the Moyka, and from many other points along all of the waterways where there are steps leading down the embankment.

Restaurant Cruises

There are several restaurant boats that sail up and down the Neva, allowing passengers to enjoy views of the city's embankments over dinner.

Favorite organizes private dinner cruises along the Neva river for couples and groups. Tickets start at 600 roubles per person, excluding food. The cruises last one-and-a-half hours and take in all the major sights along the river.

Those who like the idea of restaurants on water but fear the onset of seasickness might prefer the city's stationary floating restaurants, such as the eccentric **Flying Dutchman** (see p187), which combines several restaurants serving Russian, Japanese, French and Italian cuisine. There is also a fitness centre and beauty salon on board.

Frigate Blagodat, moored at Petrovskaya naberezhnaya, offers spectacular views over the Peter and Paul Fortress (see pp68–9) and Troitskiy most. The Veter (meaning "wind") restaurant and the Empire of Passion and Summer Garden banquet halls are the historically themed dining rooms on board.

Water buses on the Griboedov

Water Buses

Water buses operate in St Petersburg during the summer months. They carry up to 12 passengers and are meant to run from 8am to 9pm at 15-minute intervals, but are in fact highly irregular.

The line has stops at Petrogradskaya naberezhnaya, the Bronze Horseman, the Summer Gardens, Finland Station and Staraya Derevnya. There is also a service from Finland Station to the island of Kronshtadt.

In theory, the boats are a great way to see the city for a bargain price, but the service is sadly highly erratic and so cannot be relied on as a form of transport.

Tickets

Tickets for all boats can be bought on board. For Neva cruises, they are sold at kiosks on the piers in front of the Admiralty and the Hermitage. Hour-long sightseeing tours along the rivers and canals usually cost about 600 roubles. Children under seven may be allowed to travel for free, while older children may be given a discount. Tickets for the water buses are cheaper, costing about 100–180 roubles.

DIRECTORY

Anglotourismo
Tel +7 921 989 4722.
W anglotourismo.com

Astra Marine
Tel 320 0877.
W astra-marine.ru

City Excursion Bureau of St Petersburg
Ulitsa Yefimova 4a. Map 6 E3.
Tel 312 0527.

MIR Travel Company
Nevskiy pr 11. Map 6 D1.
Tel 325 2595.
W mir-travel.com

Neptun-boat
Tel 924 4451. W neptun-boat.ru

Russkiye Kruizy
Prospekt Morskoy Slavy 1.
Tel 333 1343.
W russian-cruises.ru

Restaurant Cruises

Favorite
Marata ulitsa 10. Map 7 B2.
Tel 244 6006. W teplohoder.ru

Frigate Blagodat
Petrovskaya naberezhnaya 2.
Map 2 E3. Tel 327 2508.
W fregat-blagodat.ru

Flying Dutchman
6 Mytninskaya Embankment.
Tel 313 8866.
W dutchman.ru/restorani

Travelling Beyond St Petersburg

Every weekend during the summer, and even in winter, many locals leave the city. They head for their *dacha* or for the woods, to gather seasonal fruits and vegetables, go cross-country skiing or visit one of the former imperial summer residences. Buses and suburban trains operate frequently throughout the year and are the usual means of transport to sites out of town. Peterhof and Kronshtadt are the exceptions in being accessible by hydrofoil across the Gulf of Finland. Foreigners tend to take coach excursions out of town but, with planning, travelling independently can be part of the fun.

Hydrofoil arriving at the Hermitage landing stage

Interior view of one of St Petersburg's suburban trains

Suburban Trains

Train travel is the most comfortable way to visit most of the outlying sights. Tickets can be bought from the local cash desks (*prigorodnyye kassy*) at each station, where a timetable (in Russian) is displayed. Return tickets are no cheaper than two singles. Note that smoking is prohibited, and that between the hours of 10am and midday there is often a break in the timetable.

Getting to Tsarskoe Selo and Pavlovsk

Trains for Tsarskoe Selo (Pushkin) *(see pp154–7)* and Pavlovsk *(see pp160–63)* depart every 20 minutes from **Vitebskiy Station**. The line was originally built for the royal family to reach their summer residences and the station is a marvellous example of Style-Moderne architecture. The ticket office is on the right of the main building. All local trains take about 30 minutes, stopping first at Tsarskoe Selo (Detskoe Selo), then Pavlovsk.

At Detskoe Selo station, the 382 and 371 buses go to Tsarskoe Selo, stopping near the palace. On foot, it is about a 20-minute walk from the station to the estate.

At Pavlovsk, the train station is opposite the entrance to the park, through which it is a pleasant 30-minute walk to the palace.

A host of minibuses run to Tsarskoe Selo (Pushkin) and Pavlovsk from Moskovskaya metro station in St Petersburg. They provide a reliable and convenient alternative means of transport to the train.

Passengers boarding suburban train at Vitebskiy Station

Getting to Peterhof and Oranienbaum

The most enjoyable and by far the most scenic way to reach the imperial summer palace of Peterhof is the 45-minute trip across the Gulf of Finland by hydrofoil. The service runs from early June until early October and sets off from the second landing stage outside the Hermitage *(see p86)* where a weekly timetable is posted. Generally, hydrofoils operate every hour from 9:30am, with the last boat returning at 6pm. It is cheaper to buy a return ticket (for about 800 roubles) than two singles. While it is much more expensive than the train or bus, it is worth the extra cost for the comfort and the view.

On arrival, a fee is charged to enter the lower park and this ticket is needed to get back into the park to return by hydrofoil.

The hydrofoils to Kronshtadt and then Oranienbaum (Lomonosov) are actually part of the water-bus network and are used by commuters in these suburbs. Accordingly, it costs about 100 roubles one-way to Kronshtadt, and another 50 roubles from there to Lomonosov. Hydrofoils to Kronshtadt depart from a boat pier in front of **Finland Station**, and from Kronshtadt pier another boat goes to Lomonosov.

There are suburban trains for Peterhof *(see pp150–53)* and Oranienbaum *(see pp148–9)* departing every 20 minutes from **Baltic Station.** The trains that reach Oranienbaum are those destined for Kalishche, or Oranienbaum itself.

For Peterhof, get off the train at Novyy Petergof (40 minutes from town), from where it is 10 minutes to the palace on bus 348, 350, 351, 352 or 356.

At Oranienbaum, turn right out of the station and walk about 200 m (650 ft) to the main road. Almost directly opposite is the entrance to the park, and from here it is only a 5-minute walk to the Great Palace or into the heart of the park.

An efficient minibus service runs passengers to both Peterhof and Oranienbaum and is located outside Avtovo metro station.

Getting to Repino and the Gulf of Finland

For Repino (see p148) and the Gulf of Finland, trains depart every 20 minutes or so from **Finland Station**. Tickets should be bought at cash desks within the main building. Avoid any train marked Beloostrov or Krugovoy.

At Repino, cross the main road, head down the hill towards the Gulf of Finland and turn left onto the asphalt road until you reach Penaty.

Bus No. 211 also runs to Repino and stops right outside Penaty. Buses to Repino leave from Chernaya Rechka metro and tickets are bought on board.

Getting to Novgorod

Coaches leave for Novgorod (see pp164–7) every 2 hours from the **Coach Station**. The journey takes 4 hours. There are also at least two daily trains from **Moscow Station** that take 3 hours (be warned that there is no toilet on the train). An alternative is to book a guided tour (see p224).

Driving out of St Petersburg

Car hire is available from companies such as **Hertz** and **Europcar**, but driving is not recommended. Firstly, there is no need, as the public transport network is excellent and inexpensive, and secondly, the local driving culture and

St Petersburg's Suburban Rail Lines

suspicious traffic police do not make for an enjoyable time on the road.

To drive in Russia, a notarized translation of a foreign licence is obligatory, as well as international insurance and documents proving you have the right to be driving the car: for example, registration documents or a hire agreement bearing your name.

Traffic police (see p214) have the right to stop you and check your documents. If a policeman points his baton at your vehicle and signals for you to pull over, you must do so immediately, regardless of whether you have committed any violations. The police may not issue on-the-spot fines for minor infringements – such as having a dirty number plate, not having a first-aid kit, or more serious offences such as drink-driving. (Drivers are not allowed to drink any alcohol.)

The proper procedure is to issue a ticket requiring payment within a month at any branch of Sberbank, though the traffic police are notorious for preferring to receive bribes than to issue official fines. For a minor infringement, such as not wearing a seatbelt, a fine may be around 500–1,000 roubles.

DIRECTORY

Train and Coach Stations

All train enquiries
Tel 055.

Baltic Station
Балтийский вокзал
Baltiyskiy vokzal
Nab Obvodnovo kanala 120.

Coach Station
Автобусный вокзал
Avtobusnyy vokzal
Nab Obvodnovo kanala 36.
Map 7 B5.
Tel 766 5777.

Finland Station
Финляндский вокзал
Finlyandskiy vokzal
Pl Lenina 6.
Map 3 B3.

Moscow Station
Московский вокзал
Moskovskiy vokzal
Pl Vosstaniya.
Map 7 C2.

Vitebskiy Station
Витебский вокзал
Vitebskiy vokzal
Zagorodnyy pr 52.
Map 6 F4.

Car Hire

Europcar
Pulkovo Arrivals.
Tel 385 5284.

Hertz
Pulkovo Arrivals. **Tel** 454 7099.

ST PETERSBURG STREET FINDER

The key map below shows the areas of St Petersburg covered by the *Street Finder*. The map references given throughout the guide for sights, restaurants, hotels, shops or entertainment venues refer to the maps in this section. All the major sights have been clearly marked so they are easy to locate. The key below shows other features marked on the maps, such as post offices, metro stations, ferry stops and churches. The *Street Finder* index lists street names in transliteration, followed by the Cyrillic (on the maps, Cyrillic is only given for major roads). This guide uses the now reinstated old Russian street names, rather than the Soviet versions *(see p219)*. Places of interest are listed by their English name.

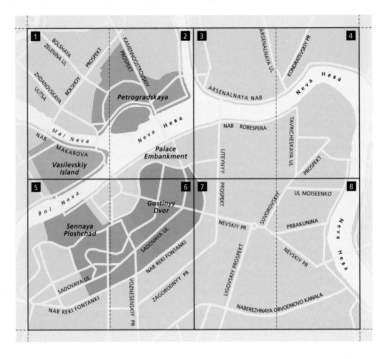

0 kilometres 1
0 miles 1

Key to Street Finder

▢ Major sight	✚ Hospital
▢ Place of interest	▣ Police station
▢ Other building	✚ Orthodox church
▣ Railway station	✚ Non-Orthodox church
Ⓜ Metro station	✡ Synagogue
▦ Tram stop	☾ Mosque
▦ Trolleybus terminus	═ Railway line
▦ Bus terminus	«45 House number (main street)
▦ River boat pier	

Scale of Map Pages

0 metres 300
0 yards 300

Street Finder Index

Abbreviations & Useful Words

ul	ulitsa	street
pl	ploshchad	square
pr	prospekt	avenue
per	pereulok	lane
nab	naberezhnaya	embankment
	most	bridge
	sad	garden
	shosse	road

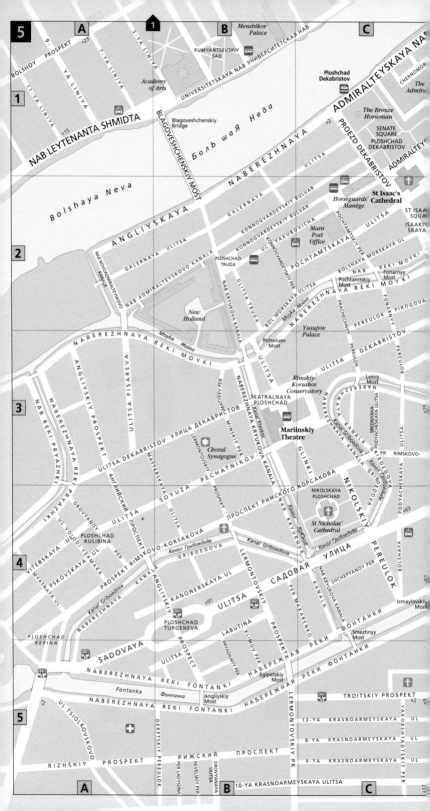

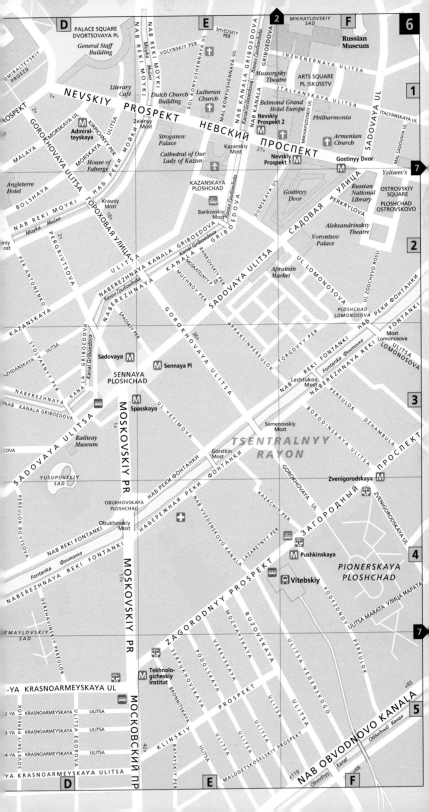

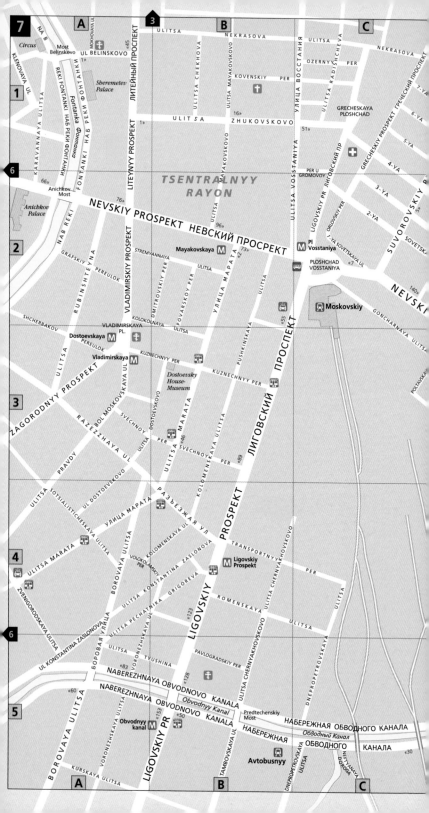

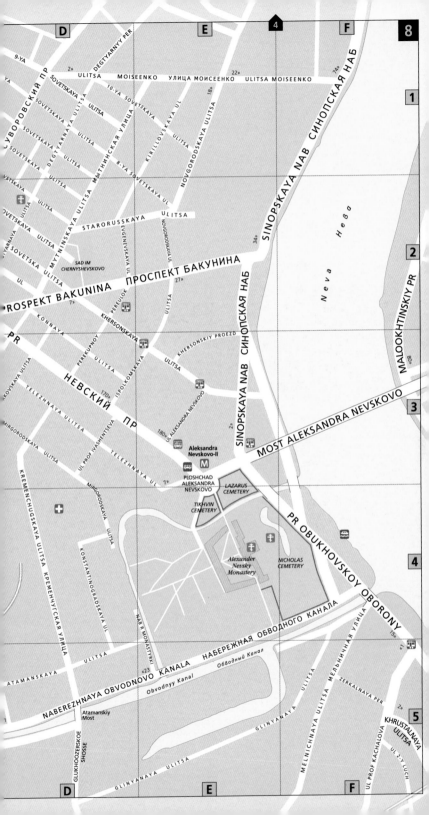

General Index

Acknowledgments

Dorling Kindersley would like to thank the following people whose contributions and assistance have made the preparation of this book possible.

Main Contributors
Christopher Rice holds a PhD in Russian history from the University of Birmingham. He and his wife Melanie, also a writer, first visited Russia in 1978 and have been returning regularly ever since. Together they have written numerous travel guides to the city, and to a variety of other destinations, including Prague, Berlin and Istanbul, as well as the *Eyewitness Travel Guide to Moscow*.

Catherine Phillips is an art historian who arrived in Russia in 1985 and has lived there ever since, moving to St Petersburg in 1989. She covered major events for British and American TV and radio during the early years of *perestroika* and authored and contributed to some of the first guides to the new Russia. Today she concentrates on translating and editing scholarly texts and writing for works of reference.

Additional Contributor
Rose Baring began to study Russian at the age of 12. She has an MA in Modern History and divided her time between London, Moscow and St Petersburg for much of the early 1990s. She has written guides to St Petersburg, Moscow and other destinations, including the *Eyewitness Travel Guide to Istanbul*.

Special Assistance
Dorling Kindersley would like to thank Marc Bennetts (walks writer), Anastasia Makarova (fact checker), Hilary Bird (indexer), Ian Wizniewski (food and drink consultant), Valera Katsuba (photo permissions), Marina Maydanyuk (researcher), Oleksiy Nesnov (language consultant), Victoria Rachevskaya (language consultant), Agency Information Resources for helping with research, Yuliya Motovilova (St Petersburg Tourist Company) and the staff of Peter TiPS.

Proofreader
Stewart J Wild.

Relaunch and Revisions Team
Namrata Adhwaryu, Emma Anacootee, Gillian Allan, Douglas Amrine, Jasneet Arora, Liz Atherton, Subhashree Bharti, Stuti Tiwari Bhatia, Andrei Bogdanov, Laurence Broers, Shura Collinson, Lucinda Cooke, Vivien Crump, Dawn Davies-Cook, Hannah Dolan, Alexandra Farrell, Claire Folkard, Chris Gordon, Freddy Hamilton, Susanne Hillen, Paul Hines, Leanne Hogbin, Vicki Ingle, Cincy Jose, Sumita Khatwani, Priyanka Kumar, Kathryn Lane, Sam Merrell, Deepak Mittal, Shubhi Mittal, Fiona Morgan, Jane Oliver, Reetu Pandey, Helen Partington, Marianne Petrou, Pure Content, Amir Reuveni, Ellen Root, Luke Rozkowski, Alison Stace, Avantika Sukhia, Ingrid Vienings, Matt Willis, Veronica Wood.

Additional Illustrations
Claire Littlejohn, John Woodcock.

Additional Photography
Valentin Baranovsky, Andrei Bogdanov, Victoria Buyvid, Shura Collinson, Andy Crawford, Neil Fletcher, Steve Gorton, Paul Miller, Ian O'Leary, Rough Guides/Jonathan Smith, Jon Spaull, Clive Streeter; KOMMERSANT Photo Agency: Yevgeny Pavlenko, Sergey Semyenov.

Photography Permissions
The publisher would like to thank all those who gave permission to photograph at their establishments, including hotels, museums, churches, shops and other sights, too numerous to thank individually.

Picture Credits
Key: a-above; b-below/bottom; c-centre; f-far; l-left; r-right; t-top.

The publisher would like to thank the following individuals, companies and picture libraries for their kind permission to reproduce their photographs:

Aeroflot: 220cr; AISA, Barcelona: 20t, 46cla, 108tr; AKG, London: 18, 22bl/cl, 22–3c, 27tl, 28clb, 29c, 30br, Erich Lessing 30bl, 31ca, 39bl, 44cl/bl/bc, 45br, State Russian Museum, St Petersburg 107crb; Alamy Images: Art Directors & TRIP/Vladimir Sidropolev 210cl; brt Russia 83cra; Danita Delimont 116; PE Forsberg 214crb; i food and drink 184cl; ITAR-TASS Photo Agency 158-9; Jon Bower- art and museums 66; Daniel Korzeniewski 208-9; Art Kowalsky 10cl; Frans Lemmens 218cla; Dov Makabaw 223br; Medioimages 10br; Dmitry Mikhaevich 61crb, 175tl; RIA Novosti 62bl; Robert Harding Picture Library Ltd 140cr; Robert Harding Picture Library Ltd/ Sylvain Grandadam 182cla, 183tl; Russ Images 126; Neil Setchfield 186bl; studio204 218br; Peter Titmuss 13tc, 140br, 212tl; Universal Images Group/DeAgostini 98; Lilyana Vynogradova 104-5, Patrizia Wyss 170cl; Alfa-Bank: 216bl; Anglotourism.com: 224tr; Ancient Art & Architecture Collection: 47cr; APA: Jim Holmes 95tl; Axiom: Jim Holmes 155cb.

Valentin Baranovsky: 86clb, 87tl, 203tl; Ian Bavington-Jones: 132tc; Baklazhan Restaurant: 191br; Belmond Grand Hotel Europe: 178bc, 180cl, 189bl, 190tl; Yuri Belinsky: 33tl; Bridgeman Art Library, London/New York: 155cr; Forbes Magazine Collection 30–1c; State Hermitage, St Petersburg 23cr, 26–7c, 27cl, 88cla/bc, 89tr/bc, 90cb, 91tr/bc, 92ca/bl, 93tl/c, *La Danse*, Henri Matisse (1910) © Succession Henri Matisse/DACS 2011 89c; Private Collection *20th Century Propaganda Poster 1920*, D Moor © DACS 2011 31tr; State Russian Museum, St Petersburg *The Cyclist*, Natalya Goncharova (1913) © ADAGP, Paris and DACS, London 2011 42br, *Portrait of Princess Olga Konstantinovna Orlova*, Valentin Alexandrovich Serov (1911) 106cla; Tretyakov Gallery, Moscow 21cla, *The Circus*, Marc Chagall, 1919 © ADAGP, Paris and DACS, London 2011 47tl.

Camera Press: Roxana Artacho 87bl; **Demetrio Carrasco**: 6b, 17b, 38cla, 55bl, 82bc, 95cra/br; **Central State Archive of Photographs and Film Documents, St Petersburg**: 44tr, 74c, 112crb, 120bl; **Jean-Loup Charmet**: 25tl; **Christie's Images**: 84bc; **Corbis**: Bettmann/E. O Hoppe 120crb; Dean Conger 54cra, Antoine Gyori 141t; Rob Howard 183c; ITAR-TASS Photo/ Shamukov Ruslan 220cl; Bob Krist 203bl; Library of Congress 30cla; Michael Nicholson 154tr; Gianni Dagli Orti 8–9, 121bl; National Geographic Society/Jonathan Irish 2-3; Jose Fuste Raga 224bl; Steve Raymer 33crb, 120br, 140cla; State Hermitage, St Petersburg 26bl; State Russian Museum 27bl.

Dom Berga: 193tr; **Dreamstime.com**: Anoli50 144; Antartis 34; Amos Chapple 56-7; Dimbar76 110bl; Ivanukh 76; Oleg Kovalenko 58; Mardym 13b; Paha_i 212c ; Sailorr 12bl; Konstantin Semenov 134; Svglass 215tc, Voltan1 168-9.

E T Archive: Bibliotheque Nationale, Paris 19clb; Hermitage, St Petersburg 90cla, 91tl.

Fotolia: Dmitry Vereshchagin 229tl.

Getty Images: Hulton Archive 45tr, 120cla, 123c, 184tr; The Image Bank/Harald Sund 11br; **Giraudon**: State Russian Museum 45cr, 107cra; Tretyakov Gallery, Moscow 167crb; **Gosti Restaurant**: 188tl.

Michael Holford: 20cb, 21c, 23bl; **Hotel Dostoevsky**: 175cb.

Interior Archive: Fritz von der Schulenburg 5c, 163crb.

Kea Publishing Services: Francesco Venturi 94 tr/bc, 95bl; **David King Collection**: 31tl, 32tl, 47bc, 71bc, 131cr.

Lonely Planet Images: Jonathan Smith 11tr, 141crb.

Mary Evans Picture Library: 21br, 23tr, 24crb, 25crb, 26cl/br, 27br, 28tl, 31crb, 64bc, 163bl; **Paul Miller**: 53cra.

Neptun-boats: 228cl; **Novosti (London)**: 22br, 23tr, 28br, 29tr, 32cl, 33c, 45tl, 52c, 53br, 80bl, 167cl.

Oronoz, Madrid: 24tl, 45bc.

Park Inn by Radisson Veliky Novgorod: 172br, 177tr; **Plodimex Aussenhandels Gmbh, Hamburg**: 180cr/bl; **Pushka INN Hotel**: 179tr.

Natasha Razina: 154br, 155tl; **Renaissance St Petersburg Baltic Hotel**: 174c; **Rex Features**: V. Sichov/Sipa Press 32cr; **Robert Harding Picture Library**: 86cla; **Rocco Forte Hotels, St Petersburg**: 171br; **Ellen Rooney**: 55cra, 81tr, 85br; **Russian Railways**: 221tc, 221bl.

Gregor M Schmid: 52br; **Shinok Restaurant**: 192bl; **Vladimir Sidoropolev**: 184br; **St Peter Line**: 222tr; **St Petersburg Metro**: 226br, 227cl; **The St Petersburg Times**: 219tc; **Skat Prokat**: 225cr; **State Russian Museum**: 7cr; *Blue Crest*, Wassily Kandinsky (1917) © ADAGP, Paris and DACS, London 2011 41br; 95tr, 106clb/br, 107tl, 108cla/br, 109tl/bc, 112bc.

Travel Library: Stuart Black 87br; **Tsar Restaurant**: 190bc; **Tsarskoye Selo State Museum**: 142-3.

Vedensky Hotel: 176bl; **Visual Arts Library**: 46br; State Hermitage, St Petersburg *L'Homme aux bras croisés*, Pablo Picasso (1905) © Succession Picasso/DACS 2011 93br; 125cl.

Front Enpaper: Dreamstime.com: Ivanukh Rcr; Oleg Kovalenko Lcl; **Alamy Images**: Danita Delimont Lbc; Jon Bower- art and museums Rtc; Universal Images Group/ DeAgostini Rbc.

Map Cover: **AWL Images**: Nadia Isakova.

Jacket: Front and Spine t **AWL Images**: Nadia Isakova.

All other images © Dorling Kindersley. For further information see: www.dkimages.com

Phrase Book

In this guide the Russian language has been transliterated into Roman script following a consistent system used by the US Board on Geographic Names. All street and place names, and the names of most people, are transliterated according to this system. For some names, where a well-known English form exists, this has been used – hence, Leo (not Lev) Tolstoy. In particular,

the names of Russian rulers, such as Peter the Great, are given in their anglicized forms. Throughout the book, transliterated names can be taken as an accurate guide to pronunciation. The Phrase Book also gives a phonetic guide to the pronunciation of words and phrases used in everyday situations, such as when eating out or shopping.

Guidelines for Pronunciation

The Cyrillic alphabet has 33 letters, of which only five (а, к, м, о, т) correspond exactly to their counterparts in English. Russian has two pronunciations (hard and soft) of each of its vowels, and several consonants without an equivalent. The right-hand column of the alphabet, below, demonstrates how Cyrillic letters are pronounced by comparing them to sounds in English words. However, some letters vary in how they are pronounced according to their position in a word. Important exceptions are also noted below.
On the following pages, the English is given in the left-hand column, with the Russian and its transliteration in the middle column. The right-hand column provides a literal system of pronunciation and indicates the stressed syllable in bold. The exception is in the *Menu Decoder* section, where the Russian is given in the left-hand column and the English translation in the right-hand column, for ease of use. Because of the existence of genders in Russian, in a few cases both masculine and feminine forms of a phrase are given.

The Cyrillic Alphabet

А а	a	*alimony*
Б б	b	*bed*
В в	v	*vet*
Г г	g	*get (see note 1)*
Д д	d	*debt*
Е е	e	*yet (see note 2)*
Ё ё	e	*yonder*
Ж ж	zh	*leisure (but a little harder)*
З з	z	*zither*
И и	i	*see*
Й й	y	*boy (see note 3)*
К к	k	*king*
Л л	l	*loot*
М м	m	*match*
Н н	n	*never*
О о	o	*rob (see note 4)*
П п	p	*pea*
Р р	r	*rat (rolling, as in Italian)*
С с	s	*stop*
Т т	t	*toffee*
У у	u	*boot*
Ф ф	f	*fellow*
Х х	kh	*kh (like loch)*
Ц ц	ts	*lets*
Ч ч	ch	*chair*
Ш ш	sh	*shove*
Щ щ	shch	*fresh sheet (as above but with a slight roll)*
ъ		*hard sign (no sound, but see note 5)*
Ы ы	y	*lid*
ь		*soft sign (no sound, but see note 5)*
Э э	e	*egg*
Ю ю	yu	*youth*
Я я	ya	*yak*

Notes
1) Г Pronounced as *v* in endings -oro and -ero.
2) Е Always pronounced *ye* at the beginning of a word, but in the middle of a word sometimes less distinctly (more like *e*).
3) Й This letter has no distinct sound of its own. It usually lengthens the preceding vowel.
4) О When not stressed it is pronounced like *a* in across.
5) ъ, ь The hard sign (ъ) is rare and indicates a very brief pause before the next letter. The soft sign (ь, marked in the pronunciation guide as ') softens the preceding consonant and adds a slight *y* sound: for instance, *n'* would sound like *ny* in 'canyon'.

In Emergency

Help!	Помогите! *Pomogite!*	*pamageet-ye!*
Stop!	Стоп! *Stop!*	*stop!*
Leave me alone!	Оставьте меня в покое! *Ostavte menya v pokoe!*	*astavt'-ye myenya v pakoye!*
Call a doctor!	Позовите врача! *Pozovite vracha!*	*pazaveet-ye vracha!*
Call an ambulance!	Вызовите скорую помощь! *Vyzovite skoruyu pomoshch!*	*vizaveet-ye skoru-yu pomash'!*
Fire!	Пожар! *Pozhar!*	*pazhar!*
Call the fire brigade!	Вызовите пожарных! *Vyzovite pozharnykh!*	*vizaveet-ye pazharnikh!*
Police!	Милиция! *Militsiya!*	*meeleetsee-ya!*
Where is the nearest…	Где ближайший… *Gde blizhayshiy…*	*gdye bleezhaysheey…*
…telephone?	…телефон? *…telefon?*	*…tyelyefon?*
…hospital?	…больница? *…bolnitsa?*	*…bal'neetsa?*
…police station?	…отделение милиции? *…otdelenie militsii?*	*…atdyelyenye meeleetsee-ee?*

Communication Essentials

Yes	Да *Da*	*da*
No	Нет *Net*	*nyet*
Please	Пожалуйста *Pozhaluysta*	*pazhalsta*
Thank you	Спасибо *Spasibo*	*spaseeba*
You are welcome	Пожалуйста *Pozhaluysta*	*pazhalsta*
Excuse me	Извините *Izvinite*	*eezveeneet-ye*
Hello	Здравствуйте *Zdravstvuyte*	*zdrastvooyt-ye*
Goodbye	До свидания *Do svidaniya*	*da sveedanya*
Good morning	Доброе утро *Dobroe utro*	*dobra-ye ootra*
Good afternoon/day	Добрый день *Dobryy den*	*dobree dyen'*
Good evening	Добрый вечер *Dobryy vecher*	*dobree vyechyer*
Good night	Спокойной ночи *Spokoynoy nochi*	*spakoynay nochee*
Morning	утро *utro*	*ootra*
Afternoon	день *den*	*dyen'*
Evening	вечер *vecher*	*vyechyer*
Yesterday	вчера *vchera*	*fchyera*
Today	сегодня *sevodnya*	*syevodnya*
Tomorrow	завтра *zavtra*	*zaftra*
Here	здесь *zdes*	*zdyes'*

There	там *tam*	*tam*
What?	Что? *Chto?*	*shto?*
Where?	Где? *Gde?*	*gdye?*
Why?	Почему? *Pochemu?*	*pachyemoo?*
When?	Когда? *Kogda?*	*kagda?*
Now	сейчас *seychas*	*seychas*
Later	позже *pozzhe*	*pozhe*
Can I…?	можно? *mozhno?*	*mozhna…?*
It is possible/allowed	можно *mozhno*	*mozhna*
It is not possible/allowed	нельзя *nelzya*	*nyelzya*

Useful Phrases

How are you?	Как Вы Поживаете? *Kak vee pozhivaete?*	*kak vee pozhivaete?*
Very well, thank you	Хорошо, спасибо *Khorosho, spasibo*	*kharasho, spaseeba*
Pleased to meet you	Очень приятно *Ochen priyatno*	*ochen' pree-yatna*
How do I get to…?	Как добраться до…? *Kak dobratsya do…?*	*kak dabrat'sya da…?*
Would you tell me when we get to…?	Скажите, пожалуйста, когда мы приедем в…? *Skazhite, pozhaluysta, kogda my priedem v…?*	*skazheet-ye, pazhalsta, kagda mi pree-yedyem v…?*
Is it very far?	Это далеко? *Eto daleko?*	*eta dalyeko?*
Do you speak English?	Вы говорите по-английски? *Vy govorite po-angliyski?*	*vi gavareet-ye po-angleeskee?*
I don't understand	Я не понимаю *Ya ne ponimayu*	*ya nye paneema-yoo*
Could you speak more slowly?	Говорите медленнее *Govorite medlenne*	*gavareet-ye myedlyenye-ye*
Could you say it again please?	Повторите, пожалуйста *Povtorite, pozhaluysta*	*paftareet-ye, pazhalsta*
I am lost	я заблудился (заблудилась) *Ya zabludilsya (zabludilas)*	*ya zabloodeelsya (zabloodeelas')*
How do you say… in Russian?	Как по-русски…? *Kak po-russki…?*	*kak pa-rooskee…?*

Useful Words

big	большой *bolshoy*	*bal'shoy*
small	маленький *malenkiy*	*malyen'kee*
hot (water, food)	горячий *goryachiy*	*garyachee*
hot (weather)	жарко *zharko*	*zharka*
cold	холодный *kholodnyy*	*khalodnee*
good	хорошо *khorosho*	*kharasho*
bad	плохо *plokho*	*plokha*
okay/fine	нормально *normalno*	*narmal'na*
near	близко *blizko*	*bleezka*
far	далеко *daleko*	*dalyeko*
up	наверху *naverkhu*	*navyerkhoo*
down	внизу *vnizu*	*fneezoo*

early	рано *rano*	*rana*
late	поздно *pozdno*	*pozdna*
vacant (unoccupied)	свободно *svobodno*	*svabodna*
free (no charge)	бесплатно *besplatno*	*byesplatna*
cashier/ticket office	касса *kassa*	*kasa*
avenue	проспект *prospekt*	*praspyekt*
bridge	мост *most*	*most*
embankment	набережная *naberezhnaya*	*nabyeryezhnaya*
highway/motorway	шоссе *shosse*	*shasse*
lane/passage	переулок *pereulok*	*pyereyoolak*
square	площадь *ploshchad*	*ploshat'*
street	улица *ulitsa*	*ooleetsa*
flat/apartment	квартира *kvartira*	*kvarteera*
floor	этаж *etazh*	*etash*
house/block	дом *dom*	*dom*
entrance	вход *vkhod*	*fkhot*
exit	выход *vykhod*	*vikhot*
river	река *reka*	*ryeka*
summer country house	дача *dacha*	*dacha*
swimming pool	бассейн *basseyn*	*basyeyn*
town	город *gorod*	*gorat*
toilet	туалет *tualet*	*tooalyet*

Making a Telephone Call

Can I call abroad from here?	Можно отсюда позвонить за границу? *Mozhno ostyuda pozvonit za granitsu?*	*mozhna atsyooda pazvaneet' za graneetsoo?*
I would like to speak to…	Позвоните, пожалуйста… *Pozovite, pozhaluysta*	*pazaveet-ye, pazhalsta…*
Could you leave him/her a message?	Вы можете передать ему/ей? *By mozhete peredat emu/ey?*	*vi mozhet-ye pyeryedat' yemoo/yay?*
My number is…	Мой номер… *Moy nomer…*	*moy nomyer…*
I'll ring back later	Я позвоню позже *Ya pozvonyu pozzhe*	*ya pazvanyoo pozhe*

Sightseeing

castle	замок *zamok*	*zamak*
cathedral	собор *sobor*	*sabor*
church	церковь *tserkov*	*tserkaf'*
circus	цирк *tsirk*	*tseerk*
closed for cleaning "cleaning day"	санитарный день *sanitarnyy den*	*saneetarnee dyen'*
undergoing restoration	ремонт *remont*	*remont*
exhibition	выставка *vystavka*	*vistafka*
fortress	крепость *krepost*	*kryepost'*
gallery	галерея *galereya*	*galeryeya*
garden	сад *sad*	*sad*
island	остров *ostrov*	*ostraf*

kremlin/fortified stronghold	кремль *kreml*	*kryeml'*
library	библиотека *biblioteka*	*beeblee-atyeka*
monument	памятник *pamyatnik*	*pamyatneek*
mosque	мечеть *mechet*	*myechyet'*
museum	музей *muzey*	*moozyey*
palace	дворец *dvorets*	*dvaryets*
park	парк *park*	*park*
parliament	дума *duma*	*dooma*
synagogue	синагога *sinagoga*	*seenagoga*
zoo	зоопарк *zoopark*	*zapark*

Shopping

open	открыто *otkryto*	*atkrita*
closed	закрыто *zakryto*	*zakrita*
How much does this cost?	Сколько это стоит? *Skolko eto stoit?*	*skol'ka eta stoeet?*
I would like to buy…	Я хотел (хотела) бы купить… *Ya khotel (khotela) by kupit…*	*ya khatyel (khatyela) bi koopeet!…*
Do you have…?	У вас есть…? *U vas yest…?*	*oo vas yest'…?*
Do you take credit cards?	Кредитные карточки вы принимаете? *Kreditnye kartochki vy prinimaete?*	*kryedeetnye kartachkee vy preeneemayetye?*
What time do you open/close?	Во сколько вы открываетесь/ закрываетесь? *Vo skolko vy otkryvaetes/ zakryvaetes?*	*Va skol'ka vy atkrivayetyes'/ zakrivayetyes'?*
This one	этот *etot*	*etat*
expensive	дорого *dorogo*	*doraga*
cheap	дёшево *deshevo*	*dyoshyeva*
size	размер *razmer*	*razmyer*
white	белый *belyy*	*byelee*
black	чёрный *chernyy*	*chyornee*
red	красный *krasnyy*	*krasnee*
yellow	жёлтый *zheltyy*	*zholtee*
green	зелёный *zelenyy*	*zyelyonee*
dark blue	синий *siniy*	*seenee*
light blue	голубой *goluboy*	*galooboy*
brown	коричневый *korichnevyy*	*kareechnyevee*

Types of Shop

bakery	булочная *bulochnaya*	*boolachna-ya*
bookshop	книжный магазин *knizhnyy magazin*	*kneezhnee magazeen*
butcher	мясной магазин *myasnoy magazin*	*myasnoy magazeen*
camera shop	фото-товары *foto-tovary*	*foto-tavari*
chemist	аптека *apteka*	*aptyeka*
delicatessen	гастроном *gastronom*	*gastranom*
department store	универмаг *univermag*	*ooneevyermag*
florist	цветы *tsvety*	*tsvyeti*

grocer	бакалея *bakaleya*	*bakalye-ya*
hairdresser	парикмахерская *parikmakherskaya*	*pareekma-khyerskaya*
market	рынок *rynok*	*rinak*
newspaper stand	газетный киоск *gazetniy kiosk*	*gazyetnee kee-osk*
post office	почта *pochta*	*pochta*
record shop	грампластинки *gramplastinki*	*gramplasteenkee*
shoe shop	обувь *obuv*	*oboof'*
travel agent	бюро путешествий *byuro puteshestviy*	*byooro pootyeshestvee*
bank	банк *bank*	*bank*

Staying in a Hotel

Do you have a vacant room?	У вас есть свободный номер? *U vas yest svobodnyy nomer?*	*oo vas yest' svabodnee nomyer?*
double room with double bed	номер с двуспальной кроватью *nomer s dvuspalnoy krovatyu*	*nomyer s dvoospal'noy kravat'-yoo*
twin room	двухместный номер *dvukhmestnyy nomer*	*dvookhmyestnee nomyer*
single room	одноместный номер *odnomestnyy nomer*	*adnamyestnee nomyer*
bath	ванная *vannaya*	*vana-ya*
shower	душ *dush*	*doosh*
porter	носильщик *nosilshchik*	*naseel'sheek*
key	ключ *klyuch*	*klyooch*

Eating Out

A table for two, please	Стол на двоих, пожалуйста *Stol na dva-eekh, pazhalsta*	*stol na dva-eekh, pazhalsta*
I would like to book a table	Я хочу заказать стол *Ya khochu zakazat stol*	*ya khachoo zakazat' stol*
The bill, please	Счёт, пожалуйста *Schet, pozhaluysta*	*shyot, pazhalsta*
I am a vegetarian	Я вегетерианец (вегетерианка) *Ya vegeterianets (vegeterianka)*	*ya vyegyetareeanyets (vyegyetareeanka)*
breakfast	завтрак *zavtrak*	*zaftrak*
lunch	обед *obed*	*abyet*
dinner	ужин *uzhin*	*oozheen*
waiter!	официант! *ofitsiant!*	*afeetsee-ant!*
waitress!	официантка! *ofitsiantka!*	*afeetsee-antka!*
dish of the day	фирменное блюдо *firmennoe blyudo*	*feermenoye blyooda*
appetizers/starters	закуски *zakuski*	*zakooskee*